GUILDFORD COUNTY TECHNICAL
COLLEGE LIBRARY

A Manual of Classification

William Charles Berwick Sayers (1881–1960)

WITHDRAWN

GUILDFORD COUNTY TECHNICAL
COLLEGE LIBRARY

W. C. Berwick Sayers

A Manual of Classification for Librarians

FOURTH EDITION
Completely revised and partly re-written by
ARTHUR MALTBY, B.A., F.L.A., F.R.S.A.,
Senior Lecturer in Classification,
Liverpool School of Librarianship.

WITH ILLUSTRATIONS AND BIBLIOGRAPHY

ANDRE DEUTSCH / A GRAFTON BOOK

OFFICE

025.4

30052

THIS REVISED EDITION FIRST PUBLISHED 1967 BY
ANDRE DEUTSCH LIMITED
105 GREAT RUSSELL STREET
LONDON W.C.1
FIRST EDITION 1926
SECOND EDITION 1944
THIRD EDITION 1955
REPRINT WITH CORRECTIONS 1959
REPRINTED 1962
COPYRIGHT © 1959 BY W. C. BERWICK SAYERS
COPYRIGHT © 1967 BY ARTHUR MALTBY AND W. C. BERWICK SAYERS
ALL RIGHTS RESERVED
PRINTED IN GREAT BRITAIN BY
C. TINLING AND CO. LTD
LIVERPOOL, LONDON AND PRESCOT

'A successful man is usually a classifier and a chartmaker. This applies as much to modern business as to science or libraries . . . A large business or work unclassified or uncharted is not a worthy organization but mere material from which a clever brain may construct one. It differs in efficiency from the ideal as a mob of men differs from a well disciplined army. Piles of bricks and mortar are not a temple any more than heaps of type are Shakespeare's works, though if "classified" and set, each in right relation to the rest, the transformation is brought about.'

MELVIL DEWEY

'As I pondered thus upon the unified nature of library service, I discovered that classification could be thought of only in relation to the part it contributed to a final goal. Again it resumed a kind of central position; but this time, instead of resuming also to separate entity, it seemed to radiate throughout the structure shafts of illumination, lighting up and strengthening all library service. It seemed to me that classification could be made to reinforce the framework of our service and prevent the whole from collapsing into a formless and undirected tangle.'

GRACE O. KELLEY

'A classification does not bring all the resources on a subject together on the shelves of a library, nor does any subject catalogue bring them all together on a table; nor does a subject bibliography. But a classification, a classified subject catalogue, or a classified subject bibliography may have a structural efficiency on which such maximal functional efficiency will largely depend.'

HENRY EVELYN BLISS

Preface to First and Second Editions

I. When I began work as a lecturer on classification at the University of London School of Librarianship in 1919 I soon became of opinion that there was need for a comprehensive statement of the whole field of classification, as the librarian was concerned with it. That expresses my purpose and the limitations I necessarily set myself then and now. The pages that follow can have no special interest for the logician as classifier, or the scientist or philosopher in the same rôle. A treatise for them would be a theoretical and historical description and exposition of all the namings and groupings of knowledge that have been attempted since the beginning of the world; a book of which the late Professor Robert Flint's *History of the Classification of the Sciences* may be considered to be an outline; and for the writing of such a work I need scarcely say that I have not the necessary equipment. What I have attempted is (1) to set out the cardinal principles which appear to have actuated classifiers when devising their systems; (2) to glance rapidly, but I hope sufficiently, across the schemes which have directly influenced, or have been designed for, the classifying of books, catalogues or other literary or cognate material, avoiding the too frequent tendency to confuse the student by cramming him with schemes which have, it may be, an antiquarian interest, but which he is not in the least likely to use; but emphasising and explaining at some length the great systems of Brunet, Dewey, Cutter, Brown and the Library of Congress – the only systems which now have any considerable number of adherents, in Anglo-Saxon, Latin and Slavonic libraries at any rate, and adding to these, for the second edition, accounts as full as space allows of the new, challenging system of Bliss and the intriguing novel one that comes to us from Madras from Ranganathan; and (3) to explain how classification affects library methods, how it is applied to shelf arrangement, book display, catalogues, files, clippings, illustrations, maps, deeds, and the other materials and operations of libraries.

II. While thus in purpose and manner the book has been written for librarians, the subject is one that has a much more universal appeal and application. I believe that experience proves that workers in almost every sphere in which the organization of materials or time is involved would derive some benefit from a study of the subject; for, in the examples which the use of classification in libraries offers, we have organizing method severely applied to severely practical ends – to the exploiting of the library stock, which phrase may stand as a sound, if seemingly unromantic, definition of the occupation of ninety-nine out of every hundred librarians.

III. To the beginner in the study of classification few things are more apparent and puzzling than the simplicity of the problem which faces the librarian and the complexity of the solutions of it that have been proposed. In brief, his problem is to arrange the books on library shelves and entries of them in catalogues in the manner which shall be most convenient for the users of the library and shall best reveal their contents. Years of study, observation and discussion have convinced him that in most cases this most convenient order is an arrangement of books by their subject matter. Out of that conviction has arisen the complexity. The questions arise:

> *When subject matter has been discovered and defined, what is the order of the subjects?*
> *What is to be done with the book which is in itself a complexity of subjects, or has no real value from the point of view of its subject content?*
> *What provision is to be made to accommodate in the order a new subject, or the new version of an old subject; in short, how can the classification keep pace with that most fluid of things, human thought?*
> *How is the book to be retained in its proper place in the classification on the shelves, and how recorded in catalogues?*

Perhaps these are the main questions, but they give rise to many subsidiary ones, and on each of the main ones there has been a flood of discussion and controversy. From the birth of libraries to the present, persistent attempts to settle them have been made, with varying success, but in no case with complete satisfaction to everybody concerned.

IV. The first part of this book consists of a discussion of principles that may govern the making of a classification. It is based on a course of lectures which I gave in 1920 to classes in the University of London School of Librarianship; these have now been revised and amplified and there is much new matter; but I fear the 'lecture' style still remains, it may be at the expense of literary quality, but I hope this will not offend. There is also, as happens in teaching, a good deal of repetition, but I conceive that this is not to be deplored. In the second and third parts of the book, I have attempted to give a glimpse of the antiquity and perennial interest of the classification problem; but I have been much more concerned to give an account of the classification systems which are in actual use in most libraries today, sufficient for the reader to understand the general scope, method and qualities of each. One cannot go further or even do so much perfectly, because full appreciation of a system can only be gained by applying and testing it for some considerable time. The remainder of the book is chiefly severely practical. It faces the position of a librarian who has been placed in charge of a library; and endeavours to show the effect of classification on the planning and working of his library, as well as giving the most general methods of classifying books, entering them in classified catalogues and supplying guides to their arrangement. I have not attempted here to supply the 'drill' in the classifying of books which is as essential to the student librarian as is the drill in his paradigms to the student of Latin or Greek. That I have already endeavoured to do in my *Introduction to Library Classification*, which may be regarded as both preliminary and supplementary to this book.

V. In revising the text a conservative method has been employed. As one of my much appreciated critics tells me with a frankness which does him credit, 'You were unfortunate in that your book (first) appeared just before the creative work in classification was done.' I was, no doubt; Bliss and Ranganathan were hard on my heels, but the first of them had not then caught me up and the second was a listener, one of the most remarkable I had, to these lectures at the School of Librarianship. Both have done work which makes the workers previously in the field seem as amateurs. But E. C. Richardson and I have both contributed in a humble way to the

A*

work of these excellent librarians and one of us lives to feel some pride and pleasure in the fact. And, after all, this book was my own, written my own way, presenting my own ideas. Others have felt with me, strangely enough perhaps, that it has a place which the books of my more learned friends do not occupy. I realized, however, that if it was to survive, drastic re-writing of some parts was essential, because I admit that the researches of Bliss had outmoded many of our notions, especially in the realm of order, and the older rules of division now seem too rigid. The essential parallelisms between the order of knowledge classifications and book classifications and the main principles of construction and application held by all of us coincide to a remarkable degree. But if Bliss and Ranganathan owe some trifling things, handsomely acknowledged, to me, I owe more to them than I am able to express here.

VI. The whole of my text has thus been reviewed. The part which concerns practice has been less susceptible to change, but it has been revised. The question of book display, which is essential to library missionary work and is good business, is touched upon, but not extensively, as its practice is a matter of the use of common perception rather than of technique; and I have considered some of the most often heard objections to classification in a chapter which is new in this second edition. I have been sometimes critical of the excellent work done by Dr Grace O. Kelley, who has been equally critical of mine, as she has every claim to be. The quotation from her chapter in *The Acquisition and Cataloguing of Books, edited by W. M. Randall, 1940,* which follows my title page represents a sentiment where we, and I hope every maker and user of classification, meet in entire harmony.

W. C. BERWICK SAYERS

1926 and 1943 (reduced).

Preface to the Third Edition

VII. Only a few words need saying about this new issue of the Manual. The first is that no work of its character could keep pace with the fermenting processes that are being created or studied in the art of arranging the manifold records, in manuscripts, books, periodicals, clippings, pamphlets, circulars, catalogues, maps, films, and whatever else may form permanently or transiently part of the stock of such repositories as libraries have become today. More discussion and experiment have been and are being devoted to the study of these than at any previous time. Meanwhile a demand for this simple work persists, strange as that may seem to those to whom the current conception of what is called depth classification, of the self-perpetuating type, prevails over all others. I have therefore left the book substantially as it was in 1944, but have rewritten some chapters. The chapter on the Decimal Classification has been rehandled and I have attempted to show not only the defects in it that obsess its critics, but also to do justice to its surprisingly capital virtues as a scheme which introduced general classification into libraries.

VIII. Science, vast as it is, is only a fragment of Being, past, present and future, which may be recorded in books; to classify accurately even that subject would seem to demand a corps of specialists perpetually in session such as Ranganathan suggests in the last chapter of his *Philosophy of Library Classification*. One may hope that such a corps can be organized and perpetuated; perhaps the Classification Research Group, set up as a suggestion of the Royal Society, of which Brian C. Vickery, one of the best equipped recent writers on the new methods, is honorary secretary, may be preliminary to this. The fact that the Fédération Internationale de

Documentation has confided the study of important aspects of classification to Indian librarians is another portent worthy of note. Meanwhile, although research work in our subject must influence all libraries, the general librarian, and more especially the public librarian, will be more than fortunate if he has the time and staff to work out his own classification. Down-to-earth commonsense suggests that for the present, perhaps for many years to come, most of us must use one of the great so-called 'enumerative' schemes that have been tried and have established their claim to be workable; and these are the schemes of Dewey, the Library of Congress, the Universal Decimal Classification and (to a lesser extent perhaps), the systems of Brown and Bliss. The student needs to know here and now how these schemes came to be and something of their construction and application. This I have endeavoured to provide and it is the sole justification for this book.

W. C. BERWICK SAYERS

Croydon, 1954 (reduced).

Preface to the Fourth Edition

IX. When Berwick Sayers first produced this Manual, he provided librarianship with a textbook that attempted to survey and explain a subject which many students, and indeed practising librarians, found extremely complex. The Manual justly became renowned for the breadth of its author's knowledge, his wise judgement on classification problems and procedures, and his discernible sympathy for younger librarians with regard to the difficulties encountered in their studies. Sayers was not only a great librarian and teacher; he was himself a pioneer in the development of the theory of library classification – its first 'grammarian', as Ranganathan describes him in the Sayers Memorial Volume. The tremendous developments of the last two decades have, however, inevitably dated many parts of his writings and this new edition attempts to maintain the original character and vitality of the Manual, while incorporating details of recent events and theories. To what extent I have achieved a grafting of the new on to the old is for others to judge. Certainly I am conscious that there are imperfections and also that, as is pointed out in the preface to the previous edition, no single work of this kind can fully keep pace with current developments in classification. If I have succeeded in blending an account of modern principles and achievement with the original text and in bringing the work up to date, I am merely repaying in part the debt which I and so many other students of the earlier editions owe to Berwick Sayers.

X. The first section of the Manual now deals with the principles of book classification and includes an attempt to consider, distinctly and simply, both the traditional theories and the modern ideas of synthesis and exact subject analysis which are influencing the study of library classification in Great Britain so profoundly. The fresh material provided concentrates more on description than on the full exposition of recent theory, as it is considered that the major task of a work of this kind is to reduce the amount of factual detail that must be assimilated in class and thus to leave more time for the lecturer to explain, with examples, modern principles of classification and to stimulate discussion concerning their advantages. It is therefore assumed that reading will be supported by appropriate tutorial and practical work in the classroom, especially with regard to the ideas covered briefly in Chapters 3 and 4. Section II abridges the older historical detail provided in earlier editions, but contains the account of Cutter's Expansive Classification and extends the description previously given concerning the development of book classification in the present century. The chapter on Classification in England has been revised and transferred to this section. Then, in section III, there is an attempt to discuss and assess the major general book classifications of today according to a common pattern.

XI. Section IV is mainly concerned with those problems which arise when a scheme is selected and applied in libraries – particularly general libraries. Finally, in section V, the task of classifying the special library is discussed and the future of library classification considered. Most of the material in this section is new to the Manual. Here, too, a brief survey of the effects of increasing mechanization upon classification in libraries and information bureaux is given; this is dealt with in much more detail in other texts.

XII. This new edition is chiefly designed to be useful as a basic text for post-graduate students and the non-graduate taking the Part II B II paper of the British Library Association. It is hoped, however, that many chapters will also prove useful to Part I students and to others. The length of the bibliography indicates that this work should certainly not be used alone by the would-be expert in classification, but I hope that the earlier expressed purpose – 'to give as full an account of library classification as a well-equipped librarian, who does not seek to be a specialist in the subject, may be expected to possess' – is still fulfilled.

XIII. The Manual also retains its original function as a survey of the work of others more than a vehicle for original thought; this necessarily means the gathering together and interweaving of a number of diverse, stimulating, and sometimes conflicting ideas. Thus my debt to the many outstanding writers in this subject is great and should be as obvious to my reader as it is to me. I am indebted also to those librarians who have so kindly provided photographs for my illustrations and to all those who have, directly or indirectly, given me advice and encouragement, or allowed me to refer to their experience in this field of librarianship.

XIV. Finally I should like to express my gratitude to my wife for her patience and continual help in the most interesting, but onerous, work of revision, and to my students – past and present – whose enthusiasm and questions tend to act as a most effective antidote to the tendency (which I suspect may attack many lecturers from time to time) to become too complacent and dogmatic about one's subject.

A. MALTBY

Liverpool, April 1967.

Contents

List of Illustrations

List of Diagrams and Tables

Principles of Classification

CHAPTER ONE

The Nature and Purpose of Classification

1. From the day when a man first assembled books of any kind or form, men have been interested in the ways of arranging them. It is merely a part of the divine instinct that 'order is Heaven's first law'; for arrangement, or classification as we call it, lies at the base of every well-managed life and occupation. As we shall see later, the clay-tablets which formed the books of the library of the Assyrian, Assur-ban-i-pal, were placed on their shelves in a considered order; and in the record of libraries throughout the ages, wherever we have any details of them, we have also evidences of the preoccupation of their librarians with this question. It is one of much interest and is simple in its basic essentials, but in the course of years has assumed a complexity which is perhaps in part the outcome of the general tendency of men to seek scientific or philosophical reasons for the processes they employ, but is also due to the rapid increase annually in the number of newly published documents. The classification of libraries may be briefly defined as: *The arrangement of books on shelves or the systematic arrangement of catalogues and similar tools in the manner which is most useful to those who read.* Classification, then, is a tool for a very simple but infinitely important purpose. If, however, a preliminary definition is easy, its full explanation and application are not so; but it is essential from the outset that we keep clearly in mind the fact that the whole object of library classification is to secure an arrangement which will be useful to our readers with the smallest complication of search or other effort for them or for ourselves. It is a technique involving the systematic grouping of books by subject and is designed to expedite

the full use of the knowledge stored in the books and other material housed by the library.

2. In this chapter we shall consider classification in the widest sense of the word and its function in our everyday activities as a prelude to the study of the need for bibliographical classification. Every classical reader knows that the word 'class' in our sense has the same meaning that was given it in Ancient Rome, when the effective nobility were arranged in six orders or ranks according to their real or supposed qualities of blood or wealth. These were the *classes* of the population as distinct from the lower orders. A *classis*, then, was made up of a number of persons having a certain quality in common. So, in our studies, a class consists of a number of things which are alike in some particular or have some quality in common by which they may be sorted out from other things and which at the same time makes their own unity. It may safely be assumed from the outset that everything in the universe is a member of some class. We can test this readily if we consider any of the common things of life – plants, animals, men, houses, streets, stones, stars, clothes and so forth. The mere mention of any one of these brings to the mind not a single object but a whole series of things which have the common name. Such a name is a *class* name.

3. We cannot reason, even in the simplest manner, unless we possess the power of being able to classify things; indeed we cannot live at all. A Wellsian picture is easily conjured up of an inhabitant of another planet, who possesses every human faculty but has had no human experience, who finds himself set down suddenly on one of our country roads. The world he has come from has none of the features of this; everything therefore before and around him is new. He walks along the road and the first object of consequence that he notices is a tree. He sees that it has a perpendicular trunk covered by a corrugated substance, that it branches off above his head, and that on these branches are rustling extremities which we call leaves. With no knowledge to aid, his eyes do not awaken in his mind memories of something like it seen elsewhere which will tell him what it is. He proceeds to experiment; he feels the trunk, and finds it solid; he plucks a leaf, somewhat surprised to find that it is easily detachable; greatly daring, he tastes the leaf, and finds it has a sweet, acid, not pleasant or unpleasant, flavour. He goes on his way, and meets another such object, but different in shape – in an accidental particular – and he repeats the experiments he made with the first

tree. His impressions of the solidity of the trunk, the detachability and flavour of the leaf are repeated. He is on the way to classification; he decides that this second thing must have a definite *likeness* to the first thing. Repeated experiments with other trees strengthen and confirm this inference. So, by gradual and sometimes painful processes, he arrives at the notion that there is a group of things every member of which is like every other in all essential particulars. If he lives long enough he may learn from man that the group has a name, Trees; but in any case he has formed an idea to which he will attach some label or name of his own in order to distinguish it. This is classification, in a broad sense.

4. It becomes more advanced classification when from repeated experiences he learns that, while all trees resemble one another in their main characteristics, some trees have darker leaves than others, some have oval leaves, others bifurcate or double leaves, some have smooth edges, some are serrated or tooth-edged; and his recognition of these differences enables him to make groups within the greater group of trees; to separate mentally the pine tree from oak, the alder from elder and birch from beech; and later he may find that fir, larch and cedar very closely resemble the pine, although they have differences, but differences not nearly so marked as the difference between the oak and pine. Later still, if his observations are continued, he will discover that even the pine tree has several kinds, the Weymouth, the Norwegian, the Italian Stone Pine, and so on. When he has reached this stage, he has co-ordinated a series of observations by the use of memory – and subordinated sub-classes to their parent class – in such a way that the sight of one pine tree calls into his mind the characteristics of all pines as distinct from other kinds of tree. He can *classify* them.

5. We doubt if a man would survive for twenty-four hours if he were entirely without this power of classifying. Imagine a man in a London street, who beheld a car knock down and injure another man and yet was unable to infer from the incident that any other car would behave similarly in similar circumstances – who could not recognise that any swift-rolling vehicle (and 'swift-rolling vehicle' constitutes a *class* of things) was a dangerous thing with which to collide! From a single incident of this kind a man with classifying power but without experience might make the error, but a second would teach him to avoid it and the first would make him cautious. But the man without the power to classify objects would be unable

to relate one car to another; experience would be of no use to him; he would probably walk quite carelessly in front of any car he saw. The example may seem ridiculous enough, but were we deprived of classifying power the circumstances might be precisely as suggested.

6. 'Classification made the ape a man' stated E. C. Richardson, meaning that it is the ability to distinguish the likenesses and differences existing between things which is peculiar to man – the higher reasoning power. However, we may be underestimating the mental powers of birds and animals, if we suggest that they are without reason. For example, the lower animals certainly have the power of distinguishing two classes of things: those that are eatable and those that are not. The beaver in his architecture shows a power which may be instinct but is very like reason. So, too, the eagle in choosing a nesting-place on great heights, usually over precipices, must in some way be aware that precipices are inaccessible. Yet it is probable that animals and birds have no consciousness of the reasons which underlie their actions and in this respect man alone may be pre-eminent; in any case these powers which seem to be merely rudimentary in animals are developed in man to a high degree; they are so even in the uneducated man; and on these considerations may rest the validity of Richardson's saying.

7. All this may enable us to reach another useful definition of classification. It is that exercise of the powers of perception and reason which enables us to assemble things in an order of likeness, and to separate them according to an order of unlikeness. There is rather more in this than may appear on the surface. The definition means not merely the grouping of things which resemble one another, but the arrangement within each group of its components according to their degrees of resemblance. To take a rough un-scientific example, which will, however, illustrate our point sufficiently. A group of dogs will contain, perhaps, many kinds of dog – greyhounds, foxhounds, wolfhounds, terriers, Irish terriers, and Scotch terriers. All these have the general resemblance which is implied by their common name – dogs. But all hounds are more like other hounds than they are like terriers; all terriers more like other terriers than they are like hounds. So these would form sub-classes within the class, dogs; but, again, a bull terrier is more like a mastiff than it is like a hound; and this relationship too must be shown in our arranging of the class. Classification, then, is not only the general grouping of things for location or identification purposes; it is also

their arrangement in some sort of logical order so that the *relation-ships of the things may be ascertained*. Here we have a vital principle in classification theory: it is one that must be constantly borne in mind.

8. Enough has been said to emphasise the truth that man's universe is so great and complex that on first appearance it is a chaos, a tangle of things to which he has no clue and of such extent that he can obtain no grasp of it unless he provides himself with some sort of map. This map of things is a convenient expression for a scheme of classification. The whole universe of thought and objects must be put into some order by the mind and that order must be recorded. Not only the whole universe, which means everything; even the single sciences are far too extensive for our comprehension until we have made some sort of map of their territories. Much of the study of man has been of what may be called a classificatory kind; that is to say, it has been concerned with observing and recording the apparatus, structure, habits and purposes of things with a view to their accurate description; so that we may name them adequately and understand them. Indeed Thomas Carlyle once said, with much justice, that the greater part of knowledge consists in the giving of right names to things. Such study and research reveals the various likenesses which things have, and by these the things tend to be assembled into classes. By likeness, we mean the quality or qualities in things which enable them to be substituted for each other, as for example, the cartridges in a particular type of machine gun, the cards used in a catalogue, or pennies. Each of these re-presents the companions in its class to a high degree. It is clear that there must be many ways in which things are alike; the likenesses stressed in a particular classification will be those which best serve the purpose of the maker of that classification.

9. Richardson asserts, without qualification, that 'the things in nature are already classified', and from this we may infer that what man has to do is only to trace out the order of that classification and to record it. We shall see in succeeding chapters that the history of book classification shows that librarians have a tendency to return continually, with some fascination, to the idea that the classification of knowledge – the accurate mapping out of ideas and objects in the world around us – is the essential basis of a book classification. That there are differences between the book classification and the know-ledge classification is obvious to simple perception, but the re-

semblance between them is even greater. Thus it can be seen that the ideas of Richardson, Bliss, and others, and the current interest of some members of our profession in the philosophical theory of levels of integration within the universe, are all attempts to ensure that a book classification will be both helpful and durable by corresponding closely to a scientific organization of knowledge. There are not wanting those who declare that there is no order in nature apart from the human mind that conceives it, yet this is surely a vain speculation of Berkeleyan sort which declares that things only exist in as much as the human mind perceives them. More valid perhaps are those objections which suggest that the natural order is too complex for any man's classificatory map to suit us all, that the order of nature defies the classifier because it is never static, or that book classification in particular presents many examples of items which 'cut across' orthodox subject disciplines. Yet, when all such objections have been considered, we can at least say that nature offers man some clues concerning the organization of the multiplicity of objects which surround him. We do know, for example, that in the natural world animals with a backbone form one group and those without another: that plants with flowers are one group and flowerless plants another; that some birds live mainly in the water and that some are exclusively land creatures, and so the process may be extended. The mere recognition of such likenesses and differences as these is an act of classification and the common-ness of the process is patent. It may be well, however, to say that while classification is necessary to knowledge, it is only a method of approaching it. Much of the difficulty that is found in classifying (and this is especially true of book classification) arises from a want of knowledge either of the subjects we are endeavouring to arrange or of the use that will be made of the completed arrangement. We cannot classify an object or idea without knowing at least some of its qualities, and we cannot classify accurately or with any degree of finality without knowing a great many of its qualities. We could not, for example, classify dogs without knowing what dogs are, and still less could we sub-divide them into their many species. Observation must first tell us the main characteristics of dogs: and having some view of these the classifying process is to arrange them. In like manner, we cannot classify books by subjects unless we know what they are about. That seems trite enough when thus stated; but the statement is not at all unnecessary.

10. Our rough definition of classification as the arrangement of things according to their degree of likeness has served to lead up to a much more extended and now classic definition. It was first enunciated by Huxley, has been modified by Jevons and added to by Jast:

> By the classification of any series of objects is meant the actual or ideal arrangement together of those which are like and the separation of those which are unlike; the purpose of this arrangement being, primarily, to facilitate the operations of the mind in clearly conceiving and retaining in the memory the characters of the objects in question, and the recording of them that they may be conveniently and quickly referred to; and secondarily, to disclose the correlations or laws of union of properties and circumstances.

This can be explained more simply perhaps. Classification is primarily a mental operation. When we say we arrange things we mean that we place them in an order which corresponds with an idea or series of ideas in our minds; we could not arrange things in an order which did not thus exist in our thought. To do this we have mental pictures of the things we are to arrange. That is *ideal* arrangement, indeed this mental process is the true meaning of the term classification. *Actual* arrangement is the placing in order of objects that we can see or touch, such as botanical specimens, or coins, or, of course, books. We may anticipate later chapters here by stating that one of the main problems in bibliographical classification lies in the fact that an actual arrangement of tangible objects is involved. A book may have links with more than one subject field, but it can have only one place in a scheme of classification designed for the arrangement on the library shelves.

11. To return to our present theme, it will be seen, we think, that the classifier is concerned not only with external things, the manifestations of the natural universe; he has a whole universe within himself – of emotions, thoughts, percepts, concepts, ideas – which he must also reduce to order. Some of man's thought is really external to himself, having been derived from others; his thoughts, for example, on current happenings are too often merely the reflection of the leading article in the newspaper he reads; but for most useful purposes we may regard them as his own. This

subjective, intangible matter is equally to be controlled and set in order. Man cannot communicate his opinions or knowledge readily unless the ideas represented are first arranged in his own mind. So the definition might read 'Classification is the arrangement of things themselves or of our mental picture of things'. This gives us a valuable point for consideration, which may be put in the form of a question: 'What is the material of classification?' The reply is – everything. We can classify not only tangible objective things; we can also arrange impressions, ideas, notions; we can and must arrange things which exist, have existed, or may exist. Thus classification clarifies thought, advances investigation, shows gaps in the sequence of knowledge and promotes discovery; revealing, as it should, the relationships of things, it enables a more or less complete survey of knowledge to be made.

12. In many ways a classification, when committed to paper, can be compared to a map. Its task is to provide for the field of knowledge or part of it, as comprehensive and clear a statement as the cartographer is able to make of a territory of the earth. For just as a map makes clear the relationship between place and place so a classification strives to show the relationship of each branch of knowledge with other branches. Likewise just as the map may stress physical, geological, meteorological, economic, or other features, the features stressed by a classification must be determined by the purpose for which it is made and the needs of those it is designed to serve. Yet, in a sense, a classification is more complex than a map. The globe of the earth is, as it were, fixed; the countries may change hands indeed but they do not change position; while in a classification topics may grow or diminish in importance. They may abandon their relationships with certain subject fields and forge new links with others. In short, the problem of organizing them is complicated by the fact that knowledge is in a constant state of flux.

CHAPTER TWO

The Value of Classification in Libraries

13. Classification is a key to knowledge; because it is clear that if we arrange things in a definite order, and we know what that order is, we have a very good map of, or key to, these things. What is the purpose of this and what does this mean in relation to librarianship? *Merely that classification is the basis of all order in handling literature and its record.* That is a large statement, but it is one capable of conclusive proof. Books are a class of things, when we take into our view all the objects in the universe; and when we separate books from all other things, merely as an assembly of books, we have performed an act of classification. But it is a very elementary one. A huge room full of books is, in fact, having regard to the welter of things they are written about and the many forms and sizes they take, about the nearest representation of chaos that we can imagine. That is to say, if they are not classified in some way apart from their mere separation from things which are not books. Unless they are classified we cannot discover without immense loss of time what books there are on chemistry, history, theology, poetry, or transport, for example. Some libraries are of this kind, or they are arranged by some accidental characteristic such as the colour of the bindings of the books. When the purpose of the books is that they shall be seen and not read, this is an excellent arrangement. Otherwise it has nothing to commend it. Some libraries have arranged books by size. This makes the library look very neat, but it would mean that if we had ten editions (say) of Milton they would be in ten different places. Examples can be multiplied. Again, if we arranged the books by their printing types (typography), the results would be similarly valueless, except for the student of typography – for whom, be it remarked, it might be a perfectly essential arrangement (but

B

only if the books are regarded as 'museum specimens', and not as having any other meaning). In a rather similar manner, if we arrange books by the language in which they are written, we get a very wide separation of *subjects*; although, again, if they are arranged for the student of language who is interested *only* in language, that would be a perfectly justifiable arrangement. Chronological order by date of publication or by date of accession is another method which could be considered. Older libraries sometimes employ a fixed chronological order of books within very broad subject classes. Again, however, it is an order without real utility for readers or librarians, as we shall see.

14. Yet another possible arrangement, which appeals to some people and is certainly superior to the methods so far considered, is to group books alphabetically by the names of their authors. This will almost certainly suffice for fiction. It also has a definite value for the private library owned or used by the student who knows all his authors, and he often prefers this arrangement. If we know, for example, that Charles Darwin was a great naturalist, we know that under his name we shall find works on natural science. But the author order tells us nothing about naturalists of whose names we may be ignorant, and it is no disparagement of the ordinary user of most libraries to say that he is usually unacquainted with authors. We must therefore rely on our catalogues to cater for the author approach to knowledge and adopt a different system for the arrangement of books on the shelves. An alphabetical subject order might be employed for the latter task. This does have the merit of locating information on a particular subject for us and, even in a university library where many items are asked for by the names of their authors, it would be superior to the alphabetical author arrangement in grouping books conveniently for use and thus saving time. Unfortunately, the alphabetical subject order also has limitations. Firstly it is difficult to decide how specific our terms should be for such an arrangement; secondly the problem of synonymous terms must somehow be solved; thirdly, and this is the most important factor of all, the alphabetical sequence results in the scattering of related subject material. We may, for instance, get such an arrangement as:

Abbeys	Battles
Accidents	Bible

Adhesives	Bombing
Agriculture	Bowls
Angling	Buildings
Animals	Bulldogs
Architecture	Cabbages, etc.

The order is not altogether without use, but it is obviously most imperfect. Our random selection of examples proves this. Abbeys have no relation to Accidents, but they have to Architecture. Books dealing with Angling or Bowls would be more usefully placed near to general works on games and recreations. In other words, subjects are not systematically related to one another in this arrangement. Each topic is separated from kindred subjects unless, by chance, the alphabet happens to bring a few related topics together. If we were only concerned with *locating* material perhaps this would not matter. But because, to adapt a phrase of Richardson's, 'use is the watch-word of arrangement', it is essential that the organization on the shelves of a library should reflect the use made of books, not only enabling material on a specific theme to be speedily located, but also *subordinating each specific topic to the appropriate general one* and showing the most important *relationships* between subjects. Thus a classified subject arrangement is essential in most libraries.

15. This leads us on to the natural question – what is the subject of a book? It becomes clear that to classify accurately and precisely we must place each book under its *specific* subject, for it is only in this way that we can arrange library material in a helpful sequence on the shelves. Within each major subject field, the sequence should begin with general material and proceed slowly to more and more specialised branches of the subject, the exact order being determined by an accurate analysis of the subjects of books and by observing the needs of specialists in each sphere of activity. Thus a history of the town of Leeds should be classified as such and not hidden away with more general material under British history, or even the history of Yorkshire. The helpful order of the history class should then enable the enquirer to see the material on the 'History of Great Britain' as a whole, then to survey works on the 'History of York-shire', or of other counties, and finally to encounter specific works dealing with the history of single towns, or even areas within towns. Each town will be subordinated to its parent county; each county to the country as a whole. It thus becomes relatively simple to broaden

or narrow down a search for relevant information. The same procedure must be followed in other subject fields, the exact subject of a book being expressed in the classification in each case. Ranganathan defines the phrase specific subject as being 'that division of knowledge whose extension and intension are equal to those of its [the book's] thought content'. That is to say, we must beware of selecting, when classifying, a theme which is more general than the true subject of the book with which we may be dealing. The student will discover that Ranganathan's *Elements of Library Classification* is most lucid and useful in explaining this particular point of classification theory.

16. We find that, where a rightly designed classification exists, librarian or reader may go to a definite set of shelves and see at their beginning the books dealing with the subjects which are preliminary to or are the foundation of the sought subject; find, following these, the books on the subject itself; and, following them in turn, the books on the subjects which develop from that subject. If classification is applied in a catalogue or bibliography the entries of books in it will be similarly in order. In later chapters we shall consider fairly definite views, expressed from several standpoints, on the best methods of achieving a classified order of the optimum helpfulness.

17. It must be recognised, however, that alphabetical order is not to be entirely rejected. Bliss has said that 'alphabetic arrangements ... are illogical and unsystematic, everywhere dispersing related subject matter; they are the very antithesis of classification'. This statement is a little too harsh and was made with the intention of refuting the claim that alphabetical order was superior to the classified subject arrangements. But there is no reason why alphabetical order should not be used, to a certain extent, within a classification scheme whenever it is the most sensible method of sub-arrangement or whenever it can bring about a more useful grouping than can a classified sequence. These occasions, it must be confessed, are (with the exception of alphabetical order by author for fiction) destined to be comparatively rare. But many libraries introduce alphabetical order into the biography class to produce an alphabetical sequence of great lives and most libraries have some material – pamphlets, current periodicals, street directories, trade catalogues, or publishers catalogues, for example – which may lend itself to an alphabetical arrangement. Within the classification, alphabetical order by author is used as a final method of arrangement

for a group of books classified at the same location and there may be occasions when alphabetical arrangement by *topic* within a class can prove superior to further sub-division on systematic lines. This last point, as we shall discover later, is well illustrated in the Library of Congress scheme. Special libraries may also find use for alphabetical systems of organising knowledge and this is attested to by the increasing use of methods of co-ordinate indexing, which are described in Chapter 25. So we find that librarians do make use of alphabetical order by subject, or by author, or even by title, when necessary. This, however, does not detract one iota from the claims that have been made for the value and overall efficiency of systematic subject classification in libraries. For the bulk of our material, the best arrangement is the classified one, especially if serious reading is being done or a reference and information service is being provided.

18. A subject classification of this kind has the obvious value of economizing time and energy, always provided that it is constructed in a way which closely reflects the use made of literature. It is an economy in the mere finding of books; for it is clear that if all the books and other materials on a subject are assembled as nearly as is physically possible at one place there will be an important saving of time in the obtaining of a general view of the literature. By relating subjects in a rational way it ensures that, if we have few books immediately available on a particular specific subject, we will find near to these volumes on the shelves other material on related themes which may well prove helpful in assisting readers. A chapter in a more general work nearby may prove of great value in providing the reader with the knowledge he requires. Likewise systematic classification assists the librarian in recording issues, in creating special subject displays and, by showing the strength or weaknesses of his collection in any subject field, in book selection and stock-building.[1] But classification is not limited in its use to the arranging of books on shelves. It has even more an *analysing* use, in the making of classified entries in catalogues. For example, in the card catalogue, a card can be filed under every subject with which a book is in any important way concerned. That catalogue then becomes a more or less complete record of all important subjects dealt with by a book (and these may not be indicated by the titles of books or revealed by the places which they occupy on the shelves). The economy value of

---

[1] W. H. Phillips provides a useful list of ways in which the classification is helpful. *Primer of Book Classification.* 5th ed. 1961, p. 23.

this is clear. How many a research worker, inventor, thinker, writer, has wasted an immense time in finding out and in solving for himself facts and problems with which other workers have already dealt! Were only the results of former labours recorded in classified catalogues, many such men would be saved from the effort of duplicating work that has already been done, and from the vexation of discovering their waste of energy. Life is too short to allow the neglect of classification!

19. The foundation of the library is the book; the foundation of librarianship is classification. Without classification no librarian can build up a systematic library; one, that is to say, which represents adequately the field of human learning as it is recorded in books. Think of the difficulties facing him – if he is honest in his work – in an unclassified library. He must gather together temporarily all the books on any given subject from all parts of his library, every time he wants to add to the strength of that subject or – what is equally important in all but the greater libraries which aim at completeness and never discard books on account of age or for the usual reasons which prompt withdrawal in libraries of more modest size – weed out books which have become obsolete. We fear that much inefficient work has resulted from want of classification. Those in charge of larger libraries have sometimes advocated the close classification of entries in catalogues, but have favoured broad or simplified classification for their shelf arrangement. The reasoning on which this advocacy is based is not convincing. At any rate general libraries arranged upon the open-access system are impossible to work without adequate shelf classification and most special libraries have found that they need a detailed scheme if their bookstock is large; otherwise readers would be lost in an unclassified welter of books. If, then a library cannot be built up, or revised, without classification, and if students and readers can get no comprehensive view of the literature of subjects without it, the vital character of our subject is easily revealed.

20 Yet, despite the clearly demonstrable advantages of employing systematic subject arrangement, bibliographical classification is not without its critics. The famous nineteenth century logician and economist, W. S. Jevons, considered the subject classification of libraries to be impossible because of the complex way in which knowledge is presented in books. In his *Principles of Science*, he wrote 'Classification (of books) by subjects would be an extremely

useful method if it were practicable, but experience shows it to be a logical absurdity. It is a very difficult matter to classify the sciences, so complicated are the relations between them. But with books the complication is vastly greater, since the same book may treat of different sciences or may discuss a problem involving many branches of knowledge. A good account of the steam-engine will be anti-quarian, so far as it traces out the earliest efforts at discovery; purely scientific, as regards the principles of thermodynamics involved; technical, as regards the mechanical means of applying those principles; economical, as regards the lives of the inventors ... In regard to literary works, rigorous classification is still less possible. The same work may partake of the nature of poetry, biography, history, philosophy, or if we form a comprehensive class of belles-lettres, nobody can say exactly what does or does not come under the term.'

21. This rather lengthy quotation might suggest that we have undertaken a fearsome and impossible thing in presuming to classify our books; we ought, we suppose, to leave them in unordered arrangement (if that be not a contradiction of terms), with only an author index; and, therefore, to leave them in such manner that they are accessible only to the man who knows every author in the subject in which he is interested, and, when his memory or know-ledge fails on this point, they will be inaccessible to him as well! The late L. S. Jast said 'This statement of Jevons reminds me of the keeper who went up to the trespassing angler with the remark, "My man, you can't fish here", and who received the reply, "But I *am* fishing".' Librarians, in their wisdom or unwisdom, have trespassed on Jevons's precious waters and have shown that they can classify. But, coming as the statement does from so excellent an authority, we must examine it, and clarify our minds in regard to it. From the librarian's standpoint, the hypothetical book may deal, indeed, with all the subjects that Jevons enumerates but it is, after all, a 'book on the steam-engine'. Remembering the rule that convenience governs all classifications, he asks himself to whom the book will be most useful; for whom, primarily, it is meant; and according to his answer he will place the book – in this case – in engineering. Again, in pure literature, or belles-lettres, it does not matter much if we do or do not know the qualities of the books included or the subjects of which they treat – because their importance does not lie in their subject matter, interesting though that often is and must be in works

of enduring character, but in their pattern as form or mode of expression; and in classifying them we adopt this characteristic and ignore altogether their subject matter. (We shall come to this question of occasional classification by form in a later chapter.) We ought to examine Jevons's statement in relation to the time at which it was made, and to the lack of knowledge of libraries which it unfortunately shows. In 1874 there were few reasonably good library schemes; hardly any of the libraries of England were classified, and those that were could not boast of anything wonderful in their arrangement. Moreover, Jevons seems not to have known of the schemes and methods laid down in Edward Edwards's *Memoirs of Libraries*, published sixteen years earlier than his own book – which is not remarkable as the readers of books on librarianship are select indeed; had he known them he might have modified his statement.

22. One hesitates to accuse so logical and orderly a mind as Jevons of confusion; but he *has* confused the functions of classification with those of cataloguing. Perhaps this is hardly a fair way of putting it, since his criticism is aimed at the classified catalogue – the actual classifying of books on shelves was a performance of which he had probably never heard. But even here his objection seems to rest upon the belief that only one entry for a book is made in a classified catalogue. A classification does not try to place a book among others on the shelves according to all its subjects, but only by the predominating, or most convenient of the subjects with which it deals. A book deals with a topic from forty sides; very well, if we had the means, and lack of imagination, we could buy forty copies of this book and place one under each of the forty places in our classified arrangement; but one need hardly say that the number of libraries achieving such a feat will not be great. Our book is, in fact, a concrete, indivisible thing, which will go into one place on the shelves; and that place, as we have just affirmed, must be the one most helpful to the user of the book. In the catalogue the book can be entered directly, or by reference, under every subject in it which is of enough importance to justify such entries. There we are handling not the book but written or typed cards or slips which represent it and these we can multiply as fully as reason and convenience dictate. We shall have something more to say about the value of the classified catalogue later on. Here it will be sufficient to add that Jevons' hypothetical book would have to be a remarkably encyclopaedic view of the steam-engine to justify an entry under

each of the topics he names; we therefore reiterate most strongly that books can and should be classified.

23. Twentieth-century critics of classifications in libraries have taken a different approach from that of Jevons. They have drawn our attention to the difficulty of classifying in subject fields where our own knowledge is scanty; to the fact that no classification can gather in one place all that a reader may need on a subject; to the inability of a linear, or one-dimensional arrangement on the shelves to reveal the complex 'family-tree' relationships that exist between subject fields; to the difficulty of producing a bibliographical scheme which can keep pace with the development of knowledge, especially the rapid technological strides that have been made in our own lifetime; and to the problem of accommodating over-sized books in any classified sequence. Such librarians have usually accepted that, for general libraries at least, systematic shelf classification is necessary, but have questioned the value of detailed arrangement. A prominent critic has been the American writer, Dr Grace Kelley, who has suggested that exact classification usually leads to long notations and may defeat its own ends by its complexity. She suggests that general libraries should be content with broad classification, relying on a detailed dictionary catalogue to carry out the further subject analysis of our stock. This solution has its own problems for the complexity of these catalogues is causing increasing concern these days in the United States. But Miss Kelley's conclusions and those of other opponents of close, or specific classification, will be considered in Chapter 22. Here it will suffice to say that, although even the best book classifications are unable to bring together on the shelves *all* the material which a reader may need, classification is far more successful in assembling non-fiction books for use that any alphabetical system or arbitrary scheme of shelving. Indeed our libraries have long ago rejected the once popular method of fixed location, which involved the numbering of shelves and the permanent allocation of each book to a certain spot on a particular shelf, in favour of relative location, which enables books to be moved about so that new volumes can be inserted in the most appropriate place in a classified sequence. The result has been that the open-access library especially owes much of its efficiency to the flexibility and usefulness of its classification system.

24. Yet much remains to be achieved. If the student is inclined to think (especially if he comes from a small public library) that too

B*

much stress is placed on classificatory principles, on terminology, and on the importance of a useful systematic order, in the following chapters in this section, he must consider how a faulty and inadequate arrangement will hinder the effective organization of material and the discovery of relevant books or information particularly in large and specialised collections. To abandon the search for better principles and new or improved classifications would be to evade the challenge of housing and exploiting the world's expanding literature – to evade in fact the essence of the practical librarian's work! We need good bibliographies and reference aids in our efforts to organise and retrieve knowledge; likewise we need to be constantly seeking ways to improve our catalogues and classification systems and to overcome, whenever possible, their imperfections in order that our bookstocks may be efficiently and fully employed and this with the minimum expenditure of time and labour on the part of the reader. Although no classification can eliminate the need for good staff with a thorough knowledge of the stock and an appreciation of readers' requirements, a sound scheme will speed up the work of an information service by displaying clearly the structure of each subject field and will facilitate the confident handling of enquiries; thus, to a large extent, staff time and labour is saved through classification also.

CHAPTER THREE

Traditional Theories of Library Classification

25. Having decided then that the absolute necessity for systematic subject classification in the vast majority of libraries is recognised, how can a bibliographical scheme best be constructed? It is no disparagement of the pioneers – Dewey, Cutter, Brown and others – to say that, in the early years of open access libraries, classificatory practice forged ahead of theory. Despite the fact that three of the important general schemes were available, or in course of preparation, by the end of the nineteenth century, the first systematic attempt to set down the *theory* of library classification did not come until 1901. This was Ernest Cushing Richardson's book entitled *Classification*. The views of this American writer were to be supported, broadly speaking, by his fellow-countryman, Henry Evelyn Bliss and also by the early editions of this Manual. They rely chiefly on the idea that classifications of knowledge, or parts of it, similar to those constructed in the past by scientists and philosophers such as Linnaeus, Bacon, Coleridge, Comte and Spencer, provide us with the essential basis for the making of a book classification. The latter, it is suggested, is fundamentally a classification of knowledge or ideas with the addition of certain auxiliaries necessitated by the complexity of knowledge as found in book form.

26. The older ideas on book classification also owe much to the principles of classification as taught by logicians. The major principle originally expounded was that classification should start with knowledge in its totality and divide it up into classes. The process would continue until division was exhausted, but two classes only would appear at each stage of division and one of these would be merely

the negation of the other. The older book classifications that are still in use today rejected this notion of dichotomous division, but leaned heavily nevertheless on the idea of starting with large subject fields and dividing them up, using one characteristic at a time, so that eventually they had attempted to list all departments of knowledge in a systematic sequence moving, from the very general to the highly specialised, in a series of regulated steps. This nineteenth-century approach certainly imposed limitations upon book classification. Nevertheless some of these earlier ideas still have much value for us; as one modern writer puts it, 'it is a mistake to consider that they cannot usefully complement other principles . . . however limited they are certainly not invalid'.[1] Unless we appreciate them we shall obtain a rather distorted picture of the Decimal Classification, the Congress Classification, and other great schemes which were constructed or begun in a period when librarians virtually had only the findings of philosophers and logicians and their own tentative experiments, or those of colleagues, to guide them. The ideas borrowed from the rules of formal logic assume that, in a general classification designed to cover all departments of knowledge, we will break down a collection of books into organized subject groups using one *characteristic* at a time. The characteristics used in division will enable us to assemble things according to their degree of likeness to make a specific class. To use a formal phrase, a classification proceeds from terms of great *extension* and small *intension* to terms of great *intension* and small *extension*. Or, more simply, it proceeds by taking class terms which connote great areas of subject matter and divides them by gradual steps into terms less and less extensive until division is no longer possible or necessary. In logical terms, each class is said to be a species of the one immediately above it in the hierarchical chain and a genus in relation to the one below. This process, in which one characteristic only is used as the dividing principle at each stage, will eventually enable us to enumerate all branches of knowledge in the form of an organized 'family tree'. For example, in the class Commerce, we might have:

[1] J. R. Sharp, *Some Fundamentals of Information Retrieval*, 1965, p. 33

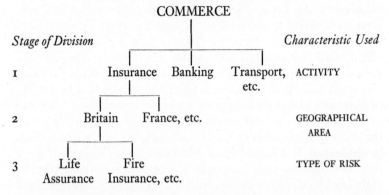

COMMERCE

Stage of Division				Characteristic Used
1	Insurance	Banking	Transport, etc.	ACTIVITY
2	Britain	France, etc.		GEOGRAPHICAL AREA
3	Life Assurance	Fire Insurance, etc.		TYPE OF RISK

A classification schedule then is a series of terms arranged in orderly rows or columns and our diagram shows how certain characteristics of division might be used to split the Commerce class into organized groups. Division has been pursued here under the topic Insurance; the classes Banking, Transport and other divisions of Commerce could, of course, be also further sub-divided and in this way we could itemise any specific theme, showing it in a vast 'tree' containing all branches of knowledge, as a part of the more general class to which it belongs. Division is, in one sense, the exact opposite of classification or grouping. Yet, paradoxical though it may seem, we must divide our larger classes in order to obtain more specific groupings each consisting of closely allied material. The same methods can be used when making a special classification but, in this instance, the 'tree' will be confined to the departments of the specialised area of activity. Thus our classification, based on the rules of logical division, moves in systematic stages from general subjects, like Commerce, to specific ones, such as (and we can visualise this if we imagine our diagram in extended form) 'the value of a fire insurance policy in 1966 for business firms in Britain'.

27. The links which this older approach has with the Greek logicians and the distinction between natural and artificial classifications are no longer of significance for us; in this edition of the Manual, therefore, references to the 'Tree of Porphyry' and the 'Five Predicables' have not been made. But the characteristics, or principles of division, illustrated in the diagram are important, for they tell us some vital facts about book classification. First of all the characteristics employed must be essential to the purpose in view. It is evident that, for example, if I make an arrangement of my

possessions, it is because I want them in the order which will make them most useful or agreeable to me, and that condition governs all classification-making. Thus the maker of a book classification (now often called a classificationist, as distinct from a classifier – the person who applies a scheme to a particular collection) will select characteristics which are relevant for the organization of knowledge in libraries and will try to apply them in the order which will result in the most efficient final arrangement possible. With this in mind, the order of application of the characteristics in our diagram could be challenged. Is it best to divide Insurance first of all by the type of risk and then use the geographical characteristic or vice-versa? Only our knowledge of the use made of books can answer this kind of question satisfactorily for us; but it is a vital question and the final efficiency of any scheme will rest upon it.

28. Another point which arises is that each characteristic should be exhausted before the next is used. For if we apply two or more characteristics *at the same stage of division*, we have a muddled state of affairs which is known as *cross-division or cross-classification*. Thus, in our diagram, if we used the characteristics of insurance risk and geographical area at the same step of division a confused arrangement would result and we should not know, for example, whether to place an item on 'Life assurance in the U.S.A.' under

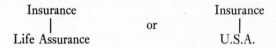

However, our diagram avoids this problem by using only one characteristic at a time and it would apply this exhaustively before the next was used. Thus the hierarchy for the above example would be:

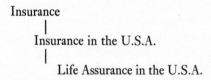

According to the strict rules of formal logic, cross-classification is a state of affairs to be avoided at all costs for it may well result in doubt in the classifier's mind and consequently in the scattering of a number of items on the same theme. However, it will be found that

it does occur at times in the established bibliographical schemes. This is often unfortunate in practice, as can be seen from the Education class in the Decimal system, but is not always necessarily a fault; the way in which knowledge is presented in books does bring about a certain amount of overlapping of categories. Indeed the question of whether a book classification should resort to cross-division or not depends entirely upon the requirements of literature. No theoretical canon or standard is so sacred that it cannot occasionally be ignored in the interests of a more helpful arrangement. But, of course, when cross-classification is adopted, it is up to the classificationist to justify the chosen arrangement; if it leads to books on a particular specific subject being separated, it cannot be condoned.

29. We may leave our diagram now to consider a different kind of lesson which the earlier writers on book classification have succeeded in imparting to us. This is that classification must be non-critical. It will easily be recognised that there is a tendency in men to view all things in relation to themselves, but this tendency should be resisted when carrying out the work of classificationist or classifier. This can be pointed out by examples more easily than by much assertion. The Decimal Classification treated Palmistry, Astrology, and Spiritualism as Delusions through several editions; likewise, in the Literature class, it once arranged nine important writers under each chronological period, gathering other authors of that period together as 'minor writers'. These indignities have been removed in modern editions, but critical classification can occur in other ways. An author may represent views which are anathema to the individual classifier; for example, he may write a book like Brandes's *Jesus Christ a Myth*, or on some political question from a violent political bias. As classifiers our views and likings have no place in our work; Brandes's book is a life of Christ, however distasteful to the Christian; the political book must likewise be placed with other books on its subject even if we think it ought to go under treason or in some other limbo for the unspeakable. The result of critical classification is to scatter material on a single subject because of the author's beliefs. It will result in a kind of cross-division which can never be commended as it leads to the dispersal of allied material and indeed to general confusion on the shelves.

30. We mentioned at the beginning of the chapter the views of E. C. Richardson, who argued that book classification rested on a classification of knowledge. It is convenient here to round off our

consideration of the traditional theories by considering his views, and those of his opponents, in a little more detail. Dr Richardson argued that if all knowledge could be systematically mapped out, according to the recognised rules of division, to form a complete classification of ideas, this map could be used as the basis of a book classification. Jevons, of course, had drawn attention to the complex way in which knowledge was often presented in books (indeed it is the point on which his whole argument against book classification rests) but Richardson maintained that books were no more complex than the objects and ideas to be found in the universe around us. 'A book', he says, 'could hardly be more complex as to subjects than a lump of rock may be as to elements.' Richardson also suggested that there is a true order of the sciences and that a good book classification should follow this order, that is discernible in nature. 'In general', he tells us, 'the closer a system can get to the true order of the sciences and the closer it can keep to it, the better the system will be and the longer it will last'. The fact that his book was reprinted in 1964 indicates that it still has some validity and importance in library classification studies.

31. Richardson was seeking a philosophical basis for library classification but, in many ways, his ideas are a reflection of the age in which he lived. The 'order of nature', as envisaged by Richardson (and also by Cutter and to a lesser extent by J. D. Brown) is essentially an order of progression from simple to complex things – the evolutionary order which excited so much attention in the late nineteenth century. Although Richardson and these other advocates of the idea that a classification of knowledge forms the basis of a bibliographical classification took care to stress the fact that book classification must be based on book usage, there is a danger that this approach to the problem may become over-theoretical. Richardson's ideas were challenged in a series of provocative articles by the librarian of the British Patent Office, E. Wyndham Hulme, which appeared in the *Library Association Record* in 1911–12 and were subsequently reprinted as an A.A.L. booklet. These carefully reasoned articles were, unfortunately, never completed. The librarian's use of classification was declared by Hulme to be without any real affinity with scientific and philosophical schemes. He writes: 'all classifications may be divided into two groups, (a) mechanical, (b) philosophical. The former, to which book classifica-tion belongs, deals with the mechanical assembling of material

objects into classes, while the latter are concerned with the ordering of our ideas of things'. He praised the Library of Congress Classification which is closely based on the actual stock and requirements of a very large library and coined the phrase *literary warrant* to describe the need for a book classification to be based on knowledge as recorded in books. Hulme's own scheme designed for the Patent Office Library is still used there and is now being revised by members of the British Museum staff. His approach is essentially pragmatic, suggesting that a library classification should be built up gradually from observations of the use made of books, rather than by following a pre-conceived map of knowledge based on the classifications of the philosophers or a 'will-o'-the-wisp' true order of the sciences.

32. He goes on to say: 'As a rule mechanical classifications are left unco-ordinated; but when, as in the case of book classification, a systematic co-ordination of classes is introduced, this operation must always be of secondary importance. If, therefore, we were in agreement with Dr Richardson, that the co-ordination of book classifications should follow the true order of the sciences, we should still be unable to acquiesce in his dictum that the test of the efficiency and permanent value of such classifications was to be found in the degree in which the order of their classes approximated to those of the higher type'. Hulme brings out his results in the phrase that a library classification is like a jig-saw puzzle in which the classes are the parts to be fitted together. This example does not seem to serve his purpose well, since the problem of the jig-saw puzzle is to reassemble the parts of an existing pattern; it is not a design made up by the solver as he goes but a series of bits cut from an existing design which, when all put together, form it. A classification made in this way would therefore be the assembling of classes of things in an order which already existed and the example could be equally well used to support Richardson's doctrine that nature is classified and the business of the classificationist is to find clues to enable him to distinguish the parts and to fit them together again – to sort them into a coherent whole. But, whatever we may think of Hulme's views, it is certain that he has left us one of the best definitions, or succinct descriptions, of book classification. It is, he says, 'a mechanical time-saving operation for the discovery of knowledge in literature. Books are our theme and the discovery of knowledge in books, by the shortest route, our aim and object.'

33. In the first thirty years or so of the present century, however, there was much more support for Richardson than for Hulme. Of the early effective library classification schemes, only Congress, and perhaps to a much lesser extent the Decimal Classification, reflected the idea of literary warrant. The majority of librarians accepted the viewpoint that a book classification could be made by building up a map of knowledge, based on the principles of logical division, by adding certain auxiliary features, and by modifying the map to make it suitable for bibliographical purposes. The idea that there is a scientific order, discernible in nature, that can be followed, was acceptable to most and indeed the notion is still held by some modern writers.[1] In H. E. Bliss these theories found their greatest and most learned advocate. He also maintained that book classifications should reveal the way in which specialist workers in the various fields of knowledge arranged their material and the way in which subjects are studied and taught – the 'educational and scientific consensus of opinion', as he rather ponderously expressed it. Writing in the 1930's, he indicated his dissatisfaction with the book classification schemes then available which, he believed, failed to group material in a way which would satisfy the specialist or scholar. He writes: 'There are indeed two kinds of classification, on the one hand the logical, natural, and scientific, on the other hand the practical, the arbitrary, the purposive; but for library classification we should join these two hands ... to make the classification conform to the scientific and educational organization of knowledge is to make it the more practical ... a library is ... a temple of knowledge, and its classification should be, not a haphazard, ramshackle structure, but an internal edifice worthy of its environment and itself of intellectual and educational value'. This quotation sums up Bliss's theories well. He believed that a knowledge classification could be used to produce a book classification possessing both scholarship and practical utility and he was later to test his ideas in a scheme of his own.

34. More will be said about Bliss and concerning these other early pioneers in the chapters on the historical side of our subject. There has indeed been much wrangling as to whether a classification should be mapped out and then offered to the world of librarianship for general use, or whether it is better for libraries to make a scheme

[1] For example, the Russian, B. M. Kedroff. Quoted in D. J. Foskett. *Library Classification and the field of knowledge.* 1958. p. 14.

of their own, or adapt an existing one to suit their own 'literary warrant'. Yet these early explorations into the theory of bibliographical classification showed that, on one point at least, classificationists and other librarians were more or less unanimous. They accepted the fact that a book classification should start with knowledge in its entirety and gradually break it down into classes and sub-classes by the application of a series of characteristics, thus eventually listing all topics in systematic fashion. This approach is inevitable if we regard our classification as a 'family tree' which follows, at least in part, the rules of division accepted by logicians. Thus the older general bibliographical schemes tended to try to enumerate all subjects in this way and to provide symbols to represent each subject listed. J. D. Brown, in his Subject Classification, anticipated modern theories of building up class numbers for subjects by the fitting together of basic concepts, but he did not fully perceive the possibilities of this idea which, in the older systems, can be best seen in the Universal Decimal Classification. To a lesser extent, the Decimal Classification of Dewey and Cutter's Expansive Classification grasped the idea of synthesis, or number-building, that is to be appraised in our next chapter. The Congress Classification, on the other hand, is essentially one which tries to list all subjects and to provide ready-made classification numbers for each. It is, therefore, sometimes spoken of as the most *enumerative* of the general bibliographical schemes. But we are in danger of confusing the student, if we contrast synthetic and enumerative classifications here. It will thus be sufficient to say that, before the middle of the twentieth century, new principles were brought to light; principles that were destined to overshadow the ideas and controversies which we have been discussing in this present chapter.

CHAPTER FOUR

Modern Ideas Concerning Subject
Analysis and Arrangement

35. The older bibliographical schemes have always found it difficult to keep pace with changes in the field of knowledge for, in attempting to list every branch of learning and to provide complete class-marks for nearly all the subjects shown, they are virtually out of date as soon as they appear. And their revision has been necessarily restricted because libraries using these well-established systems are reluctant to change their arrangement drastically. They also suffer from the fact that they offer a fixed hierarchy in each subject field, which is often only one of several hierarchies which might exist. The exact classification of many documents is thus prevented; for, if a scheme shows subject B as subordinate to subject A and subject C as subordinate to B, we cannot classify A plus C without using B as an intermediary. This inherent rigidity of structure, which is so obvious in the traditional enumerative schemes, has made some librarians sceptical with regard to the future of book classification. But fortunately there are now new methods available, for the construction of both general and special schemes, which emancipate book classification from the strict genus to species relationship produced by following the rules of logical division. These methods are based upon an analytical approach which seeks to recognise the basic *facets*, or categories, produced by the application of characteristics of division to each subject field, and to provide for the combination of concepts from these categories in such a way that any subject may be specified; it is therefore possible to classify accurately, through the use of a faceted scheme, many pamphlets or periodical articles with extremely specific subjects. The newer techniques are

being tested and gradually put into practice and seem to be superior to the conventional ideas concerning the organisation of material through classification. At the risk of seeming too conservative, certain librarians might say that this has still to be *fully* proved. Nor is it easy to integrate, as some writers have tried to do, older and modern ideas in one body of theory. They have much in common certainly in that they both, for instance, rely on the application of characteristics of division to a subject field and both recognise, for the purposes of helpful order, the supreme importance of discerning which are the most important characteristics; yet, in certain respects, like Dives and Lazarus, they have a great gulf fixed between them. Indeed, if the newer ideas blended too easily with the old they would have little originality; they will repay very careful study, for they are already making a great impact in some special libraries. Yet the essence of the traditional theories must be grasped too, for these older principles can be clearly seen in most of the existing general schemes.

36. The new methods are chiefly associated with the name of the eminent Indian librarian, Dr S. R. Ranganathan and many of them were put forward, in a tentative form, in his Colon Classification which first appeared in 1933. It would indeed be difficult to over-estimate the importance of this extraordinarily prolific writer in our studies. Ranganathan had been a student of classification in England under Sayers, but many of the ideas expressed in the Colon scheme and in his other writings are essentially the product of his own fertile and ingenious mind. The main principle to be considered is one which can be seen slowly evolving in the listing once and for all of certain recurring divisions, notably for forms of presentation and geographical areas, in many of the older schemes and most particularly in the Universal Decimal Classification, but which first clearly emerges in the original edition of the Colon scheme and has been developed considerably since then. This is that classification should be entirely synthetic. Instead of attempting to list all subjects, it is argued that a book classification should merely enumerate basic concepts, arranging these in appropriate categories or facets. Every subject will consist of the amalgamation of a number of these concepts. To classify a book, we must first of all analyse its compound subject and recognise the component elements or concepts. We then employ synthesis by linking together, in a specified manner, the symbols representing these elements – thus building up gradually the

class-mark for the subject. Let us try to make the distinction between the traditional and newer methods clearer by means of examples. Consider the specific subject: 'The doctrine of Grace in Methodism in Britain during the eighteenth century'. A *completely enumerative* classification would try to provide the classifier with a complete class-mark for this, as for all other subjects. (It may be noted that the older schemes are rarely enumerative to this degree, but the method of listing all topics is essentially the major principle which they try to follow). A *completely synthetic, or faceted*, scheme on the other hand would instruct the classifier to break down the subject into its component parts and then to build the required class-mark by linking together the part representing Methodism (as a branch of Christianity in the Religion class), the part representing Grace (from the Doctrines facet of that class), the part representing Britain (from the geographical facet common to all classes), and the part representing the eighteenth century (from the Chronological facet applicable to each class). Ranganathan has likened the synthetic method of book classification to a child's Meccano set. Both provide for the fitting together of standard unit parts to construct any model or class-mark that may be required. The newer methods of book classification are also sometimes said to reflect the analytico-synthetic approach. That is to say, the subject of each book is analysed into its facets and the symbols representing the relevent elements in each facet are then fitted together to reconstruct the subject concerned. Care must, of course, be taken to ensure that the facet combination order devised for any class is the one which will produce the most helpful possible arrangement of books and documents in that class. Also if, in a particular example, a certain facet is not represented, the others will be combined in their usual order; this removes much of the rigidity of the traditional type of classification referred to at the beginning of the chapter.

37. The classificationist, in making such a synthetic scheme, would need to survey the literature of each subject field and to divide it up according to different characteristics. In any class, the total divisions arising from the application of a single characteristic constitute one facet. The individual members of each facet, isolated by the dividing process, are described as *foci* or *isolates*.[1] We can illustrate this by showing how our previous example might be dealt

---

[1] Some writers distinguish between these two terms. See, for example, C. D. Needham. *Organizing Knowledge in Libraries.* 1964. p. 72.

with, the details below being an imaginary extract from the tables of a completely synthetic scheme.

CLASS T RELIGION

Religions Facet		Doctrines Facet	
1	Buddhism	a	Faith
2	Hinduism	b	Repentance
3	Judaism	c	Regeneration
4	Christianity	d	Grace, etc.
42	Protestant Sects.		
427	Methodists		
5	Islam, etc.		

Assuming then that we find that, in the geographical facet, applicable to all classes, Britain is represented by, say, 023; and in the likewise common time facet, the eighteenth century is represented by the letter L, we will be able to construct our class-mark. The rules for the combination of foci will probably result (if no connecting symbols are used) in the class-mark T427do23L to represent our document. This, admittedly complicated, symbol assumes that we begin with the primary, or most concrete, of our basic concepts and end with 'time' the most abstract idea involved. Likewise, to very briefly consider two fresh examples, if our subject is: 'Tin mining in Cornwall' we will arrive at the class-mark by selecting the main class involved and then by piecing together the foci representing Mining in the operations facet, Tin in the materials facet, and Cornwall in the geographical facet. In similar fashion Seventeenth-century English poetry' would be analysed into the facets – Language, Period and Literary Form.

38. The Colon Classification is, so far, the only general scheme with a completely faceted structure and it will be considered in more detail in Chapter 17. Unfortunately it is a complicated classification in many ways; this is due largely to the fact that it has endeavoured to keep pace with the rapidly developing theories of its author. The other general schemes do not consciously recognise facet analysis as such at all. Some of them practise number-building, to a certain extent, but the older idea of a vast 'tree of knowledge', which eventually lists all branches of thought and experience and provides ready-made class-marks for each branch, is nearer to the aims of their compilers than are the newer theories. Consequently we have

not followed the approach of some modern writers who tend to evaluate the traditional schemes according to their ability to reveal faceted principles.

39. Yet the idea of an entirely synthetic classification has taken root in this country during the last fifteen years. Ranganathan's views were not seriously considered outside of India until they were crystallised and put forward as a new and more satisfactory basis for book classification by two capable British advocates in 1951,[1] but we now have several synthetic schemes designed for special library purposes. There is still opposition to the newer school of thought (this is clearly seen, for example, in the writings of Metcalfe) and, in the U.S.A., its influence has been comparatively slight. But it is probably true to say that most of the British librarians, particularly those working in special libraries, who take an interest in our subject, regard the faceted method as a tremendous improvement on the principles employed by the classifications which are, at present, widely used. Why is this so? We would cite above all else the fact that the clear division of each subject field into categories and the determination of the sequence in which concepts from these categories shall be combined, represents a major advance in clarifying *principles* for determining helpful order. Among the other main advantages claimed for an entirely synthetic scheme are its flexibility, its lack of bulk, and its ability to cope readily with new subjects as they arise. The flexibility of such a classification can be seen in the way in which it permits concepts to be freely combined thus enabling a wider variety of subjects to be specified than would be possible in the older type of book classification. The lack of bulk arises from the fact that a faceted scheme will not repeat recurring concepts in its schedules every time they are wanted. It will rather list each basic part once only. This reduces the size of the scheme, making it easier to handle and use. It also, incidentally, aids the memory of the classifier, as each unit part is constantly denoted by the same symbols. A synthetic scheme can keep pace with changes in knowledge more easily than an enumerative classification because new subjects often merely involve fresh combinations of basic unit parts already listed. Faceted classifications have other assets, too; these we shall consider when we come to deal with special classifications and their problems in Section Five. One disadvantage under which these synthetic, or faceted, schemes labour is that they have had

[1] B. I. Palmer and A. J. Wells. *Fundamentals of Library Classification.* 1951.

comparatively little opportunity to prove their worth, as most of our general libraries are, or so it seems at present, firmly committed to the Decimal Classification or other basically enumerative systems; there is also, as yet, no general faceted scheme available that is suitable for widespread adoption. Another disadvantage, from the student's point of view, is that the terminology associated with the new theories is rather complex. This approach to the organization of knowledge through classification systems is, in certain ways, radically different from that briefly considered in our last chapter and the use of a certain amount of 'jargon' in conjunction with the newer principles is, perhaps, inevitable. But with the growing acceptance, in certain countries at least, of the faceted classifications, the student of the subject will find it well worthwhile to master the more important terms used.

40. Modern classification theory has also given a great deal of thought to the problem of arranging complex books and documents. These are volumes which deal, not with one field of activity, but with the inter-relationship between two subject fields. Consider the following titles:

1. The influence of the Puritans on the growth of capitalism.
2. The ways in which good twentieth century literature can encourage the maintenance of ethical standards.
3. The use of statistics in the study of demography.
4. The use of a computer to determine the authorship of certain New Testament Epistles.
5. A comparison of the natural and political sciences.
6. Book-keeping for the Grocer.

It is most necessary that the student should distinguish such works at the outset from straightforward 'two-subject' books; if, for instance, a work offers information on two subjects, say kindred topics such as Electricity and Magnetism, it must be classed according to the dominant subject of the two, with an entry being made in the catalogue under each subject.[1] Our titles above are examples of a rather different problem; that of coping with volumes which deal with the *interaction* of subject disciplines, or the impact of one subject upon an entirely different one. These titles represent the way in which many books are now written and this type of work has

[1] This is considered more fully in Chapter Eighteen.

always given the classifier a great deal of difficulty – it would be interesting to hear Jevons' views on document such as these! The older schemes sometimes enumerate such complex themes, but ignore many of them completely. If these titles are a fair indication of the complexity of the subject matter they certainly pose a problem, but modern classification theory tries to deal with them by means of another of Ranganathan's distinctive ideas – *phase analysis*.

41. A phase is the portion of a complex subject which has been derived from any one class. Thus our first example above has two phases, Puritanism and Capitalism, and the others can be analysed in like manner. Various types of phase have been identified. Our first two titles illustrate the *influencing phase;* one subject field has been influenced by another. Titles three and four show the use of the *tool phase;* a problem handled with a particular apparatus or through a special method of approach. The fifth title illustrates the *comparison phase;* while the last title reveals an example of the *bias phase.* This latter type is becoming increasingly common in literature; books on a particular subject are written with a bias towards the needs of readers in another subject field. Such works can be extremely difficult to classify. Some libraries prefer to place them with their subject; others place them according to what are considered the needs of the type of reader who will use them most often. The Colon Classification contains carefully worked out methods for dealing with multi-phased books (and the student of course must clearly distinguish the facets of a single subject from the phases that are discernible in complex works). Phase analysis is indeed most useful in recognising and adequately classifying complex books. It must, however, be pointed out that a book with more than one phase can still go in only *one* place in our classified arrangement on the shelves. Ranganathan's principles together with the use made of the particular library concerned should ideally do much to decide this placing, although more and more libraries are now reaping the administrative benefits of accepting the classification decisions of a central cataloguing agency. We must, however, rely upon our catalogue to reveal the complexity of multi-phased subjects, by providing more than one subject entry for each item in this category. Any scheme based upon the principles of facet and phase analysis will still, of course, need a good catalogue to support it – probably a classified catalogue with a full subject index will be best.

42. The subject analysis of documents is certainly being put on a

much firmer and more accurate basis by the discovery of the faceted approach and the clear recognition of the problems presented by complex, or multi-phased documents. The whole object of these theories is to analyse subjects more accurately and thus to produce a more helpful arrangement. It is only through the use of these and similar principles, in special libraries particularly, that we can organize the complex web, or 'lattice structure', as R. A. Fairthorne has called it, of twentieth-century knowledge. Our debt to the advocates of the new methods, and to Ranganathan in particular, is enormous, for it is virtually certain now that any new general classification will be faceted and will try to cope with phase relationships. Colon is at a disadvantage in that, being the pioneer scheme which introduced the new methods, its efforts to apply them are sometimes laborious and unnecessarily complicated or, at least, appear so when first encountered. However, useful ideas and developments have been contributed in recent years, not only by Ranganathan, but by many others including British enthusiasts such as J. Mills, D. J. Foskett, and B. C. Vickery. With research still taking place, there seems no reason why a new general scheme, if demanded and used, should not find the solution to many of the difficulties that have plagued classificationists in the past.

43. In addition to identifying the different types of phase in the analysis of complex subjects and clearly revealing the possibilities of facet analysis, modern classification theory has revised our ideas on the nature of main classes. The older writers, as befitted men influenced by the classifications of the philosophers, laid great stress on the importance of the main classes in a scheme and the need to arrive at a satisfactory main class order. Cutter and Brown, in particular, attempt to explain the principles behind the order which they selected for the main classes of their respective schemes; the former suggests that an evolutionary order of development and progression has been used. Such claims are not easy to justify and it is now recognised that a main class itself is not easy to define, although, for convenience, we often use this term still. To say, for example, that the Decimal Classification has only nine main classes, plus one for general works, is rather misleading – an illusion created by the nature of the decimal notation. Palmer has shown that there are far more than nine branches of knowledge which may be regarded as being of sufficient importance to warrant main class status. Thus modern classificationists concentrate rather less than their pre-

decessors did on the notion of main classes and give far more time to the question of achieving a helpful arrangement within each class. It may be noted, however, that the order in which the major disciplines are arranged is far from unimportant; in this respect Bliss's Bibliographic Classification is undoubtedly superior to the earlier general classifications.

44. In determining the most helpful order within a major class or discipline we are helped by the concept of *chain and array* in classification. A chain is a line of classes which moves, step by step, from a general subject to a specific one. Thus:

>   Economics
>   Labour Economics
>   Strikes
>   Strikes in the railway industry

would represent the terms in a chain in the Economics class. An *array*, on the other hand, is a row of topics or foci which are co-ordinate in importance, or of equal rank. Thus, in the Social Sciences, a typical array might be:

>   Politics, Economics, Commerce, Law, etc.

Our diagram below indicates that, in a mapped out hierarchy, chains of classes are shown as moving downwards on the map, while arrays of classes are arranged in horizontal lines.

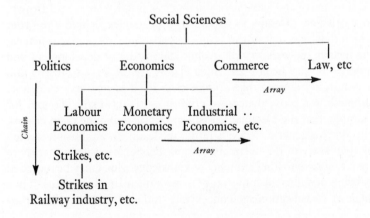

It will be seen that an array of topics of equal status arises at each step in the chain while, in a synthetic scheme, each facet consists of an array of foci and a chain of classification is formed by gradually assembling foci from the various facets.

45. The achievement of an order which is useful to the reader in a chain of classification will depend upon the characteristics of division used and the order in which these are applied. (Paragraph 27 in Chapter 3 considers this problem briefly from the traditional viewpoint). Ranganathan has suggested that a faceted scheme can achieve a helpful order in chain by applying first of all the characteristic which produces the most concrete of the facets and by subordinating the more abstract facets to it – the *order of decreasing concreteness*. Helpful order in array poses its own problems.[1] In the traditional schemes we need to arrange topics of equal status in the most useful sequence; in a faceted classification we must endeavour to place the array of foci within each facet in the most profitable order. An alphabetical sequence of co-ordinate topics or foci may be useful, but it should only be employed if there is no systematic method for the arrangement of subjects of co-ordinate rank. Geographical and chronological orders will certainly, on occasions, be of assistance; in other cases we may try to arrange our co-ordinate topics or foci in a sequence which begins with the most simple and straightforward of the disciplines involved and ends with the most complex in the group. Thus the idea of *gradation by speciality* advanced by Bliss, and considered in more detail in Chapter 16, might be useful in achieving helpful order in array in certain subject fields. The whole problem is most important because the final practical efficiency of any classification rests on the value of the systematic order which it offers; Ranganathan and Bliss have contributed much to the study of our subject in this respect and all later writers are greatly indebted to them.

46. Bliss indeed occupies a transitional place in the development of the principles of library classification. Some of his ideas are rooted in the past, but he has also offered us some suggestions which harmonise well with the findings of Ranganathan and his British disciples. His idea concerning the educational and scientific consensus is important, for it is essential that a book classification should group material effectively according to the established needs of the

---

[1] Palmer and Wells, *Fundamentals of Library Classification*, 1951, should be consulted. Chapter 4 suggests several possible helpful orders for arrays of classes.

majority of readers. Bliss's Bibliographical Classification has several classes where its creator's regard for this consensus has produced a far more scholarly and helpful grouping than is to be found in the equivalent areas of the Decimal Classification. Another contribution from Bliss has been the principle of *alternative location*. This involves the provision of two or more locations for certain subjects in a scheme of classification. A library must select *one* of these – the one corresponding most closely to its needs, and leave the alternative(s) unused. This can be extremely useful in the case of subjects which seem clearly to have two or more possibly justifiable places in a classification. So far, among the general schemes, only Bliss' own classification has applied this interesting idea.

47. Our consideration of modern principles must necessarily be extended by the student and, if he attends a full-time library school, he will probably find that his lecturer places special emphasis upon the understanding and illustration of such theories. However, we shall find these and other principles considered again in the chapters on the living general classifications. Whether a scheme is cast in the conventional enumerative mould, or whether it applies the idea of facet analysis, it will need certain auxiliary features. Notation is the most important of these for it enables us to translate the terms of our classification scheme into symbols which can be placed on the spines of books, on catalogue cards, and on various other records; but the other auxiliaries are also important. We shall consider the use of auxiliaries, and the motives which lie behind their provision, in the next two chapters.

CHAPTER FIVE

Notation

48. A notation is defined by Richardson as a shorthand sign, and that definition, although very concise, is a reasonably adequate one. In book classification it is a method for briefly indicating the class and sub-class to which each volume belongs. Almost every art and science has a series of symbols which stand in the place of terms. We meet the idea very early in our schooldays; the arabic numbers 1, 2, 3, and so on, stand in our minds for quantities or measures expressed by the words one, two, three; in all branches of mathematics figures and symbols stand in the same manner for terms, quantities, measures, ratios, etc. Even punctuation, in ordinary composition, is a notation of a kind; a comma is a symbol indicating that here you take breath; a semi-colon tells us that here we pause to introduce a balancing phrase; a full-stop is a sign indicating that the expression of an idea ends here; and so on, throughout the literary symbols: each is a shorthand sign. But the most vivid example, perhaps, that we can contrast with notation as used in book classification, is that of the symbols used by chemists to indicate chemical elements and compounds. In book classification notation is a necessary auxiliary feature, as we cannot write at full length the classification names of each subject upon every book, or against every entry in our catalogues. Librarians have therefore borrowed hints from the chemist and other similar workers and have attempted to express all classification terms in symbols. A book notation, then, is a series of signs or symbols standing for the names of terms, and forming a convenient means of reference to the arrangement of our classification. As it is merely a symbol for terms, it cannot be more important than the terms themselves; it is a piece of apparatus added to the classification. That seems trite

enough; but there have been so many wrangles about the notational merits or drawbacks of rival bibliographical schemes that one might almost be forgiven for concluding that the only thing that mattered in a classification was the notation. In fact there are many other things that matter, and notation should in no way pre-determine the structure and arrangement within any classification. Nevertheless, as it is essential to the practicability of a book classification, representing it on the spines of books and on various records and acting as the link between the alphabetical index and the scheme, it is by no means a negligible subject. We must consider carefully, therefore, the qualities which it should possess and its necessary functions.

49. A notation may be made up of figures, Arabic or Roman; of letters; of various arbitrary signs; or of a mixture of several or all of these. A notation which consists of only one type of symbol is said to be *pure;* one consisting of two or more types of symbol is a *mixed* notation. Most notations are, in fact, of the latter variety and mixed notations have been commended by both Richardson and Bliss. The outstanding example of a pure notation is seen in the Dewey Decimal Classification, (although the British National Bibliography have found it necessary to convert this to a mixed notation for their special requirements). The pure notation of numbers has definite advantages in that it has no difficulty in conveying order to us clearly and is relatively simple. It also, alas, has drawbacks in as much as it imposes a restrictive pattern upon knowledge – a pattern which makes it appear that each topic divides conveniently into nine or ten parts and that no subject has more than ten sub-divisions. Fremont Rider, whose *International Classification*, (1961), is the latest general scheme to be published, has praised the pure notation of the Dewey scheme and believes that it has made an enormous contribution to the success of that classification throughout the world. But a decimal notation has a narrow base; that is to say it can only accommodate nine topics (or ten if the zero is used) at each step of division. It is significant that Rider, in his own classification, decided to use a pure notation of letters, offering twenty-six places at each step of division. The increase in the *capacity* of the notation to house topics when the alphabet is used is enormous. However, most schemes do prefer the use of a mixed notation, beginning with letters but employing both letters and numbers to denote sub-divisions and the recurring forms in which a subject is viewed or presented. Our later discussion of individual schemes in the third

part of this Manual will show something of the many and interesting methods used by the general classifications to symbolize classes and their sub-divisions. A few examples will also be instanced in the present chapter to demonstrate the qualities and functions of a notation.

50. The features of a good notation that are most commonly accepted may be summarised as follows:

(*a*) It *must* convey clearly the order of classes in the scheme.

(*b*) It should, if possible, reveal the structure of the system, indicating which classes are of equal rank, and which are subordinate to others.

(*c*) It should be brief and simple.

(*d*) Notation ought to be easy to say, to read, and to write or type.

(*e*) Flexibility, or the power to accommodate new topics in the most suitable place, is a *very* necessary quality.

(*f*) It may have special mnemonic aids to promote and assist the librarian's ability to recollect class-marks or to construct a probable class-mark for a particular topic.

(*g*) Notation should, if feasible, fully reveal the subject content of each book.

(*h*) A completely synthetic scheme should have a notation which reveals each change of facet and phase.

Modern classification theory has queried the value of certain aspects of the traditional outlook on notation and has done much to make us re-examine basic principles. In this country, B. C. Vickery and E. J. Coates, both active members of the Classification Research Group have made some important contributions to the newer ideas and certain French writers also have been prominent in this respect. It will be necessary for us to examine the rules listed above in turn and to consider each rule, or feature carefully; some of the points listed are in conflict with others and it must be stressed that no scheme has a notation which is completely satisfactory in all these respects. It may also be remarked that ability to convey order, the revelation of the hierarchy, the indication of changes of facet and phase and flexibility are now usually considered to be functions of

c

notation; brevity, simplicity and mnemonics are its possible qualities.

51. Ability to convey order is of supreme importance. Unless the sequence of the classification is quickly demonstrated by the notation, it will be impossible to locate classes readily on the shelves or in the classified catalogue. The notation must, then, serve as an indication of the place occupied by a topic within the classification and, as such, it is invaluable in referring readers and staff quickly from the catalogue to the classified arrangement on the shelves; it is also necessary that it should demonstrate the sequence in the main part of the classified catalogue. Thus the ordinal value of the notation cannot be over-emphasised. Arbitrary signs which convey no definite order should rarely, if ever, be used; they must be rejected in favour of numbers or letters. Perhaps the former convey order most readily and it may also be thought that any pure notation will reveal the sequence of the classification more readily than a mixed one. It is dangerous to be too dogmatic about the relative merits of letters and figures in this respect and the choice as far as this feature of notation is concerned will depend largely on personal preference; we can nevertheless say with certainty that a notation which failed to reveal the classified order would be quite useless. True, some schemes, especially those designed for documentation purposes, make some use of symbols which have no apparent filing order; in these cases the classificationist must determine an appropriate order for users of the scheme to observe and follow. But all modern systems employ, for the most part, letters and figures. If they did not use one or both of these types of symbol they would prevent the librarian from clearly guiding the sequence and it would be extremely difficult for the reader to find his way easily around the organized arrangement on the shelves; it would be most difficult for staff and readers to use the catalogue freely; and the task of returning a volume to its proper place on the shelves quickly would be a laborious one. Because every practical notation *does* in fact convey order, notation is sometimes said to *mechanise* the classified arrangement – that is to say it makes the replacement of volumes in the classified sequence a simple and mechanical task.

52. In addition to its ordinal significance, notation *may* demonstrate the hierarchy or structure of the classification scheme. We use the word 'may' advisedly here. In the past, it was almost automatically assumed by librarians that the notation expressed the

relationship between topics. That is to say that as the classification divides classes into divisions, and these in turn into sub-divisions, so it was expected that the rank of any topic would be discernible from its class-mark. Indeed most people still do assume this; they think that 824 represents a class which is a division of 820, which is in turn a branch of class 800. Likewise, ABF is taken to be a sub-division of class AB, if an alphabetical notation is employed; it would be assumed also that class-marks such as 821, 822, 823, 824, or ABA, ABB, ABC, ABD, represented topics of equal status from the same array of classes. Earlier editions of this Manual would emphatically support the notation which expressed the hierarchy of a scheme; nowadays we are not so sure. Modern classification theory has shown that a non-structural notation also has definite merits. Nor do the established general schemes themselves provide us with a clear guide. They all have notations which convey order (although the schemes of Bliss and Ranganathan and the Universal Decimal Classification do include some symbols which cannot convey a sequence automatically to us). When it comes to the question of the notation expressing the hierarchy, however, we find that the Decimal, Universal Decimal and Colon Classifications attempt, for the most part, to do this; the Congress, Subject and Bibliographic schemes have notations which often make little or no effort to express the scheme's structure.

53. The benefits of a hierarchical notation may be summarised as follows:

(*a*) One normally expects the notation to reveal the hierarchy – thus confusion may arise if it does not. It is also easier to broaden or narrow down a subject search if the notation expresses the classification's hierarchy.

(*b*) A hierarchical, or structural notation, facilitates the compilation of the subject index to a classified catalogue by the procedure known as *chain indexing*. (This is described in Chapter 21).

(*c*) The guiding of the classified shelves or of the classified catalogue may be more easily accomplished if the notation is of the hierarchical type.

(*d*) It is probably easier to remember hierarchical notations than non-hierarchical ones of equal length.

Some disadvantages which should be noted are:

(*a*) It is extremely difficult for any notation to be completely hierarchical and in any case, as Coates once remarked, 'a hierarchical notation implies an unchangeable hierarchy'.

(*b*) A non-structural notation may be much briefer than a hierarchical one.

(*c*) The length of each array may be freely manipulated in a non-structural notation; thus it is far more hospitable than the traditional type of notation to the inclusion of new topics at the most appropriate point of the classification.

(*d*) It is often difficult for mixed notations (and nearly all modern systems rely on these) to reveal the hierarchy of the scheme clearly.

(*e*) A structural notation may waste symbols, as many figures or letters in a particular array may remain unused.

54. Modern research has shown that non-hierarchical notations are worthy of serious consideration, although some writers,[1] such as the late Miss Barbara Kyle, have definitely tended to favour hierarchical ones. Some of the points which we have listed above may be brought out more clearly by means of a diagram which illustrates imaginary notations – the one structural, or expressive, the other merely ordinal:

Hierarchical or expressive notation	*Subject*	*Non-structual notation*
A	Technology	A
AB	Chemical Technology	AB
ABR	Metallurgy	AX
ABRG	Non-ferrous metals	AXD
ABRGL	Light metals	AXN
ABRGLP	Magnesium	AXW

It will be seen from this illustration that the completely hierarchical notation lengthens by one symbol at each step of division in the subject chain. The notation which simply concentrates on conveying order without attempting to signify the structure of the

[1] The student who has access to the files of the Bliss Classification Bulletin is invited to consult the comments of C. B. Freeman and J. Mills in the December, 1965 issue. We consider this one of the most interesting recent discussions on this topic.

scheme, however, may not do this. In our example above with a pure notation of capital letters, the non-structural notation allocates to a sub-division of class AB the notation AX. These classes look co-ordinate but they are not; likewise AXW represents a sub-division of the class denoted by AXN and this, in turn, is actually a sub-division of the class represented by AXD. Thus, in a non-hier-archical notation, arrays can be lengthened or shortened, depending on the needs of the literature in each class – the notation no longer dictates the pattern in which knowledge must be presented in the classification. The non-expressive notation is also briefer; our class marks for Magnesium clearly indicate this. Some readers may favour the notation that clearly expresses the hierarchy as being the more logical of the two. Certainly it clearly shows which classes are of equal status and which are branches of larger classes; the benefits of this must be weighed against the need for concise notations and an alphabetical, non-structural notation can certainly achieve brevity by shortening the arrays, while the hierarchy of the classification can still be suitably indicated by indentation in the schedules themselves. The faceted schemes often have a notation which is structural in the sense that it demonstrates each change of facet, but it need not be expressive in the conventional sense. Indeed, as Crossley[1] once pointed out, the non-structural notation of Coates's *British Catalogue of Music Classification* even affords the occasional example of a well-documented sub-division being represented by a shorter class-mark than its parent class.

55. We have touched upon the interesting question of notational brevity above, but it must be understood that there will be many factors which affect this feature of notation. Bliss has said that a notation should be 'as short as is feasible' and, in more recent years, the British writer Raymond Moss has shown how long notations are difficult to retain in the mind and may well lead to inefficiency.[2] The value of brief notations should be clear to us all; if we can make two symbols, say, stand for a subject instead of three or four, it is evident that class-marks will be more easily written, typed on charging cards, catalogue entries and so forth, and remembered. In this respect, alphabetical notations are superior to numerical ones. At each stage of division, assuming a hierarchical notation is used, the decimal notation offers nine or possibly ten places, the alphabetical base

---

[1] New schemes of classification. *Library Association Record*, February, 1963, pp. 51–59.
[2] How do we classify? *Aslib Proceedings*, February, 1962, pp. 33–42.

provides twenty-six. Or, to look at the question from a slightly different viewpoint, let us imagine that a classification is based on traditional ideas and has to accommodate 17,000 topics. A pure notation of letters, if non-hierarchical and fully employed, could cope with these without ever exceeding a three letter maximum; Rider's scheme illustrates this point very well. A pure notation of numbers, however, would have some class-marks of five figure length to cope with these subjects. Thus Dewey's choice of the decimal numbers has not promoted notational brevity, although there are, of course, other factors which can be cited in its favour. The extent to which full or detailed classification is pursued will also affect this issue; any notation will be fairly long at times when dealing with highly specific themes. Yet when shortness of class-marks is considered, the tremendous *capacity* of the purely literal notation, or even of a mixed notation based on letters, must not be overlooked.

56. Simplicity of notation is closely linked with brevity, but the two things are not the same. Simplicity will depend on the length of notation but also on the type of symbol used. A brief notation relying chiefly on symbols such as squares or triangles would certainly not be simple. Any mixed notation may, in fact, be slightly more complex than a pure notation of similar length, unless the symbols of the former fall readily into convenient groups. A nineteenth-century classification, that of the American Lloyd P. Smith, employed a mixed notation which relied upon capital letters, numbers, Roman figures and some arbitrary signs; the resulting complexity made what was otherwise a useful classification system justly infamous. However, it is clear that, although the blending of symbols in the notation contributes to its simplicity, if two notations use the same type of symbol the one that is shortest will be the simpler to follow and understand.

57. It will be advantageous also to have a notation that can be quickly placed on various records and that can be easily read or pronounced. Brevity and simplicity in the conventional sense will do much to achieve this for us, but a pure notation is probably better, in this respect, than a mixed one of equal length. For instance, 624.58 is easier to say and recollect than AB73k. We may note the interest shown these days in the phonic as well as the graphic length of notations. Research has been carried out with regard to letter notations that are readily pronounceable – is this not the age of

pronounceable abbreviations? The work of the French writer Eric de Grolier is particularly significant in this respect and, of the newer schemes made by Englishmen, the London Education Classification, compiled by D. J. Foskett, is perhaps the best example of a scheme that has applied this idea. The class-marks in Foskett's scheme are certainly easy to say and recollect, but the results are sometimes rather humorous; it would seem that, while pronounceable notations might be a great asset, they also give rise to some odd or amusing letter combinations or to some undesirable allocations of letters to certain subjects and their facets. In short, the idea may have great merit yet the warning issued by Bliss in 1933, with regard to difficulties in letter notations when the letters form 'words', must not be ignored.

58. Apart from the ability to convey order, we have so far considered characteristics which a notation may or may not possess. There is, on the other hand, one attribute, or quality, without which a notation is quite valueless for modern library classification purposes. This quality has been variously named flexibility,[1] expansibility, or hospitality; it is in the possession of this feature that the notations of the living bibliographical classifications surpass those of earlier systems. Flexibility may be defined thus: *a notation is flexible if, by the addition of a symbol or symbols, any new subject may be inserted into any place in the classification without dislocating the sequence of either the notation or the classification itself.* Flexibility may be achieved in various ways and it is perhaps most convenient to list these and to consider them in turn. One rather important point may be noted here, however, before we enumerate these methods. Most schemes are flexible in that new subjects can be accommodated, but often the new topic cannot be inserted into the most *useful* place in the classified sequence; that is to say the notation is not perfectly hospitable.

59. Methods for obtaining flexibility are:

(*a*) By leaving gaps between numbers or letters. Thus, if we consider the sequences represented by different types of notation –

7273	ABHM	RK 16
7274	ABHO	RK 17
7275	ABHP	RK 18
7277	ABHQ	RK 20

[1] Mills, in his textbook, uses the word 'flexibility' to express a different idea from the above; its usual meaning is the one we have given here.

– it is clear that, if these class-marks are all in use, new topics may be inserted in the pure notations and the mixed one at 7276, ABHN, and RK 19 respectively. But this idea is crude and most unsatisfactory in practice; the gaps will soon be filled making further expansion by this method impossible. Also no classificationist can anticipate all future developments in knowledge and so there is no assurance that the gaps will have been left in the most appropriate places; subjects may have to be forced into the nearest available pigeon-hole.

(b) Another method for securing expansion in notation involves the addition of extra symbols to existing class-marks. We could thus make our first example above a mixed notation by inserting a subject between 7273 and 7274 by employing 7273A. Again our device is rather primitive perhaps; yet certainly it represents some advance on the gap idea.

(c) Similar to the above, but a more useful notion, is to recognise from the outset that a notation will be used in the decimal sense. The Dewey Decimal Classification has a notation which permits a chain of classes to be indefinitely extended thus:

$$562.1$$
$$562.11$$
$$562.111 \text{ etc.}$$

Of course, the class numbers for many of the highly specific subjects which librarians have to classify these days will be long; but this is almost inevitable in a general classification, where we must choose between a broad arrangement of knowledge as presented in books or specificity with comparatively long class-marks. We shall consider this again in paragraph 308; here it will be sufficient to stress that the decimal notation is a tremendous improvement on the gap idea in achieving notational hospitality and it is also vastly superior to notations of the integral, or arithmetical, kind.

60. (d) Yet there is certainly no guarantee that a decimal notation will allow us to avoid notational rigidity by inserting new topics in the *most appropriate place* in a scheme of classification. In fact we find that new subjects often have to be subordinated to others which are of equal rank in a classification because there is no room for them in the correct array of topics. This leads us on to consider the problem of achieving flexibility, or hospitality, in an array of co-

ordinate classes. The problem is especially acute in a numerical notation which insists upon expressing the structure of the scheme. Thus if the classes 591 592 593 594 ... 599 are all in use, how can we show a new subject, equal in rank to the topics represented by these numbers, in the same array of classes. The traditional answer was that we could not; a striking example from the Decimal Classification, which has been instanced by Foskett, is that of Electrical Engineering at 621·3, which should be shown as co-ordinate with Mechanical Engineering at 621, but which has been forced by the notational structure of the scheme into the subordinate position. Ranganathan has tried to provide us with a means for the extension of an array by means of what he terms the *Octave Device*. This involves the last symbol in each array being reserved for the special purpose of extending that array. Therefore, in a numerical notation, the 9 would never stand alone; it would serve to introduce more co-ordinate classes and a typical array might be:

581 582 583 584 ... 588 5891 5892 etc.

The idea certainly has merit and is similar to the notion employed in the 400 and 800 classes of the Dewey Decimal system where, in Linguistics for example, 420 430 ... 480 represent the major languages and minor ones are shown at 491 492 etc. Dewey does not seem to have fully worked out this idea and, in any case, the Octave Device does not solve the problem of inserting new topics at the most suitable point in existing arrays. With conventional schemes, this is only possible by some reallocation of topics. It is probably far better either to accept the fact that hospitality in array is limited, and perhaps to use a notation of letters to offer twenty-six places in each array, or to use a non-hierarchical notation which frees us from the rigid adherence to a particular number of places in each array of co-ordinate subjects. While the Octave Device encourages *extrapolation* – the addition of new subjects to the end of an array, the non-structural type of notation allows indefinite *interpolation* – the insertion of a new topic at any point in the scheme. Thus, if the notation is non-hierarchical and we have classes such as AQ and AR, a new co-ordinate class might be accommodated, say, at AQN.

61. Before turning away from our topic of notational flexibility, we must consider how this can be achieved in a faceted classification.

(*e*) Notations of faceted systems are in fact extremely flexible for

C*

they can grow in more ways than one. Traditional notations can only be extended by adding symbols at the right hand end of each class-mark or by the leaving of gaps; the faceted notation, on the other hand, permits the extension of the symbols representing any of the isolates involved. Such extension can scarcely be explained clearly without a demonstration and, although we have not yet studied the Colon Classification in any detail, it will be worth while to borrow an example from it to illustrate this feature. In this example the space isolate is introduced by a full stop and the time isolate by an apostrophe. The former is represented by numbers, the latter by capital letters. They are preceded by foci drawn from the facet described by Ranganathan as relating to the concept Personality. Thus:

R 4.56'N denotes ethics in Britain in the twentieth century
(R 4 being ethics, 56 Britain and N representing the Time isolate)
R 42.56'N stands for *Family* ethics in twentieth-century Britain.
(this reveals an extension of the focus in the Personality facet)
R 42.56124'N denotes Family ethics in twentieth century *London*
(showing further extension, this time involving the Space focus)
R 4217.56124'N denotes *Marriage* ethics in twentieth century
    London
(further extension of the focus in the Personality facet).

There are many other possible extensions with the above example; nevertheless the ones quoted should serve to show the possibilities of a faceted scheme with regard to notational hospitality. True the Colon Classification often has a complicated notation and the filing order of documents has to be carefully noted when dealing with examples such as the above; yet, from the point of view of flexibility in accommodating new topics, it might almost be said that Ranganathan's faceted approach has provided us with a new dimension in notation.

62. We now leave the topic of notational expansibility, important though it undoubtedly is, and consider some other features which a notation may possess. One of these is memory value, or mnemonic qualities. By mnemonic notation we usually mean that whenever a topic appears in the classification it is represented by the same symbols. It is quite impossible to do this for all topics or concepts, but many recurring forms of presentation, for example, can be

constantly represented by particular letters or figures. Thus, in the Decimal Classification, we tend to associate the symbol 05 with periodicals and 09 is linked with the standard sub-division which can be added to any subject number to indicate that the subject is treated from a historical viewpoint. Likewise the Decimal Classification has an area table in which each country is represented by a distinctive number. These numbers can be added to subject class-marks at various parts of the classification to indicate that a subject is confined to a particular geographical region. The continual representation of certain ideas by the same digits is useful to the librarian as it enables him to remember many class-numbers and to deduce others from the mnemonic features supplied. There are many more examples of such mnemonics in the Decimal Classification and in the majority of other schemes; examples are given in Section Three of this Manual and many more can be gleaned from an examination of the classifications themselves. Here it will be enough for us to recognise that mnemonics are not a vital feature of notation – they may help the librarian, but are rarely if ever of direct assistance to readers – and to note that there are two distinctive ways in which mnemonics can be used in notation.

63. *Systematic mnemonics* are the main type and relate to the definition of mnemonics we have already given. They occur when-ever a topic or form of presentation is continually represented by the same symbols, as in the periodicals and history examples given from Dewey's scheme above. Their value lies in the fact that the classifier quickly becomes familiar with the scheme because of the repetitive pattern within much of the notation. A synthetic scheme is particularly rich in mnemonic possibilities as each basic concept listed within a class will be continually represented by the same letters or digits. If there are exceptions to these systematic mnemonics, they are said to be variable rather than constant; most schemes, however, tend to use such systematic mnemonics as they choose to employ in a consistent manner. Sometimes, if the notation consists purely or partly of letters, we find that another type of mnemonic can be introduced; this second way of providing memory value in the notation is known as the use of *literal mnemonics*. These arise whenever a topic is represented by its initial letter or letters. Thus, to use a few examples from Bliss's scheme, U stands for Useful Arts, UE for Engineering and in Class US – Mechanic Arts and Trades – USC denotes Carpentry. Of these two varieties of

mnemonic notation, the literal mnemonics are certainly the least valuable. They can of course occur only in notations which employ letters, and in addition to this there is the danger that if the classificationist places too much value on them they may be over-employed and the preferred order may be distorted merely to gain mnemonic effect. This would inevitably lead us back eventually to alphabetical subject arrangement with its scattering of kindred topics. But the literal mnemonics may be used whenever it is possible to have them *without* disturbing the carefully worked out helpful order of subjects. The examples cited from the Bibliographic Classification illustrate just such an occasion. Bliss was far too convinced of the need for a scholarly and practical arrangement to fall into the trap of allowing the notation or its mnemonic features to detract from the carefully worked out systematic order; thus his literal mnemonics appear only when the accepted order permits and some of the mnemonic possibilities of this idea have been ignored in the interests of the sequence of topics in the classification.

64. We have said that notation may reveal the subject content of each book fully. Ranganathan would stress this point, but other writers on our subject have been more dubious about it. If we strive for what Ranganathan terms 'co-extensiveness of subject and class-mark' we will often have long notations for the specific topics in our library. He has insisted that the reader need not be hindered by these, but it is surely true to say that the longer the class-mark the more difficult it will be for the notation to mechanise the arrangement on the classified shelves. On the other hand, particularly for larger libraries, the classification must be specific; otherwise items on specialised topics will be lost among a host of volumes on a more general theme. One cannot be too dogmatic on the subject of concise notations versus specificity in classification but, as Mills has stressed, the classification must have the necessary detail for the larger or more specialized libraries that need it. Smaller libraries can always classify in less detail and obtain shorter class-marks as a result.

65. Finally we must examine the contention that a synthetic classification must reveal each change of facet or phase. Most of the existing general schemes are basically enumerative in character; only Colon relies entirely on synthesis. But if new schemes are to be made for general and special libraries, based on faceted principles, then it will be advantageous if their notations clearly show when

phase analysis has been carried out and show each change of facet in a single-phased subject. This will help librarians to break down any particular class-mark into its component parts and will facilitate indexing for the classified catalogue. There are many ways in which a change of facet can be shown. Consider the following, entirely synthetic, notations:

(a) G9; 6: 57.6734'H
(b) EpmFmWse
(c) SXLMHRY
(d) Bck806

These are once again examples which are not drawn from any published scheme. They are imaginary ones which have been selected to illustrate certain principles. Example (a) is similar, however, to a typical full class-mark from the Colon scheme; each change of facet is indicated by a punctuation mark. Thus, in Ranganathan's classification, a semi-colon introduces the Matter facet, a Colon (originally the only punctuation sign used) heralds the use of a focus from the important Energy facet, a full stop precedes the numbers introducing the concept Space and likewise the apostrophe precedes the capital letters which denote foci from the Time facet. When we come to study this scheme in detail the nature and purpose of these five categories will be explained. Here we need only say that punctuation marks of this kind are rather cumbersome as a means of showing each facet change and other methods have thus been sought in recent years.

66. Example (b) is similar to a typical class-mark from a faceted scheme for Engineering used at the English Electric Company Library at Whetstone. In this example, the use of a capital letter signifies that a new facet is being introduced. Example (c) attempts to indicate a novel idea which has received a great deal of attention from such writers on modern classification theory – the principle of *retroactive* notation. This means chiefly that, assuming an alphabetical notation is used, primary facets can be accommodated towards the end of the alphabet and each facet can be qualified by any facet preceding it; each change of facet will be shown by a reversion to an earlier letter. Thus our facets, in the imaginary example given, would be represented by SX, LM, and HRY. Some synthetic special classifications have already experimented with this idea. Its

advantages are that it eliminates the need for a special indicator digit or symbol to show the change of facet with a corresponding reduction of the length of the notation, while enabling us to readily discern the faceted structure of the scheme. The difficulty lies in the fact that the scheme must be carefully planned to make a retroactive notation feasible. One is possibly inclined to regard retroactive notation as an expensive luxury which demands the scheme to be adjusted to meet the requirements of its notation, but the idea cannot be so readily dismissed. J. Mills, who has employed it in his faceted system for Office Management has also used it in some special extensions of the technology classes of the Bibliographic Classification which he has produced in the Bliss Classification Bulletin. For instance, in the new schedule which he has worked out for nuclear reactors we have such class-marks as BEPFWQS standing for Gas-cooled reactors. Analysed this becomes:

BEP	F	FW
Disintegration of matter, atomic	Nuclear reactors	Types
Q	QS	
Introducing type of coolant	Gas coolants	

It takes time to become accustomed to notations of this kind and some may query the wisdom of adding them to a basic notation (i.e. that of the Bibliographic Classification) which is not designed to be of the completely retroactive type. Yet there can be no doubt that Mills is able to use this kind of notation skilfully to provide the scheme with some much-needed expansion and his enthusiasm for the idea is infectious. Our final example demonstrates a simpler method, but one which is scarcely practicable for most schemes. Changes of facet are indicated by using a different type of symbol for each. Therefore the facets in the example would be represented by B, ck, 8 and o6 (a number being introduced by a zero being distinguishable from other numbers). A faceted classification for literature made at the Liverpool School of Librarianship to demonstrate, in a simple way, the elements of synthetic classification to Library Association Part I students, has shown each change of facet by such a method. Unfortunately, if a subject field has several categories, the method will be quite unsuitable as appropriate types of symbol will soon be exhausted.

67. The above methods are all best regarded as interesting experiments with regard to indicating each change of facet; the

retroactive notation is the one which has received most attention. When we come to consider the problem of a faceted classification showing each change of phase in its notation, we find that Ranganathan has devised a method for this purpose which relies on the use of a zero followed by certain lower case letters. This is briefly discussed in our Chapter 17 and in more detail, of course, in the Colon Classification itself.

68. There is much more that could be said about notation, but only at the risk of overemphasising its value. Essential as it is, we must not let notational manipulations blind us to the crucial problems of helpful and comprehensible arrangement. The chapters on the various schemes in Section Three offer many more examples of the principles discussed here; we find also that notation is still being reviewed by modern research workers in the field of library classification and many older views are being somewhat modified by new findings. One firm rule is quite evident; notation must be determined by the nature of the scheme and the needs of the libraries to which the scheme is to be applied. With this in mind, we must make sure it is the servant and not the master of our classifications. As B. C. Vickery says[1] 'The only purpose of classification is to put subjects in a helpful order . . . We must make our preferred arrangement before we can mechanise it . . . We must use symbols as Humpty Dumpty used words "so that they mean just what we choose them to mean, neither more nor less".' The features of notation discussed in this chapter must be reviewed carefully with this sound advice in mind; all we can say with certainty is that the two vital attributes are the ability to convey order clearly and the power to accommodate new subjects in their correct place in the existing classified arrangement.

[1] *Classification and Indexing in Science*, 2nd edition, 1959, p. 72.

CHAPTER SIX

Other Auxiliaries Required

69. The last chapter has outlined the essential features of notation and has also discussed some of its more debatable qualities and functions. However, when we have chosen the symbols for our notation and added it to a scheme of classification we find that it is often desirable to make a further addition to the notation; this is necessitated by the fact that when several books have exactly the same class-mark they must be sub-arranged in author order. Thus we find that most librarians, apart from those with very small collections, find it necessary to attach to the end of the notation on the spine of each book an *author mark* of some kind. In many cases this is merely the first three letters of the author's surname; it enables us to achieve, within any particular specific class, an exact and convenient arrangement. We realise that BG 7 SMI comes before BG 7 STE, although both notations appear on books dealing with exactly the same topic. We may say then that arrangement within a specific subject class is mechanised by means of such author marks, or that they enable us to determine the exact position of a book on the shelves. In the United States of America, more elaborate systems have been conceived to represent the author's name after the class mark. The most famous of these is that devised by Charles Cutter and subsequently revised by Kate E. Sanborn. These Cutter-Sanborn numbers really involve the provision of a table which enables us to translate the first three letters of author's surnames into a sequence of figures; the result is that the same author order within a class is achieved but the author marks are numbers rather than letters.

70. Arrangements such as this, however, are extremely elaborate. Indeed even the usual author marks are of debatable value – although

one finds that a young student with some experience of work in a library will sometimes argue far more fervently about this comparatively minor matter than about controversies of major importance in our subject! It may be said that author marks of any kind add to the complexity of notation, fail to distinguish between writers with the same surname, and may be odd or ridiculous – to write ROT, for instance, after a class-mark on the spine of a book is hardly the best way to commend the volume to the potential reader! It can also be claimed that the author's name usually appears on the spine of the book and will enable us to achieve an alphabetical sub-arrangement within a class more easily than contractions or figures representing this name. Yet many libraries find these marks worthwhile, and it is unwise to be too dogmatic about them; we may nevertheless say that, if they are required, it now appears simpler to use the first three letters of the author's name rather than Cutter-Sanborn numbers or similar systems devised by L. S. Jast, J. D. Brown, or the great American classifier, W. S. Merrill. If the student is interested in these, or in the Biscoe Time Numbers – devised to secure final chronological arrangement within a class – he can read about them in more detail in the chapter on 'Book And Work Numbers' in the third edition of this Manual, or in other texts.[1] We must stress, however, that author-marks are a comparatively unimportant part of classification theory; they are, for instance, of much less significance in our studies than the principles considered in Chapter Five.

71. In the last chapter, we described notation as an *auxiliary* feature. That is to say it is an addition which ought not to determine the nature of the classification: to use Bliss's famous phrase, it 'does not make a classification scheme, though it may mar it'. A mere classification of knowledge, or ideas, would not require a notation; it is, therefore, an extra device needed by a bibliographical system. We must now recognise that there are other auxiliaries which are likewise required because of the way in which subjects are presented in books. Books are written presentations of thought in general or in particular; they may cover, rarely, the whole of knowledge, as a universal encyclopaedia is expected to do; they may deal with several subjects; they may take certain literary patterns, as dictionaries, essays, journals, or as poetry or drama; they may belong to a certain age or may deal with the life and thought of a particular

[1] W. H. Phillips provides a good account, *Primer of book classification*, 1961, pp. 50-4.

age; in short, they are often complicated and difficult to classify accurately. But, although the *size* of books affects our classifying (for it is quite uneconomical to shelve books of elephant folio size together with octavos), and although the contents of books may be complicated, practical librarians know that, just as knowledge can be classified, so knowledge in books can be organized by means of a systematic subject arrangement. At least sixty out of every hundred non-fiction books are in their bulk about subjects – most of them about one subject – that can be recognised, although it is not always apparent at a glance. To sum up, book classification is complex but far from impossible; it will, in fact be much easier if, in addition to notation, we employ other auxiliary features to recognise and combat the often intricate way in which knowledge is presented in books. Most of these auxiliaries are peculiar to book classification. They are:

(*a*) A Generalia Class – to accommodate works covering all or many branches of knowledge.

(*b*) Form Classes – to accommodate books in which the main interest is the pattern in which matter is written, as in poetry, drama and fiction.

(*c*) Form Divisions – to show the way in which a subject is treated in a particular book, or the point of view from which it is regarded.

(*d*) An alphabetical index – to locate terms in the classification and to indicate related aspects of a subject which may have been scattered by the classified sequence.

We must describe the functions of each of these auxiliaries in turn and, although the chief general book classifications have not yet been described, it will be useful to draw examples from them to illustrate the workings of these auxiliary features.

72. *The Generalia Class.* This class, or its equivalent, is found in every bibliographical scheme. The need for it arises because many books are polytopical. If we were merely classifying ideas it would be relatively simple to isolate those ideas and then to group appropriate ones but when we come to classify composite books, which gather together ideas on several subjects, a General Works class is an obvious requirement. It is often called in the slang of librarians

the waste-paper basket of the classification; from which we must not infer that it is a merely chaotic class. It is certainly not that: it is rather designed to house works that overlap many departments of knowledge or which are so varied in their content that they simply cannot be placed elsewhere. Emphasis must be laid upon the *general* nature of all the parts of generalia; otherwise in practical work errors will be frequent. It is clear that publications such as *The Times*, *The Encyclopaedia Britannica* and *The Spectator* are entirely general in their scope; there is no topic which may not properly come within their purview. To class works like these in Sociology, Science, or History, or in any other specific class would be to ignore all other subjects with which the publications deal. They must inevitably, then, go in the Generalia, or General Works, class. It must be recognised that a periodical, encyclopaedia, or similar publication which is restricted to a single subject must be classified with other works in that field. Thus a periodical on art goes with other items on that topic; an encyclopaedia on philosophy is likewise placed in the appropriate subject class, and so on. Generalia is thus left free to accommodate the composite, or polytopical volume which simply cannot be placed elsewhere. It is also customary for it to accommodate books which are in some way rare or special, and being valued for their special features rather than for their subject content are best set aside in a special collection. In its role as the custodian of works covering all knowledge or a very large part of it, the Generalia Class is an important auxiliary feature of any scheme; it is fair to assume that Jevons did not contemplate any such provision when he inveighed against the classification of books.

73. It will be recognised in regard to the Generalia Class that the catalogue possesses enormous superiority over classification on the shelves as an exhaustive method of treating books. The periodical, encyclopaedia, or set of transactions can be shelved in one place only in our library. In the case of very general works of this kind we will find that they are housed in the Generalia Class and that we cannot easily determine by means of the classification their full subject content. Likewise, although periodicals, encyclopaedias, etc., dealing with a single subject will be placed with that subject, we cannot expect the classification to reveal all the subjects that they contain. This is a very important problem for librarians, for the knowledge presented in journals is often important and well in

advance of that published in book form. Indeed some important contributions to knowledge may never appear in book form. Because the catalogue deals, not with the books themselves, but with cards or slips representing them, it can bring all this information to light if periodicals and other composite works are analysed and entries made under the relevant class-marks in the classified catalogue. Nowadays, of course, much of this work is done for us by published abstracting services or by subject indexes to periodical literature; yet there is still a great need for more analytical cataloguing in libraries.

74. But we have digressed from our study of the Generalia Class to contemplate the analysis of composite works of all kinds, not merely those that go in Generalia. Our earlier considerations enable us to provide a definition of a completely orthodox General Works Class. It is *one which caters for works dealing with all or many subject fields and which may also accommodate special or rare works in which the subject is less important to the librarian than other considerations.* Bearing this in mind, it will be profitable to glance at the Generalia Classes of several of the bibliographical schemes; at least one of them has extended our definition to produce rather an unusual arrangement. We may begin with the Decimal Classification of Melvil Dewey. Here the outline of the General Works Class is as follows:

000 General works	050 General Periodicals
010 Bibliography	060 General Societies
020 Library Science	070 Newspapers: Journalism
030 General Encyclopaedias	080 Collections
040 General Essays	090 Rare books and manuscripts
(left blank in Edition 17)	

The essays mentioned are collections covering a wide range of topics; if they have, in fact, definite literary merit, they must be placed in the Literature class rather than here. The only unorthodox inclusion in Dewey's Generalia Class is Librarianship. It may be argued that this is concerned with many other subject fields and the housing and utilization of the knowledge accumulated by specialists in all areas of human activity but, nevertheless, the subject is one which merits a class of its own; probably it would have received one had an alphabetical notation been used. The Library of Congress scheme has a General Works Class which is, broadly speaking, similar to the above; it is, however, strictly orthodox and was based on the arrangement provided in the Expansive Classification of Charles Cutter. In both these schemes, Librarianship is excluded from the Generalia section. The Bibliographic Classification of Bliss is unusual not for the content of the Generalia class, but from the point of view of the terminology used to describe it. Bliss has employed an alphabetical notation for the various subject classes; numbers are used to represent general material. These precede the subject classes and are known as Anterior Numeral Classes. Thus we have Classes 1–9 for Generalia, followed by Classes A–Z. An examination of the Anterior Numeral Classes will show that many of them are, in fact, locations for special collections rather than for polytopical volumes.

75. It is the Subject Classification of the British librarian, J. D. Brown, however, which has the most unusual Generalia Class. In addition to the material we would expect, it takes in all subjects which Brown considered to be pervasive of other classes; that is, subjects which are necessary to the study of every subject in greater or lesser degree, These, according to Brown, include subjects such as Education, Logic, Mathematics, a large portion of the arts, and General Science. Such an arrangement is extremely difficult to justify, although an attempt is made to do so; the 'pervasive' classes really belong elsewhere. When we come to study the Subject Classification in detail we shall have criticisms to make of this theory and its application; yet it is useful for us, even at this point, to note why this Generalia Class has been justly described as the most unorthodox one in bibliographical classification.

76. *Form Classes*. These arise because, in some books, the form of presentation is more important than the subject content. Literature is the outstanding example of a form class. We ignore the subjects of the books and arrange them into broad 'form' groups; thus we obtain the divisions Poetry, Drama, Essays, Fiction, Letters, Oratory and so forth. Now these have very diverse subject matter; for example, Dante's *Divina Commedia* is one of the revelations or mediaeval theology, Shakespeare's *Hamlet* is a great contribution to human psychology, and one could add many more examples. These may all provide background material for the serious student of history, topography and so on, but they are chiefly intended for the student of literature. Their subjects are but

subsidiary when one considers the purpose of these works, and the people who want to read them. The literary form, not the subject matter, is thus the important consideration. So we class these books in groups such as those divisions mentioned above. Yet it may be added that the placing of letters in the literature class is a Dewey expedient and it has its justification only when the letters have a strong literary interest and not always then. The famous letters of Gray, Horace Walpole, and Cowper, come into the latter category, but those of the Brownings and most other folk ought not to do so; they are the best illuminants of biography and ought to be classed there.

77. This reminds us that literature is not the only 'form class', although it is the most notable one. Biography is a form class if a separate class for great lives is created; if, however, lives of great men and women are distributed on the library shelves according to the subject fields in which the distinguished people were or are engaged, then subject classification is being performed. Likewise subject bibliographies may be scattered throughout the classification and placed with the appropriate topics; they may, on the other hand, be collected for convenience; if the latter practice is followed, a form class has been made, for they have been classified by the form of presentation – bibliography, rather than by their subjects. The master rule for the guidance of the individual classifier must be: *classify first by subject and then by form, except in the literature classes, in which form is paramount and in certain other classes where grouping by the form of presentation rather than by the subject of a book may be advantageous.* Yet it must be said that some classifiers have made interesting attempts to classify pure literature by subject. Wordsworth, it may be remembered, classified his poems as works of imagination, sentiment, reflection, narrative, and so on; but few are satisfied with the arrangement, as it is full of cross-divisions and much of the placing is purely arbitrary. In any case, perhaps he was the last person qualified to evaluate his own verse! The most common form of experiment in some modern libraries is that which attempts to classify fiction by subject; all historical novels by the period they represent, and such novels as Reade's *It's never too late to mend* and Marcus Clarke's *For the term of his natural life* at penology and so on. This arrangement has an immense interest, and is in many ways a useful one; but as the principal arrangement of the books it is thoroughly bad. For one who is interested in penology,

a thousand are interested in these books for the stories which Reade and Clarke tell, and again the law of convenience must prevail. We shall find later on that fiction can be classified in other ways also; nevertheless, it may be stressed here that plays, novels, poetry, essays, etc., are more usefully classified first of all by form, and that biographies and bibliographies may be classified by form if the librarian so desires. Much will depend here upon the nature of the library, with regard to the best arrangement of biographical material. If a helpful grouping is sought for a general library then classification by form, that is, the making of a separate biography class, may be best; on the other hand, large scholarly libraries, including public libraries with several separate subject departments, may find it best to distribute biographies by subject interest whenever possible. This will leave a small form class – Biography – for those lives which cannot be linked with one subject field and for collective biography.

78. An examination of the established general classifications for libraries will reveal that most of them recognise this problem and provide *alternative arrangements* for a topic such as biography. This gives the individual library the choice of treating it as a form class, or of classifying great lives by subject, as far as is possible. The Decimal,[1] Universal Decimal, Subject and Bibliographic schemes all cater for the nature of the library in this way; the Congress system, however, insists on the distribution of biography whenever possible. This is directly due to the fact that this scheme was compiled for the national library of the U.S.A., where this arrangement would be the most useful one. Alternative arrangements must be carefully distinguished from the idea of alternative location, as advocated by Bliss. Yet the essential thing for the student to grasp at this point is simply the knowledge of what constitutes a form class. He must recognise such a class in the division of literature, in biography, in bibliography, in parts of the language class (such as dictionaries), and indeed in parts of the Generalia Class (such as General periodicals). From the classifier's viewpoint, however, a form class creates no real problem; the material will be dealt with and classified in the usual way, and it is just as important to classify carefully and accurately in these classes as it is when subject classification is being performed. In fact, the late Dr E. A. Savage[2]

---

[1] In Edition 17, the distribution of biography by subject interest is favoured.

[2] *Manual of book classification and display*, 1946, p. 74.

has suggested that, as far as classification is concerned, literature is best thought of as a subject field, similar to the other major departments of knowledge.

79. *Form Divisions*. Most books are classified by their subject, rather than by their form of presentation. It is necessary, nevertheless, to indicate the form of presentation in the classification *after* the subject class-mark has been allocated. Thus, if we have a book entitled 'Essays on Sculpture', it is clear that we must classify by subject – Sculpture; yet it will be useful to add symbols to show that the work is in essay form. Likewise, a periodical on paint technology must be classified by subject, but it is worth while to indicate, in the class-mark, that this work is a serial publication; most modern writers regard this as akin to change of phase. Thus the essential difference between form classes and form divisions is that, in the former case, classification by form takes precedence over subject arrangement; indeed the latter may not be appropriate at all. But form divisions follow subject classification, being added to the subject class-marks on certain books and indicating the form in which each particular book deals with its subject. Most of the bibliographical schemes find it advantageous to have a set of form divisions which are constantly denoted by the same symbols and which can be applied throughout the classification with the same significance. They then become known as *common form divisions*. Those of the Decimal Classification, now known as standard subdivisions, are:

01 Philosophy, Theory	06 Organizations, Societies
02 Compends, Outlines, Textbooks	07 Study and teaching
03 Dictionaries, Encyclopaedias	08 Collections
04 Essays, Lectures	09 History
05 Periodicals	

In practice, it has been found that nine common form divisions are too few; thus the above are nowadays found in a greatly extended form in the Decimal Classification. For instance, divisions of 09 are provided and we can specify the form biography by 092. So if we do decide to distribute biography by subject, we add the form division 092 to the subject number. Thus, as Geology is represented by the number 550, the biography of a geologist might be placed in biography or at 550.92. This raises another point about the standard sub-divisions of the Decimal scheme. They are more or less applicable to the whole of the system but, quite often, they drop their zero when they are added to a class-mark ending in a nought. Indeed, if a class-mark ends in two zeros, further contraction takes place. Thus we have class numbers such as 622.05, 724.03 but 570.9, 170.5, and 506 (scientific societies), 209 (History of religion).

80. Similar divisions to the above are found in the Universal Decimal scheme; the Bibliographic Classification caters for forms of presentation, points of view and many other things in its Systematic Schedules, while the Subject Classification tries to achieve the same effect by means of its Categorical Tables. Many of the schemes also provide common *geographical divisions*, although they may not always use this term to denote them. These are similar in application to the form divisions of Dewey shown above. When a subject is limited to a certain geographical area, we can use the appropriate geographical area division after the subject number. Once again we find that the Library of Congress Classification is the exception to the general rule here; it provides form and geographical divisions, but makes no attempt to make them common to the scheme as a whole. Therefore separate sets of such divisions must be provided for the appropriate classes and the size of the classification is greatly increased. But we shall return to this theme of common form and geographical divisions in the chapters on the general library classification schemes, to find out more about the preferences and features of the rival systems.

81. Yet it may be stressed here that common form and geographical divisions, or common facets as they and similar groups of concepts applicable to all classes are called in modern classification parlance, can be extremely useful. They result in the association of recurring forms of presentation and geographical regions with certain symbols, constantly used by the classification to represent these forms or regions. This association of ideas and symbols assists the memory of the librarian in finding his way about the classification quickly and in classifying simple examples rapidly; it has mnemonic value for him. In fact the common form and geographical divisions are two of the main types of systematic mnemonics discussed in paragraph 63. It is also chiefly in the use of common form and geographical divisions, or their equivalent, that we see an attempt being made to achieve a certain amount of synthesis in the older living book classifications. For a synthetic

classification relies on the fitting together of standard parts to build up the concepts found in any subject. The older schemes, although relying chiefly on the enumeration of subjects and the provision of ready-made class-marks for each one, do use a limited amount of synthesis when they provide for the building up of a subject number by the addition of common form or geographical divisions. It is partly because the Congress system lacks common divisions of this kind that it is regarded as the most enumerative of the bibliographical classifications.

82. Finally a word may be said on form divisions with regard to the distinction made between inner and outer form. This is of less importance than the ideas considered in the preceding paragraphs; it is a notion which sometimes seems to have little usefulness nowadays, but, as it is still occasionally encountered by students of our subject, it will be necessary to briefly explain the distinction. The *outer form* is represented by Dictionaries, Essays, Periodicals and similar volumes having a definite physical form or a form of presentation that is immediately recognised; *inner form* on the other hand is a term used to denote forms such as Philosophy, History and Theory. Here the form is less clearly discernible, being closely interwoven with the subject of the book. Outer form may thus be regarded as the literary shape in which a volume is presented; inner form is subjective, the method by which the subject is presented, or the viewpoint from which an author regards a subject in his text. While most forms of presentation fall readily into one or the other of these categories, the difference between the two does not seem to have any real practical consequence. Although some books may contain examples of both inner and outer forms – for instance, 'Essays on the history of political thought' – no classification scheme takes much trouble to clearly separate the inner and outer forms in its table of form divisions or their equivalent.

83. *The Alphabetical Subject Index.* We can now turn to the last of the auxiliaries which we listed as being a necessary feature in a classification of books. This is the index, which is a necessary alphabetical key to the systematic order of the classification scheme. The latter order is more complex than an A–Z sequence of topics, but it is also far more useful; that is why the alphabetical order is, apart from its occasional use within a few specific classes, reserved for the index. It must be stressed that the alphabetical index is no substitute for a good classification. The suggestion has been made

that 'it does not matter where we classify a book so long as it is properly indexed'. This is very specious reasoning; it might be acceptable if the only purpose of classification was to make the finding of particular books an easy process. There the advantage, or merit, of a system which places books in an indifferent manner and relies upon the index, ends. It is only a *small part* of the work of classification to make the finding of particular books easy, although admittedly a most convenient and practical part. The accepted definition of classification not only implies this, it implies a cardinal purpose which this ignores – the arrangement of books so that related subjects are collocated; that is to say, so that the likeness in subject matter between them is revealed. Thus a classification cannot be justly called a good one which does not show a sequence of subjects; show on the left of a particular book, or group of books, the books that lead up to it, and on the right the books which lead away from it. This is quite elementary, indeed it is basically what we have already considered in paragraph 15; but it is most desirable that we should be convinced that classification is primarily an arrangement with a definite collocating function and not a mere random filing of books in separate subject compartments, with an alphabetical index. Ranganathan has demonstrated on several occasions the importance of classification in the systematic grouping of material. He shows that, to use his own distinctive terminology, a reader approaching the shelves should find together books which are *umbral*, or central to the subject which he seeks; nearby he must find, on either side, books which are *penumbral*, that is of marginal, or potential, relevance; then, as he moves away in either direction, he will eventually come to books on the periphery of his subject and finally to those representing areas of knowledge which are *alien*, or irrelevant for his studies. Thus the helpful and convenient order is said to be the one which follows this APUPA pattern or sequence.

84. The language employed here may seem quaint to some readers, but the essential idea should be plain. If classification does not try to relate subjects systematically it becomes a mere pigeon-holing experiment. The American enthusiast, Robinson Smith,[1] for example, once outlined a classification which used an alphabetical notation and represented nearly every subject by its initial letter. This is taking the idea of literal mnemonics much too far; notation is determining the sequence of topics in the classification! A short

---

[1] *Library World*, July 1919, p. 4.

extract from Smith's system will suffice to indicate the 'alphabetical scattering' which inevitably resulted:

A	Art	N	National, Industrial and Social Problems
B	Biography	O	Oriental Languages
C	Christianity	P	Philosophy
D	Dictionaries	Q	Quartos
E	English Language and Literature	R	Roman Antiquities
F	Fiction	S	Science
G	Greek Antiquities	T	Technology
H	History	U	Unclassified
I	Industries	V	Voyages and Travels
J	Juveniles	W	Weeklies and Monthlies
K	Knowledge	Y	Yearbooks
L	Law	Z	Newspapers
M	Modern Languages		

and with alphabetical re-divisions of each, e.g.:

L	Law	LF	Feudal Law
LA	Administration	LG	Greek Law
LB	Banking Law	LH	History of Law
LC	Criminal Law		

These, in turn, were sub-divided in a similar fashion. But every student of classification who has followed our argument this far will see that this is not classification at all; it is arrangement presumably for quick reference, but it is an indescribable jumbling of topics, the only relation between them being the alphabetical letters of the class names. It even has defects as a mnemonic arrangement, for we search our minds in vain for the possible place in this scheme of many subjects. But Robinson Smith is not the only culprit;[1] even Melvil Dewey and, later, Grace Kelley, seem to suggest that the index can atone for the faults of a scheme. Bliss has called this erroneous notion the *subject index illusion*, saying that 'no index, however convenient or necessary, can convert an arbitrary or disordered arrangement into a systematic classification'.

85. The index is, nevertheless, an essential tool. Having stressed that it cannot be expected to do the work of the classification, we must see what duties we *do* expect it to perform. A good index should carry out thoroughly two definite functions. It must:

[1] The classification offered by H. W. Parker, 3rd edn. New York, 1926, follows similar lines.

(*a*) Locate topics within the systematically arranged classification.

(*b*) Show related aspects of a subject which the classification has scattered, for no classification can bring together *all* branches of a complex subject. By collecting these 'distributed relatives', as Savage has so aptly called them, the index reveals subject relationships, albeit usually minor ones, which the classification has been forced to ignore.

In carrying out these functions the index should strive to complement, rather than duplicate the work of the scheme. It should not, therefore, repeat information which is easily accessible in the main tables. It must also be noted that it is most unwise for the classifier to try to place books in the scheme by using the index alone. Indeed it is essential that the index should be used merely as a check; the classifier must find the appropriate place in the tables and ensure that the specific class-mark chosen is correct, and that the containing general heading is a suitable one. This assumes that the classification is of the enumerative type; if, in fact, it is entirely synthetic there will be less chance of error, once the principles have been mastered. Nevertheless, the index must only be used in practical classification in conjunction with the schedules.

86. There are two kinds of index; the Relative Index and the 'one-place' or Specific index; they are inspired by opposed ideals in classification. The former gives an entry for each item in the scheme and shows, under each entry, all the aspects, standpoints and relationships from which the subject may be regarded and the class-mark for each of these. The latter suggests that there is one location only for each subject and all its aspects and thus gives only one class-mark for each entry. Both types of index include synonyms. The Relative Index has been far the more popular of the two; it is used in all the bibliographical schemes, save one, and is to be found also in countless works of reference. The Specific index (to use the name given to the other type of index by Berwick Sayers) is less bulky and superficially more attractive; in practice, however, it is a far less useful tool. It is found in J. D. Brown's Subject Classification. This attempts to locate everything on a given subject at one definite place, but in practice this is often neither possible nor, if it could be achieved, would it be useful. It is necessary for classificationists and classifiers to take into account the angles from which a

particular subject is studied (for instance, whether coins are being dealt with from the point of view of numismatics, or that of the economist – to use an example which we shall employ again later). The Specific index often fails to make this type of distinction; it ignores the different aspects of a subject, the different uses made of a commodity or material, and the different contexts in which certain subjects may appear.

87. The student may fail to appreciate this point until he has studied the index to the Subject Classification and contrasted it with those of other schemes, or until he has read more about the principles behind Brown's scheme (given in Chapter 14). Nevertheless, it is worthwhile to show the difference between the two types of index here, by means of an example from the Decimal and Subject Classifications:

Relative index (D.C.)	*S.C.'s One-place or 'Specific' Index*
Adhesives	Adhesives D 952
engineering properties and tests 620.199	
manufacture 668.3	
masonry building construction materials 691.5	
etc.	

Brown would, no doubt argue that he has distinguished 'concrete' subjects in his index and that viewpoints can be shown by adding to the subject number symbols denoting aspects, etc., from his Categorical Tables. But, in reality, his attempts to provide a 'one place' classification with an equivalent index has led to some odd groupings and separations. Dewey rashly asserted that the Relative Index was the most important feature of his classification; this is certainly not so, but it has proved a very useful tool, despite the fact that much dissatisfaction has been expressed with the index to the seventeenth edition. The so-called Specific Index, on the other hand must be taken on faith. It is sometimes accurate when it suggests that everything on a subject is to be found at one definite place, but at other times this is quite contrary to the facts. Indeed, as Mills has suggested, the Specific index may best be thought of as an incomplete index rather than a different species from its rival. It performs the location function of the index to a certain extent, but it certainly does not show the various aspects of a subject that have inevitably been scattered in a scheme – the distributed relatives of the classification.

88. *Other additions to a published classification scheme.* Apart from these auxiliary features it must be stressed that printed classifications are usually provided with an introduction which explains the origin of the system and the method of applying it. Some of these introductions give an excellent account of the system and shed light on important classification principles also although, naturally, they always have a bias towards the scheme in question. The Decimal Classification is pre-eminent in this respect, for it has a long introduction from Dewey's own pen, followed by another full one from the editor of the latest edition. But most other schemes also have good introductions and synopses of the main principles of chief divisions often follow them. In his work on this subject the student must never neglect the examination of the general classifications themselves and their prefatory remarks and explanations.

CHAPTER SEVEN

Canons of Library Classification

89. To conclude our study of the purely theoretical aspects of our subject, it will be profitable to gather together those condensed precepts of classification which various writers have enunciated. The dramatic and radical changes in the approach to library classification since 1950, both in Great Britain and in many overseas countries have made it both difficult and unwise to lay down definite criteria for a book classification and to state emphatically that the points made should be rigidly observed or taken as advice or standards of permanent value. The problem is made more acute by the fact that traditional theories of library classification are still flourishing in the older, widely accepted, schemes, while principles of a fundamentally different nature, which can only be glimpsed in most of those schemes, are generally accepted and fervently proclaimed by the advocates of the synthetic approach. In this chapter it has been found convenient to list some of the rules, or canons, put forward by some of the great writers on our subject; the student, especially, should bear in mind the fact that there are other authors of works on classification who have also indicated what they consider to be the fundamental principles on which a modern bibliographical classification should be based. Palmer and Wells[1] provide some modern principles in tabular form at the beginning of their textbook; Mills[2] offers a useful summary; and Phillips[3] indicates a list of criteria which, although it may be considered to reflect the traditional viewpoint in library classification, should satisfy most librarians. Here we shall list some of the Canons laid down by Sayers, as character-

---

[1] *Fundamentals of Library Classification*, 1951.

[2] *A modern outline of library classification*, 1960, pp. 54–6.

[3] *Primer of book classification*, 5th edn, 1961, p. 57.

istic of what might be termed the 'classical' approach to book classification; some of the important principles stressed by Bliss, whose approach might be described as 'neo-classical' and a few of the distinctive principles of Ranganathan, the herald of the newer (and to many classifiers and students most inspiring and effective) approach to library classification.

CANONS OF SAYERS

90. *As to Definitions*

There are various meanings which can be attached to the term *classification*. It is perhaps best thought of as the intellectual process by which our mental concepts or pictures of things are recognised to have likeness or unity and by this likeness or unity they are set *in relation* to one another.

As to book classification

A. Book classifications are devised for or adapted to the arrangement of books or other library material, by subject or form or both, or by any recognisable logical order. They must be made with a careful and constant regard for achieving the order most *helpful* to library users.

B. Unless deliberately created for a special subject field only they must be general; that is, they must include all topics that are the subject of books.

C. They must be capable of expansion in order that, without dislocation, they may admit new topics, or new sub-divisions of old ones.

D. They must be equipped with the necessary auxiliary features (these are described in Chapters 5 and 6).

E. They must be uncritical in their terms for subjects. In classing a book any placing that implies criticism of its subject content is inadmissible. Ambiguity must be avoided in the terms used.

91. *As to notation*

F. The notation of a scheme is a systematic and logically ordered

D

series of short signs representing the class-names in the system.

G. It may consist of any symbols that are capable of marking all parts of the scheme. It should, however, be brief, simple, flexible and mnemonic.

H. The tendency is to use alphabetical symbols for the main outline of the scheme, but to use numbers in addition to letters when sub-dividing classes.

I. Flexibility in a notation means that, as classification must permit the insertion of any new class or part of a class, so also the notation symbols must be capable of expansion to mark that insertion without dislocating the rest of the notation. This is the cardinal requirement of notation.

J. A mnemonic notation is one that marks any series of subjects or forms which recur in the scheme; each subject, form or aspect is always indicated by the same symbol, which therefore may be easily memorized.

92. *As to book classification schemes*

K. A classification scheme needs to be printed in columnar schedules in the order of the precedence of subjects, as far as that is possible, so that the hierarchy of the subjects is exhibited. (It may be noted that if a non-expressive notation is used, we may have to rely on indentation in the columns of the schedules to reveal the hierarchy of classes.)

L. The printed tables should be prefaced by an introduction explaining the methods and use of the scheme, with tables showing the outlines of its main divisions and other tables revealing its form divisions, or systematic schedules of recurring concepts.

M. A classification scheme needs continuous study and revision so that it is maintained, as far as possible, in currency with knowledge. Schemes in general use are likely to be kept so because they come under the scrutiny of regular application. (It is wise for a scheme to have an editorial body to ensure that new editions appear at regular intervals).

BLISS'S PRINCIPLES

93. These are thirty-two in number, and, in endeavouring to summarise what Bliss himself has condensed, we have probably not succeeded. The reader may consult them in Bliss's *Organization of Knowledge in Libraries*, 2nd edn., *1939*.

A. A bibliographical classification system should be logical in its construction. Such a classification is a series of classes so arranged as to show the relations that exist between them. A class is divisible into sub-classes by a specified characteristic and these may be sub-divided again and again more specifically. Each stage produces a number of parallel sub-classes which have common likeness; each stage is also obviously subordinate to the class out of which it has been divided.

B. A bibliographical classification should be consistent with the special classifications in the various departments of knowledge and with the organization of knowledge established in the consensus of scientists and educationists. For *maximal efficiency* great care must be taken concerning the *subordination* of the special to the general, and the collocation of closely allied topics. Within any group of co-ordinate classes, it may be possible to achieve helpful order by means of the idea of *gradation by speciality*.

C. Alternative locations should be provided for the arrangement of certain subjects, which have no one clearly recognisable place within the consensus of opinion, according to the needs of the libraries using the scheme. The scheme should also be expansible to admit new topics, and details in the schedule should at need be alterable.

94. *As to notation*

D. Notation is correlative to and subsidiary to classification. It should be readjustable and should be simple, short, and have sufficient capacity; these features are interrelated, for the brevity and simplicity of notation will depend upon the base of the notation. (Bliss uses a base of letters in his own scheme to increase the capacity of notation.) Mnemonics, if used, should not distort the classification. *Auxiliary schedules* may be used to represent recurrent concepts. These schedules will enable synthesis (Bliss's term is *composite specification*) to be carried out and the concepts involved will usually be constantly denoted by the same notational symbols. Where more than one of these schedules combine in minute classifications, they should show the order in which they are to be used. For these schedules the notation should be mnemonic. It should, nevertheless, be simple and avoid unfamiliar and confusing devices which are too indefinite for books although they may be serviceable to documentation. Bliss does not concur with Ranganathan in the quest to achieve exact classification even if notation becomes very long.

As to the index

An alphabetical index is no substitute for a scholarly and well-organized classification. However, the index is a very necessary auxiliary; it must give all terms used in the system, including synonyms, and show the notation for each to reveal their place in the scheme of classification. Distributed aspects of any subject must be revealed in the index, that is, a Relative index is required.

RANGANATHAN'S CANONS

95. Many of Ranganathan's distinctive ideas are explained in his books *Prolegomena to Library Classification* and *Elements of Library Classification*. He arrived at them after some years of work on his Colon scheme. They were energised, as it were, by a record reading – in a long but inspiring session, he tells us – of the two books of Bliss. The distinctive ideas of Ranganathan are those which have truly revolutionised the approach to our subject. He expounds systematically thirty-three canons; some are extensions of those of Sayers, others are completely his own. To each canon he gave a name which is an aid to memory and sometimes to meaning. These ideas include: the emphasis on the fact that an effective classification must only enumerate basic parts or concepts, which the individual classifier will piece together as required after analysing the subject of a book into its component parts; the recognition of the problem presented by books which draw on material from more than one department of knowledge – to be solved by analysis into primary and secondary phases; and a great stress on mnemonics. Ranganathan believes that the symbols of a class-mark which stand for an entity

should be the same in every part of the scheme where that entity is represented and thus be mnemonic, unless more important requirements are to be served. It would be futile to attempt to enumerate and describe all Ranganathan's Canons here,[1] but, in addition to the above, the following points may be noted as a guide to his main ideas.

A. The subject of each book must be fully revealed in the class-mark. This idea of *co-extensiveness of subject and class-mark*, as Ranganathan calls it, has been challenged by some writers on our subject. However, Ranganathan believes that, in large libraries especially, exact classification of material is essential and that a broad arrangement will only hide the specific in a welter of more general material. He also believes that a classification should have a system of book numbers to permit the distinction between two books on the same topic to be made in the class mark. Thus each book in the library will be individualised.

B. Class marks should be so constructed that symbols for new topics can be inserted at any point in an array, or added at the end of a chain without disturbance of existing class marks.

C. The schedules should provide for national variations due to local and other interests. They should be equipped with various devices to ensure that helpful order is achieved. For example, Ranganathan's own scheme uses, among other devices, the Classic Device to bring editions of classics together and, next to them, their commentaries.

D. The scheme should give the individual classifier *maximum autonomy* to construct his own class-marks for new subjects as soon as they appear. More will be said about this most interesting idea, which may have a profound effect upon the revision policies of future classification systems, in Chapter 17.

E. The system as a whole should be of the maximum usefulness to both reader and librarian. It should recognise the principles expressed in Ranganathan's five laws of library science and constantly keep them in mind. (These are: books are for use; every reader his book; every book its reader; save the time of the reader; the library is a growing organism.)[2]

---

[1] Our reader is invited to consult, if he wishes, their detailed consideration in R. S. Parkhi, *Decimal Classification and Colon Classification in Perspective*, 1964.

[2] B. C. Vickery has recently added a sixth law – 'no modern library can be self-sufficient'.

96. The reader who requires a more detailed list of standards, or canons, must turn to the original writings of Ranganathan, Bliss, and, if older theories are sought, Richardson and Hulme. All canons may seem vague when enumerated in a textbook; the acid test, of course, is how they work out in practice. It will be found, if a more exhaustive study of such canons is made, that the older writers cover a range of precepts which, in their main features, harmonise. Likewise Ranganathan and his followers are in complete agreement about the major principles upon which a modern library classification should be based. It must not be thought that Colon is the only system to employ such principles; indeed, they can be dimly seen in some of the older schemes, although not fully developed there. In addition, we now have many special classifications which deal with one field of knowledge, or with a group of kindred subjects. Most of these are entirely synthetic; they also have the advantage of using the ideas expressed in Colon selectively and of learning from its mistakes as well as from its achievement. Thus there is a distinct, some would say strong, possibility that the older ideas will be completely superseded and will disappear, very slowly in practice, as Dewey and other traditional schemes are replaced by a new and highly synthetic general classification. But this is a huge and controversial subject which can be dealt with later. Here it will be sufficient for the student of our subject to reconsider very carefully the reading he has done in this section on the *principles* of classification, paying special attention to the merits claimed for faceted classification; the need for an order throughout a classification which will be the most useful one for the reader and the way in which this is to be achieved; the possibility of enabling such an order to be varied in certain libraries, through the use of alternative locations; and the necessity of taking into account the requirements of literature when developing the divisions and notation of the various subject classes. The various ideas put forward and the terminology used should be mastered by our reader, before he goes on to read about the history of classification and the various bibliographical schemes. He may also at this stage, find it worthwhile to make a provisional attempt to decide for himself to what extent the modern principles being applied in bibliographical classification are superior to the old.

History of Library Classification

TABLE I

OUTLINE OF THREE
IMPORTANT EARLY CLASSIFICATIONS

D*

1   THE CHART OF HUMAN LEARNING, FRANCIS BACON (1623 VERSI

HISTORY (MEMORY)

  NATURAL HISTORY

    HISTORY OF GENERATIONS

    (Heavenly bodies, earth and sea, 'masses' or 'greater colleges', i.e., the four elements; 'species' or 'lesser colleges', i.e., zoology and and botany)

    HISTORY OF PRETERGENERATIONS

    'Irregulars' of nature, such as monsters, witch-craft, and marvels

      HISTORY OF ARTS (nature wrought or mechanical)

  CIVIL HISTORY

    ECCLESIASTICAL

      SPECIAL

        HISTORY OF PROPHECY

        DIVINE JUDGMENTS OR PROVIDENCE

    CIVIL HISTORY (PROPER)

      MEMORIALS (PREPARATORY HISTORY)

        COMMENTARIES

        ('C. set down a bare continuance and tissue of actions and events, without causes and pretexts . . .')

        REGISTERS

        (Here come the public acts, edicts, etc.)

    ANTIQUITIES

    PERFECT HISTORY

      CHRONICLES

      UNIVERSAL

        ANNALS

        JOURNALS

      PARTICULAR

        ANNALS

        JOURNALS

    LIVES

    RELATIONS

    COSMOGRAPHY

    (Geography, navigation, climate, geography and astronomy combined)

    LEARNING AND THE ARTS

    APPENDICES TO HISTORY

      ORATIONS

      LETTERS

      APOPHTHEGMS

POESY (IMAGINATION)

  NARRATIVE

  DRAMATIC

  PARABOLICAL (i.e., fables, allegory)

PHILOSOPHY (REASON)

  DIVINE (natural theology)

  NATURAL

    SPECULATIVE

      PRIMARY PHILOSOPHY

      PHYSIC

      (Includes astronomy and astrology)

SPECULATIVE (*continued*)

  FIRST PRINCIPLES OF THINGS

  FABRIC OF THINGS, OR THE WORLD

  VARIETY OF THINGS

    CONCRETE

    (Divided like natural history)

    ABSTRACT

      CONFIGURATIONS OF MATTER

      (Rather *states* of matter)

      MOTIONS

      (Attraction and repulsion, etc)

  METAPHYSIC

OPERATIVE

  MECHANIC

  (Applied metaphysic)

  MAGIC

  (Applied metaphysic)

  MATHEMATIC

    PURE

    MIXED

HUMAN

  PHILOSOPHY OF HUMANITY

  (Man as an individual)

    NATURE OR STATE OF MAN

    (Includes miseries and prerogatives of state and *mind and body*)

  BODY

    MEDICINE

    COSMETIC

    (Personal hygiene)

    ATHLETIC

    VOLUPTUARY (sensual arts)

      PAINTING

      MUSIC

      OTHER ARTS OF PLEASURE

  SOUL

    BREATH OF LIFE (rational soul)

    SENSIBLE OR PRODUCED SOUL

      MOTION

      SENSE

    SUBSTANCE AND FACULTIES

    USE AND OBJECTS OF THE FACULTIES

      LOGIC

        ART OF DISCOVERING

        ART OF JUDGING

        ART OF RETAINING (memory)

        ART OF TRANSMITTING

        (Here come grammar, speech, wri rhetoric)

      ETHIC

  PHILOSOPHY, CIVIL

  (Man in society)

    CONVERSATION

    (Includes etiquette and manners)

    NEGOTIATION

    (Conduct of business, personal fortune advancement)

    EMPIRE OR STATE GOVERNMENT

    (Includes economics and law)

SYSTEM OF CONRAD GESNER (8)

Praeparantes	Necessarias { Sermocinales	1. Grammatica et Philologia
		2. Dialectica
		3. Rhetorica
		4. Poetica
	Mathematicas	5. Arithmetica
		6. Geometria, Optica, etc
		7. Musica
		8. Astronomia
		9. Astrologia
Ornantes		10. De divinatione et magia
		11. Geographia
		12. Historia
		13. De diversibus artibus, illiteratis, mechanicis, etc
Substantiales		14. De naturali philosophia
		15. De prima philosophia seu metaphysica, et theologia gentilium
		16. De morali philosophia
		17. De philosophia œconomica
		18. De re politica id et civili ac militari
		19. De jurisprudentia
		20. De re medica
		21. De theologia Christiana

III SYSTEM OF BOUILLIAU (Circa 1678) or usual 'French System'

As successively modified by Martin (1740), Debure (1768), Brunet (1842), and Others

CLASS I   THEOLOGY
1. Holy Scriptures
2. Sacred Philology
3. Liturgies
4. Councils
5. Fathers
6. Collective Works of Theologians
7. Singular and Fanatical Sects and Opinions
8. Judaism
9. Oriental Religions
10. Deism, etc

CLASS II   JURISPRUDENCE
1. Introductions to the Study of Law, and General Treatises
2. Natural and International Law
3. Political Law
4. Civil and Criminal Law
5. Canon and Ecclesiastical Law

CLASS III   SCIENCES AND ARTS
1. Dictionaries and Encyclopædias
2. Philosophical Sciences
3. Physical and Chemical Sciences
4. Natural Sciences
5. Medical Sciences
6. Mathematical Sciences
7. Mnemonics
8. Fine Arts
9. Mechanical Arts and Trades
10. Gymnastics – Recreative Arts and Games

CLASS IV   POLITE LITERATURE
1. Introductory Works
2. Linguistics
3. Rhetoric
4. Poetry
5. Prose Fiction
6. Philology
7. Dialogues and Conversations
8. Letters
9. Polygraphy
10. Collections of the Works of different Authors – Miscellanies

CLASS V   HISTORY
1. Historical Prolegomena
2. Universal History, Ancient and Modern
3. History of Religions and of Superstitions
4. Ancient History
5. Modern History
6. Historical Paralipomena

CHAPTER EIGHT

Important Early Utilitarian and Philosophical Schemes

97. The object of this section is to outline the early, gradual development of classification, and especially of bibliographical schemes; it is a natural preface to our study of modern book classifications, since these owe much to the experiments made by classificationists of the past. The history of classification, effectively written, would almost necessarily be a history of all attempts to organize human thought. Since man began his long endeavours to distinguish and understand the parts of his universe, he has consciously or unconsciously formed some system in which those parts were related to one another. We need not follow here his unconscious exercise of this power of classification construction because that has been described by many logicians and psychologists. Our concern is rather with the systems which have been written down in schedules by their makers or can be inferred from their writings. Of these there are now hundreds. The most compact and convenient account of the older schemes is the 'Essay towards a Bibliographical History of the Systems of Classification' which forms a valuable appendix to E. C. Richardson's book. In this are registered, with useful bibliographical material, no less than 161 of such systems, beginning with the scheme somewhat uncertainly abstracted from Plato's *Republic* (428–347 B.C.) and concluding with that of E. Barthel (1910). All these are pure thought compilations to aid the mental plotting out of the universe of thought and of objects; in no case were they intended for practical library use. Many of them have been considered critically in Robert Flint's *A History of the Classifications of the Sciences* (1904), a work of clarity and much

learning, but somewhat difficult for the student who has not a large library at hand, because it does not set out even in outline many of the systems which it appraises. The later work, *The Organization of Knowledge and the System of the Sciences*, by H. E. Bliss (1929) has equal erudition, wider scope, more detail, and purposes to show the bearing of the systems upon a valid library system; it is therefore both parallel with and complementary to Flint, and, because of its library focus, is of greater interest in our study. It embodies at least thirty years of work and is without rival in its field.

98. Here, we shall glance at some of the older practical and philosophical systems before going on to describe, in succeeding chapters, the developments of bibliographical classification in the nineteenth and twentieth centuries. Of the value of the study of philosophical systems of classification there can be no doubt. Modern systems reflect earlier ones, and some of the terminology now used in library classification has been inherited from the past. On the other hand, the average student of librarianship cannot afford the protracted study which this side of the subject undoubtedly demands. Our consideration, therefore, will be limited to some systems as appear to have had a bearing upon the construction of library schemes, but it should be realised that the study which is here passed over can be a fruitful and even a practical one; and those who can pursue it have in Flint, Richardson and Bliss an admirable trinity of guides. The existence of the splendid essays in the history of library and bibliographical classification (2 vols., 1955–59) of the Russian, E. I. Samurin, may also be noted; these, however, have not been translated.

99. Our earliest traditions of libraries bear their account of classification. We are assured that the clay tablets in the Assyrian library of Assur-ban-i-pal were divided at least into two main classes – those dealing with knowledge of the Earth, and those dealing with the Heavens – and that these were subdivided. How the libraries of Greece and Rome were classified we do not know, but it seems safe to suppose that a race which produced the classifying mind of Aristotle would keep its books in some sort of order, and that the massive orderly mind of the Romans would use classification. 'With regard to Aristotle, Strabo has preserved the tradition that he "was the first who made a collection of books, and taught the Kings of Egypt how to arrange a library" – words which may be taken to mean that Aristotle was the first to work out the

arrangement of books on a definite system which was afterwards adopted by the Ptolemies at Alexandria'.[1] However that may be, the earliest recorded system of any dimensions was that designed by Callimachus, the greatest of the librarians of Egypt, for the library of Alexandria (260–240 B.C.). The scheme as a whole is lost, but Richardson has picked out for us certain facts and the main classes.[2] The latter appear to have been:

Poets
Lawmakers
Philosophers
Historians
Rhetoricians
Miscellaneous writers

There are hints of form and subject sub-divisions and of the fact that some of the classes at least were arranged chronologically by periods and, in the shorter subjects, alphabetically by the names of authors.

100. There is a wide interval in our knowledge after this. Schemes for the arrangement of mediaeval monastic libraries existed and are recorded by Richardson. They need not detain us, except to remark of the later ones that Mr W. R. B. Prideaux[3] in a paper on 'Library Economy at the end of the seventeenth century', says it was usual 'to divide the books into a certain number of general classes and then to place them in fixed location according to size, in the shelves set apart for each class ... The books were sometimes put under the classes in alphabetical order of the author's names. Century and nationality were also used as the basis of division'. He tells us, further, of the system favoured by the Jesuits: on entering the library, if you turned left, you beheld the resplendently bound collection of choice and exquisite authors; if you looked in another direction, you saw 'the unhappy books of the heretics placed in mourning and dirt, and indeed bound in black skins or black parchment'. The 'fixed location' here mentioned has also been referred to very briefly in Chapter 2. It is an impracticable method in any growing library; we may best consider it as a form of the

---

[1] J. W. Clark, *Care of Books*, p. 5.
[2] *Classification*. p. 89.
[3] *Library Association Record*, 1904, pp. 132–3.

once common collegiate press-marking system, discussed fully in Chapter 10.

101. Edward Edwards made a distinction in the types of library classification which is helpful, and which brings us to the central theme of the present chapter. There are, he says, library classification systems which have a metaphysical basis, and there are those which are merely practical and convenient arrangements, made without reference to any ideal order of knowledge. A system with a metaphysical origin is clearly one based upon a mental order of the things it covers existing in the mind of its compiler or, as was more often the case, borrowed and adapted from another mind: it is therefore one in which its maker had laid out some ideal order for his classes before he began to put books or other material into them. The second category of classifications observed by Edwards, 'schemes directed, more or less specifically, to the *practical* arrangement of books', begins, we may say, in 1498 with that of Aldus Manutius and proceeds through the systems of Naudé, Garnier and others to that of Ismael Bouilliau[1] (1605–98), which is generally considered to be the foundation of what is called the French System, or, alternatively, the System of the Paris Booksellers. This system, worked out in great detail and with excellent scholarship by Jacques Charles Brunet (1780–1867), became the most influential and widely used of all bibliographical schemes, especially on the continent of Europe.

102. France has always been essentially the home of bibliographers; indeed, it may be said that until comparatively recently the best works on that subject were French. The seventeenth century saw catalogues which have points of interest, amongst which may be mentioned those of Gabriel Naudé, 1643, whose *Advis pour dresser une bibliothèque* was translated by the great diarist, John Evelyn; it is a work of such liberality of ideas that it would do honour to the modern librarian. It has twelve main classes, which, because of the eminence of the compiler, deserve transcription:

Theology	Military Art
Medicine	Jurisprudence
Bibliography	Council and Canon Law
Chronology	Philosophy

[1] 'On écrit aussi, mais moins exactement, Bouillaud.' A. Cim, *Le Livre*, Vol. 9. 1907.

Geography	Politics
History	Literature

103. But we must return to the System of the Paris Booksellers, which is almost contemporary with Naudé's system and is more important from our point of view. 'The honour of originating it has been claimed,' writes Edwards in his *Memoirs of Libraries*, 'sometimes for the learned Jesuit, Jean Garnier, and sometimes for Gabriel Martin, for so long a period the most eminent of the Paris Booksellers; but the claim which is best authenticated seems to be that of Bouilliau, the compiler of the sale catalogue of the famous library of de Thou.' Edouard Rouveyre, on the authority of Gustave Brunet, claims that this outline was originated by Gabriel Martin, a bibliographer who between 1705 and 1761 had compiled 147 library catalogues. The point does not seem to be important; we must notice, however, that the system was modified and extended enormously by Brunet, who made it the basis of the classified part (volume 5) of his *Manuel du Libraire et de l'Amateur de Livres*, an important bibliography, which first appeared in 1809 and has been revised and extended many times since. The scheme has five main classes only:

1. Theology
2. Jurisprudence
3. History
4. Philosophy
5. Literature

104. In the hands of Brunet, the scheme had for its object the arrangement of a great general bibliography, in which the books are classified by their predominating characteristics. French bibliographers have been almost lyrical in their praise of the system, as is natural, seeing that so many of their bibliographies are classified by it, and it is the scheme with which they are most familiar. 'It has been reproached,' remarks Gustave Brunet, 'for not being philosophical enough or rigidly scientific. On the other hand it is clear, simple, easy and as Charles Nodier says with reason, "It embraces, without too great an effort, all the innumerable and capricious subdivisions which human ingenuity has been pleased to introduce into the literary form of books, and it is sanctioned by excellent catalogues which have become classics of their kind." ' Rouveyre compares it

with Dewey, greatly to the disadvantage of the American scheme, of which he contends, 'en Europe, en France particulièrement, son emploi serait désastreux'.

105. The full tables of the Brunet Classification occupy eighteen pages of large octavo size, with closely-printed double columns, in the fifth volume of Brunet's *Manuel*: but a reasonably detailed outline of this famous system is apparently not available in English. It has, nevertheless, great vogue in France, especially for the arrangement of bibliographies and for booksellers' stocks and private collections. So far as it is classified, the Bibliothèque Nationale bases its arrangement upon Brunet. The great and well administered public library of Sainte-Geneviève in Paris is also arranged by it, the scheme having been expanded considerably to meet the needs of modern literature, and it is assuredly successful there. It may be noted that the system proposed to the Trustees for the classification of the British Museum in 1825 is a modification of the French scheme; the scheme actually used in that great library now also bears a rather remote resemblance to it, but sufficient to suggest that it was an influence. Criticism of this system is easy from the standpoint of today, and yet difficult because, without practical experience of the scheme, it is likely to be merely academic. The obvious remark is that it is old-fashioned and is conditioned, as one might expect, by the state of knowledge in its day. The tables are far too brief and many important modern subjects are relegated to the various appendices; for example, Australia, New Zealand and Polynesia are merely an appendix to the History of Asia. The notation of the scheme is mixed, cumbrous, and obsolete; it uses upper and lower case letters and numbers and has no attractions for the modern librarian. However, this could, one supposes, be revised if necessary. The classification also lacks an index. In short, its main interest for us nowadays is not the possibility or desirability of applying it to the organization of books in a library, but in its value as a clue to the labyrinthine arrangement of many continental bibliographies.

106. It is not profitable for us to enter upon the fertile and interesting field of German bibliographical classifications, as their vogue has not been great outside the country of their origin. In what has been a standard manual of library economy in that country,[1] Dr Arnim Graesel has given a satisfactory account of

---

[1] A. Graesel, *Handbuch der Bibliothekslehre*, 1902.

systems current at the beginning of the present century. From this it would appear that the classification of Otto Hartwig (1888) has been favourably regarded (indeed this had some influence on classification in the U.S.A.), but the learned author also praises the scheme of Schutz and Hufeland (1785–1800) as one of the best. Neither of these appears to be important in comparison with the schemes selected for special consideration here; nor is it necessary to draw attention to Italian classification, although there has been an interesting attempt in that country to combine the systems of Hartwig and Dewey.[1] This much restraint is necessary in order that the student may focus his attention only upon schemes which have some definite historical significance for librarians of today.

107. We must now examine one or two important examples from the other category of classifications distinguished by Edwards – schemes having a *metaphysical* or a *philosophical* basis. Such systems would seem to deserve priority of treatment in a survey of this kind, but in chronological order schemes which do not possess this basis are found first. When we come to consider philosophical schemes we are obliged to pass over several centuries with a quiet mind, because nothing that can be so described occurs until approximately 1550. It may, nevertheless, be noted that the order of studies evolved by the universities found early reflection in Duke Humfrey's Library, the early part of the University Library at Oxford, in about 1431. Here the statutes ordained that books for the study of 'the Seven Liberal Arts and Three Philosophies were kept apart in a chest, and might be borrowed by Masters of Arts lecturing in those subjects.'[2] But the first important early philosophical system is that which is called by some 'the first bibliographical scheme'; it was created by the German-Swiss scholar, naturalist, and author, Konrad von Gesner (1516–65). Gesner's life is one of the romances of the history of learning. Son of a poor furrier in Zurich who died when his son was fourteen, Gesner at that age started out in the world in the hope of relieving the dire poverty of his mother and many brothers and sisters by the use of his pen! Coming to Strasbourg, he entered the service of Wolfgang Fabricius Capito, with whom he studied Hebrew; whence, returning to Switzerland, he was granted a small travelling scholarship which enabled him to continue his studies in France; later he became a schoolmaster in

---

[1] R. Bliss, Bonazzi's scheme for a classed catalogue, *Library Journal* 1891, pp. 5–8.
[2] S. Gibson, *Some Oxford libraries*, p.15.

his native city. A course in medicine at Basle followed, and in 1537 he received the appointment of Professor of Greek at Lausanne; but this he relinquished to continue medicine at Montpellier, to graduate at Basle, and to return to Zurich in order to commence practice. The University of Zurich made him Professor of Physics and Natural History in 1541, and this office he dignified until his death occurred, prematurely as a result of devotion to his medical duties, in a plague which swept the city in 1565.

108. In a life of little more than forty-eight years, his industry was enormous and his learning has rarely been surpassed in its width and comprehensiveness. Georges Cuvier, himself a master of zoological classification, called him 'the German Pliny'. Gesner published no less than seventy-two works on grammar, botany, pharmacy, medicine, natural philosophy and history, and was working on eighteen others at his death. His claim to remembrance, however, rests mainly upon his *Bibliotheca Universalis* (1545), which is a catalogue of Latin, Greek and Hebrew books with critical notes and extracts from the most important ones, and its supplement *Pandectarum sive partitionum universalium Conradi Gesneri Ligurini libri XXI* (1548), of which, however, only nineteen of the twenty-one books indicated in the title were published, the books on medicine and theology not having satisfied the compiler. In the *Pandects*, Gesner classified the entries according to subjects and in such manner as to make the system employed an immense advance upon its predecessors. It is classification of knowledge according to definite principles and Gesner obviously had the progressive order of studies in his mind. Philosophy, in his system, stands for the whole sum of knowledge which is to be approached through the arts and the sciences. Of the arts and sciences there are two kinds: (1) those which are primary or preparatory, and (2) those which are fundamental. Of the preparatory sciences he finds some to be (a) necessary and others to be (b) embellishments or enrichments. His necessary arts are (aa) those of discourse and (bb) mathematical sciences and arts. What he terms (b) *ornantes* (a word for which an exact English equivalent is difficult to discover) form a curious class, but are clearly a progression of studies through divination and magic, geography and history to the illiterate or mechanical arts. From these the prepared mind may proceed to his great class (2) *substantiales*, which holds the higher forms of knowledge, and connotes all forms of philosophy, metaphysical, natural, moral, civil,

economic, political, legal, medical and theological. The result is a
hierarchy of knowledge of an ideal kind in no way dependent upon
the fortuitous appearance of books in this or that subject. Brunet
remarks that the system sufficed in its time for the arrangement of a
library *bien composée*, and that Gesner, being a man of good sense,
had avoided those arbitrary combinations of different sciences into
one class which have seduced so many savants. In any case, it is the
great mediaeval attempt to relate the arrangement of books to the
educational and scientific consensus of the day.

109. There are several other philosophical systems; the only other
we shall describe here, and the one which is of most importance to
us today is the chart of human learning which formed the framework of Francis Bacon's treatise on '*The Advancement of Learning*'
(1605). The origin of this scheme may be outlined briefly. Bacon,
in laying the foundations of his philosophical system, commences
with a review of what has been accomplished in the field of learning,
and of the documents in which that accomplishment has been
recorded. The ambitious character of his project will be observed;
he is the prototype and in all ways the greatest British example of
those remarkable men of whom the world has produced about a
dozen who take the whole field of knowledge as their province; his
mind was encyclopaedic. The *Advancement of Learning* is therefore
the history of the record of thought as it was at the date of its
appearance; but it is also rather a discussion of the state of knowledge than of the books or methods themselves. Bacon rarely, and
only then by allusive methods, mentions the names of books. His
treatise is still notable, not only as an example of the classifying
mind, but because of the clarity of its logic and the beauty of its
prose. One cannot refrain from quoting the beautiful reference to
libraries as:

'The shrines where all the relics of the ancient saints, full of true
virtue, and that without delusion or imposture, are reposed'.

not because any librarian of this workaday world regards it as a
statement of the purpose of his library, but because there is a nobility
in the utterance which strikes something responsive in us all.

110. Bacon's method is subjective; and he proceeds upon a
definite principle of division that we can recognise and appreciate.
In fact, as applied to books, he is the first of all the classificationists
who is quite consistent in the characteristics on which he bases his

outline. This follows the idea that there are three distinct mental faculties, or fountains – Memory, Imagination, and Reason – and that from these flow the three emanations – History, Poetry and Philosophy. A brief description of these may be helpful. *Memory*, according to Bacon, produces History, and this is of two kinds. One records the works of nature (Natural History); the other (Civil History) the works of man. The second class shows the *imagination* working on the materials provided by our senses, 'combing, magnifying and idealizing them at pleasure',[1] from which we get Poetry and like subjects. The third class, Philosophy, is the product of *reason*. Like all other branches of this classification, it is a human science; it springs from the mind of man, not the Divine Mind. Hence there is no place for Theology, as we understand it, in this class. Bacon says that Theology consists mainly of Sacred History; it mainly goes, in this scheme, under Ecclesiastical History.

111. Bacon's recognition of three mental faculties has long since been superseded by the findings of scientists and psychologists. The scheme of classification which he proposed is, like many other classifications, a reflection of the state of knowledge in the age when the making of the system took place. However that may be, the influence of the Baconian classification has been profound. It formed the basis of the great French Encyclopaedia of Diderot and D'Alembert in the eighteenth century. 'If', wrote Diderot, 'we emerge from this vast operation, we shall owe it mainly to the Chancellor Bacon, who sketched the plan of a universal dictionary of sciences and arts at a time when there were not, so to speak, either arts or sciences. This extraordinary genius, when it was impossible to write a history of what men already knew, wrote of that which they had to learn.' Bacon's chart also influenced, apparently, the early classification of the Bodleian Library; it was the outline of the first classification applied in the Library of Congress; in 1870 it formed the plan of the famous inverted Baconian classification of Dr W. T. Harris; and, as we shall see in the next chapter, the scheme of Harris in turn strongly influenced the Dewey Decimal Classification! No other philosophical system has had such important results.

112. The study of schemes which are metaphysical or philosophical in origin may be pursued further with profit and interest by those who are interested in the systems which preceded the bibliographical classifications, but the limits which we have set ourselves

[1] R. Flint's *History of Classification of the sciences*, p. 107.

do not admit of further discussion here. The schemes of Prosper Marchand, 1704, S. T. Coleridge, 1826, not to mention the later nineteenth century systems of Herbert Spencer and Karl Pearson, may occur to those with some knowledge of the subject. Yet these, valuable and suggestive as they may be, have not exercised any direct influence on library classification as a whole, although they have played their part on the path leading to the order of knowledge at which Bliss and his supporters have arrived.

I. FIRST CLASSIFICATION

A   Works of Reference and Works of a General Character, covering several Classes
B   Philosophy and Religion
E   Historical Sciences (Includes Biography, History, and Geography and Travels)
H   Social Sciences (Includes Statistics, Political Economy, Commerce, Poor, Charity, Education, Peace, Temperance, Women, Politics, Government, Crime, Legislation, etc)
L   Sciences and Arts, both Useful and Fine
X   Language
Y   Literature (Includes Literary History, Bibliography and the Book Arts)
YF   Fiction

II SECOND CLASSIFICATION
(For a Library that has grown larger)

A   Works of Reference, etc
B   Philosophy and Religion
E   Biography
F   History
F30   Europe
F39   France
F45   England, Great Britain.
F47   Germany
F60   Asia
F70   Africa
F80   America
F83   United States
    (In F30 will be put works on Europe and any of its parts, except France, England and Germany; and in F60 works on Asia or any of its parts and so on. *These numbers are from the Local List, a separate table of numbers used to mark places in order to secure geographical sub-division of subjects*)
    History includes: Antiquities, Inscriptions, Numismatics, Chivalry and Knighthood, Heraldry, Peerage
G   Geography and Travels
    (Divided by numbers from the Local List as F)
H   Social Sciences
L   Physical Sciences
    Includes Science and Art (treated in the same book), Science (General Works), Mathematics, Physics, Chemistry, Astronomy
M   Natural History
    Includes Microscopy, Geology, Physical Geography, Meteorology, Palaeontology, Biology, Botany, Zoology, Anthropology, and Ethnology
Q   Medicine
R   Useful Arts
V   Recreative Arts, Sports and Games, Theatre, Music
W   Fine Arts
    Includes Aesthetics, Landscape Gardening, Architecture, Sculpture, Carving, Casting, Ceramics, Drawing, Painting, Engraving, Photography; Decorative Arts, Needlework, Costume, Furniture, Artistic Metalwork

SECOND CLASSIFICATION (*continued*)

X   Language
Y   Literature
YF   Fiction
    Cutter writes in regard to Music at V:
    'In the broadest sense, the Fine Arts incl Music, but as ordinarily used the phrase me Plastic and Graphic Fine Arts. The mater and methods of Music are entirely diffe from those of Architecture, Sculpture, Paint etc, and the greater part of the works on "Fine Arts" do not include Music. For th reasons I think that what connexion ther (which is chief in Aesthetics) is sufficie recognized by putting Music directly be Fine Arts.'

III THIRD TO SIXTH CLASSIFICATION
The Third Classification shows the follow extra sub-division:

A   GENERAL WORKS
B   PHILOSOPHY
BR   Religion and Religions (except the Chris and Jewish)
C   CHRISTIAN AND JEWISH RELIGIONS
D   Ecclesiastical History
E–F–G. . AS IN THE SECOND
H   SOCIAL SCIENCES
I   Sociology
J   Government and Politics
K   Legislation, Law, Women, Societies
L   SCIENCE IN GENERAL
M   NATURAL HISTORY IN GENERAL. Microsco Geology, Biology
N   Botany
O   Zoology
    MEDICINE
R   USEFUL ARTS
S   Engineering and Building
T   Manufactures and Handicrafts
U   Defensive and Preservative Arts
V   RECREATIVE ARTS, SPORTS, THEATRE, MUSIC
W   FINE ARTS
X   LANGUAGE
Y   LITERATURE
YF   FICTION
Z   Book Arts

All the letters of the Alphabetic outline are r in use except P. This in the Fifth Classifica is used for part of Zoology and for Anthropol

It will be seen that the outline is expande each successive classification, with the gro of the library to which it is applied.

A specimen of the full tables of the Seve Expansion follows:

SEVENTH CLASSIFICATION
specimen from the complete classification

LANGUAGE

Synopsis

	Language XD
	Languages XE – XY
	(Arranged by Families)
	Languages XE11 – XE99
	(Arranged by Local List)
	Oratory. Elocution XZ
.4	History of Linguistics
.7	Periodicals
.8	Societies
.9	Collections
	Language in General
	GENERAL AND MISCELLANEOUS WORKS
	HISTORY OF LANGUAGE
A	Origin of Language
AB	Brute Language
AF	Flower Language
AG	Gesture Language
AY	Psychics of Language
B	Differentiation and Classification of Languages
C	NAMES
CF	Forenames
CG	Geographical Names
D	Lexicography
E	Etymology
F	Phonology
FP	Physiology
G	GRAMMAR
H	Morphology
HI	Isolation
HO	Agglutination
HU	Inflexion
HZ	Parts of Speech
I	Noun
IW	Adjective
IZ	Pronoun
J	Verb
K	Particles, etc
L	Syntax
O	Orthography
OT	Transliteration
P	Prosody, Metre
R	Dialect
U	Universal Language
W	Esperanto
– XY	LANGUAGES
	Families of Language, Comparative Philology
A	General specialities
	etc

SPECIAL TABLES

COMMON SUB-DIVISIONS used in
First Six Classifications
Dictionaries
Encyclopaedias
Indexes
Museums

SPECIAL TABLES (*continued*)

P	Periodicals
Q	Quotations
R	Reference Books
S	Societies

As there was a danger of confusion in the notation between these letters and those of subject sub-divisions, the letters were changed to figures in the Seventh Expansion, and the order, etc, was revised. The only use of *figures* in the system is for forms, standpoints, and geographical places. Thus:

Common Sub-divisions

.1	Theory. Philosophy
.2	Bibliography
.3	Biography
.4	History
.5	Dictionaries. Encyclopaedias
.6	Year-books. Directories
.7	Periodicals
.8	Societies
.9	Collections
.10	

Then follow the numbers of the LOCAL LIST, a selection only of which is given here

11	THE WORLD
12	Voyages and Travels: Collections
13	Voyages round the World
133	TROPICS
135	TEMPERATURE ZONES
14	ARCTIC AND ANTARCTIC REGIONS
14	ARCTIC REGIONS
14	American Arctic Regions
143	Greenland
144	European Arctic Regions
149	ANTARCTIC REGIONS
15	OCEANS AND ISLANDS
151	AFRICA AND AMERICA
152	AMERICA AND ASIA
16	PACIFIC OCEAN AND ISLANDS
161	Hawaiian Archipelago
17	Polynesia
18	Micronesia
19	Melanesia
20	Papua
21	AUSTRALIA
211	W. Australia
212	N. Australia
213	Alexandra Land
214	S. Australia
215	Queensland, etc
24	ASIA AND AFRICA
25	ASIA AND EUROPE
26	EUROPE AND AMERICA
27	EUROPE AND AFRICA
28	EUROPE AND AFRICA AND ASIA
29	TURKISH EMPIRE
30	EUROPE
32	Greece
35	Italy
etc	

CHAPTER NINE

Bibliographical Classification in Nineteenth-Century America

113. The real beginnings of library classification, as we know it today, took place in the nineteenth century and most of the important steps forward were made by librarians in the United States. The modern student of the subject is extremely fortunate, in that he has, as an invaluable source book for this period, Leo LaMontagne's *American Library Classification with special reference to the Library of Congress* (1961). Here, we shall content ourselves with a sketch of the development of some of the main bibliographical systems in this, perhaps the crucial century in library history. At the beginning of the nineteenth century, the arrangement of books in the Congress Library was according to size. This is exhibited in the earliest catalogue put forth by the first Librarian of Congress, John Beckley in April 1802; it is what might have been expected from a librarian who also held the office of Clerk to the House of Representatives. At that date, the United States, as a nation, possessed in all only 964 volumes and nine maps; and the order of the catalogue ran: folios, quartos, octavos, duodecimos, maps. This system remained in vogue until 1812, by which year the Library had increased to 3,076 volumes and 53 maps, charts and plans. In this year, the second Librarian, Patrick Macgruder, ventured on a catalogue, the fourth issued, of much more ambitious design, in which the works were classified under eighteen headings which reflect those of a few well-known scholastic systems, and sub-arranged in each by size.

114. In August, 1814, occurred one of those war tragedies which occasionally scar the history of libraries. The British soldiery under General Ross – who appears to have been unaware of the existence

of the Library – burned the Capitol, and the greater part of the Library with it. At this juncture ex-President Thomas Jefferson sold to Congress his private library of nearly 7,000 volumes, a collection which was, according to A. R. Spofford, 'an admirable selection of the best ancient and modern literature up to the beginning of the present nineteenth century'. After a Congressional wrangle, in which little of the modern American library spirit, but much of the average stepmotherly English attitude to books was shown, the library was acquired. This collection was catalogued and classified by Jefferson himself, and his Catalogue of the Library of the United States, published in 1815, was based upon a modification of Francis Bacon's divisions of knowledge; forty-four divisions were employed and the arrangement of titles under each was alphabetical. It is interesting to note that this system, with further modifications, was in use until the end of the century. The modifications were made by the Librarians, John Silva Meehan, in 1861, and A. R. Spofford at a later period, but their contributions were revisions of detail alone; essentially the classification of the Library of Congress for the first century of its existence was that of Francis Bacon.

115. We shall return to the classification of the Congress Library at the end of our chapter. At this stage, it is worth while for us to move on in time in order to survey the preparatory background to the Decimal system. Decimal arrangement, as applied to book-shelves, did not begin with Melvil Dewey, nor does he claim such priority. Cim[1] tells us that in 1583 the learned Lacroix du Maine presented to Henry III a curious and singular project for the arranging of a library 'perfect in all ways'. This library was to consist of 10,000 volumes (100 books in each of 100 bookcases). The first order of these cases, numbers 1–17, was devoted to Religion; the second, numbers 18–41, to Arts and Sciences; the third, numbers 42–62, to the Description of the Universe; the fourth, numbers 63–72, to the Human Race; and so on. It will be seen that this is a vague decimal system applied not to subjects but to bookcases or shelves. All decimal systems before that of Dewey seem to have this peculiarity – they number the shelves and relegate subjects to shelves so numbered; they do not number the subjects themselves decimally. Other early systems involved giving each book a fixed place in a numerical or alphabetical sequence. The modern arrange-

[1] *Le Livre*, Vol. 4, p. 309.

ment of a library, of course, rejects all such methods of fixed location which are either completely impossible for a growing library or result in an order reflecting the order of accession of books rather than a helpful subject classification. It is far better to be able to move the books about freely so that all books on the same theme can be located together and new volumes can be inserted at the most appropriate place in the sequence of subjects. Another primitive, although much later scheme than that of du Maine, is described in a small manual of library economy by Nathaniel B. Shurtleff. This is the *Decimal System for the Arrangement and Administration of Libraries*, Boston, U.S.A., 1856, which employs alcoves with ten bays, each bay having ten shelves and both bays and shelves being numbered from 1 to 10. The notation was of a non-expansive kind not essentially related to the shelves. It bears no relation to that of Dewey.

116. The reader who is interested in other classifications in the U.S.A. at the middle of the nineteenth century will find a most useful account in Chapter 9 of LaMontagne's work. But a glance at the systems in vogue in 1874, the year in which Dewey became librarian of Amherst College, showed very little to the advantage of the librarians of the time. In England, the British Museum was classified by a free adaptation of Brunet, which still survives; at the Bodleian Library were a series of partial classifications which appear never to have been resolved into a coherent whole; the Bibliothèque Nationale had been arranged partly by Brunet, but was to a large degree unclassified; the Library of Congress possessed a variant of the system of Bacon. Dewey almost immediately realised the need for some more competent classification than appeared to be available. He therefore made a comprehensive study of existing schemes and devised his own. He tells us in the introduction to it that he was most indebted to Natale Battezzati's *Nuova Sistema di Catalogo Bibliographico Generale* (Milan 1871), and to the systems of Jacob Schwartz (1879) and W. T. Harris, the last of which was devised for the public school library of St Louis in 1870. It is not clear, however, to what extent Battezzati and Schwartz influenced Dewey's work; its relation to that of Harris is more obvious. Indeed, with the appearance of Harris's scheme we reach the vital formative years of American library classification (1870–1901) or, to use LaMontagne's phrase, we move from the 'prehistoric' to the 'historic' period in our studies.

117. Harris's system was the first of the 'inverted Baconian' schemes, of which there have been several. With modern connotations of the terms, Harris took Bacon's outline and inverted it. In its details this system was expanded in the Peoria Public Library version, which is later than the original scheme, but the outline – Science, Art and History – remains the same. A comparison of the outline structure of the schemes of Bacon, Harris and Dewey indicates sufficiently the origin of the last system:

BACON		HARRIS	DEWEY
Original	*Inverted*		
		Science	General Works;
History	Philosophy	Philosophy and Religion; Social and Political Science; Natural Sciences and Useful Arts	Philosophy and Religion; Sociology; Philology; Science and Useful Arts
Poesy	Poesy	*Art* Fine Arts Poetry Pure Fiction Literary Miscellany	Fine Arts Literature
Philosophy	History	*History* Geography and Travel Civil History Biography	History Biography Geography and Travel
		Appendix Miscellany	

Such a comparison has its purpose in our studies. It is true that Richardson remarks: 'the system itself is supposed to be in some way an adaptation of Bacon, but the relation is hardly to be discovered and it should really be counted as independent'. On the other hand, certain points in the order are susceptible to criticism from the modern standpoint, and can only be explained by a reference to its pedigree. For example, the separation of Sociology by five great classes from History to which it is more closely related than it is to any other major subject, can be understood only in this way. Again, in the Peoria classification, Philology is a sub-division of the Social and Political Sciences and ranks immediately before Natural Science, exactly as it does in Dewey; and is therefore separated in the latter system by three classes from its natural partner Literature, although Dewey suggests that some libraries might find it convenient to bring these two classes together. This debt to Bacon must be stressed, to a certain extent, because the Dewey outline does not seem to be explicable on any other ground; yet efforts have been made by writers on classification to give it a philosophical basis of its own.

118. Whatever its philosophical origins may have been, the Decimal Classification was, from the first, an outstanding success. It represented an enormous advance on earlier systems; it was based on Dewey's own survey of the needs of libraries and, no doubt, in part – in its early editions – on the 'literary warrant' of the Amherst College Library. It had a flexible notation and an excellent index; above all, perhaps, it appeared at a most opportune time in public library history, when, with the gradual introduction of open-access, librarians needed a system based on relative rather than fixed location. These reasons for its initial popularity and rapid development are considered in more detail in the chapter on the scheme. Here, it is sufficient to say that the impact of the Decimal Classification – the first of the modern bibliographical systems – was tremendous. It is incredible, and indicative of the genius of Melvil Dewey, to reflect that it was drawn up in 1873 and first published (like many great works anonymously) three years later, when its compiler was only twenty-five years of age! The introduction to this first edition contained much advice, some of which is still valid. Ranganathan has justly described this introduction as 'almost prophetic'. The second edition of 1885 gave the scheme its distinctive name, greatly enlarged the schedules and index and made minor alterations in the sequence of classes. It was this edition which cast the basic mould of the Decimal Classification as we know it today. Ranganathan has also suggested that, in a sense, the scheme was too good in that it inhibited further thought on the subject of library classification, but its very creation gave a great impetus to the development of librarianship in the United States and, in fact, the initiation of rival schemes owed much to the achievement of this pioneer classification which made relative location on the shelves of libraries the rule rather than the exception.

119. Another important system, which has not endured nearly so

well as the Decimal Classification, is the Expansive Classification of Charles Ammi Cutter. Cutter is now best remembered for his *Rules for a Dictionary Catalogue;* he was, by about fourteen years, Dewey's senior. The life-story of this divinity graduate turned librarian has been told pleasantly but only too briefly by his nephew.[1] To find the reason for the initiation of the Expansive Classification, we may begin by noting that in 1876, the Bureau of Education published a *Report on Public Libraries.* This showed that until that time classification was not a common study in America. In general, some account of various experiments is given with a few brief outlines, the only ones printed fully being W. T. Harris's scheme and the Decimal system. The author of the latter had provided in the *Report* a full account of his system, indicating that little had been previously done to secure a helpful subject arrangement of books. The Decimal Classification was, in fact, first received with some doubt as being too complex, but later occupied nearly the whole field. Yet there were some librarians who agreed with Cutter when he said; 'Its notation would not afford that minuteness of classification which experience had taught me to be needed in our library. I did not like (and I do not like) Mr Dewey's classification'. Cutter's own early experiments were with a scheme having an alphabetical notation. Yet his arraignment was not of the decimal notation only; he had his own definite ideas on the order of subjects in a classification. In due course there appeared a slender volume entitled *Expansive Classification/Part 1/The first six classifications/Boston/C. A. Cutter/* 1891-93.

120. The volume described above is out of print and not easily available; it will, therefore, be worthwhile to quote freely from its introduction in describing it. It consists of seven separate classifications; the first one extremely broad; the second less general; the third less still, and so on in progressive stages of minuteness. Cutter's recommendation is that when a library is small and likely to progress slowly, one of the earlier classifications should be applied and, as the library develops, a later expansion can be used. He says; 'I have been led to prepare a scheme applicable to collections of every size, from the village library in its earliest stages to the national library with a million volumes'. The first expansion has, in fact, only seven classes, represented by the letters A, B, E, F, H, L, and Y. The successive expansions develop this outline considerably; by

[1] W. P. Cutter. Charles Ammi Cutter, *American Library Association*, 1931.

the time we reach the fifth, the whole of the alphabet is employed, many classes being quite minutely sub-divided. Cutter actually carried the method as far as six stages in the 1891–93 volume and later to an uncompleted seventh stage. The idea of a classification that can be developed in this way is extremely interesting, when one considers the requirements of libraries of different sizes and character.

121. Unfortunately there are difficulties with this 'expansive' programme; Cutter's advice to the classifier to 'be minute, be minute, be not too minute' is rather vague.[1] Another problem is that, as this short extract from the Relative Index shows, the notation often changes as we move through successive expansions; thus the librarian may find that class-marks may need to be completely altered as his collections increase:

Plants	L	^{2}M	^{3}N	
Plastic arts	L	^{2}W	^{5}WD	
Playing cards	L	^{2}V	^{5}VM	^{6}VN
Pleading (law)	H	^{3}K	^{5}K	^{6}KW

The superior figure indicates the place of the subject indexed in the various expansions, indicating that uneconomical changes in notation are often involved. It is a matter for regret that the great cumulative index of the Seventh never eventuated.

122. Apart from the expansive principle, the most interesting feature of this classification is perhaps the idea that the order of classes reflects an order of development in nature. Cutter claims that 'The Expansive Classification follows the evolutionary order throughout, in natural history putting the parts of each subject in the order which that theory assigns to their appearance in creation. Its science proceeds from the molecular to the molar, from number and space, through matter and force, to matter and life; its botany going up from cryptogams to phanerogams . . . The book arts follow the history of the book from its production, through its distribution, to its storage and use in libraries . . . Economics, too, has a natural order – population, production, distribution of the things produced, distribution of the returns, property, consumption . . . There are many such transitions . . . They are not merely ingenuities pleasing

---

[1] Ranganathan has suggested that better advice would be: 'Be minute, be minute, be most minute'.

only to their contriver; they have a certain practical value, since they bring together books which one may wish to use at the same time.' There were several efforts to justify ideas such as these at the turn of the century; J. D. Brown claimed an order of development for his Subject Classification, although he does not use the phrase evolutionary order. Cutter's fellow-countryman, E. C. Richardson, of course, also placed great stress on the need for a book classification to follow the arrangement of the sciences. Nowadays, however, little stress is placed on this; classifiers recognise that the value of a scheme must be assessed solely on its practical achievement and not according to its success or failure in revealing a real or supposed 'natural' order of progression which, in any case, is inapplicable to certain subject fields.

123. Cutter's notation has been quoted as a pure one, but only to a degree is this the case; his Local List (a series of common divisions to indicate geographical regions) is numerical as are his form divisions. Apart from these letters are used throughout. Numbers from the Local List may be added directly to subject class-marks; form division numbers may be added to them when necessary, by means of a point. Thus

IU Schools

IU.4 History of Schools (.4 denotes history in the common form divisions)

IU 45 English schools

IU 47 German schools (these being the appropriate numbers for England and Germany from the Local List)

The form divisions and the Local List give the notation mnemonic value; they are, of course, mnemonics of the systematic kind. But Cutter also uses literal mnemonics, where he is able to do so without strain. He claimed that his scheme was 'ten times as mnemonic' as the Decimal Classification. More important, probably, is the fact that the letter notation has a great capacity for accommodating subjects with brief class-marks. His author-marks, mentioned in an earlier chapter, are another interesting notational feature.

124. Dewey once said that he wished to see a notation of letters fully tested and, at one time, it seemed that the Expansive Classification would fulfil that wish. The scheme, alas, was never completed; it

E

has been steadily abandoned by those libraries using it in the United States today, because it is now obvious that it will never be finished or brought up to date. Yet its historical importance is tremendous. The system received tribute from both Richardson and Bliss. The former regarded it as a 'really scientific work of high value'; the latter at one time attempted to develop and revise it, but abandoned the task and was content to recognise it as 'a stepping stone to the future'. Its influence on both the Congress classification and on Bliss's own system has been strong. This influence can also be discerned in an important twentieth century special scheme – the Harvard Business Classification, which owes much to the work of W. P. Cutter. LaMontagne suggests that although most classifications at this time attempted to follow an inverted Baconian arrangement, Cutter's is nearer to the spirit of Brunet. It is, he says 'the best classification of the nineteenth century'; this, coming from a modern and well informed writer, is praise indeed. Eric De Grolier also points out the merits of this scheme and the influence of its auxiliary tables. Yet today the system has no vogue at all. Perhaps there is nothing in the history of our subject (except possibly J. D. Brown's classification) which illustrates more vividly than this, the fact that a bibliographical classification is best produced by a *team* of workers and must be revised and perpetuated if it is to succeed.

125. Cutter's scheme has been discussed at some length, as it is not considered again in the next section of the Manual and because it may not be readily accessible to students. However, we shall not survey systems of lesser stature in any detail here. The reader who is interested in finding out more about nineteenth century classifications in the U.S.A. can do so by reference to LaMontagne's work. It will suffice to say that, among other systems of this period, those of Lloyd P. Smith of Philadelphia; J. C. Rowell of the University of California; and F. B. Perkins of San Francisco, are probably of the greatest significance for us today. Indeed the last named of these classificationists was a descendent of one Thomas Clap, who had done much to establish classification in the Yale Library in the middle of the eighteenth century. For our purposes, however, it will be more useful to examine the changes in the method of classification at the Congress Library that were taking place towards the end of the century.

126. By this time, the Library had reached a very high position,

in number of volumes as in character, amongst the national libraries of the world; the Librarian thus determined to commence the formidable task of providing his great collections with an entirely new and minute classification. Older libraries have made such efforts and experiments, but no national library of long history has yet accomplished the gigantic task of classifying its books according to any modern system of knowledge, or to any plan that the science of today would accept. Indeed the task is incredibly great and could only be accomplished by such a fine organization as that of the Library of Congress, where there is a large team of well qualified classifiers and adequate financial resources. Even in these happy circumstances the work has been long and arduous. The new building, completed in 1897, plus the fact that the stock of books and pamphlets by this date was in the region of a million items, brought about the decision to reclassify. The use of either the scheme of Dewey[1] or that of Cutter was considered carefully. Of these two, the latter was preferred, but it was decided that in view of the special requirements of the Congress Library and the nature of its collections, an entirely new scheme would be most appropriate. The final decision was made right at the end of the century and work on a new system, which was to be shaped by the 'literary warrant' of the vast Congress collections then began. It is strange, in retrospect, to reflect that at the time when this system was being drafted under the direction of Herbert Putnam, Richardson was writing what was to be virtually the first textbook on bibliographical classification, for the principles which he extols are very different from those which motivated Putnam, Charles Martel, and the other librarians who contributed to the discussion and planning which preceded the formation of the Congress system. A provisional outline of the Congress scheme was ready by 1901; this early draft reveals the influence of Cutter, but the system is essentially an independent one moulded around the stock and departmental structure of the library. It is, therefore, interesting to find that this period of rapid growth and development of library classification in the United States includes many systems based on those of the philosophers, but ends with one which is essentially utilitarian in character.

[1] Charles Martel's summary of the advantages and disadvantages of using Dewey's system is given by LaMontagne, *American Library Classification*, 1961, pp. 223–25.

CHAPTER TEN

The Early Story of Library Classification in Britain

127. Cataloguing, annotation and classification in a form more or less erudite have been practised in England for more than a thousand years; but there is no advantage in repeating in detail the accounts of those earlier arrangements which are to be found in the writings of M. R. James, particularly in his *The Ancient Libraries of Canterbury and Dover;* John Willis Clark, in his *The Care of Books;* and E. A. Savage in his *Old English Libraries* – writings which are most deservedly precious to all librarians. All that need be said is that the library of Christchurch, Canterbury, was classified in the twelfth century, and succeeding monastic and, afterwards, cathedral libraries, had simple, effective schemes of arrangement. The norm of all such schemes is what is sometimes called the collegiate press-marking system, which is worth brief description. The books are arranged in broad classes:

> *Class* A Grammar and Classics   *Example of division of a class*
> B   Medicine and Astrology   AA   Greek
> C   Philosophy, etc.   AB   Latin, etc.

A tier of shelves is given to each class and a shelf to each division within the class; each book within the division receives a running number. Thus a copy of the *Iliad*, occupying the fifth place on its shelf, would be marked AA5. The method is convenient both for shelving purposes and for catalogue indications, but only in a library which has finished its growth, since as each shelf is filled the scheme as a class order is overflowed and collapses. This is the glaring weakness of any fixed location method; it soon breaks down in subject fields where the literature of the library is rapidly growing in quantity. The press-marking system is in essence, the same as the 1583 system described in paragraph 115. Thus it will not do for modern librarianship, where a system based on relative location is essential; it is a form of classification for dead or dormant libraries.

128. In an interesting article which appeared in *The Library Assistant*, 1911, H. Rutherford Purnell has demonstrated that in the successive classifications in use in the Bodleian Library may be seen the growth of various forms of classification from the press-marking plan down to a curious decimal classification introduced as late as the 1880's. It was with the coming of the public library that the question of bibliographical classification became a very practical one. Edward Edwards saw this need at the very beginning, and proposed a scheme of classification, which had some influence in its day, but is now extinct. It was a curious scheme when viewed in the light of modern knowledge; there is no place in it for books on non-Christian religions, and its other omissions are serious; but it is nevertheless more interesting for its virtues than for its defects. It is to Edwards that we owe the beginning in England of the serious study of the subject. But it was only a beginning. Edwards towered above all his contemporaries both in his knowledge of book classification and in his recognition of its potentialities. He had few followers for nearly forty years. A few broad groups represented the average arrangement in the newly created public libraries. Then one or two calamities fell upon librarians. The most popular logician of his day, W. S. Jevons, declared roundly that the classification of books was a logical absurdity, and proved his argument in a manner quite conclusive to many; that this argument was founded upon a misunderstanding of the nature of library classification was not pointed out until twenty-four years later.[1] How potent his dictum was may be seen in a paper on *The Art of Cataloguing* by Dr W. E. A. Axon,[2] in 1877, in which he says 'There is a prejudice in favour of a classified arrangement (in catalogues). It has a scientific appearance and it is only when the many intricacies of the classes have to be threaded that the fallacy of these appearances becomes evident. The arrangement in proximity to each other of works on the same subject is, of course, desirable, but it should be at once confessed

[1] By Brown. *Manual of library classification*, 1898, pp. 83–96.
[2] Reprinted in *Library World*, Vol. 24, 1921–22, pp. 97–101.

that this is only possible as an aid to memory and not as a genealogical chart of human knowledge. Supposing such a logical classification were devised, the existence of so many books treating of more than one subject would invalidate its perfection'. Such a pronouncement in the day of the untrained librarian must have been a great consolation to many members of our profession, as it seemed to absolve them from learning what, in the then absence of good guides, seemed to be a formidable subject.

129. The second calamity was the invention of the ingenious and seductive 'indicator', a contrivance by means of which readers were able to tell what books were or were not available. As it is now extinct, it may be described briefly. It was for use in libraries where the public were not admitted to the shelves. It consisted of columns of numbers in a glazed frame standing on the library counter. These numbers were on a blue ground if the books were available and on a red ground if they were not. The would-be reader found the number of the book he required in the catalogue, and consulted the indicator before calling for the book by that number. The number was really written on the turned up ends of a small metal slide which fitted into a little shelf in the column of the indicator, and one end of the slide was red and the other blue. This slide held the charge when a book had been borrowed. The whole machine was thus a remarkable help to the librarian; it threw the finer work of librarianship upon the reader himself, and saved brain wear effectively. As far as it concerned classification, it seemed to make it quite unnecessary. As the indicator was arranged by a continuous number, from one to the number representing the last book added, it seemed to be the best method, as it certainly was the easiest, to arrange the books by accession numbers. Such was the magic of the indicator that the Library Association actually passed a resolution commending it to local authorities, and by so doing put back the calendar of library progress by some thirty years.

130. Few things would be more instructive, and perhaps salutary, than a candid record of the experiments in classification in Britain and America; the motives that led to them, their history, and their abandonment in some cases and the reasons for it. Such a history cannot be written at present, partly because librarians have a natural, if not quite reasonable, objection to the making public of their failures, and partly because the data is unreliable. Certainly, in Britain, the full value of classification was not realised until James

Duff Brown did the greatest service that has ever been done to public libraries by experimenting with the open access system at the then Clerkenwell (now Islington) Public Library. This meant, of course, the throwing open of the shelves to readers, and some form of systematic shelf classification is essential to such a method. Brown made such a scheme in the 1890's with J. H. Quinn; it was superseded in 1898 by the Adjustable Classification; this, in turn, was replaced by Brown's third attempt to provide a British general classification scheme – the Subject Classification. Brown's *Manual of Library Classification* was a landmark which owed much to Edward Edwards; its author was not really concerned with the theory of classification, but was the first to give a terse but comprehensive outline of the work done in the subject up to 1898 and to make it an accessible study. It is not too much to say that to Brown as much as to Dewey is due the good order which is usual in British libraries today, for Brown was a keen advocate of the newly created bibliographical systems of the late nineteenth century (although he naturally preferred his own schemes to Dewey's) and he fought tremendously hard to establish the now ubiquitous open-access methods in public libraries.

131. Contemporaneously the problem of classification had, as we have seen, been engaging the attention of American librarians; with more rapid and better results than in Europe. There was this difference too, between the English and the American public librarian. The former in his reach after distinction usually designed some piece of mechanical apparatus, an indicator, adjustable shelf book-rest, or similar article, showing an intense preoccupation with the mere machinery of libraries; his American colleague, on the other hand, devised for the same purpose a new classification or a set of cataloguing rules – one can illustrate this by pointing to the number of general classifications that have emanated from the U.S.A., although the cynical might say that this is not necessarily a good thing. It is a point worthy of speculation as to whether or not the presence of scientific methods of book arrangement and the absence of mechanism and barriers were not largely responsible for what was formerly the high estimation in which the American librarian was held in comparison to his British colleagues and the better financial conditions which his libraries enjoy; fortunately, these differences seem to be slowly disappearing.

132. It was some time before the Dewey Classification made any

real progress in British public libraries. In the 1890's, however, L. Stanley Jast, then librarian of Peterborough, came out as a champion of the scheme, and at much the same time Basil Anderton and T. W. Lyster were also its advocates. But generally there was a great fear of the difficulty and complexity of Dewey, a fear founded partly upon ignorance of the scheme itself, and partly upon the fact that until 1900[1] there were hardly any trained assistant librarians in Britain to apply it. This, in fact, led to the issue of several broad classification schemes in which some such arrangement as follows constituted the *whole* classification:

A	Religion and Philosophy	H	Language and Literature
B	History	J	Poetry and Drama
C	Travel	K	Fiction
D	Social Science	L	Miscellaneous
E	Science		
F	Fine Arts		
G	Useful Arts		

– classifications which did not classify, and by their incoherence were expected in some way to make things easier for librarian and reader. Some think that it was unfortunate, too, that J. D. Brown, the most influential librarian of the time ('the eager moving spirit' of the agitation for classed libraries, as Savage calls him) never viewed the Decimal Classification as kindly as he might have done, holding it to be too American. The schemes which he himself produced failed to win a wide market even in Britain; it is now clear that they offer no real advantages over the American system.

133. Closely allied to the advocacy of classification for English libraries, was the controversy which has been dubbed the battle of the catalogues. This really began in 1897. A paper by Brown and Jast entitled 'The compilation of class-lists', was read before the Library Association in January of that year, and this advocated that catalogues should themselves be arranged in the order of the classification scheme, with adequate indexes; the advantages of this type of catalogue, now widely accepted by librarians were explained. The controversy of that time engendered a great deal of heat and a certain amount of light, on a subject which before had not received

[1] Jast (L.A.R. 1903) tells us that in 1900 about 12 per cent only of the public libraries in England applied systematic classification to their stocks, but it was a process that was rapidly gaining ground.

adequate attention; it certainly did much to popularise classification study. From the time of its advocacy by Brown and Jast the classified catalogue has taken root in Britain, although in America the dictionary type with all its attendant and inherent difficulties is the more popular of the two by far. The *Catalogue of the A.L.A. Library*, published in 1893 at the suggestion of Melvil Dewey, did much to popularise the classified catalogue, yet today it is rarely found in the United States; this is due chiefly to the great influence of Charles Cutter, who preferred the dictionary catalogue, and to the fact that, from the beginning of the twentieth century onwards, American librarians came to rely more and more on broad classification. Ranganathan has suggested that if Cutter was alive today he would prefer the classified catalogue, but this is extremely doubtful. Indeed, there are few libraries in the U.S.A. of any stature who use this type; those of the John Crerar Library, Chicago, and Boston University Library are notable exceptions to the general trend. Yet, in Britain, the classified catalogue is the more popular and we would contend that it has several important advantages over its rival; these will be considered in a later chapter.

134. To return to the state of classification in Britain at the end of the nineteenth century, we may note that by this time the Decimal Classification was steadily becoming popular and gaining ground in open-access libraries. Brown, however, had made a scheme together with John Henry Quinn; this was useful enough in a small library, but inadequate for one of even moderate size. In 1898, Brown's *Adjustable Classification* appeared. The title, alas, is a misnomer. The scheme used a notation of capital letters, followed by numbers; gaps were left in the arithmetical sequence to permit the insertion of new topics. This classification was adopted for the time being by a few libraries, Hornsey, Croydon, and Finsbury (formerly Clerkenwell) among them. But any classification, the notation of which provides for new subjects merely by leaving vacant numbers, is certain to break down sooner or later if only on that ground; this proved to be so here. Meanwhile the subject was beginning to stimulate discussion amongst British librarians[1] and, at the turn of the century, the publication of the American writer, Dr E. C. Richardson's lectures – *Classification; theoretical and practical*, 1901,

---

[1] For instance Jast favoured a full biography class for public libraries while W. E. Doubleday argued for the alternative treatment—its distribution by subject theme whenever feasible.

E*

referred to so often in this Manual, gave the study of classification a new meaning and put heart into it. The Library Association later promoted courses for the study of library matters, and the late F. T. Barrett, and afterwards, L. S. Jast, both lectured on the subject of classification at the London School of Economics; now, of course, it is a cardinal subject in our professional syllabus and is taught at all the full-time Schools of Librarianship.

135. If the development of library classification in nineteenth century Britain seems much less spectacular than the progress made on the other side of the Atlantic, it was not completely uneventful. It is difficult for the modern student of the subject to project himself back mentally to those days of fierce controversy about indicators, catalogues, open-access and arrangement on public library shelves. Yet slowly, out of the argument and discussion, tangible results emerged; the Decimal Classification began to win the monopoly that it now enjoys in British public libraries, although it never made quite such a spectacular conquest in academic ones. Likewise, British public librarians could debate the value of the two schemes produced by Brown in the last decade of the century. The very fact that the debate and controversy existed is ample evidence of the newly acquired recognition of the importance of classification and its great value in libraries – a value that increases as collections grow in size, for it then becomes more and more important so to organize them that their contents can be fully revealed and thus fully exploited.

CHAPTER ELEVEN

The Development of Classification in the Twentieth Century

136. The first of the schemes initiated in the present century which we shall consider here is the Subject Classification, designed for British libraries in response to the frequent, but not very reasonable, complaint, which in the nineties had some currency, that the Dewey scheme gave too great a prominence to American matters. The Subject Classification was the third system compiled by James Duff Brown (1862–1914), one of the leading figures in librarianship of his own or any age. He was trained in the Glasgow Public Libraries; showed very early that he possessed originality, daring and industry; educated himself; published a musical dictionary and edited a history of Scotland when he was barely out of his teens, and in various ways displayed unusual talents, if not, on the whole, very dramatic ones. He became librarian of the Clerkenwell Public Library in 1888, and made a reputation when he introduced there the open-access system, with safeguarded methods. The controversy to which this innovation led proved that, at one time, it seemed to many that if one allowed readers in to the shelves to choose their books in a public library, one was in some way immoral and dishonest and actively injurious to the State. The matter seems laughable now; it was real enough then. Brown's Subject Classification is the only surviving British general classification scheme and is now in serious danger of becoming extinct. It will be described fairly fully in Chapter 13; here it will be sufficient to say that, in its merits and faults, it bears the marks of Brown's own strong personality. It was more successful than the other two schemes made by this classificationist; yet it has only been used by a handful of small

or medium-sized British public libraries. Savage has suggested that, with regard to Brown's tremendous ability and status within the library profession, this classification must be regarded as a disappointment.[1]

137. Meanwhile in Belgium another scheme, of a far more ambitious nature, had been initiated. This was the work of the Institut International de Bibliographie, now known as the International Federation of Documentation, and two great Belgian enthusiasts, Paul Otlet and Senator Henri La Fontaine. One of the aims of the Institut, which was initiated following an international conference of bibliographers held in 1895, was to compile a universal catalogue that should include, in a classified arrangement, every book in existence and every article of worth in periodical literature. It seems quixotic enough an enterprise; by the 1920's it was estimated that about 150,000 books were published yearly and there were at least 72,000 periodicals. Otlet also calculated that, if one included books and the principal articles published in journals the world over, there had appeared from the discovery of printing to the year 1900 some 25 million bibliographical units! Nevertheless, the conference entered upon the project; the Belgian Government, no doubt through the high influence of La Fontaine, provided funds and so became the first Government to sustain bibliography; and, for the gigantic catalogue envisaged, work began on an extension of the Decimal Classification for documentation purposes, for which special permission was received. This was the Universal Decimal Classification, a system which has been since published in many languages and has proved extremely useful in large or specialised libraries where the exact classification of literature, especially scientific literature, is demanded. U.D.C., as it is usually known, was first published in the French language in 1905. As an important living classification, and one which is extremely popular in special libraries in Europe and, to a lesser extent, throughout the world, it is a system which must be described in more detail in the next section of our work. Here it may simply be said that, with the possible exception of the system devised for the University of Halle by Hartwig, which had some influence in the U.S.A., this is the first important European bibliographical classification.

138. An individual with very different views on the organization of knowledge from those of La Fontaine and Otlet must also be

[1] *Library Review*, Autumn 1960.

considered here. The itinerant German, K. Kaiser, was not a classificationist but an indexer; yet his work is significant in our studies, for the relationship between classification and subject indexing has become very clear in recent years and indexing schemes, if soundly constructed, may well enable us to clarify our understanding of classificatory techniques. Kaiser wanted to devise a system of alphabetical indexing that would enable a piece of information to be rapidly traced whether it was part of a book, a patent, an article in a journal, or in some other form. To facilitate the retrieval of information he devised, in his *Systematic Indexing*, 1911, a method which distinguished between *Concretes* and *Processes*. Thus a piece of information on the *Moulding of Plastics* would be indexed under PLASTICS – Moulding; Plastics here being the 'Concrete' and Moulding the 'Process' applied. Kaiser's method, so briefly outlined here, undoubtedly has faults as a system of indexing. Nevertheless, it is extremely important in that it points the way towards modern subject analysis and the clear recognition of *categories*; indeed, although the value of Kaiser's work has perhaps never been fully appreciated, his distinction between operations (processes) and concretes is a valuable one, akin in some ways to certain ideas in the Subject Classification. Metcalfe,[1] who provides a concise but useful account of Kaiser's work, suggests that it has been ignored in comparison with that of others because the necessary propaganda was not available. He suggests that Kaiser's writings are still well worthy of study as the product of one of the best minds that has ever applied itself to indexing problems. Perhaps one day the work of this pioneer will receive the recognition it so richly deserves in the history of library classification and indexing.

139. In Britain, the next writer of importance is Wyndham Hulme whose distinctive ideas have already been considered in Chapter 3. Historically Hulme's writings are the natural antithesis to those of Richardson; whereas the former stressed that a map of knowledge adapted to fit the needs of books might well neglect their 'literary warrant', the latter thought that such a map was the essential basis of bibliographical classification. Hulme's ideas, as put forward in 1911, are that classification in libraries must essentially be 'a mapping-out of areas pre-existing in literature'; these he put into practice with his deputy at the Patent Office Library, H. V. Hopwood. For many years his work, too, was neglected; this was most

[1] *The subject classifying and indexing of libraries and literature.* Appendix J.

unfortunate as it contained some very important theories. Savage[1] was later to support him in the provocative and even amusing work published in 1946, and Metcalfe also pays tribute to the principles expounded by Hulme. Savage indeed, in extolling the merits of literary warrant, makes a direct attack on schemes which owe a debt to the old philosophical classifications – 'when the Gods want to destroy classifiers', he says 'they first set them to play somersaults with Bacon!' But Hulme's place in the history of library classification, unlike that of Kaiser, is now fully assured. In fact some of his leading ideas have been incorporated with modern theories and it is interesting to note that, in the twilight of Hulme's life, he met and conversed with Ranganathan; their talk is mentioned in Ranganathan's moving tribute to the British classifier.[2] Their ideas may have been different, but like all enthusiasts for this subject, they found plenty to discuss when they met.

140. In any chronological account, there is little to record in the decade following the work of Hulme and Kaiser. In 1918, the *Introduction to library classification*, by Berwick Sayers was first published as an elementary work on the subject; it was followed in 1926 by the first edition of this Manual. These works in their early editions tend to support Richardson's theories on the need for a book classification to be founded on a classification of knowledge. These are essentially textbooks; on the other hand, the *Code for Classifiers* of the United States librarian, William S. Merrill, is essentially a guide for the practical classifier. It first appeared in 1928 and its intention was and is to show the main decisions which the classifier has to make, regardless of the scheme which he is applying, and to give advice to enable him to make these decisions wisely. A year or so later, we have the writings of another great librarian from the U.S.A. – Henry Evelyn Bliss. He more than any other is the inheritor of the ideas of Richardson, but he brings to these notions a new status and dignity on account of his erudition and his extensive study of the philosophical systems of earlier centuries. His two books – *The Organization of Knowledge and the System of the Sciences* (1929), and *The Organization of Knowledge in Libraries* (1933) are not easy reading, although Ranganathan once coped with them in a single sitting! The first of these shows Bliss's debt to the philosophical schemes; the second discusses notation,

[1] *Manual of book classification and display.*
[2] *Library Association Record*, March 1956, pp. 120–22.

the principles of classification and the faults of existing book classifications. This latter work appeared in a second edition in 1939; Bliss was thus able to add a critique of the Colon classification and to revise his own theories, as he prepared his own Bibliographic Classification. We have endeavoured to summarize his canons in an earlier chapter. The depth of Bliss's learning and the extent of his research is evident from a perusal of these two large volumes, although his rather pedantic and over-precise use of words tends to serve as a stumbling block to the potential reader. His limitations seem to be the direct result of his attempt to establish the 'consensus of opinion' almost single-handed, rather than as a member of a team of experts (although his efforts were based, it is true, upon a vast amount of study and investigation) and of the fact that he devoted so much time to a consideration of principles and to destructive criticism of existing schemes that he began to prepare his own classification too late in life. In some respects, these writings anticipate modern theories; in others they cling to notions of the past. But Bliss, in any case, did not live to see the modern theories of classification firmly established, although in some ways he prepared us to receive them. We might describe him by means of the phrase used so aptly, by the poet Cowley, of the pioneer of scientific method, Francis Bacon, and say that Bliss is like 'the bell-ringer who is up early to call *others* to church'.

141. From India, in 1933, came the first edition of the Colon Classification. No other bibliographical classification has aroused either the enthusiasm or the severe criticism that have been accorded to Ranganathan's scheme. This mathematician turned librarian has shaken what we thought were the very foundations of book classification; no matter what our opinions of Colon may be, its influence cannot be ignored. Indeed, if one is not positively hostile towards the scheme, it may be regarded as the greatest stride forward, with regard to the principles of bibliographical classification, in the twentieth century. The chief ideas of Ranganathan, which were only dimly perceived in this first edition, but which were developed considerably in succeeding editions, are: the creation of an entirely synthetic scheme, the provision of a distinctive class-mark for each book in a library, the making of a scheme with the maximum of flexibility and mnemonic aids, and the provision of autonomy to the individual classifier for the creation of new class-marks. These ideas, or rather some of them, have been dealt with in cursory fashion in

Chapters 4 and 7; their detailed consideration must, for obvious reasons, be reserved for the Chapter devoted to Colon. Likewise, we shall not reconsider phase analysis and similar principles initiated by Ranganathan until Chapter 17 is reached. Yet we can stress that, although Colon is the only general classification that is completely synthetic (for it relies entirely on the piecing together of standard unit parts to construct class-marks), the older book classifications do have, to a greater or lesser extent, an element of synthesis. Facet analysis *as such* is something that they do not recognise; but the synthetic idea occurs in their notion of common form and geographical divisions and elsewhere. Yet the full impact of the ideas which Ranganathan has either unearthed, or developed and crystallised, is almost incalculable. Metcalfe, who has been perhaps his most severe critic, suggests that few Indian librarians have been influenced by his theories. Despite the fact that Dewey's scheme is still the most used classification in that country, the number of articles in Indian library journals these days which owe so much to those theories, would seem to refute this particular argument or, at least, to indicate that it is true no longer.

142. Metcalfe is certainly on firm ground, however, when he suggests that Ranganathan's greatest influence has been on British classifiers and classificationists. Although Ranganathan himself has produced many works on classification, it was Palmer and Wells' book that did much to explain and popularise the essence of the theory behind Colon. Only a year after this appeared, the British Classification Research Group was founded in 1952. The Group claims it has no definite allegiance to any published scheme; it has from the first, however, been convinced that new classifications must be entirely faceted and, by 1955, it was prepared to state emphatically that a faceted classification should be the basis of what are now usually described as 'information retrieval systems'. Such systems are used in special libraries where information, rather than books as such, is sought by enquirers. There are now available in Britain a number of entirely faceted classifications devoted to special subject fields and a new general classification based on these principles is being prepared. Colon must be regarded as merely the starting-point for these experiments; nevertheless, although it has some complexity and faults that may be expected in a pioneer work, it has done a great deal to establish methods for the construction of new schemes and thus to point the way forward.

143. Yet it would be unwise to assume that currently, in Britain, interest in the field of library classification is focused entirely on the new special schemes and the possibility of an entirely faceted general scheme made by an appropriate team of workers. In established libraries, the systems of proven value are likely to remain for many years to come and, therefore, there is great interest also in ways of improving and revising the Decimal and Universal Decimal Classifications in particular. The editorial body of the former scheme has always welcomed suggestions from users in its attempts to make the classifications more generally useful and enduring and the scheme is revised regularly. The Universal Decimal Classification is an automatic choice in many special libraries, particularly industrial libraries with scientific interests. The first edition of this scheme in English began publication in 1936; the use made of the more recent English and tri-lingual abridgements testifies to its value for the precise classification of specialised collections and for the arrangement of bibliographies, abstracts, and similar work in the field of documentation.

144. Let us conclude our rather long historical survey by, very briefly, tracing the story of library classification in the U.S.A. since the publication of Bliss's first book. Neither the writings of this classificatory giant, nor the Bibliographic Classification which he created, and which began to appear in 1940, have been very successful in the U.S.A. The Decimal Classification, on the other hand, has continued to receive great support from all libraries in America, although Congress is the system preferred in some academic libraries. In 1930, the Library of Congress, which had been issuing cataloguing cards to subscribing libraries since 1901, began to provide on these cards Decimal Classification numbers in addition to the usual Congress class-marks. This was a clear acknowledgement of the supremacy of the Decimal System in the U.S.A. and gave great delight to the ageing Melvil Dewey, who, in fact, died in the following year. The thirteenth edition of his classification appeared in 1932; this memorial edition was the last to be produced under what has been described as 'the direct author tradition', for Dorcas Fellows, Dewey's loyal helper, died a few years later and, in any case, the work of producing DC regularly was obviously a task for a vast team of specialists. Dewey had entrusted the scheme to the Lake Placid Club Education Foundation in the 1920's and from 1933 onwards the editorial office has been housed at the Library of

Congress. Edition 14 appeared in 1942, the unorthodox 'standard' edition 15 in 1951, and editions 16 and 17 in 1958 and 1965 respectively. One of the great advantages which this classification has over some of its rivals is that it possesses a sound revision policy; new editions are regularly produced with bulletins announcing proposed changes appearing between each edition. Although it is difficult to satisfy all customers, in that new users often want drastic changes, while older users of the system cannot tolerate such alteration, and despite the fact that recent editions of DC have met with a fair share of criticism, it would seem that for a scheme to be perpetuated in this way by a team of experts blessed by ample financial resources is the best possible basis for revision.

145. Yet, while the Decimal Classification has become well entrenched throughout the world, there has developed in America a certain amount of cynicism with regard to the value of detailed classification in general libraries. Dr Grace Kelley's book appeared in the late 1930's drawing attention to certain elements which affect the value of systematic arrangement, and advocating a 'wise simplification of classification' together with greater reliance on the dictionary catalogue. These ideas are reflected and even developed in the work of later writers from the United States; there is now a tendency to advocate broad classification in general libraries, detailed subject cataloguing and indexing (possibly mechanised indexing) being favoured for large and specialised collections. But then, in the U.S.A., classification has always been chiefly thought of as a tool for locating items on the shelves; the classified catalogue is so rare that one can understand, even if one does not agree with, our American colleagues' attitude towards the analysis of materials by means of exact classification. Their scepticism is healthy in many ways; any critique of detailed classification must necessarily spotlight its faults and this may eventually lead to the elimination of some of these imperfections. But is notable that although there is some interest in faceted classification in the United States, it has not had the enthusiastic response there that has been accorded to it in Britain. The broad and enumerative nature of Fremont Rider's *International Classification*, 1961,[1] is a clear testimony to the fact that most American librarians prefer broad classification on trad-

[1] Useful critical accounts of this scheme can be found in *Library Review*, Summer 1962, pp. 431–5, (by D. J. Foskett), in *Herald of Library Science*, April 1965 (M. A. Gopinath) and in *Librarian*, November 1961, pp. 177–9 (J. L. Ingham). The scheme itself should be examined if available.

itional principles, supported by detailed catalogues and indexes. More will be said on this theme later, but it may be noted that Australian thought, at least as reflected in Metcalfe's writings, is in line with current American thought on the value and future of library classification.

146. Our historical sketch in this section will perhaps have done something to reveal the development of the principles of library classification. The early bibliographical schemes are naturally influenced by philosophical charts of knowledge (the Congress system being an important exception) and, like philosophical classifications, tend to be relatively broad. They soon increase the amount of detail provided, however, and pay more attention to helpful order within classes as the growth of libraries demands a more exact arrangement. The idea of 'literary warrant' challenges the notion that book classification is merely a classification of knowledge with certain adjustments and, in the twentieth century, we find the older classifications breaking down and the recognition dawning that only the fully faceted scheme can cope with the complex problems of subject analysis which arise in dealing with so many modern documents. As in other subject fields, we discover that the early history of book classification reveals the emergence in a crude form of certain fundamental principles which, like a river, may disappear underground for a time, only to return in a fuller torrent later on. The ebb and flow of theories and ideas has left us with much on which to speculate: the possible value of 'expansive classifications'; the need to recognise 'literary warrant'; facet analysis; phase analysis; Bliss's ideas on alternative location; and so forth. Many of these notions are certain to be crucial in the development of new schemes, but all these and other ideas revealed in the comparatively short history of library classification will repay careful study by the classificationists of tomorrow.

147. We have necessarily touched upon many matters in this chapter's survey which are dealt with more fully elsewhere. No historical sketch can do more than scant justice to the interesting, and sometimes conflicting, principles that emerge with the passing of time, or to the opinions held in different countries regarding the functions and future of classification. Yet, perhaps, this section will have served to provide the student with a chronological outline of the major developments in our subject; in the next part of this Manual the six major bibliographical systems are evaluated and

considered at greater length. Here we may close the present chapter with a word of explanation with regard to Section three. It has been found convenient to refer to the six established general book classification by the initial letters of their titles; thus we shall, from now onwards, represent the Dewey Decimal Classification by the initials DC, Brown's Subject Classification will be SC, the Congress scheme LC, the Universal Decimal Classification UDC, the Bliss Bibliographic Classification BC, and Ranganathan's Colon Classification CC. We have tried also to facilitate a comparative study of the features and principles exhibited in these schemes by treating them according to a common pattern; the headings used being – Introduction; Main Features; Notation; Synthesis and Mnemonics; Index; Use and Revision; Conclusion. This has not been an easy task, but the student may find it advantageous to have the same sub-headings used in the consideration of each of the classifications. The use of the word 'comparative' reminds us that the graduate student and the non-graduate taking the Part II examinations of the (British) Library Association must be prepared to contrast the treatment of several major disciplines, such as the arts, the social sciences, and science and technology, in the six schemes. Likewise all students are once again advised that although we now attempt to provide a useful account and evaluation of these classifications in turn, and although a guide to further reading is provided in the Bibliography at the end of the Manual, there is no substitute for the actual examination of the systems themselves and for the reading of the introductory accounts provided by their compilers.

The Major General Bibliographical Classifications

CHAPTER TWELVE

The Decimal Classification

148. *Introduction.* A classification scheme which is used in all five continents, has been translated, at least in part, into several European languages and into Chinese, and has reached a seventeenth edition in English, must take priority of place in our discussion of modern library systems. That, briefly, is the record of the Decimal Classification of Melvil Dewey. Its cardinal virtues are universality and hospitality, a simple expansible notation which is now almost an international classification vocabulary, excellent mnemonic features, first-class machinery for its perpetuation, and an admirable index. It has many defects, but nevertheless has such adaptive qualities that it has survived much cogent and seemingly unanswerable criticism and has progressed in spite of it; indeed for some years to meet a real demand the Library of Congress has printed the DC numbers as well as its own on its catalogue cards. Shortly after Dewey's death, the editorial office was housed in the Congress library and the sixteenth and seventeenth editions were in fact produced by the Congress staff. As the introduction to this latest edition points out, the scheme's enormous popularity is attested to by the fact that 'titles in thousands of reading lists, book guides, and bibliographies have been arranged or their subjects identified by the Dewey Decimal Classification.' Perhaps equally or even more significant is the fact that the main classes and divisions and the essential parts of the notation of DC form the basis of the Universal Decimal Classification, with which we deal in Chapter 14.

149. Melville Louis Kossuth Dewey – which in his passion for time-saving shorthand he reduced in due time to Melvil Dewey – was born in Adams Centre, New York, on 10 December 1851, the descendant, it is supposed, of Welsh pioneers. Son of a storekeeper,

he came to librarianship through a Spartan process of self-education, a few years of teaching, followed by higher studies at Oneida Seminary, Alfred University, and finally at Amherst College, where he graduated in 1874 and became Assistant College Librarian. During his tenure of office he did many great things for librarianship, not the least of which was his fervent participation in the founding of the American Library Association. Later he became librarian of the New York State Library at Albany and there founded and directed the first 'library school'. As an organizer, pamphleteer and speaker in the advocacy of our craft he was the most energetic and fertilising personality of his long lifetime. However, just as Charles Ammi Cutter will be chiefly remembered for his *Rules for a Dictionary Catalogue*, so is the name of Dewey likely to survive in connection with his Decimal Classification.

150. DC regards knowledge as unity, which is to be divided into nine large classes; works too general in scope for any of these form a tenth class. These are properly written thus:

0.0 General Works	0.5 Natural Sciences
0.1 Philosophy	0.6 Useful Arts
0.2 Religion	0.7 Fine Arts
0.3 Social Sciences	0.8 Literature
0.4 Philology	0.9 History

The ten units of decimal division are thus reached. In practice, however, the initial 0 and point are assumed and the classes are written merely: 0 General works, 1 Philosophy, 2 Religion, etc. An extract from the introductory explanation to an abridgement of the schemes will give the salient features of DC in the words of its author: 'The classification divides the field of knowledge into 9 main classes, numbered 1–9. Cyclopaedias, periodicals, etc., so general as to belong to no one of these classes, are marked 0 (nought) and form a tenth class. Each class is similarly separated into 9 divisions, general works belonging to no division having 0 in place of the decimal number. Divisions are similarly divided into 9 sections and, it may be interpolated, sections, sub-sections and sub-sub-sections, without limit other than that imposed by the material to be classified, may be similarly divided. Thus 512 means class 5 Natural Science, division 1 Mathematics, section 2 Algebra, and every algebra is numbered 512. Its class number, giving class, division and section, is applied to every book and pamphlet in the library.

151. 'Where o occurs in a class number, it has its usual numerical value. Thus a book numbered 510 is class 5, division 1, but no section; i.e. the book treats of division 51 (Mathematics) in general and is limited to no one section, while Geometry, which is so limited, is marked 513; 500 indicates a treatise on science in general, limited to no division or section. A number beginning with o means "not limited to a class"; e.g. a general cyclopaedia treating of all 9 classes. Books are arranged on the shelves in a simple numerical order. Since each number means a definite subject, all books on any subject must stand together. These tables show the order of the subjects. Thus 512 Algebra precedes 513 Geometry, and follows 511 Arithmetic'.

152. The first edition appeared in 1876, and consisted of 12 pages of prefatory matter, 12 of tables and 18 of Index, a total of 42 pages; and of this modest work 1,000 copies were printed. It is curious to reflect that it was immediately challenged by librarians as being too minute in its sub-divisions for the arrangement of any but very large libraries. The fourteenth edition, 1942, however, consisted of 1927 pages, including index; its elephantine nature brought forth some protests and the reaction was seen in the unorthodox edition, 15. The sixteenth and seventeenth editions return to the traditional pattern, but offer the index in a separate volume. This growth suggests the enormous number of sub-divisions that are possible, because literature exists or may exist upon them, and are necessary when minute classification is undertaken. It reveals also the flexibility of a scheme which has permitted such expansion.

153. *Main Features.* Although the tiny tables of 1876 were considered to be too complex by their earliest critics, who had not yet applied them, the development which followed their use, especially by larger libraries, brought out the most enduring criticism to be made of them. Yet there can be no doubt that much of the criticism of DC is the direct result of its enormous popularity; no other scheme has been tried and tested in so many libraries and so minutely scrutinised by members of our profession. The great merits of the scheme lie in the simplicity and universal appeal of its notation, the ease with which it can be understood and applied, the fact that it is regularly revised, and the assurance, given in the second edition of 1885, that no drastic changes in the allocation of

numbers to subjects would ever be made. This last promise is, in many ways a two-edged sword; it means that the librarian does not have to contend with the problem of drastic changes in the location of subjects each time a new edition of DC appears, but it also means that a really thorough overhaul of the sequence of topics is out of the question, unless this long standing assurance is violated. Yet, by and large, the 'integrity of numbers' policy is pleasing to users of DC, who rarely welcome relocations of topics. It might also be said, when endeavouring to explain the phenomenal success of this classification that the fact that it appeared at the ideal period in the history of librarianship, a time when libraries were about to change from closed access (with its reliance on fixed location systems) to the open access principle, is a major reason for its popularity. It is certainly true that DC was firmly entrenched by the time its earlier serious rivals began to appear and that classifications, once adopted, are not to be lightly abandoned. But it is also true that DC had and has definite advantages of a more positive kind over many of these rivals. Cutter's Expansive Classification, although excellent in some respects, was never completed, LC is really only for the huge Congress library, SC has some odd features and has never been regularly revised, UDC is really only for special libraries and for bibliographies. We shall, of course, discover the emphasis, merits and limitations of these schemes in later chapters; here it is sufficient to say that for these and other reasons DC has been favoured in the majority of libraries.

154. It must be stressed that the early editions of DC represented a tremendous improvement upon earlier methods, for when this scheme first appeared many books in libraries were still arranged solely by size or some such artificial feature. DC has not only proved more successful than its later rivals, it has influenced them greatly. For the best features of this classification have been copied by most schemes; even the modern stress on the value of synthetic classification was anticipated by Dewey, although he does not fully recognise the possibilities of this idea. Another excellent feature of his scheme lies in its adaptability. DC can easily be modified to meet the needs of different libraries and various modifications and minor rearrangements are authorised in the introduction to the schedules. The seventeenth edition points out that the scheme offers reasonably close, or detailed, classification for general libraries if the synthetic possibilities are taken into account. Any library not requiring a great

deal of detail can use the abridged version, or 'cut back' quite easily the notation of the full schedules. Thus we see that the abiding merits of the system are those of simplicity, ease of comprehension and application, universality of appeal, susceptibility to modifications, and regular production and overhaul.

155. The system is certainly not without fault; indeed some modern supporters of synthetic classification would have us abandon DC in our general libraries, although they find it difficult to suggest a suitable alternative system at present available. The main faults of DC, apart from the notational ones mentioned in paragraphs 157 and 158, are the faulty sequence of classes in certain parts of the scheme (see the divisions of 650, for example); the separation of many major subject fields which merit collection (Language and Literature, Sociology and History); the failure to bring the history and geography of a country together; the scattering of the parts of some subjects (geography is again a good example, although an attempt is made in edition 17 to unite the different branches of geography in an alternative schedule at 910); and the American terminology and general bias towards the needs of western civilisation. Again the seventeenth edition tries to come to the rescue with this last point; provision is made for other cultures and nations to be brought to the fore, if so desired. DC has also been criticised as being unsuitable for the special library, but this is really true of all general classifications. A serious fault perhaps, as we have already briefly mentioned, is inherent in the 'number integrity' idea. The removal of drastic defects in the DC sequence of topics is certainly hindered by the refusal to introduce radical change; the difficulty is that such change is impractical in most established libraries and the policy of conservative scrutiny and gradual rearrangement of the schedules to keep pace with the growth of knowledge is the one which commends itself to practically all librarians who are committed to the scheme. Of course, newly created libraries will insist upon a *modern* organization of knowledge, so overhaul of the tables cannot be too conservative. But the traditional policy has been one of evolutionary rather than revolutionary development, relocations taking place just in sufficient quantity to prevent, in the words of edition 17, 'an outmoded past from tyrannising over the future'. DC's severest critics would also point to the scheme's debt to the Baconian chart of 1605! True, this makes it seem that the roots of this classification are in the remote past, but the constant attention

of experts has succeeded in overcoming many defects in the order of classes without violent upheaval and the links between Dewey's scheme and that of Bacon can be overstressed.

156. To sum up, the features of DC are such that it is still the best scheme for public libraries and most other general libraries will also unhesitatingly accept it. When Fremont Rider, in the introduction to his *International Classification*, described DC as 'the most marvellous bibliographical tool ever devised for the use of the library world', he was bestowing praise on a rival system which is rare among classificationists, but he was surely expressing the enormous debt of the profession, and this on a truly international scale, to the genius and tenacity of purpose of Melvil Dewey.

157. *Notation*. We have described virtues and defects as much as features in the comments above. But, with DC, this is perhaps justifiable as the features of the scheme are well known or can easily be seen in operation. The notational qualities illustrate extremely well many of the merits and faults of this great classification. We may note, first of all, that the choice of numerals, although making the scheme universally acceptable, placed a great barrier on its capacity to house subjects. DC has always attempted to reveal its hierarchy in the notation; this restricts it to nine places at each stage of division (assuming that the zero is used to introduce standard sub-divisions, or form divisions as they were formerly called). This 'decimal procrustean bed' has received a great deal of criticism. The cramped nature of the notation is intensified by the fact that the original apportionment of numbers to subjects was in many cases faulty. Recognition of this and also of the difficulty of change is clearly shown in the introduction to the latest edition: 'to reapportion the notation so that it would be equally hospitable to all disciplines and subjects held by libraries today would require the development of a wholly new system and would only establish a base for other inequities of a future that today cannot be imagined, just as much as the world of 1965 could not be imagined in 1876'.

158. Because of this faulty apportionment, in the light of modern needs, many subjects, especially in sciences and technology and in other rapidly developing fields of knowledge, are burdened with long numbers – a direct result of the overcrowding in the classes concerned. Other classes, in more static subject areas, are relatively empty and offer concise notations for the topics concerned. The scheme offers advice, however, for coping with long numbers; it

must be confessed also that the notation can be expanded indefinitely and that the average class-mark is easily recollected – the pure notation may contribute something to this. Although the scheme, like two others, was named after a notational feature we would not agree with the editor of the system that this is its 'greatest strength'. It is, however, despite the acknowledged lack of capacity of numerical notations, a good feature in many respects. Dewey may have restricted the development of his scheme in some ways on that eventful morning in the Amherst College chapel when he decided upon the decimal system, but his choice did much to make his classification internationally acceptable.

159. *Synthesis and Mnemonics*. The synthetic element of the DC notation can be seen in various ways. First we have the use of number-building through the common form divisions, or standard sub-divisions as they are now called. They have been outlined already in paragraph 79 and probably had their origin in the Generalia class of the scheme, for they closely resemble it. Recent editions have greatly extended these and the seventeenth lists the standard sub-divisions in the index volume, providing in all over one hundred such divisions. A sample may serve to indicate their variety:

–016   Indexes and bibliographies
–017   Professional and Occupational Ethics
–018   Research methodology
–0182 Statistical method
–0184 Operations research
–0186 Case Studies
–019   Psychological aspects

These can be used, as appropriate, throughout the scheme and are always to be introduced by their one initial zero, unless they are added to a class-mark ending with a nought; in such cases the zero of the form divisions usually disappears. But if *subject* sub-divisions are introduced by ·o under a particular number, then .oo introduces the standard sub-division. Thus a History of Pharmacology is 615.09 but the History of Mathematics is 510.09, as 510.1–510.9 are used for *subject* sub-divisions.

160. Synthesis is also achieved by the use of the area table (formerly the common geographical divisions). The divisions in this table are based on the country numbers of classes 930–999. In

edition 17 they are not provided with a distinctive introductory digit to indicate that geographical division is to take place. That is to say that when we are instructed to use them we merely add the part of the number which *follows* the initial 9. Thus the subject *social clubs* is denoted by 367 and we are told to place the history of this subject at 367.9. The history of social clubs in the United States would be 367.973, the 73 being the distinctive number for the U.S.A. in the area table. To use another illustration, *Music festivals* are classed at 780.79 and we are invited to subdivide further, if need be by the use of the geographical area table. In this table, the distinctive number for London is 421 (because the history of London in Class 900 is at 942.1). Thus Music festivals in London will go at 780.79421. It must be pointed out that the area tables can only be used in this form where an invitation to employ it appears in the schedules. If no instruction is given and the classifier wishes to divide a subject by a geographical region, he must introduce the regional number by 09.

161. A third and most important synthetic element in DC is seen in the instruction, frequently given in the schedules, to build up a number by dividing like some other part of the scheme. For example the number for *Teaching and Teaching Personnel* is 373.11, but this can be extended as the instruction 'divide like 371.1' is provided. Thus *the duties and responsibilities of teachers* would be classified at 373.1141. Likewise, to select another example of the application of this most useful idea, *Poultry production* is 636.508 and we are invited to sub-divide further by the instruction 'divide like 636.08'. Thus *chicken breeding* would be 636.50824. The 'divide like' instruction has always been a potent tool for notational synthesis to achieve the exact classification of subjects in DC; in the latest edition we find that over 2,600 entries have this 'built in expansion', an increase of over 1,800 on edition 16. Thus there is a new stress on synthesis for those libraries which find it useful; such expansion being, of course, quite optional as no library need follow the 'divide like' instructions unless it wishes to do so. Sometimes when this type of advice is given we are invited to 'divide like 001 to 999'. An example of this is seen at 016 where subject bibliographies may be classified in this way. Thus a Bibliography of Science would be 016.5, a Bibliography of Maths 016.51 and so forth. Of course, for those librarians who prefer it, it is permissible to distribute such bibliographical material by subject interest, adding in this case the

appropriate standard sub-division for bibliographies to the subject class mark.

162. All these synthetic devices have the effect of adding to the memory value of the notation. For it is clear that, by means of their constant repetition with the same significance, the standard sub-divisions and area divisions will have mnemonic effect. 42 is not always England and Wales in the scheme, nor does 73 always denote the U.S.A. But England and Wales and the U.S.A. are constantly denoted by 42 and 73 respectively when these geographical areas are to be added to a subject number. Thus we have here an example of systematic mnemonics. The DC notation also achieves mnemonic power by the similarity of the numbering used for certain kindred classes. Thus 913–919 are the numbers used for the geography of various countries; this block of numbers has divisions which are based on those of 940–999 which cover the history of the same countries. So we find that in class 900 the *History* of *Switzerland* is 949.4 and the *Geography* of the same country 914.94. Or, to look at this in a different light, if we imagine 9 as denoting History and 91 Geography, we merely need to add to these the appropriate area table number (494 in the case of Switzerland). The Language and Literature classes show a similar parallel structure in their major divisions; likewise we find that the divisions of the various languages and literatures are based on those of English Language and Literature. The student should look carefully at classes like these and note the mnemonic effect gained by the similarity of the notational pattern.

163 *Index*. It has been shown that decimal classification is older than Dewey's experience with it. He tells us, however, that he is not interested in the priority of its invention, but continues, 'extended investigation by others fails to show this most important feature of the system – the Relative Index, on which all else hinges – had ever been used as here to index by a single reference most diverse material'. The index is certainly a valuable contribution, and original in the form in which Dewey uses it, but, apart from the facts that no classification can hinge merely upon an index, and no relative index can show all the possible relations of subjects, it is clear that the most significant contribution which Dewey made to class-ification was not the index but the process of decimal division itself, by which the symbols 0 – 9 are divided by 0 – 9 and again by the same method indefinitely. Bliss rightly criticises Dewey's claims

about the importance of the index, but the alphabetical key to the schedules is essential of course and the DC index is relative, that is it reveals most of the aspects of any concrete theme which the classification has found it necessary to scatter.

164. The eighteen pages of the first Relative Index had expanded when the fourteenth edition was reached to 738, and it had become a vast alphabet of about 80,000 terms. It is now published as a separate volume, but following some criticism of the index to edition 16, the seventeenth edition has tried to reduce the bulk of the index somewhat. Many of the entres of the sixteenth edition have been replaced by *see* references thus:

> Gaseous
> > fuels *see* Industrial gases
> > illuminants *see* Industrial gases

There are many *see also* references too in the index to the latest edition. The most important terms are shown in heavy type and relocations from edition 16 are shown by a dagger preceding a class-number in the index. A plus sign following a number in the index indicates that this can be expanded, if required, by means of the 'divide like' form of notational synthesis in the tables, which we have already described. This new index will continue to irritate some classifiers, but we are assured by the editors that, although it demands a certain amount of effort on the classifiers' part, it can be a most useful tool as a key to the classified tables. More than ever, we are told, it is dangerous to attempt to class by the index alone. The DC index, if properly used, is a work of considerable suggestive value, although the experimental form of the index to the seventeenth edition will not be repeated. All indexes in other schemes have to some extent followed the model of those in the early editions of DC, although in the case of the Subject Classification of Brown the influence is comparatively slight.

165. *Use and Revision of the Scheme.* The most striking testimony to DC lies in the fact that it is by far the most used general library classification in the world. The standard edition indicated that, in the United States, DC is used by about 96% of public libraries, 89% of College and University libraries and 64% of the special libraries. This position of near monopoly has not changed a great deal in the last decade or so; the fact that in less than seven years

over 30,000 copies of edition 16 were sold (about 30% of these went to some 90 overseas countries) testified to this. As far as the revision of the system is concerned, we find that new editions are published approximately every eight years. Revision of detail and relocations in these are conservative in comparison with, say, the Universal Decimal or Congress schemes; on the other hand, there are users who complain about the alterations which are made and, by and large, DC seems to steer fairly well the difficult course between the Scylla of introducing drastic notational alterations and the Charybdis of failing to keep pace with knowledge. The bulletin issued to subscribers between editions and entitled *Decimal Classification Additions, Notes and Decisions* is a useful pointer to changes which will be incorporated in the schedules as soon as possible. The editorial body of DC seem to be especially attentive these days to the complaints and suggestions of practising librarians and will gladly listen to the advice of the scheme's users; thus there is every opportunity for the consumer to put forward his ideas with regard to proposed improvements.

166. A word about the preparation of the last four or five editions may be in order. Dewey left actual library work some years before his death in 1931, but he kept the management of the scheme, although other editors supervised the various editions. A feature of DC, at least from the sixth edition, was the use of a phonetic simplified spelling which increased in unlikeness to that of ordinary folk with each successive edition. This did much, we are certain, to interfere with its acceptance by some would-be users. The Lake Placid Club Educational Foundation, which was another enterprise of Dewey's, has cared for the classification during the years since 1924, and for some years after Dewey's death, until ill-health prevented, his policies and practices were continued by his chosen editor and loyal fellow-worker, Dorcas Fellows, who produced the thirteenth memorial edition in 1932. This was a considerable expansion of the twelfth in parts. The revisions, however, were never radical and balanced; its editors made expansions to meet the obvious needs of knowledge, but side by side with some of the most modern schedules, as, for example, the alternative tables for Psychology in the 1932 edition such obsolete schedules survived as that for Photography. The bulky fourteenth edition may be passed over, but a word must be said about the 'Standard' fifteenth edition. A new editorial committee was given 'the difficult task of modernising

F

DC' and 'in 1945 the pattern of the new revision was furnished by instructors in library schools and by librarians in a variety of libraries in North and South America and in Great Britain'. Nevertheless the policy of reducing the size of the schedules and seeking uniform expansion of classes for the needs of medium-sized libraries does not seem to have been very successful. Nor was the index to the Standard edition satisfactory; in fact it had to be reconstituted at the last moment to satisfy librarians in the U.S.A. This edition must be regarded as a brave attempt to modernise DC and has been described as its first true revision, but the general reaction to it is well reflected by the article from the pen of Thelma Eaton[1] suggesting that it was virtually a new classification and that DC, as Dewey had conceived it, was thus dead.

167. Edition 16 returned to the traditional pattern, dropped most of the relocations and restored details which its predecessor had rejected. It tries to reconcile the conflicting aims of stability of notation and provision for new topics, but is more successful with regard to the former goal. It is in two volumes and was the first edition to be actually prepared by the staff of the Library of Congress. Work had taken place under the Congress roof on the perpetuation of DC since edition 13, but editions 16 and 17 are the product of a team resulting from the combination of the staff of the Dewey Editorial Office and the DC section of the Library of Congress Subject Cataloguing Division. Edition 17 also continues the traditional pattern of DC but contains many new and interesting features, some of which we have already noted. There is a welcome stress on the need for classification to offer a helpful, filiatory sequence and not merely provide 'pigeon holes' for books and documents and we are reminded that DC is a classification for the arrangement of material on the shelves of libraries and not a tool for the rapid retrieval of information from highly specialised documents. Provision has been made in certain parts of the scheme for division by more than one principle; thus an effort is made to extend the very limited resemblance which DC has always had to the modern methods of faceted classification. Nevertheless, it must be stressed that, despite the use of synthesis, especially through the increased use of the 'divide like . . .' instruction, DC is still fundamentally an enumerative classification. For smaller libraries there is an abridged

---

[1] Epitaph to a dead classification, *Library Association Record*, November, 1966, pp. 428–30.

version (ninth edition 1965); a guide to the use of the scheme is also published by the Lake Placid Club at intervals.

168. *Conclusion*. It will be seen that the system lags behind modern theories; the wholehearted supporter of the clear analysis of the elements which make up a subject into definite categories, or facets, is likely to be tempted to regard such an enumerative system as almost antediluvian in many respects. Yet no classification devised in the nineteenth century and at all concerned with number integrity could hope to be completely abreast with modern theories of classification or with modern knowledge. The fact remains that DC works well in a very large number of libraries. Some librarians may be lethargic or apathetic (although we often find that those who bandy these words about are the very ones who are *not* faced with the enormous task of reclassifying a collection of books but are anxious that others should reclassify), but the profession as a whole is too concerned about efficiency to make do with a tool that is hopelessly inadequate. Thus DC survives and thrives because, despite the arguments of its critics concerning real or imaginary faults, it is still the best classification for public and probably for college libraries. No other system has been able, in practice, to offer a decisive challenge or to prove its theoretical superiority for the arrangement of such collections.

169. That the Bacon-Harris schemes, to which Dewey was partly indebted for his order of subjects, do not coincide with the modern view of subjects and studies is admitted, but any scheme of the so-called enumerative type cannot move its classes with every shift of knowledge. Tested by the Canons given in Chapter 7 of this book and those provided elsewhere there are indubitably many faults. The scheme certainly reflects the needs of a capitalist society and a Christian culture, although, as we have remarked, the seventeenth edition does attempt to provide for a library to bring its own nation and culture to the fore if it so wishes. Again the limits of the decimal base are continually proclaimed and the British users sometimes grumble about American bias and terminology. A formidable critic is Bliss, who attacks what he calls the *subject index illusion;* the inverted Baconian order as unphilosophic and impractical; the important main sciences as separated and mangled; the notation as ill-proportioned and uneconomical; and shows many other faults as causing confusion which revision and continual expansion have only increased. The scheme has also been criticised, in more recent years,

by Foskett, who complains about the rigidity of its framework, and by Coates.[1] On the other hand, many critics insist that the great merits of DC be recognised also; as the American H. H. Young[2] points out, it has many excellent and lasting qualities.

170. No one now rushes to defend DC on the grounds of the modernity of its order or the brevity of its notation. The curious fact remains that more and more libraries throughout the world continue to use it, many of them modifying it; somehow it works. We should certainly fail in our appreciation of services rendered if we did not say that a scheme which has survived for ninety years in ever growing currency in spite of merited criticism must have virtues which in practice outweigh our most powerful theoretical objections. These are chiefly its accessibility, its constant revision by a large group of zealous and well-qualified workers, and the ease with which it may be applied in part or entirely to collections of books and expanded as these collections grow. The notation, despite the restricted base, has been most successful and influential. Ranganathan[3] writes: 'The most potent and lasting contribution of DC to the philosophy of library classification is the demonstration of the practicability of securing hospitality of notation by the simple device of decimal fraction notation.' The scheme is also much better equipped than many of its rivals with advice for the practical classifier; in the seventeenth edition this is shown by the long editorial introduction, by the reprinting of Melvil Dewey's original introduction, and by the usual generous use of scope notes and definitions throughout the schedules.

171. After carefully considering the DC and listening to very many comments, both favourable and otherwise, we are convinced that the oldest and most persistent one comes from the expert who wants *all* material together on his subject, whatever that may be and from whatever angle he may approach it; it is the most understandable one and, to those of us who know what library classification entails, the least reasonable. Powerful oppositon to DC has been noticeable in recent years from the supporters of the new theories; one can appreciate their zeal in extolling the merits of these theories more readily than the tendency, in certain quarters,

---

[1] *Library Association Record*, August, 1959.
[2] The enduring qualities of Dewey. In Allerton Park Institute: *Role of classification in the modern American library*, 1959.
[3] *Philosophy of Library Classification*, 1951, p. 20.

to evaluate DC solely in the light of these principles and pronounce it obsolete when, in fact, no readily usable general faceted scheme yet exists to challenge it. Meanwhile the decimal notation remains an obvious reason for the world-wide use which the system enjoys, that it is an international 'language' understood by all nations. It will need a good scheme indeed to drive out DC in general libraries. Some day it may disappear, as do all human efforts, but we now look ahead to the eighteenth edition, confident that the scheme has sufficient intrinsic merit, and certainly enough support, to endure as the popular favourite, in well-established general libraries at least, for several years to come.

CHAPTER THIRTEEN

The Subject Classification

172. *Introduction.* J. D. Brown's great interest in classification can be attributed to the fact that he realised the need for systematic arrangement and the benefits which would accrue from such arrangement and the benefits which would accrue from such arrangement in the public libraries of the late nineteenth century that had been newly converted to open access methods. By the early nineties, close classification, to quote Brown, had 'not often been adopted in Britain save in the case of a few reference libraries, and where the decimal system of Mr Dewey has been applied'. Little was then known of the Dewey scheme in any case; certainly for lending departments none of the larger libraries had adopted it: in fact, their libraries were either afraid or contemptuous; it was considered too American and too complex. This view may or may not have been shared by Brown. He was certainly no lover of that classification in later years, although he admitted that it had its merits; but he was also a man who would take a line of his own rather than follow others; a dangerous attitude for most men, but in his case having its uses. The rival scheme that Brown made in conjunction with Quinn soon proved inadequate, as did Brown's own *Adjustable Classification* (1898). Undeterred by these setbacks and no doubt provoked by the American bias of the DC and the hold which it was gradually gaining in British libraries, Brown set about the compilation of an entirely new system; SC was thus presented to the world of librarianship in 1906. A second edition was published in 1914 (the year of Brown's death), the alterations in which are useful but of no radical importance; and a third after many years of experiment and application appeared in 1939, edited by the classificationist's nephew, J. D. Stewart. This is the latest edition and revision has been

extremely conservative; indeed it retains every feature that Brown devised or adopted.

173. This third edition showed the vitality of the scheme, and that it had a certain vogue in this country, Although it has only been applied in British public libraries, all medium-sized or small library systems, many of the municipal libraries still employing it testify that it meets their needs. The classification, therefore, must be described and considered. Brown produced his scheme almost single-handed and it has never had the benefits of revisions carried out by committees, which the DC enjoyed relatively early in its history. Yet of SC there is this to be said; it is based on certain personal theories of Brown's; some of these are attractive and, as the sequel has proved, are those which other classificationists have been able to adopt and to develop. The compiler was modest enough in his claims for the classification. He wrote that he had attempted to provide 'a simple, fairly logical, and practical method' for British libraries. Its merits are that it is easily understood, can be grasped without protracted examination and study and is prefaced with an introduction, written with a great deal of sterling commonsense and embodying useful classification hints and decisions.

174. On the other hand, it seems clear that Brown did not expect SC to achieve a great deal of success; the 1914 edition makes it clear that it had, by then, acquired more support than its compiler anticipated. The strong British emphasis and the detail given to British towns in its schedules no doubt had much to do with this support. An examination of SC shows that it appears to fulfil all the requirements of a practical classification. It has a generalia class, form classes, an index, and a notation that is quite brief and simple. Yet it may be thought by classifiers who examine this scheme that Brown's belief (expressed in his Introduction) that each subject specialist will tend, no matter what the arrangement in a particular library may be, to view the whole of knowledge as though his own particular study was central, has led this great British classificationist to evade the problem of providing a sequence of subjects that is truly helpful to the majority of library users.

175. *Main Features.* Here it must firstly be said that the object of SC is to provide a 'one-place' classification. Brown writes 'I incline to think that, in book classification, the constant or concrete subject should be preferred ...' This idea is superficially attractive; unfortunately a one-place system is not feasible and, as envisaged in

SC, would not be really useful. For Brown, in pursuing this goal, ignores the purpose for which books are written and the dominant interests of readers. He selects certain concrete topics and decides that material will be grouped around these, disregarding the emphasis or viewpoint from which the 'concrete' is regarded in various books. For example, Brown treats *Money* as a concrete subject and brings books on it together, but fails to distinguish between the approach of the student of monetary economics on the one hand and the art of numismatics on the other; the two themes, although very different, are thus associated in SC. He regards *Shipping and Shipbuilding* as another concrete; this leads him to place in this class material on Freight Rates and Bills of Lading which ought to appear as a division of Commerce. In short, the purpose or intention behind books and the needs of library users have been overlooked in the attempt to group material around the selected concretes. Many of the resultant groupings are arbitrary or ones which would be better in a Relative Index rather than in the schedules of the classification. The scheme is really well-named; in one sense, at least, it is the only accepted general system that is truly a subject classification. All the other schemes break up most of Brown's concretes recognising that they belong to various disciplines and that, in classification, the emphasis or *purpose* of a book is more crucial than what Brown would call its core subject. Brown is thus guilty of over-simplification in defining the themes with which books deal, for many of his concrete topics are, in reality, several distinct activities.

176. The student who seeks further evidence of the unfortunate effects of this effort to produce a one-place system is invited to examine the unhelpful groupings of topics in certain parts of Brown's scheme, at G090–G106, for example, at H620–H720, or in Class M where Oratory and Ventriloquism are placed together. It must be stressed that unorthodox groupings do not always result from this one-place theory; yet many of the unusual collocations in the scheme can only be explained in this way.[1] The nature of the index also is to be attributed to this idea.

177. Another outstanding feature of SC, in some ways similar to the above, is seen in the attempt made by Brown to link each technology with the pure science on which it is based. Thus no

[1] The reasons for resisting this notion of 'classification by attraction' are well explained by the editor of DC edition 17. *Library Association Record*, March, 1965, p. 79.

useful arts class as such is provided; the idea is that each theory is followed immediately in the classified sequence by the appropriate application. This notion of Brown's is *sometimes* extremely useful; it is good, to quote obvious and striking examples, to have the theory of chemistry collocated with material on chemical technology and to have the principles of electricity linked with electrical engineering in the physics class. Indeed some of the wiser examples of this idea were commended by Bliss and can be seen also in his Bibliographic Classification. Brown says 'The divisions seen in most classifications in vogue – Fine Arts, Useful Arts, and Science – are examples of the arbitrary separation of closely related 'subjects'; and goes on to declare that 'as the systematization of science and teaching improves, the separation between physical basis and practical application, hitherto maintained, will no longer be insisted upon'. An order of 'scientific progression' is therefore used, applications which are derived from a science or other base being placed as so derived. Unfortunately this theory that every science or art springs from a definite source is applied over-zealously in many subjects with a consistency which becomes embarrassing.

178. This means that the root science is shown and then there follows all its possible applications; these are succeeded, in turn, by another 'pure' science, which is followed by all its applications and so on. We have thus, to quote some examples from Classes B–D, Physical Sciences:

> C200 Heat
>   201 Combustion
>   206 Ovens
>   210 Boilers
>   215 Chimneys
>   216 Chimney-stacks
>   217 Steeple Jacks
>   218 Fireplaces
>   225 Fire producers
>   230 Fire extinction
>   231 Fire engines
>
> C300 Sound
>   400 Music
>   500 Vocal Forms
>   520 Choir Training

F*

and this remarkable placing of Music is immediately followed by Astronomy. Somewhat similarly, Physiography leads to Meteorology, then to Storms, thence to Pneumatic engines, Aerial engineering, Aeroplanes; likewise, the subject of Time is followed immediately by Clock and Watch-making; books on Armour and Military Costume precede material on war. This bringing of the sciences in their pure state into proximity with the trades which are closely or remotely based on them may seem logical in principle and follows on naturally from the one-place idea, but it really tends to separate things which are thought of, or studied, or used, together. Thus the trades are themselves separated by a mass of written material on the pure sciences, and this, although occasionally justified, often appears to ignore the needs of readers. It may be noted too, that SC does not in every case pursue subjects from the root science to the final application; for example, Botany does not lead up, as one would expect, to Agriculture, which is, after all, an ultimate application of botanical knowledge; and, of course, the study of Mineralogy as in granites, etc., does not lead up, as might be expected on this theory, to Architecture and Building. Bliss has pronounced that the principles here adopted are good if not carried to extremes, but agrees, and indeed asserts with more examples and emphatically, that many of the groupings that result from them are neither practical nor scientific[1].

179. Another feature of SC that must be explained is that it endeavours to follow an approximate sequence of scientific development in its main outline. In the order of things it is assumed that there were first the factors *Matter and Force*, which gave rise to *Life*, and Life in time produced *Mind*, which in turn reached at length the making of its *Record*. Allowing, as all schemes must, a Generalia Class – somewhat different here from that in other systems – we thus get the base with the divisions of which it is formed.

Generalia
Matter and Force
Physical Sciences

Life
Biological Science
Ethnological and Medical Sciences
Economic Biology

[1] *Organization of Knowledge in Libraries*, p. 280.

Mind
Philosophy and Religion
Social and Political Science

Record
Language and Literature
Literary Forms
History, Geography and Biography

In the sense that this outline is developmental it may be called evolutionary, so long as the word is applied in its simple dictionary sense of a progression from simple to complex things; Bliss suggests that, in part, it crudely resembles the order of the sciences.

180. There is a striking difference between the Generalia Class of SC and the equivalent classes of other schemes and this is the next feature for us to consider. The main sections of this class in SC are:

A000 Generalia	A750 Photography
A100 Education	A790 Sculpture
A300 Logic	A900 General Science
A400 Mathematics	A950 Scientific travel and surveys
A600 Graphic and Plastic Arts	

The recognised principle of the Generalia Class of an orthodox kind is that it accommodates subjects of too general a nature to go into any other class. Brown extends this notion; he says: 'The divisions of this main class comprise most of the rules, methods and factors which are of general application and which qualify or pervade every branch of science, industry or human study. They are universal and pervasive, and cannot be logically assigned to any other single main class as peculiar or germane to it.' This is a very controversial position. Logic is surely a mental science, although logical method can be applied to many subjects; likewise, although we can photograph almost anything, we know that the subject photography should be treated as either an art or a technology. Mathematics involves the formal statement of natural laws; while the Graphic and Plastic Arts are, *on Brown's logical basis*, one form of Record. Again, Education should be collocated with Psychology or treated as a Social Science. General Science is not too badly placed, for it is near to the Physical Sciences, but Bliss wonders why it is separated from Philosophy and Logic. Indeed only the divisions

A000–099 cover orthodox General Works Class material here. We rather lose confidence in Brown's attempts to justify the theories behind this class in SC, when we are told elsewhere in his Introduction that it was not possible to find room in Class M for the Arts and they were only removed to Generalia for this reason![1]

181. Other features of SC may be considered more briefly. We find that, in the classes O–W History and Geography, one substantive number only is used for each country, while its history and geography are regarded as standpoints from which the country, as a subject, is viewed. This logical and useful arrangement has much to commend it; many consider that the absolute separation of the history and geography of each country in DC is a defect of that scheme. A further interesting innovation is the treatment which SC gives to Literature and Biography. In the Class N, for literary texts, Brown abandons the linguistic and chronological arrangements of Dewey and other classificationists and simply provides four great form divisions – Fiction, Poetry, Drama, and Essays. Under each of these he has headings for collections in the various forms, but following these come all individual authors in one alphabetical sequence. Thus, in Poetry, Beddoes, Browning and Byron follow one another without relation to period, and Wordsworth and Coleridge are far apart. Likewise, Dante, Darley, and Davidson are together, the language in which their work was written being disregarded. The same A–Z arrangement applies in the other form groupings. It has some 'finding value' in a popular library; yet it surely ignores the claims of the student and serious reader who presumably wants to study a period of literature, or the literature of a specified country, more often than the works of any one author. Turning to the huge class, Individual Biography, we find another long alphabetical sequence. Brown arranges great lives in A–Z order by the names of the persons written about and not as in DC where the biography class arranges them according to the subjects which they are or were most concerned in life. An alternative arrangement in SC is to distribute individual biography, by subject interest, throughout the scheme.

182. *Notation*. The reader will have realized, from examples already given, that the notation of SC employs a single capital letter. It may be pointed out here that Y and Z are surprisingly excluded

[1] It may also be noted that subjects like Logic and Education were given a much more orthodox placing in his Adjustable Classification of 1898.

from this alphabetical base; the remainder of the notation is, in general, a consistent three figure one, running from 000–999 with occasional gaps for insertions. There is a grave lack of flexibility here and Brown suggests that further expansion could be achieved through the use of decimals; however, it is unfortunate that the numerical part of the notation was not originally organized on decimal rather than integral lines. The notation conveys the chosen order of the scheme quite clearly; little attempt if any is made to convey the place of subjects in the classification's hierarchy. Faulty apportionment of notation has resulted in too much room being given to History and Geography at the expense of other topics – especially technological ones.

183. *Synthesis and Mnemonics.* Brown's main tables might seem to provide no advice on number building and to list no aspects or standpoints from which a subject may be regarded. However the absence of common sub-divisions from the main tables is one of the features peculiar to this scheme. Such divisions representing recurring forms of presentation are provided separately and most liberally in a list which Brown called the Categorical Tables.[1] Here we have a list of the necessary forms and standpoints which will be needed throughout the classification together with many others which will be needed only for certain classes. By listing these once and for all in a separate table, Brown has greatly reduced the bulk of SC; had he repeated these recurring concepts every time they were needed the scheme would have been inflated to enormous proportions. The numbers representing the various aspects are separated from the basic class-marks by means of a point. This will be made clearer by the use of examples:

I750.1 denotes a Bibliography on Leather Manufacture. (.1 being the Categorical Table number for bibliography).

L855.375 stands for the Development of Retail Trading. (.375, the Categorical Table number for growth and development having been added to the class-mark for Retailing.)

K404.41 indicates the Biography of a Saint. (.41 is the Categorical

---

[1] This phrase is not to be confused with categories or facets. As used by Brown it stands for the aspects from which a subject may be regarded or the forms in which it may be presented. De Grolier and others have drawn attention to this terminological problem.

Table number to be used for biography by libraries preferring to distribute such material by topic whenever possible.)

D705.954 represents Essays on Physical Chemistry. (.954 being the Categorical Table number for essays.)

This last example shows us that there are many standpoints listed in the Categorical Tables: indeed, in the third edition of SC, there are no less than 980. Many of them, of course, do only apply to certain classes in the scheme; on the other hand, each aspect is constantly represented by the same number and this has mnemonic value for the librarian in the case of aspects, standpoints, and forms of presentation, that are needed throughout the scheme. It must be stressed that the point which introduces the categorical number is not a decimal point and care must be taken not to regard it as such or to read the numbers decimally as we do in DC. It is a separating device only, and when we do meet with a book or catalogue entry which is marked with any SC class-mark of which the point is a part we know immediately that some viewpoint or aspect of a topic is treated in the book concerned. These Categorical Tables may appear to some to be unduly lengthy and in need of reorganization; they are, nevertheless, an interesting synthetic feature of SC. The theory that whenever a term appears in a number of classes it can be taken out of the main tables and included in a list of recurring concepts is pursued quite extensively by Brown.

184. Geographical division of subjects is a necessity in all schemes; we have seen how this is achieved in DC already. Brown secures a similar result by adding the number from the History and Geography class directly to the number which it is desired to divide. Thus, if we wish to classify a work on the *Botany of Berlin*, we take the class-mark E172 Local Floras and add to it the number for Berlin, making a resultant notation E172S725; and to this number, if the circumstances require it, the categorical number can be added; thus the *History of the Flora of Berlin* is E172S725.10. The notation thus permits synthesis to a high degree; it is also quite definite and not unduly long. Similarly, to quote Brown's own examples, D398V222 is the *Geology of Arran*, L185So is *Freemasonry in Russia*, J851Ro is the class-mark for books on the *Cathedrals of France*. In the last two examples it is seen that the geographical number is contracted; Sooo is the full symbol for Russia, but the second and third noughts add nothing to the

significance of the number and are to be omitted when it is used for the geographical division of other subjects. If need be, two subject class-marks can be joined in like manner to these examples. Thus *Unemployment in the Shipbuilding Industry* could be B650L118 or L118B650.

185. One problem that does arise from the use of this synthetic apparatus is the question of maintaining a consistent sequence; should A750.41, for example, file before A750T800? The answer would appear to be in the affirmative; that is to say a class-mark followed by a Categorical Table number files before the same class-mark followed by a geographical number. Linking subject numbers, using geographical division and, above all, employing the Categorical numbers are the main ways of achieving notational synthesis in SC; there are, however, other minor methods such as the use of the Date Table of lower case letters which is described in Brown's Introduction. The student is invited to examine this and, more important, to experiment with number building from SC himself, using the Categorical Tables and linking Geographical and Subject class-marks. He will find that the scheme is easy to apply in comparison with many of its rivals, although the results which it gives will often be far from satisfactory. Nor is the notation as mnemonic as it might be; the most used of the Categorical Table numbers have a certain amount of memory value, but the table as a whole is far too lengthy to possess great mnemonic power.

186. *Index.* The Subject Classification has a one-place or specific index, in contrast to the relative nature of the index to DC and other systems. Dewey's index not only locates each subject in the schedules for us; it shows also as many aspects of that subject as may be found in separate parts of the tables, with a location for each aspect. Brown usually gives only one entry in the index for a subject, and leaves the reader to infer that at the place indicated every aspect of that subject will be found. This hardly proves to be the case, however, as will easily be seen at *Trees*, a topic which receives only one entry in the index, but which actually appears in SC's tables at Botany, Forestry, Topiary and other places. In short, Brown's scheme has a deficient and unsatisfactory index; the in-inevitable 'distributed relatives' are not shown because it is claimed that SC is truly a one-place classification system. As this cannot be so, the indexing arrangement has nothing to commend it; it is very possibly the most defective part of the system.

187. *Use and Revision of the Scheme.* We have already mentioned that SC has only been adopted in Britain and by public libraries, although parts of it may have been used to supplement other schemes in special libraries. About thirty libraries now use the scheme, but some have changed in recent years to DC or are in process of changing. One library,[1] which had long been considering reclassification, was advised to change to DC by a team of O & M investigators who were examining the work of all the corporation departments; it was apparently considered that considerable long-term economies could be effected by using a system which is widely accepted and which is employed, although with some extensions and modifications, in our national bibliography. One of the reasons for the lack of support for SC and its gradual abandonment is, of course, the fact that Brown's personal theories sometimes lead to most unhelpful groupings; another very important reason is the lack of a revision policy. The scheme has always virtually been in the hands of Brown, and later Stewart, and the 1939 edition introduced no radical alterations, for expansion was carried out, whenever possible, 'without disturbing the placing and numbering of previously existing subjects'. The fact that there has never been a team of workers serving as an editorial body has indeed been a handicap; no scheme can be satisfactorily perpetuated nowadays without this general interest and co-operative activity. Users also like to receive bulletins between editions preparing them for changes in the next revision – SC, alas, never had such refinements. A modern edition was prepared by Mr Stewart, but was never published; the death of this stalwart worker in 1965 may well mean that a fourth edition will now never materialise.

188. This may seem most unfortunate to some British librarians as this is the one example of a general scheme created in the British Isles that has met with a fair degree of success. If, in some way, the decline of the scheme could be halted, it would be necessary to produce a fourth edition which drastically revised the schedules and terminology of SC and reorganized the Categorical Tables into groups to distinguish those aspects of general application from others which can only be used in conjunction with certain classes. This might eliminate the need for an alphabetical index to these Categorical Tables. Mills suggests in his textbook some possible methods of reform along these lines; on the other hand it is unlikely that such remodelling is now worth while. Libraries still using SC will

[1] Bury Public Library.

probably slowly decide to abandon it or else will make their own extensions and adaptations from time to time.

189. *Conclusion.* We find that the third edition of SC does not depart from any of the principles of the system as Brown devised them. Help in producing it was given by many librarians who had applied the scheme, but very few subjects have changed numbers except in the history and topographical classes. The phrase 'extensively revised' in this edition's introduction refers to growth rather than to change; users of a classification usually loathe drastic alterations and might commend the conservative method of revision employed here. Yet more adventurous reconstruction of SC in 1939 would have proved better for it in the long run. The merits of the scheme, as it stands, lie in the ease with which it may be applied and understood; the amount of space given to the history and geography of Britain (even small British towns have a class-mark of their own, but this is, of course, only an advantage to British librarians); the fact that the history and geography of any region are kept together; and the occasional advantageous collocations which result from Brown's desire to link each technology with the appropriate pure science.

190. SC's awkward groupings are overlooked by some librarians who claim that the general reader rarely complains about them; the obvious answer to this might be that library users rarely appreciate the possibilities of a good classified arrangement, but are often vaguely dissatisfied when they cannot find quickly and conveniently the majority of books which they want on a particular theme, or group of allied themes. They probably do not realise that this may well be the fault of the scheme that is in operation. The librarian, on the other hand, can quickly perceive the imperfections of the erroneous one-place idea, of some of the unusual links between pure and applied sciences as defined by Brown, of the unfortunate split in the British history class, and of the odd Generalia Class and Index. The faulty apportionment of notation means that many subjects now developing extremely rapidly have little scope for expansion in SC. In a periodical article, some years ago,[1] James Douglas Stewart suggested that the system had proved itself 'to be capable of expansion to meet modern technical and scientific developments'. This, unfortunately, would seem to be just what it has not done; many important topics in the sciences and technologies

[1] *Review of Documentation*, 1950, pp. 56–63.

and social sciences are insufficiently developed and there is little room for additional detail, yet other subjects of very limited significance have a comparatively large block of class-marks assigned to them. (Compare D265–269 with F950–954, for example).

191. The lack of revision is, almost certainly, the greatest fault of all; the very survival of the scheme as a system of more than historical interest is thus now in doubt. No bibliographical classification described in this section of the Manual illustrates more clearly the importance of regular revision through an editorial committee and the circulation of bulletins between editions. Perhaps the enthusiasm and the necessary financial support were never available; yet there is no alternative way of ensuring that a scheme will keep pace reasonably well with the growth of knowledge and will be perpetuated for the benefit of those libraries which are committed to it. Thus for the arrangement of subjects fields in which great strides forward have been made since World War II this classification is now completely inadequate.

192. It is easier to find faults with SC than with any other general scheme but, as Foskett has pointed out, these striking idiosyncrasies and omissions must not blind us to the virtues of Brown's classification. Whatever defects it may possess, it is a commendable attempt by a great British librarian to create a sound and durable system and, in addition to the merits noted above, it is often extremely adaptable. This is due to the fact that many of the subjects listed in the main tables are repeated as aspects in the Categorical Tables; because of this, *some* of the poorer locations could be avoided in practice, or extra alternative treatments are made available. Thus, for instance, *Emigration to Australia* could go at Lo83Po15 or, by use of the Categorical Table number for Emigration, at Po15.757. Cataloguing and Indexing at M150 and M160 are not well placed, but, *Indexing in the Reference Library* could be classed at M969.923, .923 being the Categorical Table number for Indexing. The wise classifier by transferring some badly placed subjects to gaps in the scheme might improve the sequence in other ways also. But, although such improvisation may help us to overcome some faults, it is best to regard SC as a scheme which was only partially successful, but which helped to pave the way for modern synthetic systems. For certainly J. D. Brown anticipated the idea of an entirely synthetic scheme remarkably well; it is this anticipation which the French writer, Eric De Grolier, has in mind when he says that SC is a good

scheme if the period of its origin is remembered. True, as Stewart once pointed out, Brown would not have been familiar with (and may not have approved of) some of the terminology used by Ranganathan. Yet the provision for the combination of class-marks and the clear recognition of recurrent aspects which can be listed once and for all, indicate that the synthetic apparatus of the scheme is quite a powerful one; Brown's ideas in this respect must have influenced, however indirectly, the maker of the Colon scheme. If the present day wholehearted advocates of faceted classification are right in believing that all good book classifications of the future must rely almost entirely on synthesis then, paradoxical though it may seem, SC – a scheme which has never been very successful and which is now even threatened with extinction – may ultimately prove to have been more important, with regard to the recognition of vital principles, than the far more widely accepted DC.

CHAPTER FOURTEEN

The Universal Decimal Classification

193. *Introduction*. This system of classification was initiated by the International Institute of Bibliography, which was formed towards the end of the nineteenth century. The Institute (now International Federation of Documentation, or simply F.I.D.), hoped to collect bibliographies published throughout the world and to build up a vast classified catalogue covering all literature. Although the task was from the start a colossal one, early omens were encouraging; financial support was given by the Belgian Government, the I.I.B. and its Bibliography Office were given premises in the Musée des Beaux Arts, and Paul Otlet and Henri La Fontaine, the originators of the I.I.B., became the secretaries. Later the collections, which became extensive, were moved to larger premises in the Palais Mondial, where they remained with an interregnum of exile in Paris during the German occupation of Belgium 1914–19, until the Belgian Government were seduced from bibliography by the British promoters of a Rubber Exhibition in 1923, who were allowed to turn out the Institute in order to use the Palais. No doubt in any but an ideal state caoutchouc will oust learning![1] The work came to a standstill for a while; then the League of Nations proposed to base its intellectual activities on the work of the Institute, so that what two nations failed to appreciate had a chance of being appreciated by the nations in concert. Meanwhile the Institute had changed its name, to express more comprehensively its purpose, to the International Institute of Documentation; and in 1937 another World Congress of Universal Documentation was held in Paris which determined that the Institute should be the world authority on

[1] So small was the interest in the fate of this patiently built-up enterprise that *The Times* refused to accept a short letter of protest.

documentation and its classification scheme the standard one. The name was changed once again to the title now used by the organization.

194. The arrangement of the cards in the vast classified catalogue obviously required a more detailed type of cataloguing than was commonly in use, wherein analysis could be carried to an almost extreme fineness. Moreover, to accomplish arrangement by subject a minute classification of infinite expansibility was a primary necessity. It was recognised that such a classification, in order to show such *nuances* as the relation of books to subjects, places, languages, epochs, etc., would demand a series of common sub-divisions much more comprehensive than those in any then existing system. The DC was adopted as the parent of the envisaged scheme, and this, in its adapted and extended form, was reaffirmed in 1937 to be the standard classification by the World Congress referred to above. In spite of the interruption of the war years, the great card catalogue contained in 1921 over twelve million entries; the F.I.D. were, however, forced to abandon this, but the UDC, as the 'Expanded Dewey' was called continued to thrive and to prove most useful for the exact classification of the highly specific subjects encountered in documentation. The first edition of UDC in French appeared in 1905; it was based on the fifth edition of DC. The second edition, also in French, was produced in 1927–33. A third full edition in German and a fourth in English were begun in 1933 and 1936 respectively.

195. The great success of this scheme in special libraries and information bureaux has created a need for national organizations to supervise its development and publication in the various languages. In Britain, the appropriate organization is the British Standards Institution, which took over the responsibilities for production of English editions in the 1940's. The full English edition is not yet complete, but we have an excellent abridgement (third edition 1961). As the full schedules in English are British Standard 1000, the abridgement is known as B.S.1000A. We have also a tri-lingual abridgement (B.S.1000B), and a Guide to the use of UDC, by J. Mills (B.S.1000C). There are, too, abridgements and parts of the full schedules, or complete editions, available in many other languages. The full English edition has concentrated mainly on Science and Technology as most UDC users are chiefly interested in these subjects or an important branch of them.

196. *Main Features.* It must be stressed that UDC is a practical classification, based on the demands of specific and complex documents rather than on the framework of any philosophical system. Its attempts to cope with the exact classification of pamphlets, periodical articles, etc., mean that its notation must sometimes be complicated. The student must always remember that this notation is designed for the arrangement of entries in catalogues and bibliographies rather than for the spines of books. UDC is of tremendous historical importance as a scheme developed on an international scale for international use and as the first system of classification devoted to the task which we now call information retrieval. It lays more stress on the detailed specification of each document's subject than on the achievement of a filing order of the optimum helpfulness for a classified catalogue, but recognises that both problems are important. From the first DC was expanded considerably and certain notational extras were provided to reveal such aspects of a work as the period of time covered, the language in which the document is written, or the fact that the work in question deals with two or more topics or with one subject's relations with another.

197. The choice of the DC as a basis for the new classification was a notable one in view of the antipathy to the system in French-speaking countries and the ascendancy of the system of Brunet. The wisdom of this decision is still warmly debated; the instrument was certainly there to hand, although in its existing form it might be inadequate. The universality of the significance of decimal numbers plus the achievement of the early editions of DC must have been decisive. Yet Savage has suggested that this choice 'heavily mortgaged' the future of UDC and several other writers have suggested that it is folly to attempt to build a system for the exact classification of scientific literature on an unscientific basis.

198. The decision having been made, and permission having been received, to base UDC on DC, the earlier classification system as a whole was taken and examined critically by a number of specialists, who 'completed, amended, rehandled, according to the necessities of their specialities', while preserving the general order and character of the Dewey original. The title of the second edition indicates well the full scope and purpose of the derived classification: *Classification Décimale Universelle: tables de classification pour les bibliographies, bibliothèques, archives, administrations, publications,*

brevets, musées et ensembles d'objets pour toutes les espèces de documentation en général et pour les collections de toute nature.

While the general order and nomenclature of DC have been preserved, the possibilities of the notation have been explored effectively. Two kinds of numbers have been employed: (1) the simple decimal numbers with which we are familiar in Dewey, which form the notation of the main tables; and (2) compound numbers, consisting of the main table numbers combined with other main table numbers and, where desirable, with signs from the auxiliary tables provided. The latter are not used if the specific classing can be accomplished by means of the numbers in the main tables.

199. Although the main tables are based on those of Dewey, they have had from the start certain distinctive features. Thus, to single out an example, Dewey's 930–999 disappeared from the main tables, and the numbers omitted – i.e., the figures after the initial 9 – were relegated to a separate geographical table in which the numbers after the 9 were written in parentheses (3–9). In the treatment of the class, all History was arranged in one sequence under 9 and all Geography and Travel under 91, the local number being given in parentheses. Thus we had this perfectly parallel arrangement:

9 (42) History of England	91 (42) Description of England
9 (73) History of the United States	91 (73) Description of the United States

and so on for all countries. Later, however, the desirability of using 913–919 for geographical marking of topography, description and geography itself, was recognised, and these numbers were restored. The geographical special table (3–9) is, as we shall see, still used for the sub-division of other subjects. More important than experimental changes of this kind is the gradual divergence between the main divisions of DC and UDC. The latter scheme has found it necessary to rearrange and reallocate many of the broad departments of knowledge as shown in the Decimal Classification, as G. A. Lloyd[1] has indicated. This divergence has been noticeable from the late nineteen twenties onwards and is understandable, as UDC must try to provide an arrangement suitable for the reliable classification of a host of varied documents in numerous special libraries throughout the world.

[1] *Comparison of DC and UDC at a minimum 3 figure level.* The Hague, 1960.

200. *Notation.* In the main tables the 'three figure minimum' method of writing numbers which is invariable in DC is abandoned for the logical contracted form. Thus class 5 Science and class 54 Chemistry are so written and not 500 and 540 as in the original. This sets free the zeros for use in the special system of common sub-divisions which are such a distinctive feature of this classification. How far and in what manner sub-division goes can be seen from a section of a science subject, External Geodynamics:

551.3	External Geodynamics
551.31	Terrestrial formations and phenomena
551.311	Sub-aerial and continental erosion
551.311.1	Facies, phenomena and erosion due to the action of temperature
551.311.11	Phenomena due to action of cold
551.311.12	Glaciers
551.311.121	Nature and origin of glaciers
etc.	

This example also serves to illustrate the special use of the decimal point, which is placed after every three figures and is merely to help the eye to read the notation. Such minute division may also be helpful to general libraries using DC in that it may help them to define some of the headings in that scheme.

201. The other essential and almost unique features of the notation will be discussed under the heading of *Synthesis*. But the student should note that UDC has attempted in many ways to increase the flexibility of decimal notations; it has, for example, shown great interest in Ranganathan's idea of the Octave Device to secure greater hospitality in array. The scheme also employs what has been called the *Centesimal Device* to lengthen arrays where nine divisions are quite inadequate. This means that instead of using the digits 1–9 to represent co-ordinate topics the digits 11–99 must be adopted for this purpose.

202. *Synthesis and Mnemonics.* The scheme has a most powerful synthetic apparatus available in a series of auxiliary tables which may be regarded as a detailed development of the notions contained in DC's standard sub-divisions and area table. These auxiliary tables are supported by a series of signs of combination and abbreviation. The full range of the synthetic devices is as follows:

Symbol	Name	Significance
+	Plus sign	Document deals with two topics
/	to	Document covers several consecutive topics in the scheme
0/9	Plain UDC number	Numbers in Main Tables
:	Colon	Document deals with the relationship between two subject fields
[ ]	Square brackets	Similar to the use of the Colon sign
=	Equals sign	Indicates the language in which a a document appears
(o)	Brackets o	Form sub-divisions
(1/9)	Parenthesis	Covers place sub-divisions
(=)	Equals sign within parenthesis	Covers sub-divisions denoting race
" "	Inverted Commas	Indicates time sub-divisions
A–Z	Alphabetical order	To be used when needed for final arrangement
.00	Point double zero	Common auxiliary division of standpoints and points of view.
-	Hyphen	Used in certain parts of the UDC to introduce special analytical sub-divisions
.0	Point zero	
'	Apostrophe	(See B.S. 1000A: 1961 pp. 10 and 25)

203. These do not all represent synthesis in the truest sense of the word; the use of final alphabetical order, for example, can hardly be described as a synthetic device. But the full range of the signs and auxiliary tables[1] does provide the UDC with an extra dimension for the analysis of documents in bibliographies, catalogues and abstracting services. Each of the signs, therefore, deserves further explanation. The plus sign is used when a work joins subject matter of about equal interest from two classes; for example, 662+669 is the combination for Mining and Metallurgy. Its use is chiefly in the catalogue, for of course in shelving books the work can go only under the first of these numbers. The oblique stroke / is a connective symbol which is used to mark the fact that such a sequence as 592/599 indicates a document covering Systematic Zoology. It is an expedient to save writing 592 + 593 + 594, etc., to 599. In filing entries arranged by UDC, a number followed by a plus would file before the same number followed by a stroke; we would then have

---

[1] We have given these auxiliary devices in the approved filing order.

the main table number alone without any synthetic attachments. Next in sequence comes the colon which, to use modern terminology, enables many multi-phased subjects to be accurately specified. Thus agricultural statistics are 31:63 in the library where statistics is the main interest, but if agriculture is predominant, the class-mark may be written 63:31. In a classified catalogue entries could be made under both topics. The square brackets are used instead of the colon on rare occasions; they are only required when the relationship between two subject fields involves one of the topics in a role which is definitely a subordinate one. Thus if, in a technical library, we classified Scientific education as 5[37], this would indicate that we did not wish to reverse the relationship in the catalogue as we considered that education was the subordinate subject on this occasion.

204. The equals sign for languages is very important; it will often be employed in documentation. It virtually replaces the 4, Language, of the Main Tables, e.g., = 2 works in English, = 3 in German. Modern languages in general are represented in the appropriate table by = 083, and artificial languages by = 089; the other languages are as in Class 4. The form sub-divisions correspond to the standard sub-divisions of DC, but are always placed in parentheses. Thus 53(03) is a Dictionary of Physics, 53(09) a History of Physics. In addition to the employment of the DC numbers in this way, ingenious developments and extensions have been made. Thus a novel dealing with socialism could go at 335 (0:823). Within brackets also go the numbers from the auxiliary table dealing with geographical areas. These are distinguished from the form divisions in that they are never introduced by a zero. The geographical divisions are based on the numbers from DC's 900 class, with extensions. Thus 385(4) denotes European railways, 385(42) Railways in England and Wales, 385(73) Railways in the U.S.A. The Race numbers operate in very similar fashion except that they are distinguished by an equals sign within the parentheses. Thus (= 95), for example, would stand for the Mongolian peoples.

205. The inverted commas as the time symbol is used to indicate the period covered by a work or, less frequently, the date at which it appeared. Examples of use are 62 "18" (05) a periodical on nineteenth century engineering, 62 (05) "18" a periodical on engineering published in the nineteenth century. The classifier can be much more specific than this with the auxiliary table for time if he so

wishes. Years, months and days can all be shown in logical sequence; thus "1906.12.25" stands for Christmas Day, 1906. Centuries are indicated by the use of two and three figures, as '03' the fourth century A.D. Dates B.C. have the minus sign prefixed, e.g., '–55' the year 55 B.C. There are also many other sub-divisions of time, as seasons, months, days, hours, and even minutes; we can also use numbers for concepts such as sunrise – '414.21'.

206. The A–Z division simply indicates the use of a letter in the notation to allow an alphabetic arrangement of subjects already specifically classed, or for making alphabetic sub-classes in such cases as chemical elements, or in popular subject fields where it is thought to be convenient. More interesting is the auxiliary table for viewpoints introduced by a double zero. This table can be used throughout the schedules where necessary and can often be taken up with great profit. To take a few examples from it; .001 represents the theoretical point of view, .007 (a useful mnemonic, perhaps, for some students) the staff viewpoint, .009 the moral point of view. Lastly we may briefly add that the hyphen and .0 are used in many places to provide special extra specialized subdivisions of a subject; the .0 cannot be confused with the common divisions of form as the latter always appear in parentheses.

207. At first view these remarkable symbols and tables give a sense of bewilderment, but their apparent complexity dissolves to some extent when we remember the simple rule that they are never used unless the matter to be classified cannot be marked suitably from the main tables. The symbols and auxiliary tables are thus optional but those who employ the scheme regularly acquire a remarkable dexterity in their use, and they have that logical intricacy which makes them a joy to certain types of scientific mind. We would again counsel our reader to remember that libraries, as such, were only incidentally in the mind of the UDC designers; minute indexing on an illimitable and infinitely expansible scale was sought, and has been achieved. We have listed these symbols in the order in which they are to be used, if required; an equally formidable problem is that of deciding upon the combination order if two or more of the auxiliary symbols are needed in conjunction with the classification of one document. Here the above order, which tries to follow an approximate sequence from the more general to the more special of the auxiliary signs and tables, will not be a completely adequate guide. We find indeed that the combination sequence is

approximately the reverse of the filing sequence. That is to say that, while a number from the auxiliary schedules for geographical areas will file before a number from the points of view table, the latter will come first if the two are to be used in any one example. This is, in fact, an important principle in faceted classification and is fully discussed in Chapter 24. But in UDC we find that the principle is not fully and clearly recognised and the ruling that the citation order of elements in a compound number is the reverse of the filing order of those elements must be followed with some discretion in this scheme.

208. It is clear from the above that the scheme is far more synthetic than either DC or SC, despite the extensive use, in the latter, of numbers from the Categorical Tables to build up class-marks. The series of auxiliary tables, each with its own distinctive method of introduction, also have considerable memory value; the languages are constantly denoted by the same number after the equals sign, the countries are constantly represented by the same number within parentheses, the time periods are continually represented by appropriate symbols, and so on. Yet these tables and the special signs used naturally add to the complexity of the scheme's notation and were severely criticized by Bliss.

209. *Index.* The indexes to UDC are of the relative kind and are highly satisfactory. The one most likely to be encountered by British librarians and students of librarianship is that of British Standard 1000A. This has over 20,000 entries including details of numbers from the auxiliary schdules. We are often referred in a helpful manner from one part of the index to another related heading. There is the usual omission of personal names and the customary, and thoroughly understandable, warning regarding the folly of attempting to use the index as more than merely a key to the classified schedules.

210. *Use and Revision of the scheme.* The use of the scheme is widespread and increases. It is estimated that there are now over 5,000 users; these include, in addition to special libraries, many libraries in colleges of advanced technology, and also many journals and abstracting and indexing services in the sciences. Among the latter we may note, for example, *Building Science, Bulletin of the Institution of Mining and Metallurgy, Electrical Engineering Abstracts, Philips Technical Review,* the *Russian Journal of Inorganic Chemistry* and the *Russian Journal of Physical Chemistry.* The last two of these

titles are published by the Chemical Society in Britain and represent cover to cover translations of Russian journals. The system is also used to classify British Standards and United Kingdom Atomic Energy Authority reports as they are published and is employed by many technical organizations in Britain, such as the Cement and Concrete Association.[1] The success of the scheme in this country owes much to the tireless endeavour of the late Dr S. C. Bradford of the Science Museum Library, who did much to produce the first edition of British Standard 1000A and who praised and recommended the scheme most highly in his *Documentation*. But, indeed, it is very popular in many European countries.

211. The revision policy of UDC is, on the whole extremely good, although necessarily very slow. The full editions in the various languages make steady, if unspectacular, progress; the quality of the abridged versions is quite commendable. In English, for example, we find that the full schedules have been published for such classes as 5, 621.3, 622/623, 669, 678/679, and 69. In addition to the work of the British Standards Institution, various other interested bodies have helped in the production of appropriate schedules; the British Iron and Steel Research Association, for example, put in a great deal of work on the schedules of Class 669 Metallurgy, and the United Kingdom Atomic Energy Authority and the International Atomic Energy Agency have devoted a great deal of effort to the production of schedules for Nuclear Science. The parts of the full edition in English which at present exist are mainly devoted to the sciences, but the abridgement is quite detailed, especially if the full synthetic apparatus is utilised; a special library might well use the relevant part of the full edition for its main sphere of interest and rely on the abridgement for topics of marginal interest.

212. On an international scale, revision is carried out by the various national committees and users are informed of change and expansion in the publication *Extensions and Corrections to the UDC* which appears every six months. Information also appears at times in the *F.I.D. News Bulletin*. Those who take an active interest in revision work will scan the so-called *P notes* which are circulated for comment and which indicate proposals for development or for the recasting of certain schedules. An interesting feature of the long-term revision policy of the scheme lies in the idea known

[1] The reader should consult the list of users given in B.S.1000C : 1963.

as revision by starvation. This means that if a topic is badly located it can be transferred to a more suitable part of the classification and the old number can be starved of material for at least ten years. After this period has elapsed, it is considered that the association of the subject with the old number will be extremely tenuous and the number can thus be set free to be used if need be with a different significance. This idea has been criticised, but is certainly not without merit; interesting parallels can be found in walks of life quite remote from librarianship and documentation.[1]

213. From time to time proposals for radical reconstruction and drastic revision of the schedules are contemplated. The UDC has always been more ready than DC to consider widespread change and reorganization and at one time it was hoped that the whole scheme could be reconstructed to give it that modernity and scientific basis which new users demanded.[2] This idea has virtually been abandoned, but there are still plans for drastic revision. Among these is the proposal to transfer the divisions of Class 4 Language to Class 8 Literature so that the former can help to relieve the over-crowding in Classes 5 and 6 and can act as a bridge between the sciences and the humanities. In all this the F.I.D. strives to heed the sometimes contradictory advice of many voices: the opinion of the various national committees, the opinions of individual users who have employed the scheme for years, the demands of potential new users. As the third edition of British Standard 1000A points out: 'In revision conflicting tendencies are inevitable: the older estab-lished users, having built up extensive UDC catalogues over the years tend to resist changes, whilst the newer and prospective ones . . . are often anxious for drastic rearrangement'.

214. Despite these problems the scheme thrives; the thorough-ness and value of the revision tends to compensate for the time lag in introducing changes; the latter is very much a by-product of the fact that the scheme is truly an international classification. In Russia its use in scientific and technical libraries is now compulsory;[3] in the United States the national committee has recommended the use of a computer to speed up the revision of the scheme. The fact that so many organizations do make positive recommendations and contributions is a high testimony to the scheme's success. In some

---

[1] For example, J. A. T. Robinson, *Honest to God and the Debate*, 1963, pp. 7–8.
[2] See W. H. Phillips, *Primer of book classification*, 5th edn. 1961. Appendix 2.
[3] See *American Documentation*, July, 1964, p. 226.

fields it is not used alone but in conjunction with other systems. The best example of this can be seen in the way it has been combined with the Swedish *Samarbetskommitten för Byggnadsfragor* (*SfB*) scheme for architecture and building. Here the SfB schedules have been published along with the relevent classes of UDC and the integration may well prove extremely useful to those engaged in classification in this sphere.

215. *Conclusion.* U.D.C. is extremely important as the most international of the general schemes which we have at present and as a classification which, through the use of the auxiliary tables and signs, may be regarded as the first multi-dimensional classification. It is also, of the living general classifications, the older scheme which exhibits to the highest degree many of the ideas which are now engaging the attention of those involved in classification research. It is, of course, intended for documentation rather than for the book stock of a library and its somewhat unscientific structure is a great handicap; that is, most of the arguments concerning helpful order which apply to DC obviously apply also to its extension. The editors of the English edition, in their general introduction, have countered with the assertion that, although many classifications have been evolved to satisfy the ideal criterion that the order of the sequence of classes should correspond with the logical order of the concepts represented, the rapidity with which such attempts have lapsed shows the assumption to be false and the ideal illusory. This is going too far, as there is no evidence that any scheme accurately and entirely based upon the logical order of concepts has really been made and, this being so, it can hardly have lapsed. More acceptable is the statement that 'classifications which have initially been designed to meet a specific purpose are nearly always found to have a reasonably logical sequence ... The success of the DC in its original and modified form is a testimony to the qualities inherent in its structural order. It is easy to devise alternative arrangements for the main classes, but any alternative yet devised is equally open to adverse criticism in regard to its class arrangement if a suitable standpoint be selected'. Undue stress therefore is not laid on any theory of relative collocation of the main classes, as such theories are usually biased and change and, in any case, a classification is necessarily restricted in the extent to which it can represent closeness of association of groups, whereas the human mind is not so limited. There is, of course, the fact, as Bliss has shown, that what were

subordinate classes in the old classification order may in time become as important as the classes to which they were formerly subordinated, for example, psychology in relation to philosophy; but, as the UDC introduction argues, 'it is impossible to legislate for posterity in this respect', and in practice it is certainly quite impossible to redistribute the symbols at a later date merely in order to satisfy the condition that the brevity of a symbol shall specify accurately the importance of the subject represented.

216. The outstanding arguments in favour of the use of UDC in special libraries and information bureaux are based on its flexibility, the international significance of its notation, and the fact that it is used already by many other such libraries and by several technical publications. If we may quote again from B.S.1000A: 'UDC is particularly valuable where exchangeability of references is required, as in the joint issue of abstracts or information bulletins by a group of technical organizations, or the distribution of classified index cards through a specialised international centre'. In this country, the fact that it is accepted as a British Standard tells heavily with many industrial librarians, for standards are widely used in industry and all new standards are published with the appropriate UDC number; the work and enthusiasm of certain great British librarians, particularly Bradford, has also promoted its use.

217. Yet UDC certainly has faults. Users complain from time to time about faulty order, poor notational allocation or slow revision. Another fault is that it is often difficult to place a comprehensive work dealing with *all* aspects of a theme such as 'Copper' or 'Water'; the 'one-place' idea of SC is certainly more useful for coping with such items than either DC or UDC have been in the past. In a stimulating article,[1] Miss Kyle suggests that the scheme cannot be recommended to new users wanting a modern organization of knowledge; she argues that drastic changes such as reduction of the links with DC, the re-examination of the present revision machinery, and the gradual use of the alphabet in notation, might give UDC a new lease of life. The once greatest advocate of the system, the late Donker Duyvis, points out how much Ranganathan's principles owe to UDC. This is true but, as Ranganathan points out, the older scheme 'did not go the whole hog' in redesigning the nature of bibliographical classifications and he suggests that the 'new attachments were so

[1] B. Kyle. The UDC: present position and future developments, *Unesco Bulletin for Libraries*, March/April, 1961, pp. 53–64.

attractively elastic as to hide the rigidity of the Decimal Classification which it had indolently adopted as a readily available core'. There can be no doubt that, despite the provision of extensive synthetic apparatus through the auxiliary signs and tables, UDC retains the structure of the enumerative type of classification in many ways and this can be a severe handicap. As an international standard the system will not be easily replaced, but several writers think that it must be revised and developed more extensively and quickly if it is to survive the challenge of the newer systems of organization for specialised libraries and that its notation would need to be remodelled if it was to be developed as a scheme to be used in conjunction with the machine searching of literature. Vickery,[1] for example, writes 'a thorough survey of the technology schedules is needed, to pick out sections in which facet analysis can usefully be applied . . . Its size and universality will not save UDC if it is unable to advance with science and technology'.

218. But without entering further here into the great controversy of whether UDC is, or is not, the best answer to the problem of organizing knowledge on an international scale and at the documentation level, we may say that the ultimate value of the system, as compared with orthodox Dewey, lies in its fineness of specification. It is qualified as few schemes are to assemble, sort and identify the most minute material, to show subjects in all forms, physical and intrinsic, in all languages, of all times, and in all aspects. The expedients enumerated go beyond what is normally economically usable for shelf classification but, when all the adverse criticism has been seriously considered, it cannot be denied that, so far at least, the UDC has often proved a magnificent analytic and synthetic filing and indexing apparatus for bibliographies, business correspondence and the more detailed documents, notes and reports of the special library world.

[1] The Universal Decimal Classification and Technical Information Indexing, *Unesco Bulletin for Libraries*, May–June, 1961, pp. 126–38.

CHAPTER FIFTEEN

The Library of Congress Classification

219. *Introduction*. For ninety-seven years after its foundation in 1800, the Library of Congress was housed in the Capitol at Washington; and at the end of this period, as may be readily supposed, its collections exceeded by far the space there available. It came into its new and magnificent home in 1897, a separate building of ample and handsome proportions having the orthodox huge domed reading room, something resembling that of Panizzi at the British Museum, and ample space for marshalling the various divisions of the stock and correlating their contents, which consisted of about one and a half million volumes and pieces, with annual accessions approximating to over one hundred thousand. The first four years in the new building were years of organizing work of the first order. They saw, to quote the *deus ex machina*, Dr Herbert Putnam, 'the collections, formerly indiscriminate, divided into certain main groups and in large part arranged and digested; most of these groups conveniently located; and the physical equipment and personal service appropriate to each determined, and in part provided. They have seen determined also, and initiated into each group, a system of classification which not merely recognises present contents but provides elastically for future development; and catalogues which, also elastic, when brought to date will exhibit adequately the collections as they stand and be capable of expansion without revision'.[1] They saw, too, the establishment of the Library of Congress printed catalogue card, a standard card which could be obtained by other libraries, and which made the Library the greatest bureau for the distribution of catalogue entries in the world; and, by combination of architecture, cataloguing, classification and an

[1] *Report of the Librarian of Congress for the Fiscal Year ending 30 June 1961*, p. 5.

ingenious and effective book-carrier system, the most rapid book service in any national or other large library came into being at Washington. We are, of course, only concerned with one factor in this remarkable result, the book classification which came into existence during these four years.

220. It might have been expected that the Library of Congress would have adopted either DC or Cutter's Expansive Classification, when the decision was made to abandon the Jeffersonian system employed in the nineteenth century and to reclassify according to a more practical and flexible arrangement. No doubt the idea was carefully considered; however, the circumstances of the library were thought to require special treatment and an independent classification was determined upon and gradually constructed. Its design was governed from the first by the actual and probable content of the Library. This last statement is important, because no other general system has been based upon the actual review and individual examination of such a large and representative collection of books. The comment of one writer that 'classification has preceded notation' means much more than the words seem to imply. All schemes have taken their rise from a collection of books large or small, augmented by the classificationist's knowledge of other books. These were classified first and the schedules made afterwards. But owing to the comparative smallness of the basic collection of books it is fair to say, in these other cases, that their structural plans bear the impress of that limitation, and their notations were constructed before the systems were applied to the great mass of books to be found in the larger libraries. In the case of LC all the books had their places in the schemes before the notation was constructed. The comment quoted does not mean that the staff started the great task of classifying the Library of Congress without having first made a general plan; but it does mean that the plan was sufficiently fluid to permit of reconstruction when experience gained in the preliminary stages of arrangement demanded a reconsideration of the original design.

221. *Main Features*. It must be stressed that this classification is essentially a team product and that, in many ways, it is best thought of as a co-ordinated series of special classifications. Each major class is published separately and is virtually independent of the others, having, for example, its own form and geographical divisions and index. The classes formulated have largely been influenced by the

Library of Congress building and by the needs of the various subject departments which it houses. The outline of LC was not published until 1904 although, as Keith Davison points out in his booklet on our subject, Class Z had appeared at a slightly earlier date; the scheme had thus been maturing for some five years. A comparison of the original edition of the outline with the latest version, indicates that several changes have since been made. One class – Religion – has been completely remodelled during the twentieth century; some subdivisions have been transferred to other classes and important adjustments have been made to other divisions of the class. Such changes as these are demanded by the expanding collections. In the *Report of the Librarian* for 1901 Dr Putnam explained that 'The system of classification thus far applied is one devised from a comparison of existing schemes (including the "decimal" and the "expansive") and a consideration of the particular conditions of this Library, the character of its present and probable collections and its probable use. It is assumed that the departments of history, political and social science, and certain others, will be unusually large. It is assumed that investigators will be more freely admitted to the shelves'. It is clear, from a comparison of the two schemes, that the books in the Congress Library were first arranged in class groups corresponding to Cutter's Expansive system and this structural basis has been largely maintained in the final scheme. Yet it must again be stressed that the Congress approach is essentially a practical one; if, at times, it leans heavily on Cutter's ideas, it makes no claims at all to follow a 'scientific' or 'evolutionary' sequence; indeed LC deviates, when necessary, from Cutter's notions quite readily in order to serve the special needs of the vast Congress collections.

222. Hints as to the general procedure followed by the team of classifiers are given in the prefaces to several of the published classes. These make it clear that the whole enterprise has been aimed at producing a scheme which is 'tailor-made' for the Congress stock, the work being done in these years of initiation under the direction of the chief classifier, Charles Martel, and ultimately under the supervision of Putnam himself. The classification as originally founded has been recast, when circumstances so demanded, in the light of experience. It has always been extended and remodelled with the actual books of the Congress Library under consideration. It is doubtful if any other bibliographical system has been subjected

to such rigorous criticism and careful review. That is what is meant when it is stated that 'Classification has preceded notation'. A glance at the outline of LC on the folding chart, at the beginning of this chapter, will show that this is not as arbitrary as some critics would have us believe. If we regard books and book usage as the deciding factor in our major groupings we have to admit that the sequence, although it makes no claim to be logical or scientific, does group related bibliographical material most effectively.

223. The fact that there is much to be said for the order of LC from the bibliographical point of view has resulted in the classification being praised by Hulme, Metcalfe, and others as the one widely used system which is based on the literary warrant of the library which it primarily serves. Other schemes have been made, of course, with the existing bookstocks of libraries in mind; yet no other general scheme that has been widely applied has actually been moulded and shaped so closely by the literature housed in a national library. The theoretical approach, whereby we map out knowledge first of all and then adapt the resulting map to meet the needs of books, was positively rejected in favour of a gradual building up of a classification which consistently regarded the character and use made of books in the Congress Library. Dr Putnam has stated: 'The system devised has not sought to follow strictly the scientific order of subjects. It has sought rather convenient sequences of the various groups, considering them as *groups of books*, not as groups of mere subjects'. The words which we have placed in italics are important, since this is just what Hulme meant when he first formulated the idea known as *literary warrant* in 1911. Putnam's words indicate that the way in which knowledge is presented in books should be paramount in a bibliographical classification.

224. The original outline of the Congress system has since been developed with great minuteness; and the method of that development cannot be exhibited by mere description. We note particularly the enormous amount of space given to American history, to the Social Sciences and to Language and Literature. Classes A and B present little deviation from earlier schemes in their context, but one novelty in each is worth mentioning. AZ is the general history of knowledge and learning, and this scheme is the first to provide a place for such general works on the history of scholarship. In B, the finely conceived Psychology and Metapsychology section deserves close attention. C is general history and biography and introduces

the historical classes proper, D, E, and F. Class G comprises Geography, Anthropology, Folklore, Manners and Customs, and Sports and Amusements. The inclusion of recreative arts here is unusual and noteworthy. The class acts as a link, by way of culture and customs, between the historical and social sciences. H to L are the important classes dealing with the political and social sciences. Of these, the arrangement of J Political Science may here be glanced at. It affords a 'national' method of grouping (familiar in the treatment of literature), conjoined with a chronological development, in complete contrast to the 'topical' method so familiar to users of DC. Classes M Music and N Fine Arts call for no comment, except that Landscape Gardening is omitted from the latter and appears as a division of Agriculture at SB. P Language and Literature is an excellent example of LC's insistence on practical convenience in arrangement; the major literatures are clearly defined and in almost all circumstances there is a wise preference for chronological division immediately after the division by languages. This helps to keep together the texts of a versatile writer.

225. Class Q Science is a strange companion for Literature; it follows the arrangement of the Decimal Class 500, but with the already quoted exclusion of Anthropology. R Medicine and S Agriculture are fairly orthodox, although the latter includes Hunting and Angling. The great class T Technology divides logically into four groups: Engineering and Building, Mechanical, Chemical, and Composite, respectively. The scheme is rounded off by Military and Naval Science at U and V – they merit separate classes in a system of this character – and by Z Bibliography and Library Science. This class might as well go first as last; it is comprehensive in character, serving the Library of Congress well, no doubt, although it is not particularly well developed; the letter notation here differs from the character of that in the rest of the scheme and the original notation was so closely numbered that the latter day expansion of library science has resulted in considerable recourse to decimal sub-division.

226. The student should study the classification and not be content with a necessarily cursory description of this kind. He will find that LC is a very detailed scheme; this is only to be expected of a classification designed for a national library of such size. It must also be pointed out that the scheme was really only made with the Congress collections in view; that is to say, it is not a system for

universal use like DC or UDC. Many other librarians have found it worth while to employ the system in its original or in an adapted form; nevertheless, it should be remembered that it should be chiefly assessed according to its efficiency in arranging the stock of the Library of Congress for this is far and away its primary task. It would appear to be extremely satisfactory in this all-important respect. Yet it has more than passing interest to librarians in charge of other large collections, particularly those which are heavily weighted in favour of social science literature.

227. One other feature of the scheme that can be mentioned here is its treatment of biography. This, as we have noted already is a controversial subject to classify in that it may be collected or scattered at suitable locations throughout a scheme. In most classifications an alternative is provided; biography being distributed by subject interest or being collected in either an alphabetical or classified arrangement in a large class based on the 'form' biography. LC is not as liberal as other schemes in this matter; it insists on the distribution of biography by topic whenever feasible. The relatively small biography class, which is placed at CT as an auxiliary of History, accommodates only collected biography and those lives which are too general to be linked with any one subject field. This is an interesting attribute of the system, in that DC, although still allowing an alternative method of arrangement, is favouring the distribution of biography in its seventeenth edition. It is a procedure which offers obvious benefits in a special library or in a large general library which is broken up into subject departments; yet in many of our public lending libraries the idea of keeping all biographies together might well prove more useful to the reader.

228. *Notation.* The LC notation is of the mixed variety and usually employs two letters followed by a maximum of four figures. Sometimes only a single capital letter is employed. Thus main classes are marked with a single letter, as

A	General Works	C	History
B	Philosophy		and so on

Principal divisions are denoted by an added letter, as

BC	Logic	BH	Aesthetics
BD	Metaphysics	BJ	Ethics
BF	Psychology		

and this is the limit to the use of letters in the marking of classes and divisions. The letters I, O, W, X, and Y are not used in the main outline and there are some gaps left also for insertions at this second letter stage. The combination of two letters makes for an excellent and directive symbol for all the great sections of knowledge. It is very useful to be able to direct inquirers to such groups by clear labels. 'You will find books on Painting at ND'; 'Socialism you will find marked HX'; and so on. It is noteworthy that the first completed schedule to be published, Z – Bibliography, is numbered right through without sub-letter divisions and proves highly inconvenient for direction. Further sub-division is secured by the use of arabic numerals read arithmetically, beginning at 1 in each of the main divisions. An example will serve to illustrate this:

TC Hydraulic Engineering	TC 361 Dry-Docks
TC 353 Sea Locks	TC 363 Floating-docks
TC 355 Docks	TC 365 Other special docks
TC 357 Piers, etc.	

The numbering is rarely continuous; even where there is little anticipation of further intercalation one or two places are usually left for future use. Where developments may reasonably be expected the numbering is wide open, and usually there are substantial gaps between the sections.

229. The notation does not end here, however, as one of the outstanding features of the Congress scheme is the frequent use of alphabetical order for the end-topics of a group. Indeed the wide use made by LC of A–Z order by topic within a class, whenever this is the most practical method of arrangement will be gauged from the following examples:

QD Chemistry. Metals	QK Botany
QD 171 General Works	QK 881 Metabolism
172 By groups, A–Z	882 Photosynthesis
	887 Formation of new organic matter
181 Special topics A–Z	891 Respiration
	896 Fermentation
	898 Special Plant Products, A–Z

TL Aeronautics, Airships	TS Manufactures. Leather
TL 650 General Works	TS 1045 Imitation Leathers
654 Special Projects to 1900, A–Z	1047 Special, A–Z
658 Special makes A–Z	
659 Individual ships, A–Z	

This frequent use of alphabetical order by topic is a method which has been highly praised by Metcalfe; obviously the alphabetical order cannot replace the classified one, but it can be used to good effect *within* the classification[1] when there is no obvious systematic order to be adopted. Here it has been used with enterprise and discretion and when employed in this way the method can only be commended; it is one perhaps which might be employed more often with advantage in some other systems. Further sub-division can be obtained in LC, where the gaps between numbers prove inadequate (and alphabetical order of the kind described proves unsuitable) by the use of decimals.

230. Yet the notation of LC has received its fair share of criticism and not without reason. Despite the usefulness of the two letter foundation and the fact that the majority of topics are denoted by a class-mark of two letters and three figures, or less, it is clear that the notation does not show the structure of the scheme and the hierarchy is sometimes difficult to discern clearly from the schedules themselves. It is extremely unfortunate that numbers have been employed in their 'arithmetical' or 'integral' sense rather than as decimals; this means that LC relies heavily on gaps for notational flexibility, although as already pointed out, numbers are *eventually* divided decimally if these gaps prove insufficient. Ranganathan claims that only 'the liberal size of the gaps amidst integers is postponing notational crash'.[2] Elsewhere he repeats this criticism, but softens it by recognising the many great features of the Congress Classification – 'the rigid, integral, notation came in to spoil what would otherwise have been the best scheme in existence, backed up by all the prestige, manpower and resources of the most library-minded government in the world'. While there is much truth in this particular criticism, and the flexibility of decimal rather than integral numerical notations has been proved again and again, one is not impressed with another common objection, that concerning

[1] The student should search for some good examples from the scheme, such as the long A–Z list of industries at HD 8039.

[2] *Philosophy of Library Classification*, 1951, p. 30.

G*

the length of the LC notation. It is not fair to exhibit a few extreme examples which show great length or complexity, for such are rare, although inevitable, in a scheme providing for such minutiae as the Library of Congress houses. Some idea of this specificity may be gained from the consideration of the fact that thirty-one places are provided for editions of a single work of Thomas Paine, *The Rights of Man*, which forms part of a special table on Paine at JC 177. As it stands the system is unlikely to be adopted by libraries other than extensive ones. Yet minuteness of detail need be no deterrent. Nothing is lost because one's library would use only a tenth (or less) of the enumerated places; smaller libraries can reduce the Paine numbers to ordinary proportions.

231. *Synthesis and Mnemonics*. This is by far the most enumerative of the general classification schemes. It does not employ notational synthesis through the use of common form and geographical divisions or their equivalents, nor does it make extensive use of the instruction to 'divide like . . .' followed by a reference to some other parts of the scheme. LC rather attempts to give to each country and subject its own set of geographical and form divisions; thus, instead of a common table, we have numerous sets of such divisions; a list is provided every time one is needed. It has been argued that, for example, a schedule for the Constitutional History of Russia would be quite inappropriate to that of Portugal, that a schedule for the History of Banking could not be made to suit the History of Insurance. This provision of separate sets of form divisions and geographical tables which are peculiar to the needs of particular classes has caused great enlargement of the schedules as compared with other bibliographical schemes. Indeed the bulk of LC is only partly explained by its detail; much of it is due to the tendency to enumerate a special set of sub-divisions for forms and countries each time one is required, rather than providing a single common set that could be used to build up any basic class-mark. On the other hand, the compilers of LC might well defend themselves by drawing our attention to the trouble of devising a set of common sub-divisions which would be comprehensive enough to cover all circumstances and situations which might arise in a classification of such proportions. The examples below will illustrate the individuality of the form and geographical divisions enumerated in the various classes of LC.

EXAMPLE I

HA Statistics	HB Economic Theory	HD Economic History
1 Periodicals	1–9 Periodicals	*Land & Agriculture*
9–11 Congresses	21–29 Congresses	101 Periodicals
13–15 Collections	31–35 Collections	103 Associations
16 Comprehensive	61 Encyclopaedias	105 Congresses
Works	71–74 Method. Utility	113–156 History,
17 Essays	75–125 History	General
19 History	151–195 Theory:	166–279 United States
23 Biography	General	301–1130 Other
29–39 Theory. Method	Works	countries

EXAMPLE 2

H Social Sciences Periodicals	H Social Sciences Societies	H Social Sciences Congresses and Exhibitions
1 American and English	10 International	21 International
3 French	11 American and English	22 American and English
5 German	13 French	23 French
7 Italian	15 German	25 German
8 Other	17 Italian	27 Italian
	19 Other	29 Other

232. This repetition of languages and recurring forms of presentation results in an excessive use of paper; on the other hand, it must sometimes save the classifiers time by avoiding frequent references to auxiliary tables. It must not be thought, however, that number-building is impossible with LC. It does occur, but not through the use of any table of *common* sub-divisions. Each class has its own complicated system of auxiliary tables. A selection of figures from the series of the tables at the end of this huge class H will give some idea of what these are like and how they are applied:

I	II	III	IV		V	VI	VII	VIII	IX	X
(100)	(200)	(300)	(400)		(130)	(200)	(830)	(840)	(420)	(1000)
(1)	(2)	(3)	(4)		(1:4)	(2:5)	(5:10)	(10:20)	(5:10)	(5:10)
42	81	122	161	Europe	44	52	281	251	136	421
43	83	125	165	Great Britain	45–48	54	291	271	141	431
47	91	136	181	Austria–H	49–52	66	331	301	151	471
48	93	139	185	France	53–56	70	341	321	161	481
49	95	142	189	Germany	57–60	75	351	341	171	491

The top line indicates the number of the table.

The second line indicates the *total* of numbers allowed by the table.

The third line indicates the number of divisions allowed to each country.

In the text will be found such a direction as this:

HV Social Pathology
1571–2220 Blind
    By country
1783–1796 United States
1800–2220 Other countries, Table IX
    Under each

(10 numbers)	(5 numbers)	Documents
(1)	(1)	State or Province
(3)		City
(4)	(2)	Associations
(5)	(3)	History
(6)		
(7)		Biography
(8)		Policy
(9)	(4)	By State or Province, A–Z
(10)	(5)	By City, A–Z

To classify a book on the History of the Blind in France the classifier refers to Table IX and finds that France is allotted ten numbers beginning with 161 (Germany is next, commencing at 171). The 161 is added to 1800, making 1961, which is the first of the ten numbers allotted to France. History, as shown by the table in our text, is (5), so that the precise number required is HV 1965. The smaller countries have only five places allotted to them in Table IX, Bulgaria, for instance, is 261–265, so that the History of the Blind in Bulgaria becomes $1800 + 263 = $ HV 2063. Yet even this elaborate system cannot provide for some of the extensions under country headings, and special tables to be applied in the same way, are given in the text. This occurs almost throughout HF Public Finance; similar auxiliary tables are appended to nearly all the classes.

233. In addition there are also special geographical tables alphabetically arranged. These are notably to be found in classes G, H, T, U, and V. We give a simple form:

Abyssinia	A2
Afghanistan	A3
Algeria	A4
Argentine Republic	A7 etc.

These are used after a point for dividing subjects according to the direction in the schedules: 'Local A–Z' or 'by country, A–Z'. The symbols have not a constant meaning; thus in three separate alphabetic tables A8 may mean Australia or Arkansas, A2 may mean Abyssinia or Alabama. To give an example of the application of these, we have at HJ 6082 'Texts in foreign language issued by foreign governments' which is divided as

.A2 British	.A5 Spanish
.A3 French	.A6 –Z Other, A–Z.
.A4 German	

It may be stressed, however, that although methods such as these may seem to loom large in the schedules, they arise comparatively infrequently in practice.

234. We have tried to show here that number-building can be carried out in LC through the use of a series of elaborate auxiliary tables. What the student of classification should realise is that each subject class in the Congress system has its own arrangements of this kind and the tables may vary greatly from class to class. This means that there is a great deal of enumeration of such details and the mnemonic value of the notation is small. For the chief way of introducing mnemonic features in traditional classifications is to have a few tables covering constantly recurring concepts, such as forms of presentation, and to denote each concept continually by the same notational symbols – these give rise to systematic mnemonics. Such common tables are just what LC lacks. However, there are certainly a few literal mnemonics to be found. The Generalia Class, for instance, (modelled on that of Cutter's scheme and extremely orthodox) provides us with some; occasionally they can be discerned in other parts of the scheme. It may be considered also that, from a practical point of view, the frequent use of A–Z order by topic, for final sub-arrangement within a class, is the best memory aiding feature of all. Thus the regularly occurring alphabetical sequences, which are employed whenever systematic order

of helpfulness cannot be discovered, may serve as a partial compensation for the lack of the usual kind of memory aid in the notational symbols.

235. *Index.* Each class is equipped with its own separate index. There is no index to the scheme as a whole, although the Library of Congress Subject Headings List acts, to some extent, as an alphabetical key to the classification in its entirety. The indexes are of the relative variety and a sample of their method must be given; this is taken from the fourth edition of Class T Technology:

Automobiles	TL 1–290
Alcohol	TL 217
Auto-Trucks	TL 230
Automobile Trains	TL 235
Biography	TL 139–140
Catalogues	TL 160, 200–229
Collections	TL 8
Compressed Air	TL 225
Congresses	TL 6
Design, construction	TL 9
Electric	TL 220–223
Endurance Tests	TL 290
Essays	TL 155 etc.

(some twenty more aspects are actually
listed)

Thus great detail in indexing is provided; sometimes indeed the indexes do more work than is necessary for them, duplicating the sequence of the scheme itself by listing details which could easily be ascertained from the classified schedules. The indexes, too, sometimes fail to reveal all the aspects of a subject which the scheme has scattered, especially if these are distributed throughout several classes. In part the schedules themselves compensate for this as they contain some 'see also' references, for example:

S 631–S 667 Fertilisers and soil improvement Cf. HD 9483; TA 710.

On the whole, the very full indexing of LC deserves commendation rather than criticism; when, as it is hoped will be the case, these separate indexes are finally cumulated,[1] the result will be an instrument of very great value.

236. *Use and Revision of the scheme.* The classification, as has been stressed, was really only intended for the Congress Library, but it has also been employed with success elsewhere. It has been part-icularly popular in academic libraries and, in the U.S.A., is a serious challenger to DC for the arrangement of such libraries. It is used by such large American libraries as the University of Yale at Connecticut, the University of Michigan at Ann Arbor, and the University of Chicago and has recently been warmly recommended to medium-sized and large Canadian academic libraries.[2] About a dozen university libraries and one or two special libraries in Britain employ LC in an adapted form. Its use in the National Library of Wales was chiefly due to the advocacy of that great supporter of literary warrant, the late A. J. Hawkes, who had just been appointed as an assistant librarian there in 1912, when it was selected as the classification to be used. It is found necessary, in this great library, to transpose Wales and the United States of America in the schedules, so that the vast amount of space given in LC to the history and geography of the latter are made available for Wales. The scheme, if we are to judge by one comparatively recent account,[3] has been a great success in that library; one can understand this, for the detail and practical emphasis of the tables must benefit most serious students. Other outstanding British users include Edinburgh Public Library and the British Library of Political and Economic Science.

237. The revision is continuous and often more drastic in character than that received by the Decimal Classification. The completion of the scheme with the publication of Class K Law is still awaited, but several other classes have been overhauled and remodelled at frequent intervals. Details of classes so handled are given in the Librarian's annual reports and, as in the case of DC and UDC, there is a periodical publication (Additions and changes to the Library of Congress Classification), which announces coming developments and alterations. By and large, therefore, the policy for the perpetuation of the scheme seems to be an excellent one and its

[1] LaMontagne points out that a start was made on this in 1947. *American Library Classification*, 1961, p. 339.

[2] See the reference, in our bibliography, to Gattinger's article.

[3] G. Walters, Cataloguing in the National Library of Wales, *Library Association Record*, April, 1963, pp. 151-5.

extensions are planned by expert workers with adequate financial backing. These extensions, of course, take into account the growth of the literature in the various classes and the expansion or contraction in importance of various subject fields as this is reflected in the nature of the stock of the Library of Congress. The production of a simple guide to the use of the classification, like those possessed by DC and UDC, would be an additional help to users.

238. *Conclusion.* The theorist, with a determined set of canons for the guiding of his judgement, in considering the Library of Congress Classification, is confronted at the outset by the declared intentions of the designers. These have been modestly stated; far too modestly indeed, when one considers the colossal nature of the task undertaken and the resultant achievement. It was not the first attempt to apply minute systematic classification to a very great library; the late E. A. Nicholson attempted it for additions at the Bodleian. It is the first time however, that a scheme has been gradually built up and published as it advanced. If the results fail in some respects to meet certain critical tests, the achievement is nevertheless undoubted. Conventional theories require that a classification shall be a microcosm of all knowledge, an atlas of the field of learning in which all the territories are clearly defined and their relationships affirmed; but when such theories are applied to book classification they are immediately conditioned by two further considerations – the manner in which knowledge is related in books and the facility with which that knowledge is made available to the users of books. It is the users' point of view that has primarily to be kept in mind, for it is for their benefit that the books are classified. It is for this reason that the searching criticism of the Congress scheme, based on theories of the relationship of the several parts of knowledge, which Bliss has given it in his treatise on *The Organization of Knowledge in Libraries*, seems to fail. It is said that the main classes are not as effectively arranged as those of the Expansive Classification; yet it can also be claimed that some of the changes made by the Congress classifiers in adapting the basis of the EC actually improve the sequence. But the criticism is, in any case, of no great moment, because of the individuality of the classes; each major subject class may be thought of as a library in itself as large as or larger than most other collections of books. The order is usually extremely helpful within the individual classes, despite the rather odd placing of Sports and Games in Class G. Even Bliss is constrained to admit that

the 'six classes Q–V are well grouped and are, for the most part, well sub-divided'. We are inclined to make the same comment of the aesthetic group, M to P. To admit, however, that the scheme in reality is a series of large special classificatons is not a disparagement in view of its immense size and compass. One man designed the general outline and supervised the working out of the schedules, but that working out was accomplished by specialists in the various classes, and in the result they have produced a remarkably cohesive whole.

239. One has to acknowledge the very practical attitude of the team of compilers, resulting in the undeniable fact that this classification is a most important contribution to the wonderfully rapid service of the Library of Congress. Thus, any criticism of the scheme from a theoretical standpoint tends to be corrected by its accomplishment. The classification must really be judged on two distinct counts. As an arrangement for the Congress collections its efficiency is almost beyond question; as a system for use in other libraries, it suffers mainly from the detailed enumeration of topics and lack of synthesis in the conventional sense of the term, but also from the uneven size of its classes, and from the lack of a complete alphabetical index to the classification as a whole. With regard to these points, it may be noted that several libraries find that their adaptation of LC is one which enables an effective classification to be achieved. Yet many libraries would surely find the bulk of certain classes disadvantageous; Class H, for instance, described by LaMontagne as Martel's favourite, accommodates over one sixth of the total stock. The table below[1] reveals this and indicates the size of the other classes:

Material listed during the Fiscal Year 1965
(ending 30th June, 1965)

Class		Titles	Volumes	Total Volumes
A	Polygraphy	818	3,577	256,407
B–BJ	Philosophy	2,770	4,329	98,304
BL–BX	Religion	3,016	4,851	295,764
C	History (auxiliaries)	980	1,736	113,146
D	History (except America)	8,345	13,865	476,557
E–F	American History	3,184	6,064	374,223

[1] These figures include monographs, bound volumes of serials, music scores, and maps and atlases classified in the Map division.

G	Geography	2,385	4,215	147,744
H	Social Science	13,981	27,328	1,217,084
J	Political Science	3,382	9,540	478,011
L	Education	2,792	4,739	262,524
M	Music	8,412	16,194	337,528
N	Fine Arts	1,971	3,306	153,717
P	Language and Literature	21,307	28,346	952,152
Q	Science	7,213	13,652	483,827
R	Medicine	2,412	4,531	200,263
S	Agriculture	1,798	3,603	216,505
T	Technology	8,702	17,367	562,968
U	Military Science	711	1,886	108,532
V	Naval Science	688	1,646	61,087
Z	Bibliography and Librarianship	2,058	6,411	283,983
	Incunabula	nil	nil	445
	Totals	96,925	177,186	7,080,771

The Congress system, therefore, remains an outstanding example of an enumerative classification which may prove successful in some academic libraries or in large libraries devoted to the social sciences, but which is chiefly to be thought of as the classification of one great national library.

240. In that library, the scheme has now, as the table shows, been applied to well over seven million volumes, and the schedules and their indexes occupy more than eight thousand pages. Some conception of its aim and the difficulties involved in its compilation may be gained from the still valid words of the former Chief Classifier, Charles Martel, which are in the nature of an apologia justifying the experiment, but are sufficient to warn librarians with smaller resources from attempts at imitation. 'It has been the endeavour from the beginning to incorporate in the classification scheme the results of the experience gained both in the first application of the schedules in reclassification and in later continued use in classifying new books. A certain ideal was kept in view, but it was a practical one. The ambition was to make the best of an unrivalled opportunity and to produce a classification in which the theory and

history of the subjects as represented in a great collection of books should constitute the principal basis for the construction of the scheme, compared and combined of course with their presentations as derived from other classifications and treatises. It was recognised beforehand and confirmed over and over again in the course of the undertaking that no amount of preliminary study, consultation, and taking pains in the preparation of the provisional draft could produce other than a largely theoretical scheme, more or less inadequate and unsatisfactory until modified in application. A clearer and wider view of many a problem provisionally disposed of would often present itself as class after class was conscientiously worked over, discovering new aspects and relations of certain subjects or the same relations in a different light and making it desirable and sometimes necessary to revise an earlier and adopt a better solution. It may be admitted that with all the effort spent in improving the schemes in the light of further experience, an approach to the ideal in mind has been realised if at all only in a slight and imperfect degree. On the other hand, that degree might have been advanced materially if printing could have been postponed until all the schedules were completed. Many omissions, imperfections, and inconsistencies might have been eliminated if there had been more time. The responsibility for some of these may be laid in part at least upon the hindrances incidental to the conditions under which the work had to be carried out that the other services of the Library might not be unduly interfered with. Whether the principle adopted and the manner and extent of its application were in the line of progress remains perhaps for the future to demonstrate. That the attempt has succeeded in some measure is indicated, I think, by several communications which have reached us from the outside with regard to the classification, in which that element is commended and recognised as more or less distinctive of the Library of Congress system.'[1]

[1] *Report of the Librarian of Congress for the Fiscal Year ending* 30 June 1911, pp. 61-2.

CHAPTER SIXTEEN

The Bibliographic Classification

241. *Introduction*. Woven into the texture of this Manual are many yarns from the loom of that most scholarly of American classificationists, Henry Evelyn Bliss. His own writings include, in addition to BC, the *Organization of Knowledge and the System of the Sciences*, 1929, the *Organization of Knowledge in Libraries*, 2nd edition 1939, and *A System of Bibliographic Classification* (this being an outline of the forthcoming BC) 1935. Yet it is true to say that, if many of his ideas are found here, he also pays due tribute to the teaching of the Manual. He devoted a very large portion of his life to the study of classification, for his early work can be seen in a library journal for 1910 and yet BC was not completed until 1953. His earliest articles, however, all point to a new scheme of classification that he must always have had in mind, which would be based upon a theory of knowledge deduced from long and precise studies of all the methods of organization, as far as they were available to him, that man has used in the ordering of his activities and mental processes. Bliss was born in New York in 1870 and completed his education in the College of the City of New York, in which he became a librarian in 1891. He served there until his retirement in 1940, and during the latter part of the time had been allowed facilities by the College authorities to pursue the studies which have had so important an influence upon librarianship. The record of the life of such a man cannot have been dramatic; indeed Dr Campbell has made us aware of the lonely dedication of Bliss's later years.[1] Yet, in his sixties, Bliss surprised his friends by having published a volume of his poems entitled quite appropriately *Better Late than*

[1] *Library Association Record*, November, 1955, p. 461.

245. The observance of these ideas would, Bliss claimed, result in a system which reflected the requirements of the majority and recognised the general body of agreement which exists about the content of the major subject disciplines and the way in which they are studied and taught – the scientific and educational consensus of opinion, as he termed it. There is much evidence in his scheme of his efforts to arrange material wisely with this 'consensus' or majority viewpoint in mind; on the other hand, some librarians might challenge the idea that the consensus can be recognised in this way or dispute Bliss' assertion that it 'is relatively stable and tends to become more so'.

246. Yet it must be recognised that this striving to conform to the established body of opinion, with regard to the way in which knowledge should be organized, has on the whole been extremely beneficial; BC offers many useful sequences and carefully arranged classes. This leads us on to the consideration of two other important principles – *collocation* and *subordination*. The first of these simply involves the bringing together of closely allied subjects. Bliss's deep study of the earlier schemes of book classification had provided him with many examples of faulty grouping, or collocation, and he was determined to avoid such faults in his own system. Thus in BC we find a careful attempt to bring disciplines which have strong relationships into close proximity. The best example, although certainly not the only one, is seen in Bliss's efforts to collocate certain pure sciences with the appropriate technology. Brown, of course, had thought of this, but had over-worked the idea; usually, it is better to separate pure and applied sciences – there are only a few which merit collocation. Bliss realised this and he links together only those pure and applied sciences which are really likely to be required together by the majority of readers. His efforts to achieve *subordination* in BC can be seen in the way in which he carefully ensures that each specific theme is subordinated to the appropriate general one (which is, in turn, subordinated to a more general one still), and, in a rather more specialised sense, in the idea of *gradation by speciality*, or as it is sometimes called, serial dependence. This means that certain subjects draw upon the findings of others and are, in this sense, more specialised than the disciplines from which they borrow ideas. It is thus argued that, in a classification, the dependent subjects should follow the (often co-ordinate) topics on the findings of which they rely. It is an idea which Bliss derived from

his wide reading of the philosophers, especially the great French writer, Auguste Comte. The theory of Comte determined that such sciences as were simple, self-contained, and complete, preceded and influenced those which were more complex, derivative and dependent; thus astronomy, mathematics and the physical sciences went before the biological and sociological and led finally to his terminus science, morals. The British philosopher Herbert Spencer declared Comte's order to be impossible, yet his own ideas represent it closely. The notion can also be glimpsed in these words of Bertrand Russell:

'We may divide the sciences into three groups: physical, biological and anthropological ... In the anthropological group I include all studies concerned with man: human physiology and psychology (between which no sharp line can be drawn), anthropology, history, sociology and economics. All these studies can be illuminated by considerations drawn from biology ...'[1]

In book classification, and in BC especially, this notion provides us with a principle for determining helpful order, particularly helpful order in array. If two subjects are, roughly speaking, of the same status or rank, the one which borrows from the work of specialists in the other subject field should come after the other in the array.

247. Another prominent principle to be dealt with at this stage is that of *alternative location*. It may be stressed, once again, that this is not the same as *alternative treatment* or arrangement. The latter idea occurs in nearly all schemes for certain topics such as biography; it is recognised in BC in the literature class (where four alternative arrangements are provided) and for biography, of course, and elsewhere. But alternative location is a different matter and is virtually a unique feature of BC. Bliss was anxious to accommodate his scheme to meet the needs of large minority viewpoints within the consensus; he recognised that, for certain subjects there were two or more possible locations in the sequence of classes that were almost equally acceptable. For these the alternative location idea is provided. Photography, for instance, can in BC, be with technology or with the arts; Economic History can be subordinated to general history, but can also go under Economics. Religion is preferred by Bliss at P, where its associations with History and Ethics are

[1] *Icarus: or the Future of Science*, 1926, pp. 8-9.

stressed by contiguity, but another legitimate mode of thought stresses rather the associations with Metaphysics; so AJ is reserved as an alternative place, where Religion may be expanded like class P as given in the schedules. Bibliography and Librarianship may go in class Z, in class J as a branch of education, or may be placed along with generalia material. Another important group of alternatives is concerned with Applied Science and Technology. Bliss gives a preferred arrangement by which the more specialized technologies are subsumed under their parent sciences while the more general are grouped together in class U. However, alternative places are provided for all major technologies; the library applying the scheme can adopt whatever collocation is considered to be best.

248. It will be seen that these alternative locations are for variant placings sanctioned by scholarly authority, but differing from the classificationist's own recommendations. They recognise what Bliss would call the 'relativity of the consensus'. L. A. Burgess, a British admirer of BC has described the idea as playing a prominent role, 'not only in the broad outline, but in detail throughout the schedules'. Clearly a library would need to choose, in each case, one alternative and adhere to this; so that the rejected place(s) would be left blank as far as that library was concerned. Otherwise a form of cross-division would occur; some books on say, photography, would be at one place, others at the alternative location. This must not happen, for the scattering of books which deal with the same subject defeats the whole purpose of classification; what is needed is for each library to select the placings it wants and to ignore alternatives. In practical use, it will only be necessary for the classifier to record decisions; for guiding is so carefully provided throughout the schedules of BC that there is very little danger of confusion. Indeed, by and large, this novel feature, although it means that different libraries using the scheme will not enjoy complete uniformity of practice, is to be commended as a handsome concession to rival, but equally legitimate, schools of thought embraced within the folds of the scientific and educational consensus. It does allow the nature and needs of a particular library to be catered for to a great extent and some of the alternative locations given, together with the alternative treatments supplied in certain classes, solve dilemmas that face all classifiers, whatever scheme they adopt.

249. A list of alternative locations and alternative treatments permitted is given in Table 5 of Volume 1 of BC. The latter,

although not as important as the alternative locations, are worthy of comment. We may illustrate the use of these alternative treatments, or arrangements, from the Literature and Language Classes. Here we find that XP denotes the History of Spanish Literature and XQ the texts on this subject. Four alternative methods are provided for classification of Language and Literature, as illustrated here by sub-classes XP and XQ:

Method I The literature, arranged in one alphabet of authors (in this case at XQ and clearly not further sub-divided except by author's name) is separated from the history, biography and criticism (here at XP) which may be classified historically, by 'form' or otherwise (all by Schedule 5b).

Method II Historical classification throughout (in this case we should use XP only expanded by Schedules 5b and 6).

Method III Advocates method I for modern literature and method II for earlier periods.

Method IV Classification by form and content for the literature; the history, biography and criticism being classified historically. (Thus, in our example, XP would contain history, biography and criticism, expanded by Schedule 5b and XQ would contain the literature grouped by form). We may best illustrate the differences between the methods by classifying the same three books by the four methods in turn. Here they are:

	Method I	*Method II*	*Method III*	*Method IV*
Cervantes Saavedra, M de: Don Quijote	XQ.CER	XPO.CER	XPO.CER	XQG.CER
Blasco-Ibaniez, V: Sangre y arena	XQ.BLA	XPR.BLA	XQ.BLA	XQG.BLA
Roscoe, T: Spanish novelists	XPF	XPF	XPF	XPF

250. Finally we may consider here the BC equivalent to the Generalia Classes of other schemes – the *Anterior Numeral Classes*. These are divisions which precede the subject classes and cater for polytopical works and also for collections of various kinds; they are shown on the folding chart at the beginning of this chapter. Apart from their emphasis on sets and collections, they are the orthodox rejoinder to the General Works class found in DC; they are denoted

by numbers and precede the subject classes which are represented by capital letters. The same numbers can be used at the beginning of each subject class, where they are described as *Anterior Numeral Subdivisions*. Thus 6 denotes periodicals, and journals that are *completely* general in scope must go in Anterior Numeral Class 6; Class G is Zoology, and a magazine on *zoology in general* would be G6 – here the appropriate Anterior Numeral Subdivision is employed.

251. *Notation*. Bliss decided to provide a notation which utilised as its base the whole of the alphabet; further sub-division is also achieved through the use of capital letters. Lower-case letters and numerals are reserved for synthesis which is achieved through the use of a series of systematic auxiliary schedules; the numerals, of course, are also employed for the Anterior Numeral Classes which we have just described. Bliss saw the value of brevity of notation in most circumstances; he justifies his choice of capital letters for his basic notation on the grounds of capacity. He is able to show that, despite a certain amount of wastage arising from the avoidance of odd or awkward combinations of letters, or from unused alternative locations, the letter notation is able to accommodate all major topics with brief distinctive class-marks. To have twenty-six places at each step of division is indeed an advantage; Bliss reinforces this by making no real attempt to consistently reflect the structure of the scheme in his notation and, consequently, he gains extra brevity by methods similar to those illustrated in paragraph 54. He has also apportioned his notation wisely, planning classes and their sub-divisions in relation to the volume of literature, to keep down to modest dimensions the average length of symbol. In short, he has learned a great deal from the faults of the earlier schemes, DC in particular, through his extensive study and criticism of them; in BC, even some quite specific subjects have a notation of no more than three capital letters.

252. *Synthesis and Mnemonics*. In BC, notational synthesis, for the exact classification demanded by documentation, is provided by twenty-two principal Systematic Schedules. Many of these have sub-schedules appended for more detailed expansion, making in all forty-six in the revised list in Table 4 in Volume 3. As in the use of similar tables incorporated into other schemes, symbols from these schedules are added to those denoting the subject of the book; the added symbols give precision to the original placing by introduc-

ing some such consideration as external forms or locality. They can be added without confusion at any stage of sub-division by topic. Actually, only the first four Schedules are of general application; and even these are not equally applicable throughout the main schedules; the remainder are applicable to groups of classes, to single classes, or to sub-classes; but all are mnemonic and consistent throughout their field of use. Bliss indeed claims that these tables for synthesis (his own term is 'composite specification') are 'more special, more mnemonic, and more economical' than DC's ideas of number-building. Schedule 1 is for numerical sub-division (1–9) for considerations of form and closely resembles the group of nine Anterior Numeral Classes. Here is a condensed outline of Schedule 1:

1. *Reference books*, including dictionaries, glossaries, encyclopaedias, indexes, handbooks, atlases, concordances, pocketbooks, etc.

2. *Bibliography*, historical, evaluative, selective. Abstracts.

3. *History*, scope and relation. Books about the subject; its study, profession, organization, etc.

4. *Biography* relevant to the subject.

5. *Documents* and ancillary matter. Institutional and government publications, reports, bulletins, annuals, catalogues, maps, etc.

6. *Periodicals.*

7. *Miscellanies.* Collected or selected writings of several authors, essays, addresses, lectures, readings, symposia, etc.

8. *Study of the subject;* books about it.

9. *Antiquated or superseded books* or other materials or those under a superseded classification.

253. Of the above sub-divisions, Nos. 1, 2 and 6 are *constant* mnemonics, for the subjects which they represent, but the scheme allows for the remainder to be interchanged, if desired, in several possible ways; they are known as *alternative* mnemonics. This may appear a trifle strange to many readers, but we shall soon discover that one of the most characteristic features of this scheme is its

tolerance of modes of thought divergent from that of the author. If the user prefers the items in Schedule 1 in a different order, he is allowed to adopt this. (He will naturally record his decision and apply it consistently). Sub-division by Schedule 1 may be made freely at any point of sub-division. To illustrate at random; we discover from the main schedules that BOR stands for radio telegraphy, BOV stands for broadcasting, and BOY for television. Applying Schedule 1, we get such class-marks as:

BOR	1	Dictionary of wireless terms
BOR	6	'Wireless world'
BOV	3	History of the B.B.C.
BOV	6	'Radio Times'
BOV	8	The art of broadcasting
BOY	4	The life of J. L. Baird

It is worth while, in passing, to compare the length of symbol with that employed in other schemes when form divisions, or their equivalents, are added to basic class-marks.

254. Auxiliary Schedule 2 is for geographical sub-division and employs lower-case letters to represent the various localities. The schedule is used consistently throughout the scheme and is thus mnemonic. Here are a few examples:

FH	fr.	Flora of the Riviera
JCA	e.	Educational research in England
DHI	i.	Volcanoes of Italy

Schedules 3 and 4 are for sub-division by languages and by historical periods respectively; they contain sub-divisions which are represented by capital letters, these being differentiated from the main notation by means of a comma. Schedule 5 is for the sub-division of the philology of any language and its sub-schedules 5a, 5b and 5c are all clearly restricted in application to classes W–Y. Schedule 6 allows for detailed expansion under a particular author, and a similar Schedule, No. 7, allows a like facility in dealing with any personage. However, Schedules 8–22 are all limited in scope to single classes or, in most instances, to sub-classes. Their general character and utility may be illustrated by the case of Schedule 16, by which any religious system or sect (in Class P) may be mnemonically sub-divided by such considerations as: sacred books, ritual, holy places, priesthood, heresies, etc. All such schedules of *limited application* are printed with the tables of the class to which they apply.

255. Clearly the most used of the Systematic Auxiliary Schedules which we have just briefly described will have memory value; their numbers or letters, being continually used to denote recurring forms of presentation, geographical regions, etc., will have mnemonic significance. It is through synthesis, or composite specification as Bliss would call it, that we obtain such systematic mnemonics; these are the most important aid to the librarian's memory in the notation of BC. However, as the scheme relies heavily on letters, an opportunity has been taken to employ the idea of Literal mnemonics. Our examples above from Systematic Schedule 2 illustrate one application of this notion; there are many more. An examination of the schedules will reveal that several topics are denoted by the appropriate alphabetical symbol. In addition to the examples of literal mnemonics from BC given in Chapter 5, the following may be noted:

CD Chemical Dynamics
HB Human Body
HH Human Hygiene
NA North America

These are among the most striking, but there are many more listed in BC's Volume 1 Table 6. Sometimes they take a slightly different form from those given above. Thus Class B is physics and Class C Chemistry, so Physical Chemistry is given the mnemonic class-mark CB. Yet the student must remember our previous warnings and realise that this idea of literal mnemonics, if over-employed would lead to the alphabetical scattering of related themes; Bliss uses them only if the sequence of topics which he prefers permits their employment; they are thus used casually and indeed are sometimes termed *casual* mnemonics.

256. *Index*. A relative index of some 45,000 entries has been provided. It includes names of persons and places, but does not take in the possible extension of the main tables by means of the systematic schedules. Its fullness is indicated by the fact that Banks and Banking has 53 references. Bliss's introduction to the index shows his preoccupation with precision in language (for instance the term *Hunting animals* may mean animals that hunt *or* animals

that are hunted). Not all personal names are entered by any means and, on the whole, despite the care and labour given to its compilation, this index might be regarded as rather disappointing. One British reviewer[1] noticed that certain British place names are given incorrectly, for instance Ransey (*sic*), Isle of Man. One wonders how many errors of this kind a minute scrutiny might reveal. The index certainly locates topics for us and indicates many of the separated aspects of a subject, as the following short extract from it indicates.

Learning (Psychology)	IFI;	IFIB
– abilities (Education)		JQF
– of animals		GFW
– over-learning		IFIW
– process (Educational)		JEI

Yet, although it is certainly not seriously inadequate in any way, one feels that it is also not quite the first-class tool that one would have hoped to find. The emphasis on American terms is understandable, but nevertheless somewhat inconvenient, and the selective listing of the names of monarchs, artists, historical personages, etc., is hardly satisfying in that it would have been better to have listed *all* such names or to have excluded this feature from the index.

257. *Use and Revision.* The classification is used by about 100 libraries in all and has been reasonably popular in college and special libraries in Britain and the Commonwealth. It is used in Britain by such institutions as the National Book League, the Institute of Cancer Research, the Ministry of Health and the University of Lancaster. It can also be found in several education libraries, notably those of Colleges of Education and Institutes of Education.[2] This is hardly surprising, as Education was a subject which especially interested Bliss and his Class J is acknowledged as possibly the best in the scheme. There has, alas, been little or no enthusiasm for BC in the U.S.A. This is in part due perhaps to the natural conservatism of many American librarians, to the tendency of some of them to regard shelf classification as merely a quick locating device and thus to be content with older systems, and to

---

[1] K. C. Harrison in *The Librarian*, May, 1953, pp. 97–9.
[2] Lists of users appear in the *Library Association Record*, 1953–4. New users are announced in the *Bliss Classification Bulletin*.

an understandable reluctance to reclassify a large library which is already reasonably arranged by DC or LC. But it is also due in part to a failure to recognise the merits of Bliss's work, or if one prefers to think of it in another light, to the failure of Bliss and his supporters to build up a large substantial market for his scheme. Bliss had been encouraged by several British writers, by De Grolier, and by Martel and Richardson; yet from the first he met with apathy and even hostility especially from Dewey and DC supporters. This opposition in the U.S.A. was in fact never overcome. BC is used there in the City College, New York, of course, and in at least one special library, but the general lack of enthusiasm is only too clearly apparent. Bliss, more than any other great classificationist, is the prophet without honour in his own country.

258. There is no editorial body to revise this scheme and, with the passage of time, this will become a more and more serious disadvantage. There is indeed no guarantee that a new full edition of the classification will ever be published, although it is hoped that a Schools Edition will be produced very soon and the H. W. Wilson Company have been most co-operative in distributing a *Bliss Classification Bulletin* to interested parties.[1] The lack of revision does not seem to bother some librarians who declare that they can make their own extensions as the need arises, but such steps will eventually lead to serious deviations in practice between the various libraries employing BC. The best hope for the future of the scheme lies in the aforementioned bulletin which has appeared at sporadic intervals but is now a regular annual. Each issue contains some revisions and proposals for extension of certain classes; the latter can be ignored by libraries not requiring extra detail. Thus the September, 1964, issue of the bulletin, for example, gives expansions of the physical sciences based on certain supplementary schedules of the British National Bibliography. But the indifference of many users is a handicap in the production of such a bulletin. Indeed but for the energy and enthusiasm of the editors (D. J. Campbell and, in more recent years, J. Mills) it is doubtful whether it could be compiled.

259. *Conclusion.* The first reactions of librarians when the great work involved in the production of BC was completed were that it had come late in the career of libraries and that, except possibly in developing countries where new general libraries were being created,

[1] This has now been taken over by the British Committee for the Bliss Classification.

there was little prospect of its displacing schemes that had served us for so long if only on the grounds of the great cost of reclassification. The alternative prospect was that in a new world of peace that might be nearer than international indications seemed, and still seem, to promise, there should be much development, many more libraries with new buildings and new ways of regarding their organization; and in such conditions librarians would have at hand in BC a scheme unequalled in completeness, catholicity and scholarship; in the adequacy of the alternatives it provides; the brevity of the notation; the expository value of the introductions and of the notes throughout the schedules and the conscientiously compiled index. An Englishman cannot but recognise the acknowledgement made to his own countrymen for their assistance in the making and enlarging of some of the classes. In reviewing the completed scheme, British librarians (including, in addition to K. C. Harrison, such writers as J. Mills[1] and W. B. Paton[2]) agreed that it survived tests and criticisms with remarkable success and that a veteran philosopher, thinker and master-classificationist had made what was undoubtedly a great gift to library organization. Unfortunately, since 1953, certain faults have come to light. It is now clear that certain classes have not been altered drastically since the first outline in the early part of the century and that there is a falling away in standard in Volume 3 of the schedules and probably in the index also.

260. The critics in the U.S.A. were, from the start, more severe than the British reviewers. A. D. Osborn's review[3] may profitably be contrasted with those mentioned above; in its brevity as well as in its tone, it indicates the prevalent American attitude to Bliss's work. So we find that despite the erudition and adaptability of BC, it has some serious limitations. We would not agree with Metcalfe's assessment that the whole of the scientific and educational consensus is nothing more than a reflection of Bliss's personal ideas, but we must, with regret, record that this, in many ways excellent, scheme has some strange lapses and irritating faults. Many of the systematic schedules are difficult to locate, and the whole scheme is produced in a manner which, from an aesthetic point of view, is certainly unattractive. The full notation, when synthesis is used is often long

---

[1] *Library Association Record*, 1953, pp. 298-300.
[2] *Library Review*, Winter, 1953, pp. 237-8.
[3] *Library Journal*, 1 October 1953, pp. 1623-4. Similar in its conclusions to this review is the one by Mortimer Taube in *College and Research Libraries*.

and clumsy; Bliss introduced his composite specification devices at a comparatively late stage in his classification's development and their use would seem to spoil the simplicity and brevity of the basic notational structure. British enthusiasts informed us in 1953 that this scheme would offer a splendid arrangement in all fields without strain for years to come and that it could safely be recommended for adoption in newly created libraries. These remarks, although understandable at the time, must be modified in retrospect, especially with regard to the dubious revision policy.

261. In so many ways, especially with regard to its scholarly, helpful order and adaptability, this is the best general classification scheme available and is especially good for the social sciences and humanities; but we cannot overlook certain serious faults. In the last decade also, the advances made with faceted classification have dated much of Bliss's work. True, composite specification is, in one sense akin to this, but the systematic schedules have been grafted on in a rather unsatisfactory way and, like the other traditional schemes, BC does not attempt to practise facet analysis clearly; Bliss indeed repudiated this type of terminology altogether. It is difficult, at present, to see what the future holds for the scheme; another edition, produced by British users, could well give it a new lease of life and might stress such ideas as alternative location, while clearing up many of the unsatisfactory features. But, despite the years of labour involved in this classification and the fact that it is undoubtedly superior to DC with regard to the helpful order offered in many classes, it would seem destined to be unsuccessful. It could be that Bliss laboured too long in the realms of theory and in the task of criticizing older schemes; or perhaps his greatest mistake was in failing to realise the need for classifications to be built by a team rather than an individual, for although he did have collaborators, the end product is essentially his own. Whatever the cause it now seems certain that Bliss's system was produced at the end of the period of enumerative classifications – too late to displace DC as the most popular of such systems and too soon to benefit from modern ideas. BC will remain popular in a number of libraries, but if it is to be evaluated as a possible scheme for very widespread use it must be confessed that, probably through no fault of his own, Bliss faltered on the brink of a new era – leaving his classification a hostage to fortune.

(based on the arrangment

I OUTLINE OF MAJOR SUBJECT DISCIPLINES

z	Generalia
1	Universe of Knowledge
2	Library Science
3	Book Science
4	Journalism
A	Natural Sciences
B	Mathematics
C	Physics
D	Engineering
E	Chemistry
F	Technology
G	Biology
H	Geology
HZ	Mining
I	Botany
J	Agriculture
K	Zoology
KZ	Animal Husbandry
L	Medicine
LZ	Pharmacognosy
M	Useful Arts
Δ	Spiritual Experience and Mysticism
N	Fine Arts
O	Literature
P	Linguistics
Q	Religion
R	Philosophy
S	Psychology
Σ	Social Sciences
T	Education
U	Geography
V	History
W	Political Science
X	Economics
Y	Sociology
Z	Law

II EXTRACT FROM THE LIST OF ANTERIORISING COMMON ISOLATES

(Similar to common form divisions of the traditional type of scheme and applicable before the Space facet)

a	Bibliography
c	Concordance
d	Table
e	Formula
f	Atlas
k	Cyclopaedia
m	Periodical
v	History
w	Biography

III EXTRACT FROM COMMON SPAC ISOLATES

4	Asia
5	Europe
53	France
54	Spain and Portugal
55	Germany
56	Great Britain and Ireland
561	England
56121	Surrey
56163	Lancashire
56175	Yorkshire
562	Wales
563	Scotland

IV EXTRACT FROM COMMON TIMI ISOLATES

L	1700 – 1799 AD
M	1800 – 1899 AD
N	1900 – 1999 AD
P	2000 – 2099 AD

Particular years can be specified by the us number after the capital letters.

V

The foci relating to the concepts Personality, and Energy naturally differ greatly from class. In each class, a facet formula is give the foci within each facet are enumerated
For example:
Class K Zoology
Formula – K (P): (E) (2P)

FOCI IN (P)

1	Invertebrata
2	Protozoa
21	Sarcodina, etc

FOCI IN (E) CUM (2P)

lition, Volume 1, 1960)

lass G Biology, with the following
ns:
lation to young ones
urting

MBOLS USED TO LINK PHASES
OMPLEX SUBJECTS
eral phase relationship
s phase
nparison phase
erence phase
uencing phase

XAMPLES OF SOME CLASS-MARKS
INED
43 Memory in adolescent boys
 Personality and Energy facets of Psychology

 Mineral resources of Germany
 from Personality facet in the Geology class
owed by the appropriate focus from the
on Space facet)
8 .56163 'N66 Textile Printing in Lancashire
5
from Personality and Energy facets in the
 Arts class, followed by relevant foci from the
on Space and Time facets)

hat the filing order is the reverse of the facet
ation order. For example, the Time facet
fore the Space facet. Thus
 'N66 Textile Printing in 1966,
 file before the previous example.

les of class-marks obtained for complex
ts:
bYZ
 Economics for Social workers
is an instance involving the bias phase)
gR1
nfluence of logic upon library classification

 is an example involving the influencing

CHAPTER SEVENTEEN

The Colon Classification

262. *Introduction*. Each country in turn seems to produce a distinctive librarian who is the prototype of his profession. Edward Edwards and James Duff Brown in Great Britain, Dewey in America, Graesel in Germany, de Lisle in France, Paul Otlet in Belgium, are examples which come to mind without any thought of slighting their compatriot librarians. India would probably choose Shiyali Ramamrita Ranganathan, born 1892, and recently honoured, in his retirement, as National Research Professor of Library Science. His life indicates a fantastic capacity for sustained effort and a remarkable single-mindedness for the cause of librarianship. After graduation, he lectured in Mathematics in the Government College, Madras, 1917–20, and from then, 1920–23, was assistant professor of mathematics in the Presidency College, Madras. Without prior library experience he was then appointed Librarian of Madras University Library and was sent to England to study methods at the British Museum. There the Director suggested to him the advantages of the University of London School of Librarianship. At the school at that time he found the only subjects which really inspired him were library administration and classification. The original author of this Manual was lecturer in the latter field and gave Ranganathan the advice which he recalls in *Abgila*, 1953, March, page A 141, to read library economy, to work for a month in a public library and, with that experience, to visit different types of libraries. He proved to be a most alert, critical and enquiring student, knowing exactly what he wanted and travelling England for it, as he has travelled much of the world since. He returned to Madras as one with a mission for the improvement and extension of libraries for his people in town and country. He was a founder of

the Madras Library Association and in 1928 delivered a university extension course to nearly one thousand teachers on library science, which led to the founding in the following year of the first Madras Summer School of Library Science. Thereafter for twenty years he combined with his librarianship at the university his headship of the school. The next two years he spent as university librarian and professor of library science at Benares Hindu University; and from 1947–55 he was professor of library science at the University of Delhi, which university bestowed its doctorate upon him as 'the father of librarianship in India'. In his retirement he still continues to develop his ideas on the theory of classification and to write with enthusiasm and vigour on this theme.

263. The need for the development of librarianship in India acted as a tremendous spur to Ranganathan in his younger days. The teacher in him was accompanied by an urge to write of his experiences, experiments and speculations; so much so that he set out apparently to rewrite the whole of librarianship, first in terms of Indian necessities and to instil the library idea into countrymen not well aware of them, and gradually to promulgate his theories on a world basis; he became in consequence the most prolific writer on the subject. He assured his British lecturer that he felt a specially constructed classification was necessary for India and was warned of the long and Herculean labour involved in the construction of a scheme and in the task of keeping it up-to-date. Dewey also tried to dissuade him, pointing out the merits of accepting a system which had been tried and tested, but Ranganathan was undeterred. He felt that the fact that so many libraries made alterations to DC indicated that the scheme was not altogether successful. His Colon scheme was soon in being, was tried out in his own university library, and was published in two slim volumes in 1933. His first substantial book, however, had been his *Five Laws of Library Science*, 1931. Between the first and second editions of CC he read the theoretical writings of Bliss and enunciated his own theory in *Prolegomena to Library Classification*, 1937, in which he expounded twenty-eight Canons of varying importance. In his *Library Classification: fundamentals and procedure*, 1944, he produced an extensive body of classificatory exercises and a number of novel terms, most of which are now part of the standard vocabulary of modern classification theory. Of his other books, we would particularly commend the *Elements of Library Classification;* as a straightforward account of

Ranganathan's work it is best read first by the student who wishes to consult these writings. *Classification and Communication* is a most readable and challenging work, and perhaps the most mature summary of Ranganathan's classificatory labours is given in his *Philosophy of Library Classification*. But there are numerous books and periodical articles from his own pen which seek to explain his distinctive ideas on our subject. CC itself is now in its sixth edition, 1960.

264. Certain fundamental ideas and goals lie behind all Ranganathan's work in the classificatory field and these can be discerned in even the early editions of CC. They include his insistence that bibliographical classification should consistently obey the five laws of library science; the desire to fully express in a class-mark the subject of a book and then to add a distinctive book mark, thus individualising each book in the library; the wish to create a classification which would adhere in uncompromising fashion to definite principles; and the idea that the individual classifier should be given the maximum opportunity to anticipate revision in the published tables of the scheme by constructing his own class-marks for new subjects as these arise. His zeal for the establishment of a helpful, filiatory, order is seen in his rejection of the earlier book classifications and his constant striving to improve his own. CC has many highly distinctive features and consequently the next part of this chapter, which is devoted to a description of these, is necessarily rather long.

265. *Main Features.* CC is not a series of tables setting out, in graduated fashion, a conspectus of the whole universe of thought in a continuous sequence with each subject developed from its broad outline to its most specific parts and with a notation for every subject so listed from the most general to the most minute; it is not, in other words, an enumerative scheme. As our preceding studies have shown, the other classifications have their main tables worked out enumeratively, although most of them provide for notational synthesis and extra detail through systematic and mnemonic schedules which develop and qualify all or some of the subjects in those main tables. Ranganathan, however, has produced an *entirely* synthetic system; every subject is recognised as consisting of a number of basic parts. In each subject discipline, CC lists the appropriate basic parts or isolates and organizes them into categories or facets, each category consisting of those concepts produced by a single characteristic of

division. Class-marks are constructed by the combination of the isolates or foci from the various facets in the order prescribed by the scheme. Several punctuation marks are used to link these foci from the different categories together. The tables are, in Colon language, like the parts of a Meccano set which, by the use of nuts and bolts can be assembled as required for many different constructions. The elements, or foci, from the tables can be linked in numerous combinations, the punctuation marks serving as the nuts and bolts, so to speak. Through the use of these tables by the classifier experienced in the principles governing CC, everything significant in the subject of a book can be expressed in the final individualising number which it receives and one can classify many more compound themes than it would be possible for any scheme to feasibly enumerate. It may be pointed out also that, as CC tends to list recurring notions or aspects once and once only, the classification schedules are much less cumbersome than those of the traditional schemes; by trying for the most part to list all subjects, the older classifications obviously repeat many basic concepts again and again.

266. The subject outline of the Colon system is of traditional canonical character as indicated on the folding chart at the beginning of this chapter. In *Prolegomena* can be found a rationalisation of this outline in the manner which we expect of classificationists, but Ranganathan seems not to stress its value overmuch, being far more concerned with helpful order within each subject discipline. He adds, in the first edition of *Prolegomena* (page 210): 'the order of the main classes in the lay-out of a scheme of classification is not of much moment as long as it is reasonably tolerable'. The outline can be criticized to some extent; no perfect order in the first array of classes is indeed achievable, but the framework of BC offers a rather more useful and scholarly sequence of major subject fields.

267. It is, however, the entirely faceted structure of the scheme within these major disciplines that merits closest attention. Within each of the classes above we find concepts or foci conveniently arranged in categories. The classifier must therefore analyse the subject of the book with which he is dealing, select the relevant main class, and then build up a class-mark by piecing together each appropriate focus, using the connecting symbols indicated. Volume 1 of the sixth edition, designed for macrothought (relatively broad areas of knowledge or book classification) is divided into sections. The first section is a detailed introduction to CC, the second the

H*

234 / A MANUAL OF CLASSIFICATION

actual tables, the third section offers special schedules for sacred books and the classics. The classifier new to the scheme should use the schedules in close conjunction with the advice given on the application of the various classes in Part I. The discussions of faceted classification in our Chapter Four and in other modern texts on our subject may also provide useful guidance as to how to attempt practical work with CC.

268. We find that Ranganathan has found it possible to relate all facets to one or another of five fundamental concepts; Personality, Matter, Energy, Space, and Time. These are usually written merely as PMEST. There has been dispute over these even among supporters of faceted classification and Vickery has suggested that there are other fundamental concepts which govern division. We are only concerned here, however, with the arrangement in CC and it is the PMEST formula which indicates the sequence in which the foci from the several facets should be combined. Space and Time simply denote geographical and chronological divisions. A common set of each of these is provided, the former being denoted by numbers and the latter by capital letters. As they apply to the whole of the scheme, they are listed at the beginning of the schedules. The foci in the other categories differ from class to class. The category Energy always denotes an operation, a process, or a problem to be solved; Matter is represented by materials; Personality, more difficult to define succinctly, is best thought of as the core of any subject. When foci from all five categories are present, the PMEST formula gives us our combination order or order in chain. We begin with Personality, the most concrete category and move through the others according to the formula, until we come to Time, the most abstract of the five concepts concerned. There are also principles which determine the order of an array of foci. But let us try to make facet analysis, or the analytico-synthetic approach as it is sometimes called, clearer by means of a simple example from the sixth edition of CC.

269. Imagine that the subject to be classified is *A popular description of the marsh plants of Great Britain*. We must first of all analyse this subject into its facets. The book must go in the Botany class and the foci are obviously *marsh plants* (belonging to the personality category), *popular description* (which falls into the Energy category) and *Britain* (Space category). Matter and Time are not represented here, so the combination orders will be PES. We find that in class G in CC our class-mark will be:

$$G\,9515 \quad : \quad 13 \quad . \quad 56$$
$$\text{(P)} \qquad \text{(E)} \quad \text{(S)}$$

It has been noted that the facets involved are divided by punctuation marks. These are useful indicators as they enable the various facets to be quickly recognised. The primary facet (personality in most examples) always follows the main class letter and is represented by numerals used in a decimal sense, although no decimal point is provided. Matter, when represented, is introduced by a semi-colon. The colon introduces the important Energy facet; Space and Time are introduced by a full-stop and an apostrophe respectively, but can be readily distinguished as the Time divisions are represented by letters, while those of the Space facet, like most of the other foci in CC are indicated by numerals. The classifier thus arrives at the class-mark above by selecting 9515 as the number for marsh plants from the Personality facet, adding the number for popular description from the Energy category; and, finally, introducing the number 56 for Britain from the geographical facet.

270. The facet formula is complicated by the fact that the classifier may be faced with examples which bring facets from all five categories into play; more important, he may find that some of the five fundamental concepts occur more than once in the faceted pattern of any topic. Ranganathan has catered for such examples by the concept of *Rounds and Levels*. It is recognised that two foci relating to Personality may sometimes be required before the introduction of Energy. In such an instance there is said to be more than one *Level* of Personality. On the other hand, the Energy facet may give rise to a recurrence of facets relating to Personality, Matter, Energy or all three concepts. When these arise after the first Energy facet, we are said to have a second manifestation or *Round* of facets. The probable facet formula for fairly complicated subjects in any class is shown at the head of that class in Colon. Thus in Class W, Political Science, we have the formula: W(P), (P2): (E) (2P). This means that after the initial W we may have a number from the Personality facet, then a second Level of Personality, then Energy, and then a second Round of Personality. (Space and Time, of course, are indicated at the beginning of the schedules and do not need to be shown at the head of each class). The student will be well advised to fully master the essence of the idea of facet analysis and the Ranganathan notion of the five fundamental concepts before

trying to grasp the notion of *Rounds and Levels*. But a more intricate example may be helpful to some in explaining how this latter idea is put into operation in CC. Let us consider, this time, the specific subject *Attempts to eradicate the problem of poverty in Scotland in the 1940's*. Our main class is, in this case Y Sociology, and the subjects must be analysed into the concepts – poverty; cure or treatment; Scotland; 1940's. Once this is done we perform the necessary synthesis. We find that poverty is the primary facet here, although it belongs to the problem, or Energy, category. It is represented by 434 and introduced by a colon. Eradication is an Energy facet from the second *Round* and is also preceded by the colon sign. Scotland is, of course, represented by the number from the common isolates in the Space category and is introduced by a full stop, while the common time isolate for the 1940's is introduced by an apostrophe. Thus our class-mark is:

$$\text{Y} \; : \; \underset{\text{(E)}}{434} \; : \; \underset{\text{(2E)}}{64} \; . \; \underset{\text{(S)}}{563} \; \underset{\text{(T)}}{\text{'N4}}$$

We have again indicated the categories under the class-mark in order to show that here we have two Rounds of Energy, but that Personality is absent (the symbol for the major problem, poverty, needs to be added directly to the main class symbol) and Matter is likewise not represented. It may merely be added that the colon, originally the only punctuation mark used in CC and the reason for the name of this classification, is still the most important of the punctuation signs in one sense for it introduces the 'pivotal' Energy category which may well initiate a whole new *Round* of facets.

271. The student should also note that there are rare examples in CC of an arrangement in which one of the categories is divided in an unusual way. This may arise because, for example, certain of the foci in the Energy facet may denote processes which only apply to some of the foci in the Personality facet. They would, therefore, follow the appropriate Personality isolates immediately, and the remainder of the Personality isolates would be enumerated after them. This is known as the use of *differential facets*. Another, perhaps more striking, example of the employment of this idea is in a class like Literature, where it would be unhelpful to provide a single list of chronological divisions as the various languages would each need to be qualified by their own appropriate set of divisions in

the Period facet. Thus differential facets arise each time a primary facet cannot be sub-divided throughout by a *single set* of divisions from a secondary facet. Each focus in the primary facet may need to be qualified in a distinctive way; hence the adoption of differential facets. Vickery[1] quotes Medicine and Agriculture as the CC classes in which this notion has been most fully developed. The idea need only be used, of course, when it is strictly necessary to provide diverse sets of foci in the minor facets of a subject because the major ones simply cannot justifiably have their foci all sub-divided in the same way. But in most fields of activity, fortunately, this type of problem does not arise.

272. Far more important from the student's point of view than the recognition of the principle of differential facets is the understanding of the idea of phase analysis. This we briefly considered in paragraphs 40 and 41 of Chapter Four. Colon was the first system to distinguish this problem clearly, for although, as Ranganathan points out in some of his books, the traditional schemes sometimes enumerate multi-phased subjects or sometimes make a tentative effort to enable them to be specified through number building, there is no real attempt there to lay down systematically a principle which will enable us to deal with *any* complex subject of this kind and to distinguish each *type of phase* in the notation. In the introductory part one to the sixth edition of CC, we find that the problem is most clearly defined and dealt with. Each such book must first be classed by the symbols denoting the facets in its primary phase; the secondary phase can then be introduced by means of an assigned lower-case letter introduced by a zero – the digit indicating a change of phase. Thus we have, to borrow an example from the influencing phase:

COgU Geophysics (or the influence of geography on physical science).

The student should perceive that it is most helpful to accommodate such documents in the scheme near to the beginning of the class represented by their primary phase. The above item, for instance, is obviously specialised in relation to items dealing solely with the physical sciences and should follow them in the classified sequence, but it deals with the influence of a subject on the physical sciences *as a whole* and, therefore, should precede the volumes which are restricted to special branches of this field. It should be

[1] *Faceted classification*, 1960, p. 33.

noted, in conjunction with Chapter Four, that the Tool phase, one of the main types of phase which we distinguished there, has been abandoned as such in Colon; this problem is now dealt with by means of certain common energy isolates which can show how a particular method of treatment is applied to a subject. CC retains, however, the other important types of phase – influencing, comparison, bias, which we mentioned earlier; it also recognises a difference phase, which would be seen in such a subject as: '*the difference between the philosophical and religious notions of evil*'. Multi-phased subjects should be distinguished from similar complex documents which deal with the interaction of two subjects drawn from a *single* class of knowledge, e.g. *the influence of the poetry of Henry Vaughan on William Wordsworth*. Such a subject is said to demonstrate an *Intra-facet relationship*.

273. The other main features of CC are seen in the careful enumeration of the various principles that can be used to achieve a helpful sequence of topics in array or, in Colon terminology, a helpful order of foci within any facet and in the number of special 'devices' provided. With regard to the former, it must be confessed that there is a stress on helpful, filiatory order throughout the scheme, and it is of course essential that foci, or isolates, should be grouped within their appropriate category in the sequence which offers the optimum advantage. Several possible orders may be applied – evolutionary, geographical, chronological, an order based on the literary warrant of the subject concerned, or even alphabetical order, are among the possibilities suggested. The final choice is determined in each class of CC by the needs of that subject field, as reflected by the literature of India. The devices include the Octave principle (which we have already considered in the Chapter on notation and which the F.I.D. obtained permission to use in 1948 in UDC, if necessary), the Subject Device, the Chronological Device, and the Classic Device. The intention of all of these is to bring about the exact classification of documents and obtain the most useful sequence possible. The Classic Device, for instance is used to bring the various editions of any classic and commentaries relating to it together in the sequence; the other Devices we have mentioned are said to be used for the sharpening of a focus in any facet, that is for the achievement of precise classification. It is hoped that they will enable the classifier to develop the intension of existing isolates without waiting for further instructions in this matter from

the classificationist. The wise student, however, will study the possible application of at least one or two of these devices in CC itself.

274. *Notation.* Turning away from these novel and intriguing features, we find that the notation of Colon is extremely mixed. It relies heavily on numbers, but when fully employed uses letters, brackets, Greek symbols, and punctuation marks also. It reveals Ranganathan's constant insistence on the necessity for an ultimate economy of 'co-extensiveness of subject and class-mark' and is most hospitable to new topics. It is sometimes long and complex; this is usually when the documents with which it deals are compound or complex ones. It is expressive of the structure of the scheme to a greater degree than the notation of any other general bibliographical system and clearly shows each change of facet, demonstrating also (although a little less clearly) change of phase. Opponents of the scheme often suggest that the notation is impossibly long; this may well be because they have seen a few very long notations from CC which denote highly specific documents. In other cases, the notation is as short as that of rival systems. Ranganathan has suggested[1] that long notations do not bother the reader. He argues that just as the passenger in an aeroplane is not concerned with the way in which the engine works providing he reaches his destination safely and reasonably promptly, so the reader is not concerned with the notation if he can find the book or books he wants quickly. This particular analogy is rather misleading; although the notation is, as Ranganathan contends, primarily a tool for the librarian, the reader must use it to go from the catalogue to the shelves and he will need to follow the notational sequence to determine the order of material on those shelves. True, Ranganathan might say that the catalogue is a staff tool and that good plans of the library and shelf guides will be far more use to the reader than the notational symbols; nevertheless most librarians believe that the readers should use the catalogue and it seems desirable that, for both reader and librarian, the notation should be concise in as many cases as possible. Ranganathan is surely on safer ground when he points out that the small library which wants simple classification and short notation will obtain it, as most of its books there will deal with simple, straightforward subjects; the larger library, coping with specialized material and employing

[1] *Prolegomena to Library Classification*, 2nd edition, 1957, pp. 281–2.

classification in depth must, it seems, accept the longer class-marks for many of its documents. Ranganathan indeed sees in notation the possibility of an international language; in Colon, therefore, it is always used with great precision. It is succinct in the broad fields of macrothought, but it does not, to use the classificationist's own phrase, 'shirk the challenge' of the exact classification of more difficult material.

275. *Synthesis and Mnemonics.* CC is the one general scheme which is entirely synthetic; indeed we have inevitably considered this 'main feature' already. The older, conventional schemes, of course, are not entirely enumerative; DC perceives the value of number-building, SC has great possibilities in this direction, BC has elaborate tables for the task (although Bliss seems to have been slow to realise the necessity for the provision of such tables), and UDC, through its auxiliary signs has tremendous synthetic potential. It might be said also for example, that the use of the Colon in UDC is virtually the clear recognition of one form of phase analysis. But only Ranaganathan has produced a fully faceted classification for the whole field of knowledge as yet. Colon is the one general scheme which clearly recognises the need for the breaking down of subjects into their constituent parts, the listing of each of these parts once and for all by the classificationist in its appropriate category, and the provision of rules for the fitting together of the parts from the various facets. The enumeration of basic recurring concepts only, rather than of all known subjects, has greatly decreased the size of the schedules of CC. Thus we find that synthesis is achieved through facet analysis, phase analysis, intra-facet relations, and also through the use of a table of *Anteriorising Common Isolates* (similar to common form divisions), and one of *Posteriorising Common Isolates* (Personality and Energy foci applicable to many classes) listed with the common Space and Time Isolates at the front of the schedules.

276. The tremendous mnemonic value of such a formidable synthetic apparatus must be remarked upon. Each isolate is denoted by a distinctive symbol whenever it is used as part of a class-mark; thus, as far as systematic mnemonics are concerned, CC has a notation with more memory value than any other general classification scheme. The student should notice that CC has other mnemonic features. There are no literal mnemonics as used by Bliss but, in addition to the mnemonic effect obtained from the listing of basic

isolates in the schedules, an attempt has been made to develop a new form of mnemonic. These unscheduled mnemonics, or *seminal mnemonics* as Palmer and Wells dubbed them, take the form of a list of entities associated with a particular digit. The introductory part of CC shows that Ranganathan has tried to gather together certain allied concepts into groups and to represent each grouping by one of the digits 1–9. The digit 1, for example, is associated amongst other things with unity, God, the world, and so forth. The method as at present set out appears to be highly subjective, but the aim is to provide a guide to the classifier who is confronted with a new subject and who wishes to anticipate the incorporation of this subject into the tables of CC. Thus if a new subject cropped up and most of the isolates revealed by the facet analysis of this subject were listed in the schedules, the individual classifier, it is claimed, should be able to anticipate the number for the remaining isolates by reference to the table of seminal mnemonics. Therefore, if the new isolate dealt with unity or a related theme, the classifier would realise that 1 was the appropriate digit for it; he would be able to work out the decision of the classificationist in advance!

277. Ideally this method would result in various classifiers in different libraries being able to deal with newly created subjects without waiting for the next edition of the classification and yet achieving identical results. The *self-perpetuating classification* which would result from the complete development of such an idea is still some way from us, however. It would be extremely difficult in practice to obtain complete agreement with regard to the associations of ideas with digits; indeed Colon tells us that it is highly desirable that all foci formed by this device should be considered at meetings of users of the scheme. Even if agreement could be reached in this direction, it would seem unlikely that all classifiers would independently apply these seminal mnemonics perfectly or that all new subjects coud be immediately correctly placed in the scheme by means of them. The cynical might even be inclined to dismiss this idea altogether as indeed Metcalfe, perhaps the severest critic of CC tends to do. Yet the notion is a most ingenious and interesting one; it is significant to note how A. J. Wells was able to select suitable digits for the foci in the Energy facet of a classification for packaging through the use of this idea.[1] The careful reader of CC will observe

---

[1] This is discussed in R. S. Parkhi, *Decimal Classification and Colon Classification in Perspective*, 1964, pp. 469–70.

for himself also how often in the tables of the scheme a concept is represented by the digit which we would anticipate if we were familiar with the seminal mnemonics. Thus, for example, in the Common Time Isolates, lower case p represents a meteorological period and p5 the wet season; the list of seminal mnemonics shows liquid and water among the ideas associated with the digit 5, so this is obviously a logical choice for 'wet season'.

278. *Index*. This may be regarded as a Relative Index but it differs from the normal type of index in that it merely shows where standard parts, or foci can be found in the schedules; the class-marks obtained from the linking together of such parts are not given in the Index. We have entries such as:

Lending 2 (E),62.   X (P),62(E),1
Partnership Z (P2),315

Our two random examples indicate that the concept 'lending' occurs in class 2 Library Science where it is denoted by 62 in the Energy facet; it also arises in class X Economics where, in the Personality facet it is also denoted by 62, and in the Energy facet by 1. Partnership occurs only in Class Z Law, where it belongs to the second level Personality facet and is represented by 315. The overall effect appears to be an economical and satisfactory one; the index can certainly not be used alone, but then no index should ever be so used. In CC it is a useful key to the various basic classes and their isolates and is truly complementary to the schedules of the classification.

279. *Use and Revision of the scheme*. This classification has, like BC, suffered from the fact that it arrived in the world of librarianship at a time when most general collections were committed firmly to earlier systems. Indeed Dewey, as we have remarked, had done his utmost to dissuade both Bliss and Ranganathan from creating their own systems. Colon is, however, used in an increasing number of libraries in India, although its use elsewhere is slight. In Britain, it has been employed in the Library of Christ's College, Cambridge, where several important oriental collections are housed. It appears to work quite well there and the staff comment favourably on the memory value of many schedules, although some classes, such as F and X, give rise to difficulties. Metcalfe suggests that many Indian librarians are indifferent to Ranganathan's theories or

sceptical concerning them; yet it is certain that the increasing volume of library literature from that country testifies to the impact which the principles behind Colon have made on many of the younger generation of librarians. The use of CC's distinctive principles can, of course, also be seen in Britain in the number of special classifications, constructed on completely faceted lines, that are now becoming available.

280. The revision policy of CC has left much to be desired. Editions have been produced regularly and radical changes have sometimes been made to incorporate new theories and developments of older ones. In recent years, the scheme has consisted of a volume for the classification of books and we have been promised, with each edition, further schedules for microthought or documentation purposes. These depth-classification schedules have not materialised, although several relevant articles have appeared in *Annals of Library Science* indicating how CC could be suitably developed and extended. The fact is that this is very much a one man classification and owes a great deal, not only to Ranganathan's ingenuity but to his amazing fund of energy and enthusiasm also. The idea of a self-perpetuating classification has not been fully developed; indeed it is possibly unattainable. In this case, CC may suffer from its lack of an editorial board to carry out systematic revision based on the needs of users and developments in the field of knowledge.[1] There is no official bulletin announcing proposed changes or additions and, it must be confessed, any librarian using the scheme would be likely to disregard many of the changes made on account of their drastic nature; no well-established library can easily incorporate wholesale changes into its classification system. It may be noted, in this respect, that at Christ's College, Cambridge the fourth edition of CC is used and no attempt is made to recognise ideas introduced in later versions unless these can be acknowledged without undue difficulty. It may be observed that the recognition of the five fundamental categories, for instance, was not introduced until the third edition; also, as we have already observed the Colon was originally the only punctuation mark used to separate facets, but there are now several others. These changes are commendable in one sense; they do, however, make things more difficult for a library which has adopted an early edition of the scheme. It might

---

[1] The volume by Ranganathan in the Rutgers University series tells us that an editorial board has now been formed.

even be argued that CC has the advantage over DC in changing and keeping up-to-date because it is not so widely used. For it is the generally accepted scheme that cannot afford to introduce significant alterations or structural changes.

281. *Conclusion*. One is conscious that the methods behind CC are so different from those of the conventional schemes and that the terminology in some ways is so complex that it is difficult for a writer to do the scheme justice or explain it to his satisfaction in a single chapter. Ranganathan's own books, (read, apart from the *Elements*, chronologically) do much to familiarise us with his distinctive ideas and terms and the overlap or repetition that occurs inevitably to some extent in these volumes also helps to drive home the essence of the more important theories. CC offers the enormous advantage of the completely faceted approach; the clear rules for the formation of subjects from the constituent elements represented by the foci in these categories enables the classifier to specify many modern subjects which are difficult to fit into the less plastic enumerative framework of older systems. CC is a slim volume also in comparison with the older schemes, as unit parts rather than composite subjects are enumerated. This lack of bulk should facilitate the use of the scheme once the basic principles have been grasped. The system now has many capable advocates, but Dr Ranganathan himself is still among the most active of these, his energies and perspicacity apparently undiminished, urging us to seriously consider the advantages offered by a faceted general scheme and indicating that reclassification can be achieved in established libraries by the method of using the new scheme for new accessions and much used older volumes and leaving the little wanted stock arranged in a parallel sequence by the superseded classification. Despite this insistence upon the value of the osmotic method of reclassification as he calls it, CC is having the same difficulties in gaining recognition in practice that are met by other comparatively new general classifications.

282. Bliss, although he appreciated some of Ranganathan's ideas, was a rather harsh critic. He questioned the need, even in documentation, for such lengthy and formidable symbolizing as CC's complete specifications carry; they are certainly unlikely to be used in ordinary libraries. The importance of the Colon system lay, he felt, in what Ranganathan would describe as its wholehearted recognition of the synthetic principle and its provision (through

phase analysis) for the specification of complex subjects. He considered, however, that 'its systematic devices and its complicated pseudo-mnemonic notation are too much of a burden for any bibliographic classification'. Nevertheless, he concludes, 'the erudition, insight and ingenuity of the author are truly admirable'.

283. Other critics draw our attention chiefly to the difficulty of the terminology, the emphasis on the East and on Indian library requirements, the problems arising out of the considerable changes made from edition to edition, and the failure of Ranganathan to acknowledge his debt to the older systems – UDC in particular. There is more than a grain of truth in at least some of these complaints. The Eastern emphasis of the scheme is understandable; it is perhaps, as Foskett suggests, based on a recognition of the 'literary warrant' of India. This does not, of course, prevent us from applying the same principles to classifications designed for the Western civilization. The difficulty of the scheme and its terminology are, in part, acknowledged by its classificationist, who insists that nevertheless the extra effort made to master it will bring more than adequate rewards to the classifier and that part of the difficulty lies in breaking free from the shackles imposed upon our thinking by the older enumerative approach to classification. The debt to UDC is certainly evident but, as De Grolier[1] says, 'In relation to UDC a certain number of improvements are noted, probably greater flexibility, more hospitality'. The UDC use of synthesis is not as thorough as that of Colon; the older scheme is tied to an enumerative framework and does not clearly recognise a facet formula. De Grolier justly adds that Colon 'presents also some great gaps, especially in the classes relating to the physical and natural sciences and to their applications'. As we shall see, this hinders its adoption in many special libraries. But perhaps the greatest objection to the use of the scheme lies not in this, nor in the notation employed (which is sometimes long and awkward), nor again in the fact that CC appeared long after other schemes had been generally accepted, important though these factors may be; it lies rather in the difficulty encountered in coping with any classification which, chameleon-like, alters considerably as the need rises. The constant deletion of unsatisfactory features and grafting on of new ideas make CC essentially a vehicle for experiment rather than a working classification.

[1] *A study of general categories applicable to classification and coding for documentation*, 1962.

284. Bliss suggests that 'the system is well worthy of study by those who contemplate constructive developments in bibliographic classification'.[1] This appears, in retrospect, to be a colossal understatement, for CC, and particularly the analytico-synthetic methods associated with it, have influenced recent classification study greatly, even to fascination. Even the modern American writer, J. H. Shera,[2] thinks Ranganathan's the most fertile mind that has addressed itself to the problems of library classification, but he points out that CC's severest critics are prepared to dismiss the system in the words used by Carlyle of seventeenth century England – 'grand unintelligibility'. If we ignore the prejudice of some writers and examine the scheme objectively, we find that the chief aims of this classification are to rely on an almost entirely synthetic structure, to promote in every way possible the achievement of an helpful order on the shelves, to deal with complex subjects according to definite predetermined rules, and to ultimately produce a method so condensed and so perfect in operation that every user will automatically give the same call-mark to a book (even to one on a new subject) without reference to the classificationist. The enormous impetus given to classificatory research, on an international scale, by the system cannot be overestimated; much of this is considered in a later chapter. Indeed it is now clear that the methods are greater than the scheme itself, for these principles point the way forward to the making of new schemes both general and special. CC does not merit the remarks bestowed upon it by its keenest adverse critics, but it is clearly not satisfactory as a general classification for universal use. Its greatness, and the genius of its creator, lie in the fact that the ideas which can be seen in the classification, and those which are still evolving, open up new vistas of the bibliographic schemes of the future. It is too soon to state emphatically that the faceted classifications will ultimately prevail in nearly all libraries; the problems of reclassification and the challenge of machine retrieval systems will affect this issue. But it is clear that CC, despite its complications, has provided a refreshingly stimulating approach to our subject. It is not the classification of tomorrow but the schemes which have that privilege, in special libraries particularly, are likely to owe an incalculable debt to the pioneering work of Dr S. R. Ranganathan.

[1] *Organization of Knowledge in Libraries*, p. 304.
[2] Classification: current functions . . . In *The Subject Analysis of Library Materials*, edited by M. F. Tauber, 1953.

The Practical Application of a Classification Scheme

CHAPTER EIGHTEEN

The Rules for Classing Books

285. In this section we consider some of the problems which arise when any published scheme is applied to an actual collection of books. Some of these problems affect all libraries, but we are especially concerned here with those affecting general, and particularly public, libraries; the question of classification and indexing for the special librarian will be dealt with separately in Section Five. The nature of these difficulties and the solutions proposed will depend in part on the classification scheme that is selected; for the vast majority of public libraries this is DC, but LC has been adopted, or more strictly speaking adapted, by many university and certain college libraries, and in some academic libraries BC and even UDC are to be found. Yet many of the problems covered in this and the next few chapters are ones which will inevitably arise whatever system is applied; there is perhaps a case for dealing with some of these early in a textbook on classification, since the student with some experience of library work will already have encountered a few of them. But it seems wisest to consider principles first of all, next to see these in operation in the six living general schemes, and then to contemplate the application of the schemes, the links between classification and administration, and the factors which hamper the working of a bibliographical classification. Although our studies, as covered by this book, are concerned chiefly with the *theory* of classification, we must not allow theory to transcend the requirements dictated by experience, thus neglecting the task of resolving the difficulties which arise in its application. This Section, therefore, is concerned with the uses and problems of classification rather than with theoretical matters.

286. In the present chapter, we consider some of the rules to be

followed in practical classification. Many years ago, L. S. Jast asserted that 'it is one thing to have a satisfactory classification and another to have a satisfactory classifier'. Although satisfactory classifiers are now available, the implications of the assertion remain. It is quite safe to say that few persons can classify in a practical manner who have not studied how to do it in relation to the actual working of a library. If classification were a recognised science, with laws as immutable as the accepted laws of Nature, it would be a relatively simple task to get out precepts and even codes for practical classing. Despite the methodical approach provided by its theory, it is not; it is an art in which, in several cases in a year, an exercise of personal judgement is required. All rules are conditioned by this fact; indeed, the most important 'rule' – *place a book where it will be most useful* – is hardly a rule at all, for it involves a number of considerations. Useful for whom; the general reader, the student, the non-reader whom we wish to attract? Again, if at present a placing seems to be useful, is that because of some temporary factor or is the attraction to a particular place real and likely to last? The newcomer to practical classification must not despair, however. Most schemes have provided us with useful advice on their application; they also often reflect, in the organization of each subject field, the needs of the professional workers in that subject. Thus adherence to their instructions will provide us with placings which are of permanent value to most library users, providing the following practical rules are also observed; these, therefore, should be studied carefully.

1. Place a book where it will be most permanently useful.

2. Class by subject and then by form of presentation, except in the form classes, where the precedence is always given to form.

3. When a book deals with two subjects, classify under the dominant subject; if this cannot be ascertained, class under the first. Likewise, if a book deals with not more than three divisions of the same subject, place it in the one that is most prominently dealt with, or – if the treatment is of equal importance – in the one dealt with first. If the book deals with more divisions of the subject than three, place it at the general heading which covers them all.

4. Place a book at the most specific heading that will contain it.

5. When a book appears on a subject which has no stated place in the classification scheme, determine the heading to which it is most nearly related and place it there. (The exact application of this rule may depend on whether a new edition of the scheme in question will soon be available or not).

6. Avoid placings which are in the nature of criticism. (We have also considered this in the Section on principles.)

7. When two headings clash, make a decision as to which is to prevail; record this decision, for future reference.

287. We shall comment below on some of these rulings. To them may be added one or two other points of advice, which are hardly rules, but which deserve attention and which consolidate or add to the remarks above.

1. Always consider the predominant purpose or tendency of a book when classifying.

2. Books pro and con any subject go together at the subject.

3. Always have a reason for your placing of a book.

4. Index *all* decisions; this will make the practice of your library clear to its future classifiers and will enable a system to be applied in a consistent manner.

288. As we classify for the benefit of our readers, Rule 1 should be self-explanatory; since we class a library normally by subjects, the need for Rule No. 2 should also be clear. We determine the subject of the book by the main tables and place it there; then add to the subject class-mark the appropriate qualifying symbols to indicate the method by which the subject is presented. The difficulty is that we cannot always determine what the subject is without some examination and thought; and even then, there is a possibility of error – books are often one thing in appearance and another in actuality, which explains in part Jast's assertion which is quoted above. A good classifier will have some knowledge of the subjects with which he deals but, although we may have educated classifiers, we cannot have omniscient ones. The main, the crucial problem in classifying is the *subject of the book* which is to be classed; and there is

no royal road to determining that in all cases. Some sixty per cent of books, however, are on specific, easily recognisable topics, and on these the classifier can work fairly rapidly. The remainder will demand a closer scrutiny, and we can only suggest a simple, commonsense procedure. The classifier must read the preface and list of contents, scan through the index in some cases, and note the authors qualifications and emphasis. Only very elusive works, refuse to yield their subject and their purpose to this method. Bliss instances an example which may illustrate the point just made: 'If a book on Scotland is not mainly geographic and historical, but consists of descriptive and narrative chapters together with a mélange of literary and scientific observations and reflections on the national traits and institutions, also considerable social philosophy in the last chapters, the judgement is indeed complex and the decision may be uncertain'. But surely, from first to last, this is a book on Scotland!

289. One warning which must be kept in mind when we are classifying is: Never class a book by the face value of its title-page; the results of doing so would often be ludicrous, as certain quite hoary jokes in literature, and in classing itself, prove. The shepherd who bought Ruskin's *Notes on the Construction of Sheepfolds* was acting on the same principle as the classifier who places by title only, and reached a similar result. A modern work, like C. N. Parkinson's *The Law and the Profits*, might likewise be badly placed if the title was read carelessly! Such warnings are surely scarcely needed by the careful student. Perhaps a more difficult book is that which has a metaphorical or allusive term for its title, a form of title to which Ruskin again was especially addicted: titles such as *Fors Clavigera*, or *Unto this Last*, convey absolutely nothing to a classifier at first sight, and some of them have to be read, at least in part, before the subject can be discovered; alternatively, in certain cases, a reference work can be consulted to discover quickly the subject of the book concerned.

290. One Rule which demands comment is No. 3, which involves the composite book; that is to say the book dealing with a number of subjects. It was this type of work which led the early thinkers on classification to despair of the worthwhile application of the process to books. Here the catalogue must rescue from neglect those topics which are necessarily out of sight when a book dealing with more than one subject is placed, as it must be, with the dominant topic. If the book deals with subjects from many *different* branches of

knowledge, it is clearly to be put in the Generalia class, and common-sense must determine the extent to which the labour and expense of analysing its contents in the catalogue is necessary; often it is not, but very occasionally a very important contribution to a subject is in a book which cannot be classed at the subject. It is, however, most undesirable to load a catalogue with superfluous and irritating details of chapters on matters which have been dealt with already as well, or better, in monographs. While the truly general work must go in Generalia, the practical classifier must be satisfied that a book really is general: many supposedly general works have a dominant subject in them: are really better at, say, science, history, or some other major discipline. The book which deals with two or three subjects is a more simple problem. It is placed at the subject which is treated most fully in the book with extra entries in the catalogue under the other subjects.

291. Probably the most exasperating book of all to classify is that which appears to have an equal right to go into two places in the classification. It may be that such a book deals with a new branch of knowledge and we cannot easily determine to which subject field this new theme is best subordinated. On the other hand difficult books of this kind are more likely to be those which deal with two or more subjects not clearly and distinctly, but in a way which con-siders the impact or influence which one subject has on others; these we now call multi-phased books. The book which deals with, say, Drawing and Painting is a straightforward two subject work and can be dealt with according to our Rule 3; the increasing over-lapping of disciplines in the present century presents the classifier with many examples that are much more complex than this, how-ever. We must therefore apply phase analysis and distinguish the book with two or three distinct phases from the work which merely provides information on two or more topics. Mills[1] lists rules to be followed in the classing of multi-phased subjects. We must, first of all, recognise the type of phase involved; *The influence of the theory of evolution on Christian belief* is obviously an example of the *in-fluencing* phase and must be classed under the subject influenced. The examples relating to the *tool* phase usually reveal the appropriate placing to us readily enough; those illustrating the *comparison* and the *difference* phases are rather more complicated and the primary phase must be carefully selected in each case from an examination

[1] *A Modern Outline of Library Classification*, 1960, p. 161.

of the book involved. But perhaps the most controversial of all the multi-phased works are those which belong to the type designated by the title *bias* phase.

292. A few examples will make the difficulty clear. If we have works such as:

> Ethics for the Businessman
> Book-keeping for Grocers
> Arithmetic for the Electrical Engineer

Where do we place them? These are all, undoubtedly, books on a particular topic written with a bias towards the needs of a particular class of reader. Most supporters of modern classification theories would agree with Mills, who suggests that the chief phase in examples such as these is the subject: ethics, book-keeping, and arithmetic, respectively. He argues that these are the dominant, or core, themes and that if this principle is followed *all* readers will find these books; it may also be thought that the Grocer (to take an example which we used also in an earlier chapter) will *expect* to find material on book-keeping in the accountancy section, that the Engineer will not go to his usual part of the library when he wants a book on arithmetic, and so on. Traditional theory, however, as can be seen in many works on our subject, often argued for the alternative placing, although it did not clearly identify the problem of phase analysis, as such, at all. This is an argument which we feel still carries weight, at least with regard to some examples.

293. From the point of view of providing a strictly subject classification and obtaining clear principles for such, modern theory is correct on this point. Yet the purpose of these books would seem to suggest that they are *only* intended for Businessmen, Grocers, and Electrical Engineers. The best placing, therefore, might well be the one which takes account of the topic and its bias, on account of the fact that such books may have no real interest for anyone other than the readers in the category to which they are addressed. If this is so, then we should surely collocate the simple account of book-keeping, designed especially with the problems of the grocery store in mind, with other material which the Grocer might possibly need. The Colon Classification would have us follow the idea which is supported by Mills and others, but most schemes allow the individual classifier some choice in this matter. The decision of CC means that

we must consider a subject such as *Educational Psychology* as an example of bias phase; that is, a work on psychology with a bias towards the field of education. Ranganathan would have us classify this under Psychology, but it is surely more useful in the Education class or, at least an alternative should be provided. Of course, one must always be *consistent* in selecting the primary phase with examples involving any form of phase analysis; thus *all* material on book-keeping for Grocers must be kept together at one of the two possible locations. In DC, for example, we can classify *Ethics for the businessman* under Ethics or under Business. If the latter place is preferred, we denote Ethics by the standard sub-division 069. There are now also sometimes satisfactory places enumerated for such topics as *Maths for the Economist* (placed at 330.182[1]). In short, there is every facility to class according to the type of reader served when this is more useful than a strict subject placing. We would argue that it is the Businessman, and the Economist respectively who will most frequently need our last-named examples and will expect to find them located alongside other material which they use regularly. The use made of books must determine what we must do; Mills points out, quite rightly, that placing by interest rather than topic can be abused, but possible abuse of an idea must not deter us from selecting the placing where we know a book will be sought by the majority of the readers who may want it.

294. Nevertheless it may be stressed that these are *complex* cases. With most books the classifier has merely to take the work and to note its subject and the treatment of that subject – its form of presentation. He then, if he is using one of the traditional schemes, turns to the schedules and considers:

(a) What is the main heading embracing the subject?
(b) What is the appropriate division of that broad heading?
(c) What is the specific place within the division?

It is wise to adopt this, or a similar approach, if one is to be certain of the best placing. To use the index alone may well be misleading, for we may select from it a place which does not reflect the emphasis or context of the book which we are classifying. Consider the following examples from DC:

---

[1] A sixteenth edition placing which, alas, is not provided in Edition 17.

1. 394.1   Drinking customs of the world.
2. 641.874 Light wines for autumn dinners.
3. 663.52 Whisky distilling.
4. 613.81 Influence of whisky on hearing and seeing.
5. 614.34 The control of whisky production.
6. 178.1   The moral evils of drinking whisky.

Classing from the index, rather than from the tables might well result in the wrong aspect being selected; but if we check our placing under the containing heading, we can be sure that the right place with regard to the *emphasis* of the book has been chosen. In SC perhaps one could class from the index alone, for documents such as the above would be gathered together at one 'concrete' place. This is a simple method, but often an unhelpful one; we prefer the arrangement of other schemes where tables and index must be used together.

295. Another rule that may be briefly commented on is No. 4, which indicates the desirability of specific classification. This problem is discussed in our next chapter also, but here we may say that such specific classing is an ultimate economy, in that it makes for the accurate separation and definition of topics. A library which classed all its histories of England at one number, for example, and failed to provide sub-division by periods and places, would have so large and miscellaneous an assortment of volumes under the number that the effectiveness of the collection would be gravely impaired. Thus classification in some detail is needed in all but the very smallest general library to separate each specific theme from more general ones; without this detail the material wanted might well be hidden in a mass of other books. The special library which uses a general system will certainly need all the detail that is available in the scheme for the major subjects in that library's collections. Indeed the only real objection to specific classification would seem to be that it is so often linked with long and cumbersome notations.

296. Naturally, in all our practical classification, we use every reference book that may serve as a tool in the work. It is elementary that a well-equipped cataloguing room has good dictionaries of languages and of as many subjects as possible, collections of other library catalogues and, as important as anything, the principal schemes of classification. Most of these give good advice to the best procedure to be followed by those wishing to apply them; the advice given in their introductions is often also of a more general nature and

will be worth bearing in mind by the cataloguer whatever system his library employs. Since 1950, the British classifier has had the benefit of the type of centralised service which his American colleagues have enjoyed for many years; the *British National Bibliography* first appeared in that year, under the editorship of A. J. Wells. It is a classified weekly list of new British books with appropriate cumulations and saves a great deal of time; most British classifiers now rely on the DC numbers given by the BNB, although they may occasionally alter these slightly. They are, therefore, left with more time to classify older books that are added to stock and overseas publications. In the years since its inception, this work has proved an invaluable reference tool to librarians in many ways; one of the most important of these is its role as a readily available classified list of new books, the task of classification being done for the benefit of all by a team of well-qualified workers.

297. An older reference tool which is still useful as the only work of its kind is the *Code for Classifiers*, produced by the American W. S. Merrill, in which various problems are dealt with. This was first published in 1928, with a second edition in 1939. It is the one code which is virtually independent of any single classification scheme; it attempts to draw on the advice and experience of many classifiers in the U.S.A. with regard to difficulties which arise whatever system is applied. For example, although the problem of phase analysis is not clearly recognised, the Code does in fact deal with many situations which fall into this category; it discusses also the long-standing controversy with regard to the alternative treatments of biographical material and gives assistance by dealing with the difficulties of classifying in some major subject fields. So, despite its age, it is still a handy desk book for those concerned with practical classification and should be examined by the student. Some of the textbooks on our subject give also advice on practical work to a certain extent; Ranganathan's *Elements of Library Classification* is, perhaps, pre-eminent in this respect, although the advice given really relates to an entirely synthetic scheme and this book is best used in conjunction with CC. It has been suggested that the recognition of the newer principles in book classification makes a tool like Merrill's code obsolete; this can scarcely be true when most of us, whatever our opinions of the modern theories, are firmly committed to DC, or another of the traditional schemes. The Code is, in fact, invaluable as a tool which recognises and comments upon most of the

I

major problems which occur in the application of any scheme; indeed most librarians believe that a new edition of it is much to be desired.

298. Merrill's Code is described by its sub-title as dealing with the 'principles governing the consistent placing of books in a system of classification'. This leads us to consider the final point which we wish to make with regard to practical classification; the fact that consistency is essential as indicated in our Rule 7. There is no point in having several books dealing with exactly the same theme scattered because there is more than one possible location for this theme and different classifiers have chosen different locations. This means that if we put our book on *Ethics for the businessman* under Ethics, it would be foolish to put the next book we have on the same topic under Business. The classification must collect together material on each theme; thus consistency in our decision-making is imperative. Books with more than one phase will create problems for us, but there is no point in adopting different solutions each time a particular problem occurs. Likewise, if we use BC, we must accept, for certain themes, *one* of the alternative locations provided and adhere to this choice. In deciding where to place a book on a new subject or a complex work having more than one phase, we will be assisted by Merrill and possibly by the BNB or other aids. Yet it is well worthwhile also for the classifier to index, in the interests of consistency, every decision he makes in regard to subjects which are new to him and to the classification. The place selected for a new topic, not yet mentioned in the schedules, should be written in the index of the scheme so that any future book on that subject coming into the library may be placed consistently. If certain principles are clearly followed by a library and these and any special decisions made are recorded, then future classifiers in that library will be readily able to determine what has been done before and there will be no danger of two or three books on exactly the same topic being scattered. Indeed it is probably better to put all the books on a subject at an unwise location, so long as that location is clearly indexed, than to put some in the wrong place, and later, acting on better judgement, to place subsequent books in another location – the right one. In the first method the books on the subject are at least all together, and the reader will forgive many theoretical mistakes if he gets that important advantage. It is therefore necessary throughout to be sure of what has been done previously, so that the desired consistency may be achieved. If the early location employed by his library for a

particular subject is thought by the classifier to be faulty he must, when dealing with a new book on this theme, transfer the older material to the superior location in addition to placing the new volume there. Such a step will only be feasible if the principles followed by the library and decisions previously made have been noted and are clear to see. This we may say that although we do *not* accept, because it derides every *real* purpose of classification, Dewey's view that it does not matter much where a book is placed as long as that place is definitely indexed, we do accept the view that it is even more confusing to have several places for books on the *same* subject.

299. The rules given in this chapter are merely a tentative effort to provide a guide to the practical classifier; they should be used in conjunction with the advice given in the introduction to the scheme concerned and with the other aids which we have described. The advice here is chiefly concerned with DC and the other traditional schemes; the classifier who uses a faceted classification would need to modify it to some extent, although many of the points dealt with are significant for both enumerative and synthetic classifications.

CHAPTER NINETEEN

Classification and Library Administration

300. Every librarian when placed for the first time in charge of a library will, if he is wise, face the question of the arrangement of that library before he engages in any other important tasks in connection with it. Even if his library is not in actual existence, and has yet to be built, he will settle with most considered care two points: whether or not the library shall be classified, and, if he decides in favour of classification, by what scheme it shall be done. It is rather late in the day, not only in public libraries but in academic and special libraries also, to advance arguments in favour of the classified as against the unclassified collection: no modern librarian who has any sound knowledge of the purpose of libraries and of the tasks they have to perform will, except perhaps in certain small and highly specialised libraries, hesitate for a moment in deciding in favour of classification. But once he has decided to classify, he is confronted with a number of important practical problems, mostly of an administrative nature, the solution of which is vital to the future of his library.

301. The first concerns the design of the library building. It is necessary to point out that the classified library requires more room than one which is unclassified and, if possible, a simpler mode of planning. In an unclassified library additions of books can be made to the shelves at any part that may be convenient: such adding cannot alter the significance of an order which does not exist; and usually the empty shelves will stand ready for new books at the end of the collection, because in the library of this kind the books are usually arranged in numerical order by accession number. In the classified library it is desirable to leave spaces at the end of every subject on which a number of books have been written, and to the

literature of which frequent additions may be expected; or, at least, spaces should be left at the end of each class, in order that additions may be accommodated without too much movement of the general arrangement. This is a mere economy of time. Theoretically – seeing that books which are arranged by subject are independent of the shelves – the space may be left at the end of the whole collection; but this would involve the pushing up of thousands of volumes in a library of even moderate size whenever books were added, and in practice that would be out of the question. It is clear, then, if space must be left at the end of each class, that more shelves must be provided than would be necessary in the unclassified library.

302. These considerations are affected by the fact that a public library system is a complex of branch libraries, each possibly having a Junior Department as well as the Adult Library; likewise all central public libraries have reference departments and a few now have a series of subject departments. The university library too, may be faced with the problem of several sequences, especially if many departmental collections exist. There is the further complication that library stock is not confined to books; many libraries house pamphlets, periodicals, gramophone records and a variety of specialised material. Another simple factor which must not be overlooked is that size plays a large part in the final arrangement of books. It is obvious that large books, quartos and folios, for example, cannot stand side by side with octavos and smaller books on the same shelf without a loss of vertical space that few libraries can bear. So, although it is an accidental feature as far as the subject classification of books is concerned, size is the principal factor in book arrangement. Mere economy of space – a most valuable commodity in the modern library – makes it obvious that books of elephant folio size cannot stand with octavos and certainly not with duodecimos on the shelves; every scheme of arrangement is therefore a series of parallels governed in the first place by the size of the books. This difficulty must be recognised; it must not, in any circumstances, deflect us from the task of providing the most helpful subject arrangement possible. The librarian must also, in planning the arrangement of his library, remember that books are published in unequal proportions as regards size; one cannot forecast with accuracy how much space will be required in a given time for each size of books. The shelves, therefore, of a classified library should be adjustable, so that, as the number of any one size of book grows,

these shelves may be adjusted vertically to accommodate them. Usually at least two sequences are necessary; these are the sequence of octavo and smaller volumes, and the 'oversize' section. The latter may need further sub-division, particularly in reference libraries.

303. At this point, it is useful to distinguish between the librarian's use of the terms *broken order* and *parallel arrangement* or *parallel classification*. The former expression indicates some disturbance of the strict classified sequence; thus if the library uses DC and the large classes Language and Literature are brought together for convenience, broken order is employed. This is the obvious example; the student who has been observant when visiting libraries will find many more, but, perhaps none that occurs more frequently than this. Broken order, then, occurs when adaptations are made to the scheme in use. It also arises when special displays are created and material is drawn for these from many parts of the classification scheme. The whole object of broken order is to arrange the bookstock more effectively and to promote the use of books: it should be applied wisely, for often the order selected by one of the great classificationists, although imperfect, is more useful than many of the rearrangements produced by librarians, apart from those exhibited in temporary and attractively presented book displays. One occasionally sees examples of so many unjustified 'breaks' in the classified sequence that 'shattered order' is the phrase that leaps to mind! The normal and oversize sequences that we were previously considering are examples, not of broken order, but rather of parallel classification – two or more 'complete' sequences are involved. Likewise we see parallel arrangements in the different departments of a library with their various sequences. It is best, within each department, to shelve oversize volumes in an entirely separate sequence, although some libraries like to reserve the bottom shelf in each bookcase for such 'parallel' material. However, the main point to be stressed is that the existence of many separate sequences in a classified library does not invalidate classification. There is a vast difference between searching through two or three collections of material on a subject (because the books concerned are of different sizes, or because a distinction has been made between reference and lending material), and searching hopefully, but almost endlessly, through a huge unclassified collection or series of collections.

304. A word or two is needed on the selection of a classification

scheme. It should, by now, be sufficiently clear that classification has a very decisive bearing not only upon the arrangement of the books on the shelves, but upon the planning of the library building, the character of its departments, and on the method of working. So important is a right decision at the outset that no apology should be necessary for emphasising this fact. A library is a most complex machine, in which changes present disheartening difficulties if they are not foreseen; and the better its organization from the point of view of the public, the greater are the difficulties any change involves. Consider an example. For complete service, libraries classify books on the shelves; the class number also appears on catalogue entries, on the back of the book, on the back of the title page, in a shelf list or accessions register and on other records in public lending libraries (depending to some extent on the charging system in use). It is clear that an alteration of the class-mark for one book only would mean quite a lot of work especially in a library system where a union catalogue is kept at each branch. If, therefore, it becomes necessary to change a whole library, or even a whole class, the cost in labour and money is really formidable. Thus preliminary thought, a careful regard for the probable future of the library, and the choice of a classification which, because of its flexibility and adaptability, will meet all reasonable possibilities, are economic necessities. Never be misled into the position of a librarian who thinks some inferior scheme, perhaps easy to apply, 'will do for the present'. Look well ahead.

305. We are on more delicate ground when we come to select the best of the well-established existing general schemes; there is no guiding rule adequate for all libraries and every type of reader and reliable estimates of the cost of employing any one of the rival systems are difficult to obtain. One can readily believe that academic libraries may find DC inadequate or even lacking in the necessary scholarship. LC or BC may thus be preferred there. Some would also have the public librarian reject DC, but they rarely suggest a satisfactory alternative; indeed objections of one sort or another can be found to any general scheme that we know. But the choice must be made and it is good sense to point out that there are distinct advantages to readers when many libraries are similarly arranged. (This, of course, can only be so approximately; no two libraries are ever likely to reach identical placing of all books). Recent changes in local government areas have proved the benefit of neighbouring

authorities using the same system; there may be much reclassification otherwise when amalgamations take place. There are also advantages in the reader finding in, say, the Birmingham Public Library the system to which he has become accustomed in Manchester. It seems, therefore, right to some to accept the widely used DC, simply in order that the library may form, as it were, one more branch of the great national library of which every library in every town may be considered to be a section.

306. Of course, there are counter-arguments. Uniformity in this respect tends to disregard the character and the 'literary warrant' of individual collection. It has been suggested also that the adoption of a uniform system of classification throughout all libraries would be quite unsuitable to the special librarian and would generally eradicate or stultify initiative. There is, nevertheless, a very strong case nowadays for uniformity as much as possible in general libraries; the administrative advantages of this are overwhelming and the librarian whose initiative is circumscribed by his classification must have very little initiative. Time alone can reveal whether this means that DC will become yet more popular for the classification of general collections or whether it will be slowly driven out by a new general scheme made on faceted principles; we return to this theme in our later chapter on classification research.

307. When the choice of a system has been made, it should be studied root and branch; its outline, hierarchy, method of subdivision, notation, index and mnemonic features should be thoroughly grasped. In spite of all our preparatory study this is no easy task; the newcomer to classification is apt, in the traditional schemes especially, to place a book without checking back from the sub-division to the main heading under which it appears. Another prevalent mistake is to crowd books on subjects for which there are headings in the sub-divisions into the main class. One also sees even worse elementary mistakes. Notations are copied incorrectly or are confused, historical numbers being mistaken for geographical ones, for example. A study of the scheme in its entirety would prevent many errors of this kind; what is more important, it would suggest the full possibilities of a scheme, which are often greater than appear on the surface. Classificationists will often plead that such a thorough study will convince us that their scheme offers as good an arrangement as we are likely to get and that unauthorised adaptations are thus to be shunned; be that as it may, the classifier should certainly

take pains to fully comprehend the scope and character of the system which he elects to apply.

308. *Broad versus Close Classification*. There then arises the question in general libraries: should the chosen scheme be used as it stands or only in part? If our library is not a large one is it necessary to go, say, further than the first thousand places – the three figure position of DC? Would not further sub-division mean unnecessary minuteness with the attendant disadvantages of long class-numbers? Further, even if there is a real advantage in minute classification, is this not neutralised for the reader because he cannot understand or remember the figures of a long class-mark? Some arguments for broad classification with extra detail in the catalogue and some of the critics of close or specific classing are considered in Chapter 22. Here we merely cite the view of one American writer[1] who argues that 'classification like the mathematical symbol π is never perfect no matter how far extended'. However, many librarians who advocate a limited use of a classification scheme do so on grounds which should now be negligible. The constant growth of libraries makes reasonably specific placings inevitable in all collections except extremely small ones or, perhaps, in an old cathedral or similar library, which is complete and will never increase in size. The reader is not so unintelligent as some librarians appear to think; he can usually understand numerical or alphabetical notations unless these are extremely long. When he is unable to follow the sequence, it is usually because the guides and other aids with which the library should be furnished, are lacking or inadequate. The *practical* point to bear in mind is that classification should be carried as far as is necessary to define and segregate the subject matter of the books; otherwise specific themes will be intermingled and hidden in a broad containing class. Sooner or later, in nearly every growing library, the full classification will be needed and alterations to class-marks on older stock and records involve a great deal of work. Thus to classify closely, if not an immediate practical necessity, may well be an ultimate economy provided that the library adheres to the classification originally selected; no librarian enjoys retracing his steps to extend classification symbols allocated, say, ten years ago, which are now discovered to be too general for his collections. Cutter's Expansive Classification was an interesting experiment in

[1] R. B. Downs in his paper 'The administrator looks at classification'. In Allerton Park Institute: *The Role of Classification in the Modern American Library*, 1959.

I*

both broad and close classing, but his advice 'be minute . . . be not too minute' is not altogether conclusive, because it is difficult to say what being too minute means. The more positive rule, 'Classify a book in the most specific heading that will contain it' is preferable; because, if this is observed, it must bring the whole classification into play. Ranganathan, with much justice, speaks with contempt of 'the regression to broad classification, even to the abandonment of classification . . . as if saving shelf space is the summum bonum of library service'.

309. The librarian of a very small collection may abandon the rule indicated above, provided that he considers the *potential growth* of his stock. Broad classification may occasionally be used in special libraries in circumstances described in our next section; in the public library it is often encountered in the Young People's Department where it is quite adequate to provide the younger reader with a simplified plan of the system in use and enables him to comprehend, without undue effort, the elements of the method librarians use to arrange material. Broad classification is, of course, encountered elsewhere in practice; sometimes in circumstances where it can scarcely be condoned. The smaller municipal library system and the tiny branch libraries in a county service are the obvious examples of its just use. DC, in particular, is quite adaptable for service in such small units, as the editor's introduction to its seventeenth edition points out.

310. James Thompson of the University of East Anglia has advocated a broad arrangement as sufficing for the needs of the new British university libraries.[1] One expects, of course, the author approach to be the dominant one in such academic libraries; in fact one sometimes finds that a subject catalogue is not supplied. Yet, although the undergraduate will be concerned mainly with authors and with specific references recommended by his lecturers, he will surely seek out other material on his subject from time to time. The needs of the post-graduate research worker in university libraries should also not be ignored. Thompson quotes authorities, chiefly American ones, to support his views; the reaction in Britain can best be gauged by the nature of the correspondence that followed his article. To our way of thinking, the approach which he suggests, although in some ways understandable, is an evasion of the real problem. The ever increasing flow of literature, the increasing

[1] *Library Association Record*, September, 1963, pp. 327–30.

demands being made upon our scholarly libraries and the expansion of the number of university places are all factors which tell against his argument. The academic library of the future will surely need a good subject catalogue, but the classification must play its part also; a reasonably specific arrangement will thus be imperative to gather together material on any specialised theme and, therefore, to save time and effort.

311. *Use of alphabetical order.* When broad classification is adopted, it may be worthwhile to sub-arrange items in each broad category by alphabetical order of topic; alternatively, A–Z author order may be employed. The first of these two methods is, of course, extensively used in LC, which certainly does *not* make use of broad classification; it is, however, also a process which could be adopted in a small library, alphabetical subject order within a broad class being preferred to further systematic sub-division. We observed in Chapter 2 that alphabetical order of one sort or another is useful for the arrangement of certain categories of material and that, at times, it is a helpful method of sub-arrangement within the classification. The essential thing is that a library must not use A–Z order merely because it is simple or easy to apply; the alphabetical arrangement can only justifiably replace a classified one if we are sure that no loss of efficiency results. When the detail of the systematic order is unwanted, when there is no obvious systematic method of arrangement to apply, or when it does not seem necessary to show closely the relationships between specific topics; these are the occasions which call for the use of alphabetical arrangement. Alphabetical author order for fiction, and as a means for the final arrangement of a number of books on the same specific topic *within* a class, is common; if a large biography class is maintained, the great lives may be arranged in alphabetical rather than systematic order. The smaller public library may also apply the notion of broad classification, categories of a popular kind such as motor cars, gardening, outdoor sports, etc., being sub-divided at an early stage by the A–Z sequence of topics. And, of course, A–Z order may be used for some 'non-book' material also; it will inevitably take some part in the organization of knowledge, as an alphabetical catalogue of some kind is indispensable. Yet usually, particularly in our larger libraries, the role of A–Z order in shelf arrangement for non-fiction is a comparatively small one. The National Lending Library for Science and Technology at Boston Spa affords an excellent example of the

extensive use of alphabetical order in arrangement. This is, however, to be regarded as a special case; a library which consists chiefly of long runs of scientific journals can scarcely be considered as a typical example of the stock and needs of most collections. We repeat once again that the A–Z order, whether by author, title, or topic, is only to be used in most general libraries when the classified order is obviously unsuitable. The fast-growing library should be classified closely; the task takes no longer than broad classification and the job is done once and for all. Therefore, the various general schemes of classification must supply the necessary detail for such an arrangement. Those libraries not needing all this detail can easily ignore such sub-divisions or provision for synthesis which they consider to be superfluous.

312. *Adaptation.* The student must take care to distinguish between broad classification and the alphabetical method of sub-arrangement. They may indeed be used together, but there is no reason why a scheme should not, in fact, classify in some *detail* before resorting to alphabetical sub-arrangement by topic or by author within its classes. However, we may leave this theme here and consider another administrative problem which the librarian faces when he applies a scheme. Should he apply it as it stands, or will he be well advised to adapt it to his own library's needs and adjust classes which he considers to be awkward or inadequate? As modifications are often made in schemes, this question deserves thought. It is curious that the librarian mind is so constructed that it likes 'nibbling at classification schemes' – to use the phrase of J. D. Brown. In part this is due to the weaknesses of one kind or another that a librarian can see in the scheme he has chosen; few schemes, indeed, do not seem capable of improvement in some way when we have tested them. Yet a distinction should be made between adaptation recognised by the classificationist, or by the editors of a scheme, as reasonable adjustments and those modifications which are unauthorised as far as the classification's editorial body is concerned. A former editor of DC, D. J. Haykin, once asserted that many of the complaints about that system arose because librarians were not prepared to take it as it stood, but insisted upon making their own adjustments; one can see Haykin's point of view when he suggests that, if this is done, it is not fair to blame DC for the unhappy results. Thus most librarians will be well advised to make only those modifications which are suggested in the introduction to

the scheme as possibilities (BC with its alternative locations is especially generous in this respect); other adaptations are likely to prove misleading and, if the classification is widely used, much of the commendable uniformity of practice between libraries will be lost as a result of these novel alterations. As the editor of a leading American journal on our subject wrote recently: 'We would never recommend wholesale or impetuous revision or "adaptation" of classification schemes. Too many libraries have faced or are facing expensive reclassification because of past improvisation. Once tampering with numbers has begun the movement accelerates and the innovator finds himself (and his successors) committed to moving farther and farther away from the source'.[1]

313. The modifications which are usually made involve the bringing together of such subjects as Language and Literature in DC and the association, in the same system, of the History and Geography of the same country. There are various ways of achieving the latter; they mostly result in an arrangement such as

> 942.21 History of Surrey
> T42.21 Travel in Surrey

Here the divisions 914–919 have been abandoned and travel books go into the History section, being distinguished from history books by the replacement of the digit 9 by the letter T. It is also customary to remove fiction from the classified sequence, whatever the scheme used, and to shelve modern fiction in an alphabetical arrangement by author. In some public lending libraries there is a small collection of quick-reference books, separated from the rest of the stock, without regard to the place of each reference work in the classified sequence as a whole. Thus adaptations often lead to the state of affairs which librarians describe as broken order.

314. One finds occasionally that adaptations of a more ambitious kind are made. For example, special collections in general libraries often demand some adjustment of the scheme employed, as we point out in Chapter 23. The university library using LC often makes extensive adjustments to it in order to make it more suited to the requirements of such a library or, in this country, to counterbalance the understandable American emphasis[2] of the Congress scheme.

---

[1] Esther J. Piercy, *Library Resources and Technical Services*, Fall, 1965, p. 413.

[2] The library of the University of York has, in fact, adapted DC to meet its own special requirements and 'literary warrant'. (See J. Stirling's article in *Journal of Documentation*, September, 1963.)

Yet sometimes the public library which has adopted DC will attempt more ambitious reconstruction of that classification, for the arrangement of its general collections, than has been described in our last paragraph. Obviously some related material is scattered in DC. If any librarian possessed the knowledge and industry to make it a really one-place classification, in the best sense of the term, he would do a great service to classifiers; yet the system would then no longer be Dewey's, but a new classification, to be studied as such. As it is, librarians are often inclined to complain about this fault or that, but only rarely does the public librarian make a drastic change in the system. One example of the more adventurous type of adaptation in the past was the arrangement worked out for the Geography Class of DC by Stafford Public Libraries. This involves the re-allocation of certain numbers to allow the various branches of geography – economic, human, physical, and so forth, to be brought together. The resulting arrangement can be regarded as an ingenious attempt to overcome the general dissatisfaction with the treatment of this subject in DC. It could well have been argued, when the adaptation was introduced, that it put Stafford out of line with the general practice in the classification of geography in British public libraries and, as we remark more than once in this chapter, there are great administrative advantages in having a more or less uniform system of classification throughout the country in libraries of the same type. But the Stafford arrangement has been perhaps partly vindicated by the fact that the latest edition of DC has found it necessary to offer an optional alternative arrangement under 910.

315. Yet, by and large, we must incline to the view that if a system is, like DC, widely used and acknowledged, it is best used as it stands for the arrangement of general material; adaptations should not go beyond those permitted by the scheme's introduction. Indeed to write a full history of all the modifications of this or that system which have been made to answer the convenience of librarians would occupy an inordinate space and would not serve any purpose except usually to show the futility of the work; in short, adaptation is to be shunned unless the reasons for the modifications are very powerful ones indeed. The only reasonable exception to this advice is the local collection or other special material.

316. *Reclassifying a Library.* Perhaps an even greater issue than that of adaptation is the possibility of reclassification. If our stock is arranged according to a system which is rapidly becoming obsolete

and a better method is readily available, should the change be made? This question does not admit of a ready answer. Some would offer the glib reply that a library should always be prepared to change the classification system and should face up to the challenge of employing the best methods available, discounting temporary inconvenience; others will offer the equally unsatisfactory retort that reclassification of an established library can *never* be economically justified, or cannot even be contemplated by a busy librarian. The answer lies somewhere between these extreme views. A librarian faced with the possibility of accepting a new system must carefully consider its long term advantages with regard to the scholarly and satisfactory arrangement of material on the shelves and of entries in catalogues. He must also weigh up the cost of a change in terms of time, labour, the problem of altering many records, and the task of maintaining a service to readers while the reclassification process is being carried out. The actual financial cost of the operation is also important; it is most unfortunate that, despite some discussion on the subject, we have no fully reliable published estimates of either the cost of classification itself or the expenditure involved in reclassifying a substantial collection. In this country certain public libraries have changed from SC to DC in recent years and some academic libraries have abandoned obsolete systems for more flexible ones of their own devising. Librarians in many countries face this problem and are inevitably reluctant to embark upon such a programme of work because of the number of volumes which have to be re-examined and reallocated by the classifiers and because, and several librarians consider this to be the key factor, no established general scheme has as yet a clear-cut advantage over the well entrenched DC for public libraries and indeed for many academic libraries. The latter, it is true, especially university libraries, do often prefer an adapted form of LC or a good 'home-made' system; one of the best examples of the latter is the scheme made in the nineteen fifties by Kenneth Garside for University College, London, and based on faculty reader interest.

317. If the problem of changing over hundreds of classified volumes to the new scheme is considered the major difficulty and the librarian is otherwise convinced that reclassification is a necessity, the answer may lie in adopting a fresh scheme for new accessions and regularly-used older material only, while adhering to the older system for the arrangement of most of the material already in

stock. This would avoid allowing the methods of the past to prevail over and dictate to the needs of the present and future, without giving rise to so much reorganization. It is a notion which Ranganathan has called the *osmosis method* of reclassification and it has been adopted in some libraries. It results in an arrangement where there are two parallel sequences for a time representing different classifications (apart from any parallel arrangements which may exist within each of the two schemes). Gradually, however, the older system will be driven out by the preferred classification and will eventually only be found in stackrooms where the reserve stock and rarely used material is arranged. This method is surely the most painless way of injecting a new method of arrangement into a well established library service. It is not ideal, but it does tend to abolish the argument that reclassification is unthinkable because thousands of volumes will need to be changed over to the new system. On the other hand, many librarians will, it must be confessed, be very reluctant to reclassify even if this method is contemplated. There are obvious disadvantages in employing two different schemes side by side for a number of years and these cannot be lightly disregarded. Dr D. J. Campbell has suggested that the osmosis method is unsuitable for special libraries and can best be practised in collections which retain much obsolescent material.[1]

318. American writers on our subject have been especially quick to see how uneconomical the reclassification of a medium-sized or large existing library usually is. In such an instance, the work involved in changing the scheme can only be justified if the subsequent advantages are truly enormous. Thus several libraries using a totally inadequate system might now change to DC to have the benefits of a better scheme and the advantage of employing the classification now used in most general libraries. But an entirely new classification which tried to supplant the Dewey Decimal system would have a much more difficult, although not impossible, task. As Professor Maurice Tauber has pointed out on several occasions, the onus in this matter really lies with the makers of a new system, who must prove that reclassification by it will yield long-term, durable advantages. Perhaps it is best for any new classification to fully prove its worth in newly erected general libraries, before those committed to an older system are called upon to seriously consider

[1] Making your own indexing system in science and technology, *Aslib Proceedings*, October, 1963, pp. 282–303.

change. We return to this theme in Chapter Twenty-seven.

319. Let us imagine, for a moment, that a long-established library *does* decide to reclassify. How could this operation be accomplished with the least possible disruption of its services to readers? We can only sketch here the procedure which might be followed, but this may be sufficient to indicate how the task could be approached. First of all, a space must be cleared to house the reclassified volumes in their fresh arrangement. Next the classifiers must attack the older system class by class, transferring material from each class in turn to the appropriate part of the new arrangement. The latter will grow slowly in the space provided and fresh space will soon become available as large gaps arise in the older sequence. As material is transferred, the appropriate records in the catalogue must be altered and the book stock in the older arrangement must be gradually contracted so that space is available where it is most urgently needed. Eventually all the stock, or all that the librarian decides to reclassify, will have been removed to the new sequence which will soon grow with extraordinary rapidity. This 'gigantic game of chess', as C. D. Batty once described it, will certainly involve a great deal of effort. If the task is pursued too rapidly, there is a risk that errors will be made and old class-marks left undeleted in the catalogue; it must, therefore, progress steadily, but relatively slowly. At all times books must be available for the reader. Thus all staff must be kept informed of the state of the huge task and must know which class has been removed from its old sequence for reclassification at any particular time in the operation; they must know also which subjects have already been reclassified. Although the staff will be burdened with extra work at such a time, the library should certainly display a notice informing readers of what is happening and inviting them to seek help if they cannot find any item which they may require during the transitional period. One sometimes finds at times like this that the reader appreciated the old system more than one suspected!

320. *A Centralised Classification Service*. Finally in this chapter we shall consider the possibilities of centralised classification. Most municipal and county library systems have a central department where cataloguing and classification for the system is carried out; what we have in mind here, however, is a central organization that can perform this work on a national scale, employing an expert team of classifiers and solving the awkward problems of the classification of complex books for each individual library. The idea of course is

by no means a new one – the Library of Congress has done this type of work in the U.S.A. since the beginning of the present century; it implies, however, that most libraries will use the same classification scheme and that they will employ it with few adaptations. In other words, if the individual library is to reap the full benefits of such a service, it must be prepared to accept, to a large extent, uniformity in classification. One might repeat also that such uniformity is certainly a boon in library administration if neighbouring public library authorities amalgamate and their stocks are blended; in such cases a great deal of extra effort, and that of a most laborious kind, would be called for if the combining libraries employed different classification systems or used widely different versions of the same classification. In like manner, uniformity of classification facilitates participation in schemes of subject specialisation.

321. Despite the fact that the McColvin Report pointed out the need for a centralised cataloguing and classification service in Great Britain, there was a delay in securing such a service; fortunately, this has been provided now for some years by the British National Bibliography. This publication provides a weekly list of new British books classified by DC; most libraries in this country save a great deal of time by obtaining many of the class-marks needed for their stock directly from the B.N.B., leaving their own staff to concentrate more on the classification of overseas material. This, naturally enough, is another great reason for the continuing popularity of Dewey's scheme in British libraries.

322. There has in fact been some controversy over the method of classification employed by the Bibliography, as the various issues of the Library Association Record for 1960 and the August 1961 copy of the news-sheet *Liaison* demonstrate. The B.N.B. makes extensions and alterations to the orthodox DC. The former include the use of certain UDC devices and the employment of the figure one in square brackets after a class-mark to indicate that it is considered that the extent of the sub-division in DC is inadequate; the latter can be seen in the use of lower-case letters in place of the common form divisions of DC. It is claimed that these modifications are necessary to bring about a more helpful arrangement of entries in the larger cumulations of the Bibliography and to serve its long-term needs; yet many librarians seem to think that it would be best for B.N.B. to use the DC in its orthodox form rather than to act as a denaturant in this way and Custer has made the position of the DC

Editorial Committee quite clear in this matter of unauthorised adaptation.[1] There can be no doubt, however, that these modifications and especially the attempts to provide extra specificity and greater notational synthesis have been employed by the editor, A. J. Wells, with the interests of the future of the Bibliography at heart. The alterations can often be ignored by those libraries not requiring them and the lower-case letters can be converted back to the orthodox, numerical form divisions, if necessary. It would seem that most libraries using B.N.B. suffer little inconveniences from this unorthodoxy in classification; on the credit side, the Bibliography does, despite a few minor drawbacks, provide us with an excellent key to new British books and it offers the classifier great economies plus the benefits of uniformity of classification, to a large extent, with other B.N.B. subscribers.

323. *Conclusion.* The themes dealt with in this chapter will repay a much closer study than has been possible here. They represent most of the major issues and possibilities that confront the librarian in the selection, application, and administration of a general classification scheme. Some of these issues call for careful judgement from the practising librarian, with the peculiar problems of his library being considered in the light of the information given in this manual and in other texts. The student should think most carefully about the subjects and problems considered here; the bibliography relating to this chapter will indicate some further sources of information, but it is necessary also, indeed vital, that topics such as adaptation, reclassification, broad versus close classification, and others should be considered critically in the light of one's own ideas and observations.

[1] *Library Association Record*, December, 1960, pp. 406–7.

CHAPTER TWENTY

Guiding and Display Work

324. In a library which operates on the closed-access principle it is possible, when once the books have been placed on the shelves in their correct order, that a very simple indication of that order by means of a guide card to each class in addition to the writing of the number on the backs of the books will be a sufficient guide for the staff to the location of any particular volumes. However, in open-access libraries, a much more extensive treatment of the shelves is necessary. The classified arrangement will be unfamiliar to the library user; to ensure that material is quickly located and the collection fully exploited, the librarian must provide a series of guides to act as the link between the familiar but unhelpful alphabetical approach and the little known but far more helpful classified arrangement. There is a real danger that, unless the systematically arranged sequence is well guided, the reader in public and even in academic libraries will fail to find his way quickly to the particular book, or section of the library, that he needs. We are convinced that there are still many libraries which provide insufficient guidance to their classified arrangement or which offer notices which are amateurish, vague, or completely inadequate. The reader need not know much about the classification in order to reap the benefits which it offers; good guidance can enable him to grasp the elements of the arrangement and find his way about the library quickly and easily. We find nowadays that retailers are forced to study consumer requirements closely if they are to sell their products; likewise librarians must study the customers' problems and requirements if a first-class service is to be offered. There can be no doubt that one of these requirements is a good standard of guiding, especially with

regard to larger collections. The reader needs a number of clues to and indications of the classified arrangement. These are:

1. A good catalogue.
2. A plan of the classified library.
3. Class guides.
4. Bay and shelf guides
5. Individual book guides.
6. A printed pamphlet.
7. Personal assistance whenever possible.

Postponing the description of the catalogue as a guide, for this receives separate treatment in the next chapter, we may consider the function of the various guides in turn.

325. *Overall plan.* One of the best guides to the shelf arrangement as a whole is a plan, showing the positions of the bookcases and giving the numbers and names of the main classes contained in them. Ideally a large plan of this kind will be placed in the entrance foyer, or be given some other prominent location in the library. The reader will be given a broad, overall picture of the classified arrangement through this plan and he will ascertain from it the approximate location of any topic. Small reproductions of such plans, say, of postcard size, are sometimes published so that readers may possess their own copies. But we are more concerned here with the large bold plan which the library exhibits near to its entrance. There are many possibilities for a plan of this kind; one of the most interesting innovations along these lines has been at Luton Public Library, where a large plan of the push-button type has been provided. An illustration of the Luton plan is shown opposite page 284. The reader selects the subject he requires and presses the appropriate button on the plan. The area of shelving in which books on this topic can be found then lights up on the plan. The plan at Luton covers both the ground floor and the gallery of the Central Library; over 500 topics are listed in its alphabetical index.

326. *Class Guides.* Many of our other guides are affixed to the shelves or bays and are, as we have indicated, an alphabetical key to the systematic arrangement. A class guide is one which is placed at the top centre of a bookcase, or at the beginning of a large class on the shelves. Sometimes it is merely a bold statement of the class number and subject, such as

300 SOCIOLOGY

or it may set out the main divisions of the class, possibly with reference to parallel classifications, as

300 SOCIOLOGY	
300 Social Science	360 Social Welfare
310 Statistics	370 Education
320 Political Science	380 Commerce, Communication
330 Economics	390 Customs, Costume, Folklore
340 Law	
350 Public Administration	

See also the 'oversize' collection for books too large to be shelved here.

These class guides may take various forms, but they should always be colourful and attractive to encourage readers to take notice of them. Obviously much artistic taste and ingenuity can be given to to such bold signs; it is well worth-while to have such detail as perfect as possible.

327. *Bay and shelf guides.* Large classes which occupy several bays of shelving require closer guiding; and the most convenient units to guide are the bay, or tier and the individual shelf. Much experiment and ingenuity has been expended on such guides, and many forms are in use. The idea behind these guides is that they shall reveal exactly what a bay of shelves contains and what is on each particular shelf. They may be placed at the end of the bay in the form of a framed notice, on the shelves in the form of blocks, or they may be provided in the form of a series of narrow strips which can be attached to the edge of the appropriate shelves. It may be noted that the 'block' idea consumes a great deal of shelf space and thus the other methods are usually to be preferred. It is possible also that the large bay guide can make the reader aware of allied subjects that, unfortunately, are housed in some other part of the classification system. Great care must be taken to ensure that all such bay and shelf guides are moved as the stock in each section expands, as it always will in a living classified library. There is no point in guides which are misleading because a class has extended its boundaries and left the guide badly positioned. Yet, alas, this

situation is still encountered in a few modern libraries. Typical shelf guides are those illustrated below:

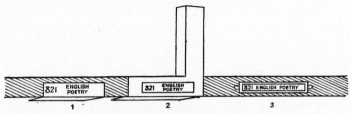

Shelf Labels:

1. Shelf label in xylonite holder.
2. Metal label holder combined with book-rest.
3. Ordinary brass screw-on label holder.

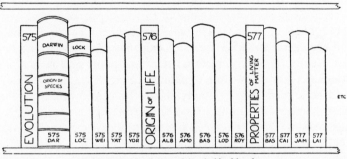

Subject Guides inserted in shelf of books.

328. *Notation.* After each bay has been clearly guided and shelf or topic guides have been liberally provided, further assistance is provided by guiding the individual through the notation of the classification in use. Every book must clearly bear its class-mark on the back of the cover. This class-mark reveals its position in the classified arrangement and is the link between the entries in the catalogue and the shelf classification. Some controversy has arisen about the position of the notation and, while such controversies as 'up or down the spine' or 'the top versus the bottom of the spine' may appear reminiscent of certain portions of the novels of Jonathan Swift, there is a good case for uniformity of practice in that the library looks neater if all notations appear, say, two inches from the bottom of the book. Occasionally, however, exceptions will need to be made. All we really wish to demonstrate here, however, is

that notation is itself a guide to the classified sequence; providing it is not too long and that the symbols which it employs have ordinal value, the reader should be able to follow it fairly well.

329. *Blocks indicating absent volumes.* It has been ingeniously suggested that in a perfectly organized classified library every absence of a book from its place in the main classified sequence would be indicated. Where the collection is divided firstly by the size factor into octavo, quarto, and folio sequences, the main sequence is necessarily the first of these. A guide called a 'dummy' may thus be placed among the octavos at the place where the larger volumes would have appeared had their size permitted a single classified sequence to be maintained. This dummy resembles the wooden or other blocks sometimes used as shelf guides. It has the same fault that it eats up space on the shelves; and space is, despite the essential truth of a quotation from Ranganathan's pen in our previous chapter, sometimes one of the most precious, least-easily spared things in a library. Dummies are now comparatively rare in shelf arrangement. Other forms of guidance can draw attention to the existence of oversize material and the dummy may be confused with blocks serving as subject guides, if these are employed. Also, it could be argued that a dummy should be placed on the lending library shelves every time a book is borrowed or is absent for any other reason. The work which this would entail makes the proposition unthinkable. It is therefore far better to rely on the other guides described so far to show to us and our readers the whereabouts of a particular class, the content of each bay and shelf, and the exact location of each individual volume. If a 'dummy guide' is provided it will resemble the one opposite.

330. *Printed pamphlet.* A most useful guide to the modern library, especially one with several departments is the printed pamphlet or brochure. This may give a general conspectus of the library's services and can give a simple explanation of the method of arranging material on the shelves coupled with notes on how to find a book through the catalogue. The catalogue should also be separately guided, but the advice given in a printed pamphlet of this kind can be most useful nevertheless. There are many examples nowadays, in both public and academic libraries, of introductory guides in pamphlet form. They are usually to be found by the entrance or near to the catalogue and the reader is invited to take one away with him. Here again the librarian must consider carefully the most

effective wording of the advice given in such a pamphlet and must ensure that it is attractively presented and that the reader is encouraged to take it and read it through.

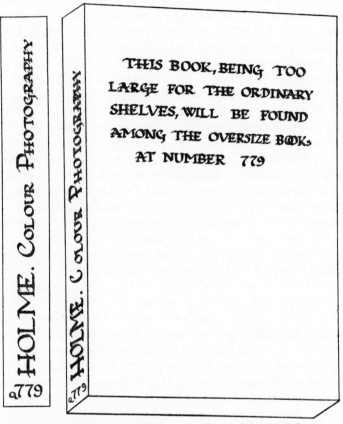

A 'dummy' book: a cross-reference from Octavo shelves to shelves for oversize books.

331. *Personal Guidance.* The best form of guidance that the reader can possibly receive is that given directly by the staff. In these days of mass advertisement we find that printed guidance is sometimes ignored (although that is no reason for not providing it, for it will often prove helpful). No amount of guidance in the form of notices and pamphlets, however, can be regarded as a substitute for direct assistance from members of the staff. If possible new readers should always be given a brief description of the library services and its

method of arrangement. The Reader's Adviser or other members of
the staff should always be willing to explain to the users of the library
how to find a book in the catalogue or on the shelves. The extent to
which this advisory service can be given will depend, of course, on
the number of staff available for professional work: it is because, in
many libraries, there are not enough staff available that we have to
rely so heavily on the other forms of guidance. But direct personal
assistance is the best type of guidance of all and should be given
whenever possible, although the other methods cannot be neglected.
Personal help can make a world of difference to the impression of
the library services which the reader receives and to the way in
which he understands how to use these services intelligently.

332. The good librarian will select appropriate guides for his
library judiciously. There is no point in overburdening the reader
with notices, but there is likewise no excuse for failing to provide a
reasonable standard of printed guides. The size of the library and the
type of reader concerned with its services must be taken into account
and as much direct help must be given as possible. After this personal
aid has been given, the reader's ability to find his way about the
large classified library will depend largely upon the other guides
described here. R. L. Collison has suggested that effective guiding
results from a commonsense policy in this matter plus an ability to
see things from the reader's viewpoint. We would agree with this,
but would stress most strongly the need for librarians to put themselves in the reader's position and test the efficiency of their printed
guides by imagining themselves coming to the library for the first
time in search of a book. Better still, for it is always difficult for the
professional librarian to pretend that he is new to his library, some
regular readers could be asked for their views on the quality of the
guiding; they may well provide helpful suggestions which will
enable us to demonstrate the classified groupings more powerfully
and effectively and thus to offer a better service to our customers.

333. *Display Work.* It is time for us to consider the other theme of
this chapter, which is the value and purpose of display in libraries.
Any open access library in which the stock is well presented and
guided, is a book display in the widest sense of the term: our best
advertisement of our capabilities as librarians is reflected there.
Indeed one writer has said classification is 'a backroom technique
devoid of all value unless completed by a positive endeavour to
advertise and circulate the book stocks on which it has been em-

ployed'.[1] The larger, more adequately lighted, appropriately decorated and conveniently, even comfortably, furnished our public rooms are the finer is the book display. We usually employ the word *display* in a more restricted sense than this, however. It is adopted for a special exhibition of books and other material on some particular topic or theme. This may well be a theme of current or local interest; in many cases, however, the display has been formed to gather together related material that the classification has scattered. No scheme can collect in one place (and this should by now be obvious to our reader) all the material relating to a subject; nor can it reveal all subject relationships, although the good scheme will demonstrate the most important ones. Occasionally, the library may wish to exhibit together the 'distributed relatives' of the classification and a book display offers an excellent opportunity for doing this. If the DC is the scheme in use, for example, an exhibition of material on *Psychology* could bring together books from many parts of the classification. In addition to the obvious material from various sectors of the 100 class we might have relevant books on religious, industrial, criminal, art, social, educational, and sales psychology, scattered in various divisions of the classification. The display will gather together this kindred material, for a short time, and indicate its presence and the relationship between the different aspects of this topic. Likewise a display can be created on a particular country, the object in this case being to collect, from various classes, books on its history, geography, language and literature, political and economic life, religion, science, art, and culture. Lives of some of the great men from that country can also be included in the special temporary display. Thus displays are an outstanding example of the wise use of *broken order*.

334. These displays may be maintained for a week, a month, or longer. Much will depend upon the popularity of the exhibition of books and, if the department concerned is a public lending library, on how easily the display can be replenished as material is borrowed. Sooner or later the books must be returned to their correct place in the classified sequence for it is here that the most permanently useful sequence of topics is, or ought to be, revealed. Our displays are designed as short exhibitions which show other possible groupings from time to time. These exhibitions are designed to serve, or promote interest in, a special occasion. The active librarian has his

[1] R. S. Walker, *Librarian*, February, 1958, pp. 21–8.

finger on the pulse of public thought, watches world activities, keeps a calendar of the anniversaries of great men and events, knows what is going on in central or local government, and so on; and while these things are hot news he endeavours to illustrate them by book displays. He is also concerned to keep before his readers good books, from the classics to works on subjects that would be neglected by most people. The suggestibility of the general reader is very great; he prefers the judgement upon books of other people to his own so long as it is not obtruded upon him unsought and without tact. The best illustration of this is the crowd, always to be seen in the busy public library, around the section where the returned books are put while awaiting reshelving. The good librarian will try to help such people through displays, but it must not be thought that display work is to be confined to the world of public librarianship. College libraries can often produce effective displays, especially those which gather in the distributed aspects of an important topic; here, as in the public library, such exhibitions can stimulate interest in a subject and in the library itself.

335. One of the best books on the subject of display is that of Savage;[1] although published twenty years ago, it is still of value for the way in which it reveals the individualistic ingenuity and enterprise in book exploitation which he has always shown. Dr Savage calls our attention to the display work done in stores and calls for more 'sales initiative' from librarians in this respect. The full implications of his advice have never been grasped by many qualified librarians although the general quantity as well as the standard of display work has increased enormously in recent years and one now finds many central public library departments and branch libraries, not to mention college libraries, where the publicity value of temporary but attractive displays is fully appreciated and where many interesting experiments in this direction are being made. It may appear invidious to quote examples in this context but a reference must be made to the West Riding County Library service, where excellent 'shop window' displays in branch libraries are an accepted feature and where other exhibitions on a variety of themes are first-class publicity for both the value of reading and the merits and range of stock of the county library. This library has a department devoted to publicity and display work and this is directed by a qualified librarian; staff with appropriate art school

[1] E. A. Savage, *Manual of book classification and display*, 1946.

The 'push-button' type of plan used in Luton Public Library.

A typical window display at a branch of the West Riding County Library.

experience have, however, been recruited to assist in the creation of posters and suitable dummy figures. The artistic flair of the staff means that many such models and posters can be made to support and enhance displays at both headquarters and the branch libraries. It is quite astonishing for the uninitiated to discover how really first-class display work can be carried out with the aid of comparatively inexpensive tubular structure, such as Raphic and Abstracta, and to learn how effectively lettering for displays can be produced by means of such material as polystyrene. In the hands of librarians with ability and initiative, these displays must do our profession a power of good.

336. It is outside our province to enter into the field of library advertising to which, as a subject, perhaps book display really belongs. Yet it needs no demonstration that if the librarian is to perform one of his services, which is to create readers, he must lure them, if that be not too smug a term, into reading what he believes they ought to read and otherwise might not read. A whole book can be devoted to the ingenuities of library staffs in making displays. They can consist of just one book, or a very small grouping, supported by colourful posters and other relevant items. Larger groups, as, for example, a display of 'the best sellers of the Victorian era' may occupy a whole room. Engaging invitations to people such as 'Why not learn a language?' with the books on some popular languages shown, or – and this though not especially connected with classification is the most popular of all – 'Books the librarian has read and recommends', are the sort of thing contemplated. (This is a whimsical success when one remembers that the average public library reader credits the librarian with having read every book in his library!) The field is without limit.

337. Displays, of course, need not be confined to the library premises. It has been suggested that shopkeepers may permit the use of a window for displays occasionally. We do not think such a concession is to be expected from the only stores in which it would be really effective, but an empty shop may often be available and the opportunity then must be too good to miss. Displays can also be made at local society meetings, bazaars, exhibitions and so forth. All displays, however, should be appropriate and should be planned with care. They should make use of suitable background, good and efficient labelling, and should use colour with taste. There is much to be said for expert help with the posters and other artistic features

that go with a book-display. Home-made labels, ill-drawn diagrams, ineffective wordings are all to be shunned; such work is at best time-consuming for the assistant librarian and for every library with a budding artist on the staff there must be many who have members of staff who think of themselves as such. There is a world of difference, as some of our senior librarians have found to their cost. Thus it is often wise to seek aid from the local College of Art, or even to employ staff who are specialists in this kind of work. This, as we have seen is done in the West Riding, but many authorities may consider that they are too small for the acquisition of such staff to be economical and worthwhile. There is no reason, of course, why neighbouring libraries should not co-operate in this matter and employ display staff jointly; indeed there is great scope for experiment in this sphere of our activities.

338. But we have wandered from the subject of display in relation to book classification. It is best thought of, in this context, as something which is complementary to the organized and permanent arrangement on the shelves; it is useful in displaying helpful groupings which must often be ignored and in publicising the services of the library. Indeed displays may help to serve as a guide to the library's resources and its potential; in this respect, they are closely connected with guiding, the theme of the earlier part of our chapter. The most successful displays are always staffed unobtrusively and, although they offer great scope to the librarian's imagination, commonsense and courtesy to the regular, serious reader might suggest perhaps that not too many exhibitions of this kind should be made at any one time. They could mean the removal of important books from their proper places on the classified shelves, and these may be missed by readers who really need them much more than the fortuitous recruit to reading who may be won by book display.

CHAPTER TWENTY-ONE

The Classified Catalogue

339. With the exception of personal assistance, the best guide to the contents of a classified library is an effective catalogue. It is an indispensable key to the stock in a library of any size and, whatever form it may take, it must provide some means of showing what books are available in the library on each subject, and by each author. This Manual does not attempt to cover the subject of cataloguing but, as the classified catalogue involves the application of a classification system just as much as the arrangement on the shelves, and as the catalogue is an excellent guide to the arrangement on the shelves, it is necessary to devote a short chapter to it here. Like most British librarians, we are supporting the classified catalogue against the rival type – the dictionary catalogue. The latter has been extremely popular in the U.S.A.; a fact which perhaps illustrates as clearly as anything can the disillusionment of librarians in that country with highly specific classification. For the dictionary catalogue relies on the alphabetical approach to knowledge, while its rival follows the order of the classification scheme in use, with certain alphabetical keys. Before describing the classified catalogue in some detail and briefly contrasting it with its rival, it must again be stressed that the catalogue is a most important tool. It caters, as we have indicated, for author and subject requests; it may also provide entries under editors, translators, titles, series, and so forth. It is customary for the main entry, at least, to give a fairly detailed description of the book being catalogued for the benefit of the reader and librarian.

340. We make no apology for considering at this point the ways in which the catalogue and the classification in use are complementary tools for the organization of knowledge in a library. Although some

of the points made in this paragraph may seem self-evident, it is certain that students of the subject often overlook several of them; they should be constantly borne in mind in our studies. The shelf classification is concerned with the arrangement of books themselves – tangible objects which can only go in one place on the shelves; the catalogue, however, deals with entries representing these books. Thus if a book deals with, say, three subjects, it can only have one place (under the dominant subject) in the shelf arrangement; in the catalogue, *three* subject entries can be made. The catalogue will also clearly reveal works which the reader may not find on the shelves because they are out on loan, or away at the binders, or shelved in an oversize sequence, or forming part of a special book display. The catalogue is also more varied than the classification in that the latter caters only for the subject approach to knowledge; the catalogue does this also but, in addition, it provides author, title, and other entries to aid its users. It can thus be seen that, although comparatively few readers in most general libraries use the catalogue, it has great merit and certain advantages over the classification scheme; this is equally true of both classified and dictionary catalogues. Of course, it must be stated that the shelf classification has, in some respects, advantages over the catalogue. It deals with books and not with mere entries and most readers prefer to get to the books as quickly as possible; they do not wish to consult a catalogue but rather to browse at the shelves. If neatly arranged and well guided the classified sequence on the shelves can be of inestimable value to the reader. Those readers seeking a book by a particular author, however, or those wishing to find all the books which the library has on a particular subject, may well find that they need to consult the catalogue. But then, of course, these are not rival tools; they are intended to assist each other in the arrangement and retrieval of knowledge and the wise and well instructed reader will make good use of both classification and catalogue.

341. Our main object here is to explain the nature and advantages of the classified catalogue. Let us consider first its nature, or method of construction. It consists of three sequences: the main or classified section; the author index; the subject index. The principal sequence will contain at least one full entry for each book in the library; these are filed according to the class mark. A typical example would be:

821.912

ALLOTT, Kenneth *editor*

The Penguin book of contemporary verse, 1918–60;
new revised edition, selected with an introduction
and notes, by Kenneth Allott.
London.   Penguin Books.   1962
   413 pp.   18 cm.

The alphabetical subject index will serve as a key to this classified
sequence; it consists merely of a list of topics together with the
relevant class-marks. Thus, for the above example, our subject
index entry might be:

ENGLISH POETRY : 20th Century   821.912

The phrase *alphabetical author index*, often used to denote the third
sequence of the classified catalogue, is really a misnomer. This is
not an index in the truest sense as the subject index is; it is rather
an author catalogue with brief entries not only under authors,
joint-authors, editors, illustrators, etc., but also under titles and
series, when necessary. For the above example, it is likely that the
following entries would be made in the alphabetically arranged
author sequence:

ALLOTT, Kenneth *editor*

The Penguin book of contemporary verse, 1918–60.
Revised edition. 1962
   821.912

Penguin book of contemporary verse, 1918–60 edited
by Kenneth Allott. Revised edition. 1962
   821.912

K

342. Many books, as our reader will have fully realised by now, have more than one subject. Unless they are truly polytopical, the classified catalogue will endeavour to show, in its principal sequence, added subject entries for their themes that have been ignored in the shelf classification. Thus, if a book dealt with *British Local and Central Government* and was shelved in DC at 352.042, then the main catalogue entry would be made under this class-mark. But the classified sequence would also have an entry for central government, the secondary subject in this case, arranged as follows:

```
351.0942
(shelved at
352.042)    Author

                    Title and date
```

It will be noted that these secondary entries *must* make it quite clear to the catalogue user that the class-mark under which they are filed differs from that which represents the chief subject of the book and at which the book is actually shelved.

343. The cataloguer may go further than this and analyse the contents of composite works in his catalogue. The case against analytical entries, which deal with some part of a book as distinct from the book as a whole, has always been that they consume time and catalogue space, may rarely be helpful, and may even confuse the reader who employs the library catalogue. On the other hand, the subject analytic especially may help to fully reveal the resources of the classified library. Analytical entries fit quite readily into the classified catalogue; author and title analytics for parts of composite works will go in the alphabetical author sequence, while the subject analytic will be placed in the principal section of the catalogue in a similar manner to the added subject entry. An example will, once again, serve to make this clearer:

Subject Analytical Entry

332.61
(shelved at
at 650)   WARSON, Ronald

The Stock Exchange
(In Modern Business Training. 1965
pp. 239–255).

Subject Index Entry for above

STOCK EXCHANGE   332.61

Thus if the reader wants books on this theme, he consults the alphabetical subject index to obtain the appropriate class number. He then searches at that number in the classified sequence where he will find, in addition to entries for whole books, entries for significant *sections* of volumes – such as the one in our example.

344. We have, with the exception of references, described the nature and content of the three sequences of the classified catalogue. This type of catalogue has many advantages to offer the subject enquirer and the librarian who seeks to provide an information service. It is easier to compile than the alphabetically arranged dictionary catalogue, for the latter, although it covers the same range of entries, demands the very careful selection and rejection of possible subject headings. Ease of compilation is obviously a secondary factor with regard to our catalogues; yet it is not one which should be discounted, especially as the modern librarian has so many demands made upon his time. More important nevertheless is the function of the classified catalogue in revealing, in addition to the items available on any specific theme, entries dealing with closely related subject themes. The enquirer who wants information on a specific topic only is well served by either type of catalogue; the dictionary catalogue, through its principle of specific entry, ensures that the relevant data will be extracted and the classified catalogue refers the reader to the appropriate point in the main sequence from the alphabetically arranged entries of its subject index. If, however, the reader wishes to survey what is available on a

broader theme, or on several allied topics, the dictionary catalogue will usually rely very heavily on 'see also' cross-references to enable this to be done. These references will demand the exercising of the principles of classification to a large extent in that, to refer from a general to a specific subject, we must mentally or literally construct a hierarchy of subjects showing the relationships of one to another. Its classified rival, on the other hand, will use classification principles more fully and will automatically group many of the allied entries because of the systematic nature of its chief sequence. Thus the classified catalogue enables items on a specific theme to be rapidly traced and also collocates related subject entries, thereby achieving what E. J. Coates[1] has described as the subject catalogue's dual objective.

345. It may be admitted that no catalogue can collocate *all* related material and that the reader may often only wish to see what is available on a specific theme. Advocates of the dictionary catalogue point out that it is readily understood, needs no alphabetical indexes, and sometimes (paradoxical though this may seem) collocates related subject entries which the classified catalogue would disperse. This occasional dictionary catalogue collocation of like entries arises through entry under geographical area, or through the choice of a subject heading which gathers in related material from many parts of the classification scheme. Again it may be argued that the classified catalogue's efficiency is limited by the scheme in use; that the alphabetically arranged subject catalogue is the one which is truly complementary to the arrangement adopted for shelving material. That there is some truth in these statements is obvious to all; the great and continuing success of the dictionary catalogue, especially in the U.S.A., is a powerful testimony in this direction. But we are not convinced that these arguments are conclusive; on the contrary, it is suggested here that the classified catalogue is the superior tool for reader and librarian.

346. With regard to the ability of the reader to understand the classified catalogue, we suggest that the reader's comprehension of any catalogue will depend chiefly upon the encouragement and help which he receives in using it and on the amount of printed guidance provided. For specific subject requests there is, as already noted, little or nothing to choose between these rivals; it is the request for information on a wider field that is the acid test. Here, the essential

[1] *Subject catalogues: heading and structure*, 1960.

collocative nature of the classified catalogue is surely decisive, even though it is not always adequate in this respect. The dictionary catalogue sometimes offers collocation, but it does not do this nearly so often as the classified type. For relating entries, the usual dictionary cataloguing device is the use of the 'see also' reference. There may be as many as twenty or more of these references away from certain subject headings and the enquirer soon tires of the almost interminable directions from one heading to another. If he is willing to persevere with them all he is often frustrated by finding the same books listed under two or more of the headings or, when his task is completed, he is never really confident that all the relevant data has been extracted from the catalogue. Both types of catalogue, have their supporters; it is perhaps unfortunate that Dr Ranganathan, as a keen advocate of the classified catalogue, has also said that he believes the catalogue is purely a staff tool. This opens up the way for adherents to the rival school of thought to suggest that the reader cannot understand and will not employ the classified catalogue. We have tried to expose this fallacy by pointing out that, apart from staff usage, the number of catalogue consultations made will depend heavily upon the help and guidance provided for the reader in this matter.

347. Having expressed our preference for a classified sequence in the catalogue in addition to the systematic arrangement produced by the classification of books on the shelves, we must now consider for a moment the alphabetical subject index to a classified catalogue and its method of construction. The index is a very important key to the classified sequence and it is important that it should be constructed in the most useful way possible. Indeed, as the librarian who favours a dictionary catalogue will be quick to point out, many readers will only use the alphabetical part of the classified catalogue; that is to say they will consult either the author or subject index and will then go directly to the shelves at the class-mark indicated, thus missing added and analytical subject entries and information about books that are on loan or in the sequence of oversize volumes. This objection is worth considering; it is again best countered by urging librarians to explain the nature of the catalogue in use more clearly to the reader. But the subject index is indubitably valuable and must be made with care. There is really little excuse for merely providing the index to the classification scheme as a substitute, although some libraries do this. A subject index of one's own can be made fairly

rapidly and it is not very space consuming for, once an entry has been made for a topic, it will stand in the index for *all* the books on that specific theme in the stock of the library. To rely instead on the published index to the classification in use may have three disadvantages: it will confuse readers by listing subjects and class-marks not represented in the stock of that particular library; it will not recognise any modifications to the scheme in use, whether authorised or not, that have been made by that library; and, from the British librarian's viewpoint, if the scheme emanates from, say, America or India, it will employ terms in its index that may seem rather strange or ambiguous to readers in this country.

348. For these reasons, the librarian should always construct his own subject index to the classified catalogue; having decided upon this he must then determine the best method to adopt. Traditionally this meant selecting specific subject terms at random, considering the needs of the type of reader using the catalogue and indexing separately any synonymous terms which arose. In more recent times, an attempt has been made to rationalise the whole process of subject indexing for the classified catalogue by means of what is now known as *chain indexing*. This technique, like so many of the modern ideas in this subject field, stems from the writings of S. R. Ranganathan; it is now well documented, as our bibliography indicates. It links the indexing process closely with the chain of progression from general to specific in the classification scheme in use. The indexer begins with the most specific step in the notational chain and works his way back to more general terms, indexing each step in context. Thus, if we consider the specific topic in DC

Wedding Etiquette   395.22

we find that the chain of classification leading to it is:

> 390 Customs
>   395 Etiquette
>   395.2 Etiquette for special occasions
>   395.22 Wedding etiquette

Our index entries will be four in number if the chain procedure is used here:

Weddings: Etiquette	395.22
Marriages: Etiquette	395.22
Etiquette	395
Customs	390

With regard to the above, the following points should be noted:

(*a*) The indexer may sometimes find that the classification is not sufficiently specific and that he needs to add some steps of division in order to cater for the precise subject with which he is dealing. This does not occur in our example but, in DC for instance, one often finds it necessary to show the *same* class number alongside the last two or three links in the verbal chain because of lack of specificity in the classification.[1] Thus we may have a chain that ends, for instance:

Industrial Sanitation	628.5
Smoke Control	628.53
Smoke and Smog Prevention	628.53

(*b*) The indexer must watch for synonyms. If these occur, it will be necessary to make two or more entries to correspond with the appropriate step of the notational chain; thus, above, we have indexed both marriages and weddings against the class number 395.22.

(*c*) There may be steps in the notational hierarchy which are unwanted for indexing purposes, either because no enquirer is likely to search under the appropriate verbal terms or, more likely, because of faulty *subordination* in the classification scheme in question. Such steps are known as *unsought links*; in our example 395.2 is an unsought link, as the phrase *special occasions* is too vague to merit an index entry.

(*d*) These should be distinguished from *false links*, which arise when the notational chain is lengthened without an appropriate verbal term being supplied. In DC, for instance, if a zero is needed to introduce a standard sub-division or geographical table number, it is clear that this zero represents a notational extension for which

---

[1] The use of the device [1] after certain DC numbers in the B.N.B. is a recognition of this occasional lack of specificity.

there is no verbal equivalent. It is merely an indicator that form or geographical division is about to be employed.

349. It will also be noted that some of the entries in our example contain a qualifying term after the word or phrase indexed; this is often useful, especially if a topic can crop up in more than one context. In this way, we can distinguish between, say, MARRIAGES: ETIQUETTE at 395.22 and MARRIAGES: STATISTICS at 312.5. The student may think perhaps that the provision of four entries for a single book in the alphabetical subject index is excessive. It must be remembered again, however, that once these entries are made they will stand for *all* the books which a library has on this theme and they will also cover any books represented by earlier steps in the chain of classification involved. Thus ultimately it is certainly no less economical to use chain indexing than to rely on other methods and the chain procedure has certainly offered a more systematic foundation for subject indexing.

350. The advantages of chain indexing are that it offers a logical procedure for the making of a classified catalogue's subject index; it can be used to *complement* rather than duplicate the work of the classification. By citing the parts, or facets, of a subject in a different order from that adopted by the scheme (for instance, while the classification follows the order general to special, the index lists each specific term *followed* if necessary by a more general one to show its context) the chain procedure helps to ensure that the indexer selects all helpful terms under which a reader may justifiably search; older methods have often been rather 'hit or miss' in this respect, but this technique does much to bring 'distributed relatives' together in the index. On the debit side, it may be said that the ease with which the chain procedure can be followed will depend, to a large extent, on the system of classification in use. Colon is ideal in this respect; in schemes which use non-hierarchical notations, it is far more difficult to ascertain, from the gradual expansion of class-marks, the chain of progression from general to specific subjects. By and large, chain indexing seems to offer favourable results; it does ensure that appropriate entries are made and provides a splendid opportunity for the indexer to support the classification by listing the parts of a compound subject in a different sequence from that used by the scheme, thus catering for alternative approaches to a subject field. This feature and the possibilities of a 'rotated index' to a faceted classification are admirably dealt with in

D. J. Foskett's introduction to his *London Education Classification*.

351. Our survey of the technique known as chain indexing has necessarily been a rather cursory one; we now turn our attention to a final problem – that of guiding the classified catalogue adequately. The importance of good guiding for both shelves and catalogue has already been stressed. With regard to the latter, the librarian must (unless he is in the fortunate position of having enough staff to give direct personal assistance to enquirers on all occasions) aim at ensuring that the reader is able to consult the catalogue readily and accurately. An explanation of the way in which the catalogue operates, given when the reader first joins the library, is the best form of guidance. The printed pamphlet, which we mentioned in the last chapter, should also be prominently displayed and will contain a simple account of how to find books through the use of the catalogue. A bold, but attractive, notice, on or near to the catalogue, is another necessity. This should explain the nature of the catalogue and its sequences as briefly and simply as possible. The individual drawers of cards, or cases of sheaf slips, should also be clearly guided; this involves the indication of the content of each drawer on the outside, and guide cards of full, half, one third 'cuts' etc. showing the major divisions within each drawer or tray.

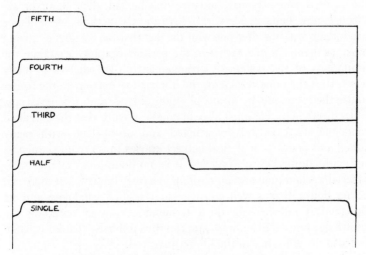

FIFTH

FOURTH

THIRD

HALF

SINGLE

Guide Cards: the various 'cuts' or tab sizes are indicated.

K*

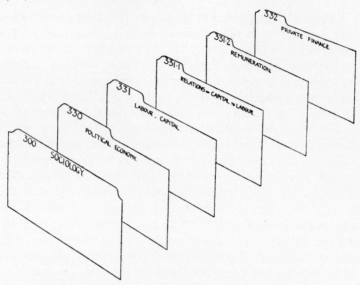

Guide Cards: with actual Sub-divisions indicated by size of tabs.

352. The latter, 'internal' guidance can be well provided in a card catalogue, where possibly cards of different colours could also be employed; it is not so easily achieved, unfortunately, if the sheaf catalogue is used. But at all times the librarian should try to offer all the printed and personal guidance that he can. The major break-through now being made with regard to new methods of catalogue production will not alter one whit the fact that the catalogue can and must, as demonstrated earlier in the present chapter, overcome the limitations of the systematic arrangement on the shelves in many ways; thus the onus rests with the librarian to encourage the reader to use the catalogue, by means of clear guidance and, whenever possible, direct help. He must also, of course, ensure that the classified catalogue itself is well-constructed and up-to-date, with many added and possibly analytical subject entries in its main sequence, and with comprehensive indexes. It is, no doubt, an exacting task, especially when time is at a premium in a busy library. Yet there can be no doubt that a well constructed classified catalogue and its alphabetical indexes can do a tremendous job in revealing the knowledge housed in a library and can thus publicise that knowledge and also the efficiency of the library involved.

CHAPTER TWENTY-TWO

Limits and Problems of Book Classification[1]

353. It seems worth while, at this stage in our studies, to consider in more detail some of the opinions concerning the inadequacies and imperfections of bibliographical classification. We have not, it is to be hoped, turned a blind eye to these at any point, but it is now necessary to review more thoroughly the objections to systematic classification by subject, as the method of organizing knowledge on the shelves of a library and in library catalogues. Without doubt, one of the most powerful objections to DC, or to any other of the general classifications, is that it has difficulty in dealing adequately with the problems of special libraries or even with the arrangement of specialised material in general collections. This particular disadvantage is the subject of our next chapter and is dealt with also in the final section of this Manual. Here our task is to examine and evaluate other objections to the classified subject arrangement. Since the time of Jevons, bibliographical classification has certainly not lacked its critics; this is, perhaps, to be regarded as a healthy sign, an indication that there is a constant appraisal of the technique and a striving for improvement, for no librarian believes that his classification is perfect – his creed is simply that it is far better than any alternative method of organizing his stock to facilitate the ready exploitation of recorded knowledge. Let us, however, examine now the ideas of the twentieth-century critics of subject classification and note some of the most important limitations with which our classifications have to live.

[1] The 1944 edition of the Manual contained a chapter on the failures of classification based on an article by Berwick Sayers which had appeared in the *Library World* in 1942. The chapter was omitted in the third edition, but has been restored here in a revised form. A.M.

354. First of all it must be confessed that a classified library consumes more shelf space than an unclassified one of the same size. This arises from the fact that, in the chronologically arranged library, new accessions can be simply added to the end of the existing sequence, whereas when subject classification is adopted, space must be left at the end of each class and sub-class for new material on each theme to be inserted at the appropriate point in the classified arrangement. This factor will always be with us, but no librarian now considers it to be a major objection to classification; we have already recorded Ranganathan's statement to the effect that it is foolish to be too frugal with regard to shelf space and, in any case, the extra room consumed by the classified collection is very small in proportion to the benefits offered. Another inconvenience which arises, and one which the student of our subject must always remember, is that broken order and parallel classification affect the application of our classifications. The impact of the former is best seen in the creation of temporary exhibitions and in groups of 'quick-reference' material. With regard to the latter, it must be said that there is no such thing as a library which is able to get all its material on a given subject together at one place, unless that library has a stock so small and so much accommodation that space does not matter. The first principle in the division of books is necessarily by size; it is clearly pointless to attempt to place folio and duodecimo volumes in the same sequence – thus parallel arrangements are essential. Such parallel classifications also arise through the existence of many branches and departments in a single library system, yet who would deny that several parallel classified sequences are much more satisfactory for the location of volumes and the juxtaposition of related material than no classification at all? In older libraries, or others where readers do not go to the shelves, there is usually no close classification, although this is not always the case, and some of them possess classified catalogues. Usually such libraries have been arranged in the simple chronological order of accession. It may be thought too, that if there is a classified catalogue the purpose of classification on the shelves has been achieved by this means and shelf classification is superfluous if only the staff have access to the shelves. Consider, however, even in libraries of the closed-access type, the daily quest of readers for a number of books on a given subject; and consider, too, the time that is wasted if the librarian is suddenly required to assemble all the books he has on the

French Revolution, or Radium, or the Einstein theory. He must classify his books to the extent of the subject every time he has to answer such a requirement. Would it not be better to do it once and for all by the simple act of classifying thoroughly the whole library? The fact that we have several sequences in a classified library does not invalidate classification. As we point out in Chapter Nineteen, there is a vast difference between the consultation of three or four groups of books to see what is available on a subject and the searching hopefully, but extremely laboriously, through a whole, vast unclassified collection.

355. A difficulty which must be recognised at the outset is that the classifiers themselves may be poor, or badly trained, workers; the enormous advances made in education for librarianship are doing much to banish this limitation, but Jast's remark that it is one thing to have a satisfactory classification and another to have a satisfactory classifier must be remembered and care should be taken to ensure that the system in use is properly understood and applied. The senior member of the staff responsible for classification and for the overall supervision of this work can do much to ensure that classification is being carried out in a correct and consistent manner.

356. *Sir F. G. Kenyon's Criticism.* There are other objections arising, it may be from over-emphasis on the importance of classification and from the disappointment which is experienced when it fails to do what it is incapable of doing, or what it was never intended to do. An indictment which is worthy of attention, for it comes from a great scholar who had strong connections with libraries, is that made by Sir Frederic Kenyon.[1] In discussing 'the idols which especially beset' the librarian, he dealt with the *idola classis*. He alleges, and with examples demonstrates, that as the accepted schemes are of some complexity, the reader is unable to find his book without having first some knowledge of their intricacies. He then goes on to contend that classification fails to reveal all the material on any subject and that the larger the library is the more waste of time there is in examining all the books on the chosen subject that are on the shelves, rather than relying upon the 'bibliographies and references in other books on the subject'. He also suggests that if books are removed into carrels, or otherwise put aside for special readers, they are not in the general sequence and so are lost to the immediate seeker. Most of these criticisms can be

[1] *Bulletin of the John Rylands Library*, August, 1941.

conceded without much reservation. We have already asserted the enormous advantages which the catalogue has over the shelf classification as an exhaustive method of revealing the subjects of books, and catalogues may stand for Sir Frederic's bibliographies in this connection. Our distinguished critic quite fairly implies that the main effect of classified libraries is to get the books together on the shelves which obviously or recognisably deal with the same or closely allied subjects. Clearly, as the book is physically indivisible, it can only go in one place and that place must be the one which the classifier deems to be most useful to his readers. If he chooses this consistently, the classifier has done all that is possible with shelf classification; few libraries would even contemplate the provision of two or more copies of a polytopical volume, each to be classed under a different subject. But Sir Frederic asserts that 'where books are ordered from the catalogue by their press-marks, it is quite immaterial whether a book on astronomy stands side by side with a treatise on Rugby football'. Now if the act of classing books correctly by a scheme involved much more effort than classing them ineffectively there might possibly be some substance in this argument, but if a trained librarian is using a known system he can do the proper classing almost as rapidly as the placing for the sort of subject chaos which the alternative method seems to prefer. What possible other reasoning than that the work occupies more time can be brought against the precise placing of books by topic, providing this does not result in extremely complex notations? That precise arrangement is *less useful* is an impossible suggestion; the minute subject grouping musт have enormous advantages over every other for, except for the omniscient, it will scarcely be held that the examination of entries in a bibliography, however expert, will be better than the examination of the books themselves.

357. It may well be possible for any librarian to place too great an emphasis on any one branch of his work; our subject is a means to an end only and we would accept, unhesitatingly, Sir Frederic's concluding words: 'Classification undoubtedly has its value, but the limits of its usefulness as a guide to the student should be clearly recognised'. But we would urge that there are few students or advanced workers so equipped that they know their field sufficiently well to replace access to the books with catalogues and textbook references, especially in an age when the output of fresh literature is so tremendous. We do not, in fact, believe that Sir Frederic thought

that they could, although his words might be seized upon by others and taken to mean this. In an excellent review in the *Library Association Record* of Sir Frederic's paper, that thoughtful writer on classification (and, incidentally, great advocate of literary warrant), Mr A. J. Hawkes, assured us that the purpose of classification is not to enable the reader to find individual books as much as to find books in useful subject groups. Classification, of course, is both a locating and grouping device, but for the ordinary reader it is chiefly a method for finding a volume quickly. The reader is rarely concerned with finding *all the books* we have, in a large library, upon one subject; he wants rather *a* book on that topic and if the classification confronts him with a useful selection, he usually finds something that will serve his purpose. In the unclassified, or very broadly classified, large library such a reader would find that his search was long and exacting in most cases. As for the student who wants an exhaustive survey of the library's stock on a particular theme, his full salvation must lie in the catalogue as well as in the shelf classification; on this Sir Frederic and Hawkes both agree, but the catalogue itself may well accept the classified rather than an alphabetical arrangement.

358. *Dr Kelley's Views.* Prior to Sir Frederic Kenyon's paper, a detailed critique of close classification had been made by Dr Grace Osgood Kelley in a good book.[1] Dr Kelley must not be thought of as an opponent of classification as such; she is, rather, an advocate of simplified classification and her arguments are marshalled with a skill that is almost persuasive. Her contention, based on long and varied experience, is that detailed classification defeats its own ends and that a sensible reduction of the classification detail used for arranging items on the shelves of a library is necessary. Minute subject analysis must then be left to the catalogue and to Dr Kelley, as to most librarians in the U.S.A., this means the dictionary catalogue. The general argument along these lines is reinforced by the enumeration of thirteen 'elements' which affect the value of classification in libraries. This list includes: the fact that the growth of knowledge is always forging ahead of the arrangement provided in our schemes; the inevitable complexity of the classified, as opposed to the alphabetical, form of arrangement; the possibility that the reader will have already classified his subject field and that the system provided by the librarian may not correspond to the arrange-

[1] G. O. Kelley, *The Classification of Books*, 1937.

ment which he expects to find; the difficulty posed by the existence of long notations for many subjects; the absence of many books from the sequence, at any one time, which makes a 'perfect' classified library unobtainable.

359. It is impossible to do justice to Dr Kelley's work in a concise survey of this kind; the reader is invited to examine her book, especially the chapters indicated in our bibliography and should consider to what extent her criticism would apply to a modern faceted classification. But it is worthwhile to note that she considers that the elements affecting classification fall into two groups; these comprise difficulties inherent in classification and those arising from its practical application in a library. It is also essential to comment briefly on the examples we have chosen from the elements, to indicate to what extent these things really do impose limits upon the value of our established classifications. Firstly her argument with regard to the changing order of knowledge; there is no gainsaying the truth of this – it is a problem that faces every classificationist. We are reminded of the words of Dr Arundel Esdaile[1] when he wrote, some years ago, that, to keep up with knowledge faithfully, 'it is realised that the rearrangement (of libraries using subject classifications) would have to be repeated at intervals of at least half a century, which in the life of a library represents indecent frequency. Yet such is the truth. The divisions of science are as impermanent as the shades in a kaleidoscope'. If by 'divisions' Dr Esdaile meant the greater classes, it is not the truth; nor is it the truth of the major divisions of these classes; the reliable classification will therefore need only to change in its specific points, in its minutiae. The best available schemes do in fact have a policy of slow, but continuous, change under the direction of an editorial committee; they rarely contemplate drastic alterations, for these would not be welcomed by users. No doubt this does not remove the problem to which Dr Kelley draws our attention but, nevertheless, it seems to be the best solution unless one day we can expect to have a fully self-perpetuating system. Her other suggestion, that a classified order is more complex than an alphabetical one is absolutely true; it is also more efficient by far than the alphabetical order, with certain reservations which have been dealt with earlier. Classification is complex only to the extent that the task which it is required to perform is complex. But if the system is well guided the reader will rarely be bothered by

[1] *Library Association Record*, August, 1933, pp. 242–3.

the complexity; it is purely a problem for classificationist and classifier.

360. If the reader has already decided upon the way in which his subject field should be arranged, as Dr Kelley suggests may be the case, it might seem that there is little the classifier can do about it. However, the good classification will surely embody the suggestions of specialists and take into account the way in which experts in each field of knowledge expect that field to be organized. The consensus of opinion, as Bliss called it, is thus observed. This will mean that a reader may well find that a modern classification corresponds in its arrangement to that organization of his subject field which he has already mentally conceived, simply because the classificationist has taken the trouble to find out how specialists wish their subject to be organized, before drawing up his schedules. The other two elements that we have quoted from Dr Kelley arise from the application of classification to books. Long notations are undoubtedly a handicap; they are often the price which we must pay for specificity in classification in a large or specialised library. There is no reason, or course, why smaller libraries should not, if they so wish cut back notations by the elimination of some of the detail – providing that they take the growth of the library, as well as its present size, into consideration when classifying. The absence of books from the shelves is also cited by Dr Kelley as a factor affecting classification; it is, in that we can never, in any lending library, expect to find all the material 'in'. But this is surely to be welcomed – the library where volumes are never taken from the shelves must be a very poor advertisement for the librarian's powers of book selection!

361. Our critics should not be dismissed so cavalierly. They know as well as we do, perhaps better, that the objections to classification go deeper. They are implicit in the works of all writers on the subject and every scheme so far devised has some limitations or defects – of order, notation, or indexing – which present pitfalls to the users. Some of the older general classifications have categories which once sufficed, but are now partly superseded. Yet while admitting these things and while recognising the truth in much of Dr Kelley's argument, it must be stressed that this is really an objection to detailed classification rather than to classification as such; also we would contend that any alternative system for the arrangement of knowledge, whether on the shelves or in the catalogue, will have many more limitations than has subject classification. As far as

shelf arrangement is concerned, Grace Kelley realises this; the quotation from her which follows our title page represents a sentiment with which we wholeheartedly agree.

362. *Another condemnation*: we are treated by an American professor to the following.[1]

'The technique of arranging books for use – or, in professional terminology, cataloguing and classification – are, in my judgement, over-emphasised as techniques, especially in the case of the university library. The whole business of classification is based on the theory that human knowledge can be definitely arranged in distinct categories. As a matter of fact, scholars are always re-arranging knowledge into new classifications. For any course of instruction beyond the level of general education, the reading list will most likely draw books from many different sub-divisions of the major categories. Most books belong to many different classifications, and an extensive array of cross-references is needed in any effective catalogue.

363. 'The theory that the scholarly specialist will find all the references on his subject under one class number is a myth. No true scholar tries to locate the books in which he is interested by scanning the shelves of the library; he works from bibliographies . . .

364. 'In my judgement the whole business of classification could be practically eliminated in a small library by having no subject-matter divisions and shelving all books alphabetically by author. In a large library it might be desirable for administrative purposes to have some divisions on the basis of subject-matter; possibly in a large library this might run up to thirty or forty different categories. Within each of these the books could be shelved alphabetically by author with no disadvantages to the readers. The card catalogue would, of course, give references to the books under the appropriate subject headings. Such a step might eliminate some of the time now given to the training of classifiers. Classification would be a problem for the expert scholars in the respective subject-matter fields, and it could be readily done from one central source to serve all the libraries in the country.'

365. The criticisms here made, although stated several years ago and in some ways dated, retain a certain interest for us. They seem to rest upon the assumption that because bibliographical schemes do not accomplish the impossible task of showing all the inter-

[1] J. D. Russell, *Library Quarterly*, October, 1942, pp. 775–93.

relations of knowledge, they are therefore ineffective for every other purpose. The experienced librarian knows full well that this is a complete fallacy. It is possible that in the university library, the bibliography of a subject is a main source of choice for many students and research workers, as Professor Russell avers; in the public library, the vast majority of readers are, unfortunately, unaware of the existence of subject bibliographies, although the staff will use these to support the catalogue and classification. But the reader so often wants what is immediately available and it is the classified arrangement on the shelves which best presents the stock to, and saves the time of, the subject enquirer. Indeed ones imagination boggles at the thought of large open-access libraries with books arranged alphabetically by author within 'thirty or forty different categories'. The chaotic arrangement which would soon ensue would be a librarian's nightmare; there would also be an enormous waste of time, as books on a specific theme would have to be gathered in from all parts of the library, instead of from merely a few locations. Such broad grouping seems to suffice still in some libraries in the academic sphere; but then we firmly believe that it has been a great loss to librarianship that comparatively few of the world's national and university libraries have been handled, as was the Library of Congress, by a man with public library experience. To return to Professor Russell's criticism; we may merely add that the practical librarian of a well-used collection of any size will readily perceive that, interesting as the speculation is, especially with regard to a centralised classification service, it shows unawareness of most librarians' problems and needs. In this country at least, most of us would say that we now possibly need better and more detailed classifications rather than a return to such huge groupings as our critic suggested.

366. An idea in some ways similar to Russell's but a much more novel one, was put forward, in the same American periodical, by Lund and Taube, who introduced a scheme for a 'non-expansive classification system'. This defies all our traditions in classification; but is a most interesting paper and still worth reading. It suggests that no classification can provide adequately for future knowledge and argues that the best system would be one divided into chronological groupings. Each of these 'periods', according to its standard of learning and the type of literature produced in it, would have a separate classification based on the order of knowledge as developed

in that period. Each of the period classifications would be sealed, so that it cannot be expanded and nothing can be inserted into it except, we presume, the newly discovered books and documents of that period. The authors suggest nine parallel classifications of this kind for a great general library, each one carefully based on a close, retrospective study of the period which it covers. The result should be that the relationships between topics within these periods can be accurately expressed, or so it is claimed.

367. Once again the reader is invited to consult our bibliography and to read this highly original article for himself. Much, very well balanced, argument goes to support the system proposed. Yet we are certain that it is unworkable; it will not do for the busy modern library. We are still convinced that books from all ages, but dealing with the same subject, should be found together, as far as is possible. Nor is it clear from the article whether books *about* a particular chronological period, but produced in a later one, are to break the seal of the parallel chronological expansions and obtain admission – as the scheme is described as 'non-expansive' they will probably not. If this is so, one of the basic rules of classification is broken; can we really justify, for example, the separation of modern critical works on the various periods of English Literature from the relevant original texts? Yet the idea is both interesting and attractive; Lund and Taube make us aware of one of the deficiencies of any subject classification; the fact that it is difficult to cater for different movements and periods in history really adequately and, above all, that it is difficult to arrange the knowledge relating to our own age – for every age is best assessed and classified in retrospect.

368. Our preoccupation with critics of classification from the U.S.A. will have been noticed; that is natural enough for there is probably as much pessimism as hope in that country with regard to the future of detailed shelf classification in general libraries. Rider's *International Classification*, 1961, is really rather lacking in detail and adopts the principles favoured in the nineteenth century in that it relies totally on the enumerative approach and concentrates on obtaining short class-marks at all costs. Of course, much earlier, in his biography of Melvil Dewey,[1] Rider had told us that 'many would-be experts in classification . . . have not realised that because a certain amount of classification is a good thing, an infinitely larger amount of it is not necessarily better. It should have been obvious

[1] Chicago, A.L.A., 1944.

that the more detailed a classification is made, the more quickly it tends to become obsolete; that the more complex it is made, the more its original easily-grasped simplicity becomes lost'. There is even a surprising note of pessimism in the introduction to Rider's scheme, where it is stressed that it is meant for new general libraries; reclassification, Rider believed, is never justified unless the existing system proves completely inadequate. It would be interesting to think that IC will give a new lease of life to the older ideas, but it is scarcely possible to imagine much interest being aroused in new, enumerative, general systems. Rider's scheme is up-to-date at present, but the lack of synthesis and of a revision policy will surely tell heavily against it in coming years. Yet it emphasises the opinions of a large number of American librarians. These can be stated succinctly as believing that broad classification is best for general libraries, that class-marks should be shorter, and that synthetic systems have not yet fully proved their worth.

369. Some of these ideas can be found in the many writings of a prominent American writer, Jesse H. Shera. Dean Shera sees the future of the organization of knowledge, in large and specialised libraries at least, as lying with the employment of mechanical methods of retrieval. Machine systems are indeed becoming more popular and he thinks we must accept them gladly, as of course we must, when they contribute speed and accuracy to our library work. With regard to classification in the traditional sense, Shera thinks that it has 'been convicted by the ample testimony of its own inadequacy'. One of its greatest faults, as he sees it, lies in the fact that any classification on the shelves can only present a *linear* or *unidimensional* picture of knowledge; a true view, of course, would be a multi-dimensional one. That is to say, assuming we have a hierarchical notation, the classes 731, 732, 733, 734 · · · 739 will all have the same relationship to the parent class, 730. But the shelf classification does not clearly show this family hierarchy at all; it presents the classes in a *line* – 730, 731, 732, etc. Thus 739 is far removed from the parent class, but 731 is close to it. The linear pattern imposed by the shelf arrangement has seriously distorted, it is contended, the true pattern of relationships which the classification has tried to offer. Again, we must concede the point. No one-dimensional arrangement, and this type of arrangement can hardly be avoided in libraries, can fully reveal the hierarchy of subjects as envisaged by the classification. But the objection is, to some degree, an academic

one; bibliographical classifications have worked quite well in the past despite this limitation.

370. *Other views.* It would be certainly unjust to suggest that *all* the opponents of detailed classification are to be found in the U.S.A. We have already seen that the British writer, Thompson, advocates broad classification for our new university libraries; likewise, Stirling's article, previously referred to, tells us that, at York, broad classification is used on the spines of books but more detailed classification is demanded in the catalogue. Another writer, Raymond Moss,[1] has pointed out several flaws in the methods we use to classify material; he views our subject chiefly from the angle of an industrial librarian, but his provocative paper is worthy of study by all. Here again we find registered the plea for greater simplicity in classification methods. Moss writes 'we should cease to regard classification as a method of placing documents in the most "specific" place for all time, but rather as a continuous process of revision resulting in further division of a class only when the number of documents in that class is becoming too great for convenient administration or location'. Likewise, Metcalfe, whose ideas have been mentioned in our text in cursory fashion on several occasions reflects in his books a healthy scepticism towards some of the modern ideas and a profound regard for final alphabetical arrangement within fairly broad categories whenever a detailed grouping on systematic lines is difficult to achieve satisfactorily. There are other critics to be discovered; their ideas are usually, however, very similar to those which we have considered so far. There are very few opponents of subject classification as such nowadays; the controversy centres chiefly around the merits of broad, as opposed to close, classification and the extent to which the increasing application of machines to library techniques will contribute towards the solution of the problem of organizing knowledge for use.

371. One most interesting idea, in some ways akin to broad classification, is that of *Reader Interest Arrangement* in general libraries. This again is a notion from the United States. It involves the arrangement of stock in popular categories based upon the observed interests of readers. These often cut across conventional groupings to produce useful sections such as 'Do it yourself books'. Volumes in such groups are prominently displayed and well guided; in most cases, a book may be moved to another category if it seems

[1] How do we classify? *Aslib Proc.*, February, 1962, pp. 33-42.

to receive insufficient attention in the category in which it was originally placed. The idea may be regarded as a genuine attempt to provide a better service for readers in general, popular, libraries; it must be applied with care even here, for the broad groupings which it favours may not correspond to the long-term interests of readers. Also to move books about from one grouping to another may create serious location problems from time to time. In the larger library, and perhaps in any library providing a reference and information service, the idea does not appear to be very practicable; its existence, however, is a further indication that subject classification, as most of us know it, does have imperfections and that some librarians are prepared to explore alternative methods of displaying their stock to the general reader.

372. Certain British public libraries have experimented with the Reader Interest type of groupings, to a limited extent, in some branch libraries. A different sort of arrangement, yet one which also cuts across classification in the conventional sense is the 'service in depth' idea[1] and kindred experiments. Different again, yet in essence similar to the above, is the arrangement to be seen with regard to the stocks of certain of the departments of Liverpool Central Libraries. Like most large municipal systems, Liverpool has organized these departments on a subject basis, but it has extended the traditional conception of the subject department. In addition to Art, Commercial, Music, and Technical libraries, we find such departments as the International, American, and Commonwealth Libraries. The object of the latter departments is to collect together the language, literature, geography and history of each country. Strictly speaking, this could be cited as a practical example of cross-classification. The division by subject *and* by place at the same departmental level is virtually the equivalent to the employment of two characteristics at the same stage of division. But theoretical considerations must always be modified in the light of experience; the Liverpool arrangement, although unorthodox, has much to commend it in a municipal authority of this size and results in a very useful grouping under countries which the use of the DC in the usual fashion would not permit. It is a striking departure from the obvious modifications of the general schemes and, although the phrase 'reader interest' has not been used in conjunction with the

---

[1] There are many writings on this; see, for example, A. Bill, Patterns of public library service: a new approach, *Assistant Librarian*, September, 1965, pp. 172–4.

resulting arrangement, it is perhaps best thought of as a notion which can be coupled with that American trend. A view of one of the Liverpool departments involved, the International Library, appears in the illustration opposite page 366.

373. *Conclusion.* Our chapter has set out to consider some of the limitations of book classification, but we have digressed somewhat in order to examine the views of various twentieth-century critics of detailed classification and to consider some deviations from the orthodox classified arrangement in general libraries. Every modification or adaptation of a scheme may be regarded as a sign that it is not completely satisfactory and the variety and extent of such adaptations indicates that faults can be found in all systems. We would suggest that the main problems spring from: the size of books, resulting in the need for parallel sequences on the shelves; the complexity of knowledge as recorded in books; long and cumbersome notations; the difficulty of classifying special material or 'non-book' items; the inevitability of linear arrangement; and, finally, the constant problem of keeping a scheme up-to-date without introducing radical changes. Some of the limitations must simply be accepted; others may admit to a total or partial solution, although there is often disagreement over this. Perhaps too the development of facet analysis has, for most librarians, taken the sting from some of the traditional objections to the systematic subject arrangement of books. It might be a profitable exercise for the student to list all the factors affecting the usefulness of classification named, or hinted at, in this chapter, plus any others which may spring to mind. Yet when this has been done and when the truth in many of the criticisms made has been acknowledged, there is still no denying the fact that, in nearly every library, classification is fully justified. Despite these limitations it survives and contributes a great deal towards the efficient exploitation of our bookstocks. It is a great time-saver, because it collects books into organized groups; these groupings, although never entirely perfect, are far more useful than alternative methods of arranging material. Because of this, although librarians may wrangle at times about broad or close classification, we find few pleas for its abolition these days; its worth is proved again and again in our daily work.

374. Indeed we would ask this question: is there any librarian of long experience, who has worked in a classified library of the usual kind where readers have access to the shelves, who would willingly

say that classification, in some form, is an unnecessary or even un-desirable part of his system? Imperfect and impermanent in detail as our schemes may be, inadequate as our classing occasionally is, the benefits which we have derived from classification outweigh the defects immeasurably. To enhance those benefits by the vigilant scrutiny and progressive improvement of classification systems should be an aim of those who work in or for libraries, because the good order and effective management which many of them present today is due, in no small measure, to classification.

TABLE VIII   OUTLINES OF SOME CLASSIFICATIONS O

CHARLES MADELEY, 1904

SUBJECTS
0	Agenda
1	Constitution
2	Finance
3	Staff
4	Establishment
5	Stock: Acquisition
6	„ Registration
7	„ Exposition
8	Use
9	Report

DEPARTMENTS
M	Museum
L	Library
C	Public Rooms
D – W	Branches
X	Auxiliaries
Y	Conference
Z	Other Institutions

L. STANLEY JAST, 1907

0	General
01	Librarian. Personal
1	Legislation. Founding. Classes of Librar
2	Extension Work
3	Building
4	Government and Service
5	Executive
6	Accession. Description. Conservation
7	Departments
8	Publications
9	Other

IBRARY ECONOMY, WITH SPECIMEN SUBDIVISIONS

JAMES D. STEWART, TABULATION OF LIBRARIANSHIP, 1947

AIN CLASSES

General

Legislation and Foundation

Government and Personnel

Buildings, Fittings and Furniture

Executive and Finance

Books and Other Material

Special Material

Administration

Use of Libraries

Extension Work: Co-operation

History and Description

SECTION IN FULL

    Use of Libraries

0 Reading and aids: Adult and General

041	Psychology of reading
042	How to read
043	Fostering the use of books
044	Recreational reading
045	Reading with a purpose
046	Hygiene of reading
050	Choice of books: general
051	Choice of editions
052	Sequels
060	Courses of reading (divide as main library scheme)
061	File of prepared courses, lists
070	Readers' Advisers. Personal guidance
071	New readers: introduction to library
072	Enquiry Desk
073	Enquiries register
074	Personal register (individual readers)
075	Subject mailing lists, etc

CHAPTER TWENTY-THREE

The Arrangement of Special Material in the General Library

375. The work of the librarian would be greatly simplified if his stock were confined to volumes of books. These indeed, as the foregoing pages have abundantly shown, present many problems from our point of view, but in the main there is a ready and recognised solution for them once the art of classification is understood. The modern librarian however is the custodian and collector of many varieties of material which must be regarded as *special;* there may well be films and filmstrips to be housed, there may be a gramophone record collection in the public library, and certainly the librarian will have to cope with a wide range of maps and pamphlet material. These categories of material will sometimes demand a rather different treatment from the rest of the stock but, in certain cases at least, it is possible to cope by means of parallel sequences or by modification and adaptation of the classification system in use. Of all these items, the one most nearly related to the book is the pamphlet, a form of literature which tends to increase. Much important information does not become available in books for many months or even years; it is only to be found in newspapers or periodicals and these also are constantly increasing in number. In order to make such data accessible, it is, in most cases, necessary to collect newspaper cuttings and copies of important periodical articles not otherwise held by the library. It is frequently necessary, too, to preserve trade catalogues, handbills, and all sorts of literature which is published in single sheets. There is also the collecting of illustrations, prints, manuscripts, and deeds. This statement does not exhaust the whole of the material which becomes subject to

treatment at the hands of the librarian. In the mass, and without the most careful arrangement, it forms a chaos in which little information can be traced. Properly filed, classified, and indexed, this special material and fugitive matter may become an active reinforcement to the bookstock of the libraries.

376. *Periodicals*. Such items may hardly be thought of as special since they are found in nearly every library. From the point of view of arrangement, however, there can be no doubt that certain problems are raised. In many libraries the classification of such items would seem to be scarcely necessary. Current journals will be filed in alphabetical title order; bound volumes of back numbers are nearly always too bulky to be shelved with books, unless a great deal of space is to be wasted. They can be classified and arranged in a parallel sequence, or can be arranged in title order within such a separate sequence. The diversity of content of many bound journals is the factor which suggests that classification may be rather futile. If libraries are split into departments there may be some value in keeping say, technical journals separate from general ones, and classification will achieve this; but in many libraries it is an unnecessary procedure. It is the content of the journal that is of value and, if a reader has the exact reference for the article which he wishes to consult, the alphabetical sequence of bound volumes will suffice; if he wants to know what has been published in periodical form on a particular subject, the librarian must consult published indexes to journals or indexes of his own creation. It is here that classification can play a part. Despite the undoubted preference for the alphabetical subject heading approach in published indexing services, it must be evident that a *good* classification can be most helpful in arranging an index to periodical literature. The success of UDC in many special libraries in carrying out exactly this type of work testifies to this. We would strongly urge, therefore, that it is not the classification of journals that is important but rather the classification of the articles which they contain. In an article in the *Wilson Library Bulletin* many years ago, Marie Prevost stated 'The remedy for an unindexed periodical is not classifying but getting it indexed'.[1] One agrees wholeheartedly, except that in many cases a classified index would be more useful for gathering together references to related articles than an alphabetical one, despite the latter's use of 'see also' references.

[1] Quoted in A. D. Osborn, *Serial Publications*, 1955, p. 181.

377. *Films and Maps.* A brief word on these important categories of material is demanded. Films will not be on open-access and need not be shelved in classified order unless the collection is large. It will be necessary, nevertheless, to classify films and filmstrips so that the entries representing them can take their correct place in the classified catalogue. If a separate catalogue of films is provided, its classified sequence of entries will bring together those relating to films on the same subject; if the entries are filed with those representing books, subject collocation is likewise achieved. It will be necessary, in the latter case, to indicate clearly that an item is in the form of a film or filmstrip. There seems to be no reason why the classification used for films should be any different from that used for the bookstock. Maps are usually filed vertically in large metal cabinets. The arrangement should be one which brings together those which cover the same or kindred geographical areas, although the subject of a map may also sometimes be of great importance. Some series of maps are virtually classified for us by the carto-graphers; witness the useful arrangement of the Ordnance Survey maps in Britain which can be helpfully filed according to the numbers allocated by the Ordnance Survey and based on the 'national grid' system. Many other maps, however, will demand careful thought from the librarian if they are to be filed in a helpful sequence. The classification used for books could be applied to them or a special scheme such as that used by the Library of Congress or the one proposed in *The classification and cataloguing of maps and atlases*, by S. W. Boggs and D. C. Lewis could be adopted, if it was thought to offer decided advantages.

378. *Gramophone Records.* Such a collection, if maintained by a public library, will normally operate on the closed-access principle. The library will surely, however, follow the example given by modern stores in this direction and display the sleeves of records to permit the would-be borrower to 'browse'. The arrangement of these sleeves or of an open-access collection may, as E. T. Bryant points out,[1] be the same as for music, as far as is possible. A fairly small collection, however, might feasibly be merely divided into broad groupings – Classical Music (with appropriate sub-divisions – or, perhaps better still, sub-arranged by the name of the composers), Folk-Music, Jazz, Recordings of bird songs and calls, Poetry on Record, records designed to promote the learning of a language, etc.

[1] *Music Librarianship*, 1959, pp. 244–6.

In the United States particularly it is being recognised that, for a large or highly specialised collection, such popular broad groupings may be quite insufficient as indeed would be a general classification; close classification, perhaps according to a scheme such as the highly flexible *British Catalogue of Music Classification*, or one of the systems mentioned in Bryant's work, would then be a necessity.

379. *Pamphlets.* All libraries tend to include in their stock a large and increasing number of pamphlet publications and the problem presented in their arrangement is that they cover a very wide range of subjects but are usually too flimsy to stand on the shelves unless a suitable 'case' is provided by the binder. If a pamphlet is large enough to bear a binding which will take visible lettering on its back, and its subject matter has permanent interest to warrant it, there is no reason except that of cost, for not binding it. The ideal arrangement, surely, is to bring the bulk of library material together in one systematic and helpful sequence of subjects. Local pamphlets especially are best separately bound, if possible; they are thus better preserved and may be more safely handled. Sometimes, however, the pamphlet is not sufficiently large to permit this. Some librarians believe that such items are best classified immediately; pamphlets of related size and subject can then be bound into volumes which will stand in an approximate classified order on the shelves, while analytical author and subject entries in the catalogue will reveal the exact content of the volumes. Alternatively the pamphlets may be filed in boxes and indexed if of lasting value; some may find their way to the vertical file, which is described later in the present chapter. The rival methods have their own advantages and drawbacks and it is unwise to be too emphatic with regard to the definite superiority of any one system for coping with pamphlet material. We would merely add that several pamphlets will be government publications and we are inclined to believe that this type of material is best housed in pamphlet boxes either in classified order or in a sequence which will keep the items issued by each government department together, regardless of subject content. Periodicals issued by government departments must, naturally, be treated in the same way as other journals and the more substantial of other government publications can take their place alongside other books in the main classified sequence on the shelves. It seems wise, however, to store the slighter items in boxes; if this is done there are certain merits in employing a classified sequence, although for the

quick location of individual items the sequence in boxes according to the issuing department is more rapidly achieved and is equally effective.

380. *Classification of Fiction.* One very important category of material in public libraries which is 'special' perhaps when the question of the efficient arrangement of the stock is considered is fiction. By far the most popular method of organizing such material is the alphabetical sequence by author's name; this despite the fact that it results in a long unbroken sequence of books in many libraries. While fiction may seem to provide the most obvious opportunity for the use of a straightforward alphabetical order, it should be noted that attempts have been made to introduce a more helpful organization of large fiction stocks by means of a form of classification. To arrange fiction according to the classification employed for the remainder of the stock would definitely seem to be unhelpful to readers. In the general library, it can be argued that while specific requests may be received for a work by Jane Austen, Thomas Hardy, D. H. Lawrence, or Virginia Woolf, most people merely want 'something to read'. Moreover, how many of our general readers know if William Faulkner and Henry James – to use names at random – are English or American authors; and how many have any notion of their dates? Most libraries, therefore, remove all fiction from the Literature class, although some may favour the classification of the older novels of recognised literary merit and importance and the alphabetical arrangement of all fiction published after, say, 1920. In his *Primer of Book Classification*, W. H. Phillips argues persuasively for the division of the fiction stock into three distinct sequences: fiction published before the First World War, translated fiction, and modern fiction. Within each grouping the arrangement would be alphabetical by author. There would certainly seem to be some advantages in such an arrangement in the large and busy public lending library.

381. More involved ideas for the grouping of fiction have been advanced. Some libraries have employed broad groupings with regard to the theme of the novel, arranging alphabetically by author within each grouping. The system suggested by L. A. Burgess some years ago for the systematic arrangement of fiction has not met with a great deal of response from librarians; nor is it likely that the similar suggestions of R. S. Walker in more recent years will be enthusiastically received. The problem is that, while it is certainly

possible that the adoption of a special scheme for fiction with its own notation might offer certain advantages in grouping items in an interesting and useful way, it is obvious that in many libraries the traditional methods are sufficiently helpful and involve far less work. It seems likely, therefore, that the employment of classification for the organization of novels will be confined, when indeed it is used at all, to attempts to break up a long alphabetical sequence of authors through the use of chronological divisions as suggested by Phillips or through the employment of a few broad and easily recognisable subject categories.

382. *Local Collections.* One of the dominant interests of any public library should be the past and present of the locality in which it is situated. The librarian should strive to collect everything in literary form, whether manuscripts or printed, whether written about the town which he serves or written by those who have lived in it. Further, all public libraries should have a select collection relating to the county in which they are situated, but except in the greater counties, which might be divided for this purpose, only one library, and that the largest and most accessible, should collect literature on the county as a whole. Indeed two things seem evident about local collections; that certain librarians have underestimated their value and potential, and that others have failed to appreciate the need for library co-operation in the question of acquiring literature relating to the county to which several neighbouring municipal authorities belong. The ignoring of the latter principle has introduced an entirely unnecessary and very costly element of competition into collecting for the libraries concerned, and in some counties we have libraries less than ten miles apart which are competing in the same field to the great detriment of each other and without any corresponding public advantage. How far local collections should go beyond literature depends upon whether a town possesses an art gallery and museum. If these exist, many such articles as prints and coins may be left to them. Even in their absence, however, it is not the business of the library to collect local biology, botany, and zoology, let alone archaeological objects. But there is much to be said for the collection of prints, photographs and such engraved things as tokens, all of which have a direct documentary interest. So far as prints are concerned, there is a distinct cleavage between those which have an artistic and those which have a merely historical interest, and it is usually held that the art gallery should take the

L

ones where the predominant interest is artistic and the public library the others.

383. It may seem unnecessary to dwell on the character and scope of the local collection in a chapter where it is only possible to glance at some of the classification problems involved in the organization of various kinds of special material and yet, while much literature on the nature of the local history library exists, its importance and functions must be briefly indicated before the question of systematic arrangement can be explored. It becomes clear that, in most general libraries, if any department should have a special classification it is the local collection. Sometimes DC is adapted for the arrangement of local history and two sequences provided – one for material relating to the town, the other for surrounding areas in the county; at other times it is thought best to use an entirely separate classification for local material. The whole area of the county or town may then be denoted by the use of a single symbol; as, for example, S for Surrey, or M for Middlesex; an economy which is seen immediately when we remember that the class-mark for Surrey's history in DC at its shortest is 942.21. If it is decided to construct a scheme of one's own, the main problem to be settled is – which will be the most convenient arrangement of material on the county, by subject or by locality? That is to say, will the greater number of readers enquire, for example, for all books on the churches of Sussex, or for books on Chichester, including those on its churches and cathedral? Or, again, will people ask for the history of sport in a certain ward in a town, or for the history of sport in the town as a whole? It will be seen at once that either of the alternatives is possible; the classificationist making a special scheme for local history can decide for himself, but it seems fairly obvious that it is the topographical arrangement which must receive precedence, with further topographical and subject sub-divisions.

384. The question then arises: what shall be the topographical unit? It is surely best to arrange material relating to the county so that districts which are contiguous on the map are brought together in the classification; the arrangement for a single town might be made upon the same principle, wards or ecclesiastical parishes being made the basis of the scheme. But the nature and characteristics of the area concerned must have much bearing on this. So also, if DC or another general scheme is adapted for this purpose, the librarian must see that his extensions and adaptations suit the area and corres-

pond, as closely as possible, to the type of enquiry which the department is most likely to receive. There are many difficulties in adapting general schemes for local history collections and, in view of these and the wide variety of material to be classified, J. L. Hobbs has suggested that a synthetic classification might well be devised and applied.[1] As yet there is no classification for local material based on the modern principles now available, but any student who is interested in the problem and any librarian faced with the practical task of devising a classification should at least examine some of the special schemes which have been created for this purpose. These include the system worked out for *Aston Manor*, by R. K. Dent, R. Austin's scheme for the county of *Gloucestershire*, and the one devised by J. Ormerod at *Derby*. Of all such classifications, the system which is perhaps the one with the widest interest is that devised by A. J. Philip and published in 1953. It is not merely restricted to the needs of one area, it has a long and useful introduction and, in many ways, despite its notational complexities, it seems to be the special scheme with the greatest potential. But perhaps Hobbs's suggestion could be followed up and a synthetic scheme devised for a local collection; such a scheme could surely be adapted in other regions quite easily and it would be a most suitable medium for putting the modern principles of library classification to a worthwhile practical test in public libraries.

385. A word must be added on the treatment of certain types of material which a local collection is sure to possess. Newspaper cuttings relating to the locality must, if they give information on important people, places, or events, be carefully preserved. It is suggested that the best method for achieving this is to mount all cuttings on sheets of stiff paper and to fasten these in classified order into loose leaf bindings on the principle of a large sheaf catalogue. The full volumes of cuttings could stand on the shelves with other classified material and could contain a note to the effect that a reader wishing to examine other, more recent, cuttings on the same theme would be able to do so on application to the staff. In a similar manner, photographs, prints and paintings relating to the locality could be classified by subject or place, so that illustrations on local churches, to select a possible theme of an enquiry, would be found together. This latter type of material would not, however, normally be on open-access. Illustrations and cuttings could be filed alpha-

---

[1] J. Burkett and T. S. Morgan, editors, *Special materials in the library*, 1963, p. 83.

betically by subject heading, but in the case of the latter, if they eventually appear on the shelves in binders, the use of the same classification as is employed for the bookstock would seem to be an ultimate economy. Thus it is clear that the classification of the local history library and its diverse material is an interesting study; the person who is prepared to examine a special scheme, or the adaptation of DC that is used in the local departments of nearby library authorities, will find out far more about the peculiar problems which arise in the classification of local history than we could possibly hope to show by means of a more detailed account here.

386. *Deeds.* This is not the place to dwell upon the importance of a good system for the collecting, conserving, and recording of those documents, mainly handwritten, which are the original record of public, private, and commercial transactions and are the sources of most authentic history. Those libraries with extensive collections of such material are really in need of a qualified archivist to organize and exploit such manuscripts. For those wishing to investigate the problems involved, the work of the Public Record Office and the various reports of the British Records Association are of primary interest; outstanding also is Hilary Jenkinson's *Archive Administration* 2nd edn., 1937. Here he describes, among other things, methods of filing and storage in vogue. We quote: 'Different shapes and forms of document lend themselves to a greater or less degree to boxing and enveloping, and in some instances it may be necessary to choose between cleanliness and air, in which case air must have the first place. As a rule, however, it is possible to meet both. At the Public Record Office parchment deeds, for example, are loosely folded and slipped each into a stout, square, flapless envelope, numbered with the same number as the deed: a box, the dimensions of which in section are slightly larger than those of the envelopes, receives them in the fashion of cards in a card index; a loose lid with a deep brim closes it. For loose small documents of irregular size, or for small rolls, larger boxes of similar construction but having the lid hinged are used.'

387. *The Vertical File.* Smaller pamphlets, newspaper cuttings other than those pertaining to the locality, and a number of other items containing useful information, some of them ephemeral, may be housed in what is known as a Vertical File. Here the material is arranged in manila folders and these are placed, in classified or other subject order, in the drawers of a metal filing cabinet.

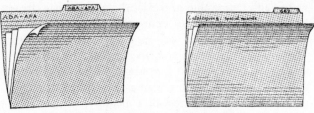

Early Form of Folder for a Vertical File.

Each item is marked with its class number and sometimes a folder is reserved for a single pamphlet while, on other occasions, several items on the same topic go into one folder.

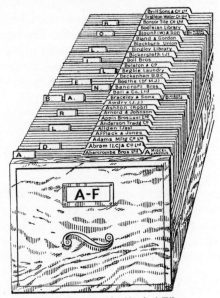

Open Drawer of a Vertical File.

It must be pointed out, once again, with regard to pamphlets, that many such items are large enough to be bound and shelved with the main classified sequence; it is only the smaller item in this category that can justifiably be placed in the Vertical File. The file may well include, however, many other items which lend themselves to storage in this way.

388. Newspaper cuttings are the commonest source of current

information and their value in the local collection has already been touched upon. Thousands of items of interest, numberless small facts, biographical hints, as well as a great deal of current commercial information, are in newspaper paragraphs which never get into books, and may be lost if they are not dealt with at the time of their appearance. In order to obtain a file of important news items it should be made the business of a member, or members, of the staff to examine all newspapers, and to extract cuttings according to definite principles of selection. Few libraries would collect cuttings for all subjects in the classification but, in addition to those on local places and themes, it can be said that all references to the dominant interests of the day in every branch of activity and thought, and biographical, historical, and similar articles, should be preserved when they are not obviously a re-hash of material which is already existing in a more convenient form in books. Economy of time and labour forbid too careful a scrutiny of articles to see whether they are completely original or not. Experience will assist the selector in choosing the right article for filing. It will be necessary to distinguish in the Vertical File, between those cuttings which are only of temporary value, and those which will not be withdrawn after a time because they form a permanent contribution to the library's store of knowledge. It will, of course, be realised too that the source of all cuttings must be shown, as this is the authority on which the information they convey is given.

389. It is, therefore, envisaged that the Vertical File will house in a further parallel classified sequence much of the material in the library which is not in book form. If the larger pamphlets are bound, or housed in boxes, the Vertical File will be relieved of much of its bulkier material and can then become a receptacle for the smaller pamphlet, cuttings, some photocopies, and perhaps some small maps, deeds, certain letters, and articles of lasting worth which the librarian has extracted from journals which his library does not bind. If all this material is placed in a series of folders, which are classified minutely and arranged in the order of the classification, we have a file of infinite mobility and simplicity, which is parallel with the whole of the book stock, may be catalogued in precisely the same way, and any material in it will usually be found by one reference from catalogue to file. Such a file is maintained wholly or partly by many libraries. To quote just one example, the file relating to business matters and economic conditions in overseas countries,

which is maintained by the Manchester Commercial Library, gives an excellent indication of the possibilities opened up by the judicious employment of vertical filing. The ideal arrangement of material is in a single classified sequence and for this and other obvious reasons we should beware of overcrowding the Vertical File; if properly used, and assuming its contents are examined and obsolete material weeded out at intervals, it is indeed a valuable method for the storage and recovery of many fragile, but important, items of information.

390. *Illustrations, Prints, Lantern Slides:*—Prints and illustrations are another example of material that is especially important to the local collection. But many libraries collect a wide range of illustrations, other than those of purely local significance. If there are too many of such illustrations for them to be accommodated in the Vertical File, then a special collection must be built up; certain libraries have managed to build up huge and valuable resources with regard to photographs, prints and other similar material. Here again, to cite merely one instance, we may note the magnificent collection of some 250,000 illustrations at Birmingham Public Libraries, many of which can be borrowed. Most libraries will need to be content with much smaller collections than this, but a great deal of useful work can be done if such material is carefully collected, mounted and preserved. Such prints and illustrations must be classified, or arranged in some form of subject order. The wise librarian will, in addition to preserving and extending his collection of illustrative material, index all important illustrations which appear in books and journals; this, although a laborious task, is one that can prove very rewarding, particularly in reference library work.

391. Lantern slides are clearly as susceptible of classification as any other kind of picture and, indeed, demand some form of it. The best method of filing, both for safety and for rapid reference, is in drawers, like cards in the card cabinet; but the slides must fit in accurately so that undue movement is impossible. Suitable cabinets are sold by firms which specialise in photographic equipment and lantern slides. The classification that is ideal is that which would serve for news-clippings, that is to say, any sufficiently minute bibliographical classification, and certainly the UDC can be used here. The classification of slides premises that the title and class-marks and any other necessary indications are written on the

masking of the slides. The slide must also receive subject cataloguing, or indexing. The chief difficulty about lantern slides is the fact they they are not used as subject units, but rather as units in a lecture-subject; they are essentially illustrations to lectures. If slides are arranged in perfectly classified order, then a set to illustrate a lecture on any subject can easily be built up. The work, however, of building up and then of demolishing directly after the delivery of the lecture takes time and is often unnecessary. It seems that in many cases the law of convenience is served best if the slides are kept in lecture sets and any other form of arrangement is abandoned. This decision is made reluctantly, but seeing that the placing together of things which are used together is the essence of practical classification, it seems to be a satisfactory one even from the point of view of the classifier. In this kind of arrangement a subject index is even more necessary. Some libraries have collections of negatives as part of their local collection. These can be classified in the same manner as lantern slides and, in order to preserve the unprotected film, it is advisable that they should be inserted into folders or envelopes before being filed in the drawers. The classmark can be written on these envelopes.

392. *The Classification of Library Economy.* All general library classifications have divisions which are devoted to the arrangement of the material of librarianship itself. Primarily these classifications are intended for the arrangement of books and pamphlets and, in view of the particular interest which the literature of his own subject has for the librarian, this material may also be regarded as being somewhat special. The librarian, however, also needs to give careful consideration to the filing of his correspondence and administrative papers, and to the arrangement and indexing of his stationery and stores. With regard to correspondence, there is no doubt that to file alphabetically by correspondent is certainly the easiest system initially, but the difficulties it presents when the whole correspondence on a particular subject is needed are too great to commend it for us in any but the smallest library, and even there it would be a very indifferent method. Alphabetical order by subject is a much more commendable method than either the above or the use of chronological order; on the other hand there is much to be said for the use of a classification system. This may seem unnecessary in view of the fact that many of the letters filed have only temporary interest or importance. J. D. Brown held that the filing of most correspondence

was a waste of time, and was caused largely by the fear of the librarian that he would lose something that might doubtfully be useful. Few will agree completely with such an extreme view, but certainly if everything is filed, letters must be weeded out frequently —at least once a year.

393. It will, we hope, be agreed that the alphabetical subject arrangement or a classified arrangement must be used for the correspondence and other administrative documents that are filed. If the latter is preferred, the librarian may turn to the appropriate divisions in one of the accepted schemes, or he may consider the use of a special scheme. Special systems for the classification of Library Science include L. S. Jast's *Classification of Library Economy and Office Papers, 1907,* the similar type of scheme proposed in the *Library Association Record, 1904,* by Charles Madeley, or James D. Stewart's *Tabulation of Librarianship, 1947.* The outlines of these classifications are given in the chart at the beginning of this chapter; the student is encouraged, nevertheless, to examine one of these schemes for himself. That of Stewart is particularly interesting; it resembles SC in some ways, but is essentially a detailed arrangement for literature on librarianship and also for papers, stationery and stores. It has a useful introduction, a mixed notation, and a relative index, and it would seem the most likely of the three systems to be used in libraries which prefer to have their correspondence organized systematically by topic. The librarian must consider carefully whether he will introduce for office papers another classification than that by which he classifies his books. There is a distinct advantage in a uniform system of classification throughout the library, although the existence of material such as we have described in the present chapter makes it necessary to have certain parallel sequences. But such uniformity is practically impossible. As a case in point the classification of local material, as we have seen, cannot be done by any general scheme of classification except by means of modifications and expansions which would produce gigantic notations. Likewise the difficulty of the sections for classifying Library Economy in the Decimal Classification and similar schemes is that these are chiefly designed for the arrangement of books rather than for administrative correspondence and papers; the Stewart or Jast classifications could cater for the latter without the mauling which a general system would need.

L*

394. If we turn from the problems of office papers to the question of arranging books and pamphlets on Librarianship, we find that most libraries consider the DC arrangement to be reasonably but not completely effective; it is, certainly, much more useful than the equivalent portion of SC, but somewhat inferior to the classifications for our subject provided in the Congress and Bibliographic systems. But the tremendous interest in faceted classification which is now so evident in Britain has borne rich fruit, in recent years, in the number of special schemes that have been made. Among these is a faceted classification for Library Science which is to be used at the Library Association Library, and which has already been applied at the College of Librarianship, Aberystwyth; this College has issued a bulletin describing its use of the scheme and proposed extensions and is eager to communicate with other potential users of this new faceted scheme, which was produced by the Classification Research Group. It is surely both a relevant and a convenient exercise for the Welsh Library School to classify material on the subjects in its curriculum by a scheme specially devised for this purpose and based on modern principles. Convenient, because the stock should surely be arranged through the use of this classification in a most satisfactory manner; relevant, because the application of the system must provide excellent opportunities for the teaching of the value of classifications which are entirely synthetic in their structure.

395. *Conclusion.* It will be evident that, of the categories of material briefly considered in this chapter, some are obviously only likely to be encountered in public libraries; most, however, will also come, to some extent, within the scope of the work of the university or college librarian. Several of the categories, despite the title of our chapter, also crop up with their attendant problems of organization and exploitation, in special libraries. The task of arranging such a wide variety of material is no light one and the student of classification should carefully consider the points that have been made here and study in more detail the classification problems of one or two of the 'special' types of material. Probably Library Science and Local Collections offer the greatest scope and interest in this respect.

The Classification of Special Libraries: Classification Research

CHAPTER TWENTY-FOUR

The Task of Classifying a Special Library

396. Many of the problems outlined and discussed in the previous section of our work will affect all libraries; we were chiefly concerned there, however, with general, and especially with public, libraries. In this final section of the Manual, the emphasis is on the special library—its material, work, and peculiar problems of arrangement; this also seems to be the best section in which to consider the nature and value of the research in classification which is taking place and to review the future of classification in libraries, for most of the great strides forward in the last decade have been made in conjunction with special library classifications. The rapid growth in the number of special libraries and the absence of suitable classifications has provided the opportunity to test the newer theories of classification in the construction of special schemes and the experience gained from the newly created classifications has thrown much light on the problems of notation, helpful order and the arrangement of highly specific and complex documents.

397. Our task in this and in the next chapter is to indicate some of the difficulties that arise in the classification of specialising libraries; to name and briefly describe some of the important special classifications which now exist, and to discuss the relationship between classification and information indexing. The reader will almost certainly realise that there are many types of special library including industrial libraries, the libraries of learned and professional societies, libraries serving research organizations, and those working on behalf of government departments, for example. He must also, if he has a general library background, learn to appreciate that the stock of a special library often puts a very strong emphasis on 'non-book' material; the periodical article, the patent,

the research report, may be just as important as the bookstock. Indeed it is often more important, in that the most valuable or most current information may be rarely found in a book. The emphasis in most libraries of this type is also different from that found, for instance, in the public library. The specialised library is serving as an information centre and often its very existence will depend upon its ability to find quickly for readers, not necessarily a particular book, but a vital piece of information. A special classification ought likewise to be defined; it is one which, rather than covering all areas of knowledge, deliberately restricts itself to one subject field or a group of kindred subjects. It may, on the other hand, be special in a rather different sense, in that it covers *all* knowledge but is designed solely for one particular type of library user. We shall be dealing here chiefly with systems which are special with regard to their restricted subject coverage.

398. These preliminary definitions may seem tedious and unnecessary, but it is wise to deal with them before considering the difficulties of classifying the special library or information bureau. It is almost axiomatic that a special library must have a special classification, because in a special library the extreme ramifications of the subject concerned are sought and no classification scheme of a general character may have set these out exhaustively or made full provision for them by means of synthesis. True, a well-constructed general scheme has in it the possibilities of expansion to any degree; however, few such systems have been expanded to what we would now call the 'documentation level' and, if the expansion did take place, the resulting notations would be extremely long. It might be thought by some librarians that special libraries ought to use general schemes whenever possible to encourage uniformity in practice; this alas is rarely feasible, unless the UDC is the general classification concerned and the library one which specialises in some technical field. In most other cases, the general scheme will not do. But we must examine the problem in more detail.

399. One of the chief reasons why the general classifications are often rejected by special librarians is seen in the length of classmarks in the general scheme for specific subjects. Thus, for example, in a special library dealing with Petroleum, the fact that the number for this subject as a whole in DC is 665.5 is a severe handicap; it is easy to see how long class-marks would be for specific aspects of this subject field. We therefore find that the adoption of a general

scheme in a special library is always notationally undesirable; true, adaptations could be made to bring about greater brevity in class-marks, but most special librarians would argue that it is best to have a scheme which allocates the *whole* of its notation to the area of activity with which the special library is concerned. It is true also that the general schemes are usually lacking in detail for special library purposes. DC and BC would certainly be inadequate for any library dealing exclusively with a technical subject; even LC, in certain of its classes, might be faulted on these grounds. Only UDC and CC attempt to meet the challenge of classification at the documentation level for all subject fields. On the other hand, a scheme specially devised to cover a limited area of activity would certainly offer the necessary specificity of classification and the notation would be carefully apportioned to fit the restricted subject field. Palmer has suggested that general schemes of classification offer more than enough detail for most special libraries in every branch of knowledge except those in which the library is chiefly interested, but that in these latter fields they are too broad. This is almost certainly true; thus what the special librarian really needs is a system which will provide a detailed arrangement for his main subject interests and relatively broad classification for other branches of activity, which are only rarely represented in his stock.

400. Pendleton[1] and Vickery[2] have suggested other reasons why the special library should have a special classification. These include the absence of really thorough and speedy revision policies in many schemes which cover all knowledge, the lack of helpful order, and the fact that the users of a special library tend to look at many other branches of knowledge, naturally enough, from the point of view of their own activity. That is to say they expect, in an industrial library for example, the dominant interest of the firm to be the focal point of the classification, other subjects being viewed in the light of their importance for specialists in this principal subject field. These factors militate heavily against the use of any general scheme in the special library world; in addition we must consider the primary function of such libraries; the need to offer a rapid and thorough information service makes the specific classification of documents, in most cases, a necessity. Pendleton believes that if special schemes

[1] *Library Association Record*, June, 1954, pp. 205–8.
[2] *Faceted Classification*, 1960, pp. 7–8.

exist and their worth has been demonstrated, the appropriate libraries would be foolish not to make use of them.

401. There are, of course, some arguments *for* the use of a general classification in special libraries and information bureaux. UDC in fact is widely used in such libraries, especially in Europe. Its appeal to the special librarian in this country lies in the fact that it is detailed and virtually provides a 'two tier' level of classification in that the special librarian in a scientific field can use the appropriate part of the full English edition and rely on the abridgement for the classification of material in marginal fields. It also has the advantage that it is used in many technical journals and bibliographical services and, again from the British librarian's viewpoint, it is supported by the British Standards Institution. The wide recognition of the work of this organization by British industry has, as we pointed out in Chapter 14, made the scheme an almost automatic choice in many industrial libraries in this country, although it has met with some serious competition in recent years. There can be no doubt that UDC provides the necessary synthesis for precise classification and is far and away the best of the general schemes for a specialised technical library, but there must be serious reservations with regard to its suitability for some special libraries. Despite its popularity and its ingenious attempt to cater for those librarians requiring a really detailed classification, it suffers the inevitable defects which all general schemes tend to exhibit when the problem of classifying the highly specialised collection is faced. Some industrial librarians would defend it most warmly but, by and large, we consider its adoption unwise if there is a suitable special classification available.

402. It is impossible to be dogmatic about this; there are so many special libraries springing up nowadays and they differ so radically in size and character that no rigid decision can be made with regard to the course they should adopt on the vital question of classification. Some may find UDC admirable; this is particularly likely if they are concerned with a field in which the full schedules are available. Yet it is certain that other special libraries will find this classification nearly as unsuitable as the alternative general systems. They must then consider the adoption of an appropriate special scheme (possibly supported by the use of UDC for marginal subject fields), the adaptation of another of the general classifications or, if a special system is not available, the librarian may need to construct such a classification for the convenient arrangement of his collections. We

shall consider these alternative possibilities here, leaving the remaining prospect – that of relying on co-ordinate indexing – for the next chapter.

403. With regard to the adaptation of a general scheme for special library requirements, there are many interesting experiments to be seen. It is possible to find variations of DC and BC and even reliance on certain parts of SC. Unfortunately, like all adaptations, the end product of such work is a rather awkward hybrid; if the specialised library is expanding rapidly and one of the general schemes will not do, it is much better to employ or make a worthwhile special system. We would rarely recommend adaptation as the best solution, for either a scheme is adequate as it stands or is never likely to prove satisfactory. The adapted general classification will almost certainly be inferior to a special scheme and at the same time the library concerned will not gain the advantages which accrue to those who use a widely accepted scheme in an orthodox fashion. With the adaptation of a general scheme we relinquish uniformity in practice, yet there may be situations when such a process *is* advantageous or when it is forced upon the librarian by the lack of a suitable special scheme and the impossibility of making one. With regard to the latter point, it should be noted that adaptations can prove quite time consuming also, for they need to be worked out carefully and their peculiarities noted for the benefit of the various classifiers. To sum up, adaptation must not be rejected out-of-hand as a possibility, but other avenues should be very closely explored before such a course is ever accepted as the best solution.

404. We may digress for a moment to note some other methods of arrangement occasionally encountered in the world of special librarianship. For instance, although such libraries might seem the natural place for very detailed classification to be employed, we sometimes find that a broad arrangement only is applied; in such cases, unless the library concerned is a very small one, a very detailed subject catalogue would be needed by way of compensation. In Britain, perhaps the most interesting account of a broad, popular, classification as used in a special library in conjunction with parts of UDC is that given by Arnold;[1] there are few industrial libraries where such systems would be acceptable, however. The preference is still for UDC in its full and orthodox form. A variation of a

---

[1] Information retrieval: a pragmatic approach, *Journal of Documentation*, December, 1958, pp. 183–9.

different kind is seen in the use of two or more classifications for different categories of stock in the special library. The best example of this that comes to mind is the arrangement in the Board of Trade Library. Here much of the material is classified by LC, as befits a library concentrating on the social sciences, but there is some use of DC also. A collection of dictionaries and other material for translators is arranged by BC, and British trade directories are grouped according to a special industrial classification. It is rare to find so many parallels within one library;[1] yet the system works extremely well at the Board of Trade, probably because the stock divides conveniently into the various categories and each is distinct and virtually self-contained. There are probably only a handful of special libraries where an idea of this kind could be exploited to advantage.

405. The next possibility with which we must deal is the employment of a special classification; there can really be little doubt that this is the ideal solution to the whole problem, if indeed a system has already been made for the subject field. It is possible that such a classification may not quite fit the exact requirements of the special library concerned, but it will nearly always be much closer to those requirements than any general system, with the possible exception of UDC. Unfortunately some areas of knowledge do not yet have a classification devoted to them. This situation has been partly rectified in the last decade in that several new classifications, each restricted to a specialised field of activity have been made. In addition to some special classifications which follow traditional principles, we therefore now have an increasing number of faceted schemes. Indeed it is the special library which is best equipped to test the value of the modern ideas as many new specialising libraries and information centres are being created and thus there is every opportunity to put the latest theories into practice. If these are the ideas of the future, then there can be no doubt that the special librarians who apply these systems are paving the way for the widespread introduction of better methods for the organization of knowledge on shelves and in catalogues; such librarians, perhaps because they are continually witnessing the need for better methods in their own concentrated field to keep pace with the flow of new literature and ideas, are certainly often more keenly aware of the need for progress than some of their colleagues in the public library sphere.

[1] The same type of situation is found in one or two British public libraries where one system is used in the reference department and another in the lending library.

406. It may be wondered why CC itself is not adopted, if the faceted approach is considered the most advantageous; unfortunately although it is the one faceted general scheme it is weakest in the very fields, mostly technological ones, where faceted classifications are most urgently needed in the Western world. Of the special classifications which are available, we may mention some that are constructed according to the older principles before noting some of the relevant faceted systems. A scheme built on traditional lines which particularly deserves mention is C. C. Barnard's *Classification for medical libraries*, originally devised for use at the London School of Hygiene but now used by some thirty libraries. Its second edition appeared in 1955. The scheme uses an alphabetical notation and is like BC[1] in that it uses a series of tables to achieve some synthesis and employs the idea of alternative locations. Some of the topics in Barnard's Generalia Class are reminiscent of the arrangement of SC, but then it is perhaps permissible in a *special* classification to place a subject like Education in Generalia. Other special classifications include the *SfB classification for Building and Architecture; the Oxford system of decimal classification for forestry;* and *Glidden and Marchus's Library classification for public administration materials.*

407. A special classification which is very different in character from Barnard's is that known as the *Cheltenham Classification*, compiled by E. S. Fegan and M. Cant, 2nd edition, 1958. This is special, not in the sense that it is restricted to one subject field, but rather because it is designed only for one type of library – that of a school or college; the name is derived from the fact that Monica Cant was formerly librarian at the Cheltenham Ladies College. The system has an alphabetically based notation; numerals are used as subdivisions of each class. The broad synopsis for the sequence of classes is: Theology and Philosophy; History; Language and Literature (much notational space is given to these topics); Science and Technology; Fine Arts. The system attempts to reflect the way in which subjects are taught in schools and allows a good deal of latitude to individual libraries in its more detailed sub-divisions; it contains useful explanatory notes for the classifier. K. Garside's classification, mentioned already in paragraph 316, is also special in

---

[1] Barnard's preface mentions his debt to Bliss's work; there is also an affectionate tribute to the great American classificationist from Barnard's pen in the *Library Association Record*, January, 1956, p. 43.

this sense; that is it is intended for a particular type of library, or rather for the special needs of a certain academic library.

408. However, as indicated earlier we are chiefly concerned with those classifications which specialise in one branch of knowledge. The growing acceptance of the technique of facet analysis in Great Britain since 1951 has resulted in a rapid increase in the number of special classifications that are now available; likewise the need for special schemes has provided an excellent opportunity to prove the worth of the new theories. It is obviously uneconomical for us to list all the special faceted schemes that have been made in recent years; it is significant perhaps that several have been constructed by members of the British Classification Research Group, while others have been devised by special librarians confronted with the immediate practical problem of providing a better method of arrangement for their library. Critics of faceted classification may argue that several of the CRG schemes have not yet been thoroughly tried and tested, but those which have been applied to a collection of documents seem to be living up to the expectations of their advocates. To give some examples of these faceted special schemes, we may quote the classifications for *Food Technology*, *Metal Container Manufacture* and *Education;* all three are the work of D. J. Foskett and this prolific author and classificationist has also been responsible for the creation of a faceted scheme for *Occupational Safety and Health*, which is used by the International Labour Office in Geneva. Of these, the scheme devised for the London University Institute of Education may be briefly commented on as an excellent example of a faceted scheme; its introduction is one of the best concise explanations of the faceted approach that we know. This *London Education Classification*, as it is called, also employs the notion of pronounceable notation which we mentioned in Chapter Five. Each isolate is denoted by three letters, the second of which is always a vowel; the student examining the scheme must not be put off by the amusing possibilities which exist here, for although pronounceable notations may prove a mixed blessing this classification appears to be an excellent one, and the introduction carefully emphasises the important point that the index to a classified catalogue must support the scheme by citing the elements of each compound subject in a way which will ensure that every feasible subject approach to documents is catered for, by the classification or the index, in the most economical manner possible. Thus the clas-

sification itself should, and probably will, fit the facets together in the most helpful order; the subject index to the catalogue caters for alternative orders and variant approaches to any particular topic within the field.

409. Other outstanding examples of special faceted schemes include the system devised for *Soil Science* by B. C. Vickery; J. Farradane's classification for *Diamond Technology*; the *Office Management* scheme of J. Mills, with its retroactive notation, O. W. Pendleton's system for *Insurance;* the E. J. Coates classification for the *British Catalogue of Music;* and Barbara Kyle's scheme for the *Social Sciences.* This last system is possibly of special interest for, if we exclude CC, it is the nearest approach to a general faceted classification, in that it covers a large area of knowledge. It is intended for use in the bibliographical publications of UNESCO and was made after Miss Kyle had carefully examined and rejected the possibilities of UDC as a social science classification worthy of international use. Some other faceted schemes are mentioned elsewhere in this textbook; the reader who wants a fairly full list is invited to consult the appendix to Vickery's book *Classification and Indexing in Science.* What is certainly noteworthy is that these schemes do not, in their facet formula, attempt to follow the ideas of Ranganathan with regard to the fundamental concepts PMEST; they rather select relevant categories based on the demands of the literature in each field.

410. Several advantages seem to be emerging from the use of these faceted systems, although the increase in their adoption is necessarily slow in that many libraries, including special ones, are firmly committed to older classifications. The faceted schemes are based on a careful analysis of the subject field concerned and the clear recognition of the vital characteristics of division. The total number of foci produced by the application of any single characteristic form a definite category (or facet) and the classificationist merely enumerates the foci within each facet in their most helpful order – this may be chronological order, geographical order, or some other sequence which offers a rational method for listing them – allocates a symbol to each focus, and decides upon the best order for combining foci from the various facets. Preliminary assessment of the characteristics of the subject field in this manner makes unwanted cross-classification virtually impossible. Also the careful control of the sequence in which the facets are to be combined to build up a class-mark for a

compound subject should certainly result in an order of the optimum helpfulness. Another great advantage is that faceted classifications make it possible to specify many subjects that cannot be dealt with accurately in an enumerative classification. An illustration may make this last point clearer. Let us consider the type of document that would be dealt with in Foskett's classification for *Metal Container Manufacture*. If an item has for its subject 'the inspection of seams on open top cans' we will classify it by lining together the foci from the Product facet (open top cans), the Components facet (seams) and the Operations facet (inspection), in this order. But supposing we wished to classify the same document by an entirely enumerative scheme. We would have to find its place in the list of terms in the hierarchy. This might appear as:

> Cans
> > Open Top Cans
> > > Seams of Open Top Cans
> > > > Inspection of Seams of Open Top Cans

Thus classification, in this instance, could be carried out just as readily by means of the enumerative scheme. But suppose that the next document to be dealt with covers 'the inspection of open top cans', 'the inspection of cans', or 'seams of cans'. The essential rigidity of the enumerative classification is at once exposed; it cannot cope with such items in adequate fashion unless terms such as 'seams' or 'inspection' are inserted into the hierarchy at every point where they might conceivably be required! The faceted classification, however, can follow its normal synthetic pattern; it will classify 'seams of cans', for example, by lining together the foci for 'cans' and 'seams' in the approved manner. The cumbersome nature of any enumerative system for dealing with the specific themes with which the special librarian must always contend means that such classifications will either fail to recognise many of these themes or will do so only by listening recurring concepts, such as 'inspection', again and again in the schedules.

411. The other advantages usually claimed for the entirely faceted special scheme are that it is easier to compile than the traditional type of classification; that it enables precise classification to be achieved; that it is less bulky as each recurring concept is listed once only in the appropriate category; also that many new

themes which emerge will, in fact, simply involve fresh combinations of concepts which the synthetic scheme has already recognised and listed. This means that the faceted scheme will not date as readily as the enumerative type; an important factor to be considered in libraries specialising in scientific and technical fields. Ranganathan sums up this last point for us in characteristic fashion:[1] 'enumerative classification is suitable for a finite and lethargic universe of knowledge, but the analytico-synthetic classification is needed for the turbulent universe of knowledge embodied in microdocuments'. Finally, with regard to the benefits of the newer approach towards classification, we may note that some British librarians have alleged that the reader in a special library understands and appreciates the idea of synthesis in classification more readily than the approach which tries to chart the whole subject field by listing every conceivable theme. Foskett, on more than one occasion, has claimed that a faceted scheme, by grouping basic concepts into categories, reflects the world of reality that scientists and engineers know and deal with; likewise, Mrs J. Aitchison, who was chiefly responsible for the English Electric Company's faceted classification for *Engineering*, indicated that despite certain faults in the synthetic scheme, its superiority and utility for a special library was clearly recognisable, by both staff and readers, after it had been in operation for a comparatively short time. Her views are, in a sense, particularly interesting as this is an excellent example of a fully faceted scheme designed with the needs of a particular industrial library in mind.

412. The choice of the special librarian with regard to a suitable classification is thus very much wider nowadays than in former years and the newer principles now being taken into account may well prove especially significant in documentation and information work. But there are, naturally enough, still some subject fields which lack a special classification, faceted or otherwise. The librarian in such cases must use a general scheme in its original or an adapted form, or make a special classification of his own. If he decides upon the latter course, he must consider carefully whether to follow the conventional pattern of attempting to list all branches of the subject concerned to form a gigantic tree of that part of knowledge or whether to reject what many modern librarians would regard as the built-in obsolescence of this approach in favour of a faceted system.

[1] In his paper at the Dorking Conference on Classification for Information Retrieval, 1957.

The latter is certainly more flexible with regard to its method of listing basic elements only and providing rules for the combination order of the concepts from the various categories. The supporters of these newer principles have certainly been extremely active in explaining and publicising their views; there are now many explanations of faceted classification, but probably the best of several possible guides to the making of such schemes is the book by Vickery entitled *Faceted Classification*, which we have already mentioned. The author points out that such classification, in its sorting of the component parts of knowledge into definite unmistakable categories, is similar in part to the rules of logical division which govern the traditional enumerative systems. He contends, however, that the results obtained from faceted classification are superior to those derived from the traditional methods, on account of the way in which each category is strictly distinguished, and because the faceted scheme provides much more flexibility for the combination of terms in compound subjects.[1] One can only add that the other major modern technique of phase analysis, which enables us to systematically extricate the strands of a complex subject, could be almost equally valuable at times in the special library field.

413. If the librarian wishes to make his own scheme on faceted principles the terms used in the subject field must be studied and noted. These must then be arranged in categories, each category or facet consisting of a list of concepts produced by the application of a single characteristic. These concepts must be arranged in the most helpful order in an array within their category and the categories will be checked by a tentative application of the analysis carried out to a fairly small, but fully representative, collection of documents. If the vital categories appear to have been distinguished, the librarian must then check to see if each basic concept likely to arise has been listed in its appropriate category. The way is then clear for the allocation of notation to the various facets (it may well be advisable to draw upon the extra capacity which an alphabetical notation offers and to provide some means of revealing each change of facet and phase in the notation) and for an exploratory testing of the completed system. Only experience with the scheme can reveal whether the classificationist has succeeded in revealing all the relevant foci in each facet; it is, of course, possible to add some later, if need be. We have already stressed that this approach eliminates all undesirable

[1] *Faceted classification*, 1960, pp. 12–13.

cross-division but, at the risk of confusing some readers, it might be added that if cross-classification *can* prove advantageous, the faceted scheme must recognise this. Vickery,[1] for instance, has shown how a concept may arise in more than one context, thus necessitating its appearance in more than one facet.

414. What is more essential is that the appropriate facets be clearly recognised and distinguished from the outset; it is also necessary that clear rules be made for the combination order of facets to keep the primary facets to the fore. In this way the scattering of related material is confined to themes of minor importance and is carefully *controlled*. The combination order chosen must be based upon the observed needs of the literature and on the typical requests for information received by the library. It will be found that the filing order of facets will be the exact reverse of the schedule order of combination.[2] We can demonstrate this as follows. In the combination (or horizontal) order, the primary facets must come first to bring about the most helpful sequence of documents or catalogue entries. But, when seeking a filing sequence for the individual elements, it is found that to reverse the schedule order is the best method. No scheme can collect *everything* that might be brought together, but if the filing order (sometimes referred to as the vertical order) reverses the combination order of the schedules it will ensure that everything on the *primary facets* is collected. Here again we see a great advantage of the faceted schemes; they enable us to easily determine which subject associations have been stressed and which ignored by the classification and to be certain that the major ones fall into the first of these two categories. (An index to the classified catalogue, constructed according to the chain procedure, will then show related aspects from the secondary facets which have been distributed in the scheme.) Thus, in CC for instance, a document involving the concepts Personality and Time would file before one drawing on the same Personality focus plus a Matter focus. Likewise in a Literature classification, worked out in outline at the Liverpool School of Librarianship, the combination order of facets is Language (represented by capital letters), Periods (represented by lower case letters), Literary Form (represented by numbers), and Forms of Presentation (represented by numbers introduced by a zero). But

---

[1] *Aslib Proceedings*, August, 1962, pp. 243–7.
[2] This is explained also in other texts, e.g., Mills, *A Modern Outline of Librar Classification*, p. 18 ff, and Davison, *Theory of Classification*, pp. 30–31.

the filing order for a selection of documents would be as indicated below:

B	English Literature
B01	A critical work on English Literature
B1	English drama (no period specified)
Bd	English Literature (1558–1610)
Bds	Shakespeare
Bds1	Shakespearean drama
Bds101	Critical work on Shakespearean drama

It will be observed that the filing order of the elements reverses their schedule order of combination in order to collect all material under each *period* rather than all material under each *literary form*. Similarly CC collects material in the Matter category by filing it after Time, Space and Energy – foci from primary facets must *file* last. The UDC has perhaps not fully comprehended this principle and its sequence as a result is not always as helpful as it might be.

415. Our chapter has indicated that there are many methods and possibilities open to the modern special librarian or information officer. He may reap the benefit of modern theory and use a faceted classification on the lines described; if there is not a suitable one available he may, if he has the time and zest for the task, make one. Alternatively he may employ UDC which, although not consciously faceted, has a very strong synthetic element, has been thoroughly tested on an international scale, and has a great deal of support. He may, again, decide that one of the other general classifications, probably in an adapted form, must be his most logical choice; there is yet another possibility open to him also, as we shall discover in the next chapter. But in Britain at least, UDC is very well established in special libraries and is not giving way too easily to the newer ideas. Perhaps, as De Grolier argues, this is because it is an institution and institutions tend to persist; on the other hand, many librarians warmly praise its great practical value. We can only conclude by asserting once again the difficulty of being dogmatic in this matter, in view of the wide variety of collections encompassed by the term 'special library'. Those responsible for the effective arrangement of such libraries must weigh up the various alternative possibilities very carefully and judge for themselves.

CHAPTER TWENTY-FIVE

Co-ordinate Indexing for Special Libraries

416. Indexing is important in all libraries; it is only in comparatively recent years that it has been rescued, however, from the position which D. W. Langridge has described so aptly as that of the 'Cinderella of Library Science'. If knowledge in books is to be discovered and used, there is a great need for the production of better indexes in many textbooks. The Library Association and the Society of Indexers have done much to encourage authors to index their text more thoroughly and the idea of the Wheatley Medal award, made annually to the person responsible for the best indexed work, is an excellent one. Good indexing is also being promoted through the influence of such publications as British Standard 3700 of 1964, which deals with the preparation of indexes and through similar publications compiled in other countries or by international bodies. The indexing of published texts is not, naturally enough, directly within the librarian's sphere and control; yet the latter's use of literature and his dealings with those who seek rapid access to the most appropriate items of published information must make him aware that many authors are still in need of persuasion and exhortation if books and documents are to yield their knowledge readily to enquirers.

417. As far as the librarian's *direct use* of indexing techniques is concerned, we have already noted the possibility of employing the chain procedure when compiling the subject index to the classified catalogue. There will be times when any librarian will find, nevertheless, that his catalogue, no matter how well compiled, will not indicate all the information that is available on a specific topic. He

will then consult relevant bibliographies, of course, but it may well be that appropriate material in his own stock will come to light, if certain composite volumes and specialised publications have been indexed. Indexes which can be kept with profit in a large general library include: an index to poetry; an index of trade names; and, possibly, an index of the names of those individuals chiefly responsible for certain government white papers. The character of the library and the published indexes available will do much to determine the nature of any special indexing that is done by the staff, but our last example is indicative of a form of index which can often be very useful; many Command Papers and other documents published through H.M.S.O. are frequently referred to, both at the time of their publication and in later years, as 'the Radcliffe Report', 'the Younghusband Report' etc., by readers who are vague as to the date of publication of the document and may even be a little unsure about its exact subject. It is material of this kind that, unless a catalogue entry or reference has been made under the personal name, can often only be *quickly* tracked down if the librarian has been sufficiently industrious to prepare a simple index to it designed for staff consultation only.

418. The theme of our chapter is concerned with the important technique known as co-ordinate indexing, but before we come to this subject, the ideas of Farradane[1] with regard to indexing may be mentioned. Like the later work of Ranganathan their aim is the accurate definition and relating of subjects. The indexing system proposed for relational analysis strives to isolate subjects which have been 'uniquely defined'. The subject terms selected, which must always be nouns, Farradane calls *isolates;* these must not be confused with the isolates or foci produced in a fully faceted classification, although they are in some ways similar. Between these isolates, certain relations are known to exist, such as causation and reaction. The symbols used in the indexing system to express such relations are called *operators*. If the isolates are combined, or qualified, by the right operators – those which express the only possible relations between them – a linear symbol called an *analet* may be constructed. Alphabetical arrangements of such analets by their first factors, it is claimed, will provide 'a complete, logical subject index . . . A classification can then be constructed by selection of deductive relations arranged in

---

[1] *Journal of Documentation*, 1950, pp. 83–9 provides the initial account; there is also reference to his ideas in Lecture 4 of B. I. Palmer's *Itself an Education*.

hierarchical form'. Farradane claims boldly that his methods result in the only true representation of the structure of knowledge and that his principles provide accurate and adequate indexing and classifying with complete flexibility. He has developed his theory in subsequent issues of the *Journal of Documentation* and time will tell whether it can prove useful for the arrangement of books; its creator is an information scientist rather than a librarian. The method is certainly interesting, but not too easy to comprehend; it seems to call for an unusual skill in defining and relating the necessary isolates.

419. We are concerned here mainly with special libraries and with systems which are more widely adopted than the ingenious methods proposed by Farradane. Some special librarians find that classification, in its accepted form, is unsuitable for their requirements altogether. Their stock may consist mainly of pamphlets, journals and reports; the number of books being small in relation to this mass of other material. Obviously research reports, patents, standards and the like cannot be shelved with books; many periodicals and reports may also need a minute subject analysis which might be possible in a large classified catalogue but would be out of the question as far as shelf classification is concerned. In special libraries, therefore, where there is a large amount of document material to be arranged and, very possibly, no appropriate special classification, the only real alternative to the UDC lies in the adoption of some form of co-ordinate indexing. The decision must be made carefully; there are, in the industrial library especially, obviously advantages in employing the highly synthetic UDC. But in the United States in particular, and to an increasing extent in Great Britain also, co-ordinate indexing systems are gaining in popularity. This indexing may be confined to the 'non-book' material in the library, the bookstock being arranged according to a classification scheme; alternatively, *all* material may be organized through the index, the shelf arrangement being a chronological sequence of accession within the various categories – books, reports, etc.

420. We shall endeavour to explain the essential principles behind co-ordinate indexing by describing the *Uniterm* system, which is the best known of the rival methods. This was devised by Mortimer Taube as a method for the retrieval of information from technical reports, although other librarians seem to have hit upon very similar systems independently. The processes involved in a simple, manual Uniterm system are as follows. Each document coming into the

special library receives a running accession number. Its subject is then thoroughly and carefully analysed and is broken up into appropriate alphabetical units or unit terms. For each of these a card is made out with the appropriate term at the head. The number of the document is placed (*posted* is the technical term often employed by librarians in the United States) on each card. The cards are then filed in alphabetical order of Uniterm and the documents are assigned to their place in an accession order sequence. This means that reports and pamphlet material can be readily stored in boxes or otherwise conveniently housed, since new material need not be placed at the most appropriate subject location but is merely added to the report or pamphlet sequence.

421. When a request for information on a topic is received and the librarian wishes to search the report collection, he must 'translate' the inquiry into the appropriate Uniterms and extract the relevant cards from their alphabetical sequence. He then searches these cards for common numbers; a number which appears on *each* card extracted will indicate that the document represented by that number covers *all* the terms, or concepts, demanded by the subject inquirer. At this stage, two points may be briefly stressed. Firstly, unlike classification, co-ordinate indexing techniques do not attempt to map out knowledge in a systematic pattern. The terms involved, which are similar to the isolates of a faceted classification, are left in the unhelpful alphabetical order; co-ordination of the required terms does not occur until a search is carried out. Secondly, the Uniterm system essentially involves the selection of single words to serve as the terms at the head of the cards.

422. Let us illustrate the technique by means of a simple example. Suppose a library specialises in the literature of chemistry and the various applications of chemicals. A document dealing with '*The use of boron in fertilisers for flower gardening*' would be broken down into the Uniterms 'Boron', 'Fertilisers', 'Flowers' and 'Gardening'. If its accession number, say, was 510, four cards would be made out, one for each term, with the accession number of the document on each. To retrieve such a publication, when required, the relevant cards would be extracted from their alphabetical file. They might yield the following information:

1

BORON

0	1	2	3	4	5	6	7	8	9
10	81	272	43	4	75	136	217	58	99
240	461	382	113	334	445	376	477	228	289
400	711	512	293	824	685	716	617	348	579
510			563		765	836	807	628	819

2

FERTILISERS

0	1	2	3	4	5	6	7	8	9
170	81	182	113	144	75	66	217	188	99
360	551	382	643	294	155	556	447	348	329
400	711			334	445	686	797	558	409
510	821			824	685		807		669
					765				

3

GARDENING

0	1	2	3	4	5	6	7	8	9
190	111	62	113	114	75	16	47	138	59
360	171	292	173	234	195	286	187	708	189
510	361		393	474	445		327		409
	641		523		765		687		

4

FLOWERS

0	1	2	3	4	5	6	7	8	9
270	221	32	23	264	125	96	287	8	399
340	491	152	113	544	605		517	68	469
510	671	602	303	734	765		607	388	669
		782						558	

We would find, by comparing the first three of these cards, that the numbers 75, 113, 445, 510, and 765 were common to each. By adding the card for 'Flowers', we would narrow down the search further and it would be revealed that the documents numbered 113, 510, and 765 were probably relevant; this, of course, includes the document for which we are searching.

423. The reader encountering here a description of co-ordinate indexing for the first time is invited to re-read our verbal description in paragraphs 420–421, after having studied the above example; he will find that, in its essence, the process is a very simple one. The Uniterm system, however, has many rivals which, usually differ from it only in comparatively minor respects. One major difficulty which arises in our system as described, and it is one which the discerning reader will have immediately noticed, is that cards rapidly become congested with numbers making a search for common numbers into a slow and tedious operation. Thus, in a library of any size, manual methods of co-ordinate indexing have been superseded by systems involving an elementary form of mechanisation. Thus we find that there are methods such as the Batten Card System (with its strong classified element), the Zatocoding of Calvin Mooers, and the so-called Peek-a-boo System. The latter, instead of relying on cards ruled into ten columns with numbers entered manually in the appropriate column according to their final digit, makes use of centre-punched cards. The other type of punched card, the edge-notched variety, is widely used in commerce and industry but is rather more involved with regard to the solution of information indexing problems, although it has been applied to such a task. The centre-punched card, unlike the edge-notched type, is divided into thousands of squares. Each square represents a number and, instead of writing a number on the card, the library staff use a punch to make a hole in the appropriate square. To search for common numbers, the cards are extracted, are carefully arranged so that each is exactly superimposed on the one beneath, and are then held up to the light. If light shows through any particular square, then that square denotes a number which is common to all the cards and which, in turn, stands for a document that brings together all the aspects involved on the cards.

424. While edge-notched cards may require the use of a metal rod to facilitate sorting, the centre-punched variety which we have just described merely rely on accurate punching and the holding up of

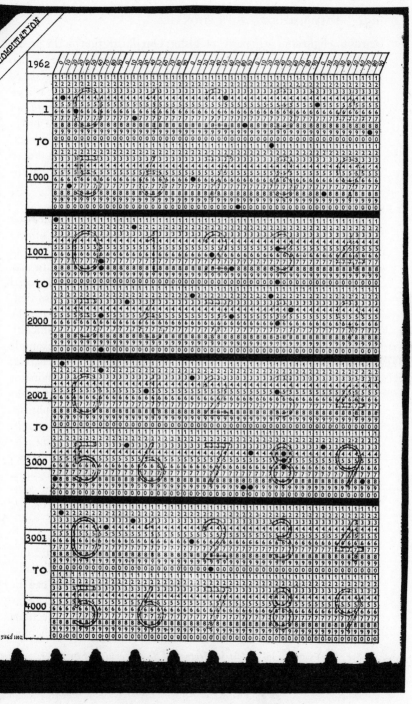

A typical body-punched card, as used at the
Library of British Insulated Callenders Cables, Prescot.

cards to a light source in perfect register. Our illustration on the preceding page indicates a method which is virtually akin to the Peek-a-boo System, but which was developed independently at British Insulated Callenders Cables Limited, at the library of their Prescot works. Each of these cards is suitable for use in the indexing of a batch of four thousand technical reports or similar documents. The broad horizontal lines divide the cards into blocks of one thousand numbers; within these blocks, the large squares represent each hundred numbers and the smaller ones the individual numbers. The identification of the latter is rendered less difficult by the use of 'zero', 'ten', twenty' and so on, at the head of the vertical columns.

425. If such cards are scanned, it will be found, for example, that documents 831 and 1077 bring together all the aspects of the subject *The computation of sag in steel-cored aluminium conductors on overhead lines*. This assumes that the two pertinent holes are also punched away on cards headed 'Sag', 'Conductors-steel cored aluminium' and 'Lines-overhead'. The reader may notice also that, although four thousand documents is the maximum that can be covered by the cards, B.I.C.C. have overcome this type of difficulty by dividing their material into chronological batches; our example relates to 1962 material only. Another feature of the example is that, unlike the Unitern method, this *Unit-concept* system, as its originator A. Johnson, has called it[1], often employs more than a single term at the head of a card. There are decided advantages in using phrases rather than single words, on certain occasions, as the indexing unit. We shall touch upon these later in our chapter; at this point, the student of our subject need merely understand the difference between co-ordinate indexing and conventional subject-cataloguing, and the difference between such indexing in its manual form compared with the methods used when centre-punched cards are employed.

426. Once the operations involved have been comprehended, it is natural that one should attempt to assess the advantages and disadvantages of such systems in special libraries. On the credit side, apart from the fact that reports, pamphlets and cuttings can be readily filed in boxes and folders in chronological sequence, we may note the fact that retrieval is very speedy. Very large collections could rely on computer searching as we indicate in the next chapter,

[1] See, for example, his article in *Journal of Documentation*, September, 1959, pp. 146-55.

but most special libraries would find that a co-ordinate index on punched cards could be made to yield its information very quickly to the human searcher; this assumes, naturally that the indexing terms or phrases have been selected with care and that the user of the index can quickly 'translate' an inquiry into the requisite indexing terminology. Perhaps even more important than speed is the ability of the index to enable *any* related concepts to be quickly brought together. A special classification, faceted or otherwise, can only arrange documents in one order. True, this order will, if the scheme is efficient, be the one which is of most value to the majority of enquirers; yet there are bound to be queries which call for the bringing together of concepts which the classification has been obliged to separate. The information indexing systems claim to overcome this weakness; any related concepts can be rapidly collocated because the index does not attempt to offer an order of optimum usefulness, but rather provides a means whereby terms from different parts of the alphabet can be quickly gathered together and whereby documents relating to the grouping formed can be speedily traced. After a search has taken place a term or phrase is re-inserted into the alphabetically arranged sequence of cards; in another search it may well be linked with terms entirely different from those with which it was collocated in dealing with the first inquiry. For this reason, many writers speak of post co-ordinate indexing; terms are not pre-co-ordinated as in classification, but are linked at the time of search.

427. A further advantage is that it is possible to analyse important documents extremely thoroughly by this method and to index in great depth. The system replaces the usual form of subject cataloguing; thus the only type of catalogue needed in conjunction with it is one which contains author entries and possibly entries for translators, editors, series and some highly distinctive titles. What is more the indexing removes the burden of the long notations that are so often the inevitable partner of the specific classification needed by technical and commercial literature in industrial libraries. Yet the reader must not imagine that, in saying this, we are prepared to withdraw any of the claims made for the classified subject approach in the organization of knowledge. On the one hand, it is clear that indexing methods of this kind are really only appropriate when report literature and pamphlets loom large in proportion to the bookstock; on the other hand it must be pointed out that, despite

M*

the reliance on verbal terms rather than notation to denote the concepts, co-ordinate indexing systems themselves make more use of classification and classificatory principles than some of their supporters might wish to confess. True, this is sometimes in a rather indirect way; yet it has been found that great advantages emerge when the index takes an alphabetico-classed form and several concepts which are very closely linked are kept together in the index by the inversion of a heading or by various verbal manipulations.

428. What of the disadvantages of such systems? We have already noted that the purely manual methods result in searching being slowed considerably because of the laborious nature of the task involved in searching for common numbers on cards which are almost filled with the numbers of documents. Punched card techniques eliminate this danger, but certain other problems remain. One very real one is that, while specific searches can be carried out, the alphabetical nature of the index makes the search for related material of a more general character, or indeed any form of browsing at the index, virtually impossible. It is true that most, or many, of the requests in a special library do demand information on a specific theme, but many rather more general documents might well contain useful information on the specific topic and thus, if this is borne in mind or if any form of a generic search is required, the absence of classification, or comparative lack of it, may prove a handicap. This problem is best overcome by thorough indexing; that is, if a general document contains important information on a more specific theme, in addition to its data on the general subject, the specific as well as the general topic should be indexed in relation to that document. The other method of minimizing this type of difficulty is to introduce, as suggested earlier, a strong element of classification into the alphabetical index. At B.I.C.C., for instance, it is recognised that, while there are various reasons for the deterioration of cables, an inquirer might want information on cable deterioration in general. This, in the B.I.C.C. Library, has involved the use of indexing terms such as DETERIORATION – RODENTS, DETERIORATION – CORROSION, etc. Therefore, if information on corrosion is wanted, the latter term is withdrawn from the index; if the enquiry is more general, involving several reasons for cable deterioration, all the relevant cards, grouped together in the index, can easily be scanned.

429. Another problem which arises is that unwanted information

may sometimes be recalled from the index. American writers on our subject often refer to this as the problem of *false reports*, or *false drops*. The difficulty is one which is especially likely to occur unless the terms for the index are carefully selected; it can be overcome to some extent by the use of phrases, rather than single words, in the index. If, for instance, the Uniterm method was used, the retrieval of irrelevant information might occur in the following way. Let us suppose our document deals with '*The use of aluminium for beer cans and of tin-plate for food cans*'. Cards might be made out headed ALUMINIUM, BEER, CANS, TIN-PLATE, and FOOD respectively. But if we have an enquiry for literature recommending, say, *the use of aluminium in the construction of food cans*, it is highly likely that our document above, although very possibly unwanted on this occasion, will be retrieved. A great deal of time and effort has been spent, particularly in the United States, with regard to ways of eliminating this particular hazard in co-ordinate indexing. Experiments have been made with a number of linking devices and research continues; yet it is our contention that the efforts made to solve this particular potential fault have been out of proportion to the nature of the problem. Recall and relevance ratios are defined and very briefly discussed in Chapter 27, but one assumes that if an inquirer obtains all the relevant information available on a specific theme he will not be unduly perturbed if the total number of documents produced includes one or two that are not really required. Even so, it must be stressed that the best way to control false sorts lies in the careful selection of terms and phrases for the index.

430. Here we come to the crucial problem; co-ordinate indexing systems stand or fall by the skill with which their vocabulary is selected and linked and the ability of the staff to 'translate' inquiries into the appropriate indexing terminology. As R. A. Fairthorne puts it: 'the first step is to ensure that different things are called by different names, the same things by the same name, only one name, and a helpful name'. This may well be the vital as well as the initial step. It is no coincidence that, at the B.I.C.C. Library at Prescot, where co-ordinate indexing has been so successful, terms for the index have been most carefully selected, a distinction being made if needed between the use of a word as a noun and the same word in its adjectival form; the fact that the senior members of the staff have some subject knowledge and have worked with the index since its inception is another significant feature.

431. It is necessary that, whatever the co-ordinate indexing system in use, a dictionary or thesaurus should be kept to show which terms have been employed; this may be particularly useful for assisting new or junior members of the staff to convert the language of the inquirer into the language of the index, but may be used by all members of the staff when the need arises. The dictionary will show, not only the terms employed, but many of those neglected also; the traditional 'see' reference will refer us away from the latter to the term needed. Such a dictionary needs to be carefully compiled and regularly evaluated if the system is to be really efficient. Indeed, although in the early days of co-ordinate indexing systems the stress was on the random choice of vocabulary by the inquirer, it is now fully recognised that the selection of the indexing language and the listing of the selected terms is a most essential part of the whole process. It may be stressed that classification again has a part to play here, for the precise definition of terms and the provision of links to show associations between them is essentially a classificatory activity. The concepts listed in categories for a faceted scheme may also help in determining the best concepts to employ for the vocabulary of information indexing. Meanwhile, research into vocabulary selection goes on, especially in the U.S.A.; but librarians in Britain are not ignoring the problem. An interesting paper by Raymond Moss[1] contains some useful facts on minimum vocabularies and the pages of *Aslib Proceedings* and *Journal of Documentation* reveal the general interest in the techniques and possibilities of co-ordinate indexing systems.

432. It is clear that such methods are destined to play an ever-increasing part in special librarianship; they have a certain interest also, of course, for the public librarian, although the latter may find he has little or no opportunity to apply them. They are, in fact methods which have been experimented with in the special departments of a few public libraries, but which have made little headway outside the special library field. There will be some special libraries where the techniques are quite inappropriate, either because it is important that material be organized in the conventional classified sequence on the shelves and the UDC or a special scheme is needed, or because it is uneconomical to divide a large collection of material

---

[1] R. Moss, *Vocabularies for Batten Card (Peek-A-Boo) Indexing* (*Liverpool Library School Occasional PaperNo. 2*), 1965. His more recent paper, *Minimum vocabularies for information indexing* is also noteworthy.

into a number of chronological sequences; the latter step may be demanded if there are many thousands of documents to be indexed and the punched cards only cover say, four or five thousand places per card.

433. The proven efficiency of co-ordinate indexing in many specialised technical libraries is indicative of its undoubted merits for the recall of data from certain categories of material; the Uniterm system has also fared comparatively well in the tests on the efficiency of classification and indexing systems conducted at the College of Aeronautics, Cranfield, under the auspices of Aslib. The character of special collections and the information needs of the library users must surely determine in the future whether more and more special libraries use such indexing techniques or whether it is, in Britain at least, the UDC or the faceted schemes which grow in popularity. UDC is still certainly the established favourite for the arrangement of these libraries, but in the long run it seems likely that the position will change. In the meantime one can only observe with great interest the attempts to mingle the advantages of both classified and alphabetical arrangement in many co-ordinate indexing systems, and the continued investigation into the methods and limitations of such systems, particularly in the United States, in an attempt to increase their efficiency further. It is perhaps regrettable that these techniques have almost solely been applied to the problem of organizing technical documents; it would certainly be of great practical value if they could be tested more thoroughly in other subject fields also, particularly with regard to the indexing and retrieval of the commercial information which is also of great importance in several industrial libraries.

CHAPTER TWENTY-SIX

Classification and the Computer

434. The subject of information retrieval affects the whole of this section of the Manual but is now extremely well documented in a variety of textbooks and articles and is covered by a separate paper in Part 2 examinations of the British Library Association. The increasing stress on the potential and actual use of computers in such work encourages us nevertheless to include a short chapter on the part which classification can play in a computer-based retrieval programme. There has, as the reader will almost certainly realise, been a strong and understandable tendency towards increased mechanisation in information work in the last decade. Punched card techniques represent an elementary form of mechanisation that is a great advance on purely manual systems; so also machine literature searching represents a further enormous development in the evolution of information indexing. Systems whereby relevant information can be rapidly traced and the appropriate references printed out by the machine, and indexes produced according to such notions as the Keyword-in-Context (KWIC) principle, would have astounded the librarians of the period immediately before the Second World War. But the torrent of new literature in all subject fields demands the constant improvement of methods designed to arrange that literature and to locate the most suitable items quickly, for with more and more documents for possible reading but no increase in reading time specialist workers will need extra assistance to obtain reliable and important new information from books and periodicals. The problem affects all subject fields; it is apparent even in the so-called static areas of knowledge such as Philosophy and Religion, but of course it is the technologist who is most aware of the danger of being swamped by the overwhelming volume of potentially valuable new

documents. The eighteenth-century Italian Jesuit, Saverio Bettinelli,[1] once spoke about an age, which might be thought of as one of 'bibliographic Malthusianism', when the birth rate of new literature would exceed man's ability to store and exploit it; such a time would surely be almost upon us in the present century[2] were not librarians and others fully aware of the dilemma and taking active steps to solve it. One of the great problems is that the purpose of classification and indexing should be to show us not only what is available but what we can afford to ignore; thus less indexing would be done if we knew exactly what to index and, in a slightly different sphere, the present day stress on the *selective* dissemination of information is a recognition of the very same difficulty. The fact that the task *is* being faced squarely and that a variety of possible solutions are being found can be seen from the increasing flow of literature on information retrieval itself; the range and value of this literature can perhaps be gauged from this chapter's lavish use of footnotes. Relevant articles now appear not merely in the obvious sources such as *Aslib Proceedings*, *Journal of Documentation*, and *American Documentation*, but in technical periodicals such as *Metals Review*, *Computer Journal*, *Science* and *New Scientist*. The magazine *Information Storage and Retrieval*, published quarterly since January 1963, also throws light on this problem, although students will find many of its articles extremely advanced.

435. We are really concerned in this chapter with mechanical methods of retrieval, especially those which involve the use of a computer, and the extent to which they affect, or rely on, classificatory techniques. For when mechanised searching is employed, it is clear that classification *can* play a large part, although it need not *necessarily* do so. We prefer that it should for, in all indexing and searching operations, a classified arrangement offers a systematic, general-to-specific approach and enables the enquirer to readily broaden or narrow down his search when necessary. Co-ordinate indexing systems involving punched cards may well, as we have seen, rely on a strong element of classification even if remaining apparently alphabetical techniques. Likewise data fed into a computer may well assume a classified form, if it can be argued that this is the form which

[1] Quoted in LaMontagne, *American Library Classification*, 1961, pp. 343–4.
[2] The logician, Y. Bar-Hillel denies this, saying that further specialisation by the growing number of scientists will solve the dilemma. See his article in *American Documentation*, April, 1963, pp. 95–8.

will facilitate the retrieval of a large number of relevant references to documents in the shortest possible time.

436. Here, at the risk of stating the obvious, it may be wise to insert a word or two concerning the nature of computers.[1] They are certainly not all-wise machines which can abstract or index documents on our behalf; what they can do extremely well is to perform a number of operations in a particular sequence at an amazing speed and make a choice between alternative sequences for us. Computers can themselves be classified in two ways; there are sequential and simultaneous computers, the former carrying out the different parts of an operation in turn while the latter would perform all the aspects of the computation at the same time. The other method of dividing computers is to recognise the essential differences between digital and analogue computers. In practice, for information work, the sequential digital computer is the only type of interest to us. As we have already stressed, the great merit of such machines lies in their ability to store a vast amount of data, and to make a search of this store extremely rapidly and efficiently, and to print out the results; they will *not* perform the subject analysis of documents, but can house an enormous number of classified or alphabetical references and scan these for items wanted for a particular enquiry at a speed which is significantly faster than the manual systems or those which rely on a simple element of mechanisation.

437. It is clear then that, if a computer is to be used for the recovery of information from an organized store of knowledge, information may be fed into it in the form of alphabetical or classified references 'translated' into spots on magnetic tape or discs. It has been estimated that for a collection of 200,000 documents, with an average of ten index terms per document, the information indexed would occupy less than one reel of Atlas or I.B.M. magnetic tape and sorting and retrieval would be extremely rapid.[2] The enormous advantages of such methods in very large institutions are obvious; we may briefly digress to observe that some conventional catalogues in the U.S.A. have been replaced by a high speed computer system and the National Science Foundation in Washington has been generous in supporting certain institutions financially in

---

[1] Particularly recommended as a readable introduction for those who seek details of the history and potential of computers is S. H. Hollingdale and G. C. Tootill, *Electronic Computers*, Pelican Books, 1965.

[2] See R. C. M. Barnes, *The present state of information retrieval by computer*, 1964.

such a task. In this country also computer technology is gradually invading many branches of library activity and some public library authorities have produced a printed catalogue by this method,[1] although there are still certain problems to be overcome with this type of catalogue. The most notable of these, from the point of view of classification, is the fact that a certain maximum number of spaces has been reserved for class-marks; yet there can be no doubt that this feature, which is certainly a limitation, can be overcome.

438. On the debit side in the arguments concerning the suitability of computers for information indexing and recovery we must note that they are uneconomical unless heavily utilised. Barnes, in the report previously quoted, suggests that they may only be worthwhile for searching 100,000 documents or more. It is also possible that time may be lost in preparing information in a form suitable for a computer search, that there might be a temptation to use a computer for prestige reasons alone, or that it may have to be shared with other departments in an organization in a way which is injurious to the library and information service. In his important book *On Retrieval System Theory*, B. C. Vickery has suggested that only a part of the operation of recalling items from a classified store can be handed over to a machine. The whole operation consists of:

(*a*) Naming the subject we are searching for in the standard terms used in the index.
(*b*) Locating the subject terms in the index.
(*c*) Locating the documents to which the machine refers us.
(*d*) The study and integration of the retrieved documents.

Vickery suggests that, at present, only step (*b*) can be mechanised and that there is no assurance that, even here, mechanisation is superior to human searching. No machine, he points out, can tackle step (*d*). Vickery certainly appreciates the advantages of automating the retrieval process in that time and drudgery can be saved, but reminds us that machines are costly and may break down and that we must be sure that the advantages claimed for such systems are truly inherent in the machine and do not arise from other factors. Similar arguments have been advanced by Foskett.

439. Such statements might, one supposes, be used as evidence

[1] See, for example, A. O. Meakin's article in the *Library Association Record*, September, 1965, pp. 311–16.

to support the contention that British librarians have been as sceptical about machine searching as some of their American colleagues have been about faceted classification. Yet not all American writers are fully convinced of the value of machine searching at present either.[1] It is certainly true that an inefficient system of indexing, whether the index assumes a classified or alphabetical form, cannot be atoned for by the use of an efficient machine. This brings us to the central theme of our chapter – to what extent can classification be used in an information index designed for computer searching? The antagonism to the idea of feeding references into a computer in a classified form stems chiefly from the fact that many librarians still associate classification for documentation with the fixed, genus to species, display of topics shown in the older enumerative systems. Vickery[2] has discussed this problem in some detail. He points out that if a machine has a 'memory unit' which will hold references to *allied* ideas then, although each item is only coded with symbols representing its specific topic, *generic* searching can also be carried out under the more broad headings to which the specific terms relate. Such general searches will often be necessary and useful data on a specific theme is often to be found in a document covering a more general topic; thus some form of coding for machine retrieval (be it facet analysis or what the Americans call *semantic factoring*) which recognises the relationships between allied terms and documents would seem to be essential. Farradane, in his paper at the 1957 Dorking Conference, argued in like vein saying that 'what is required is a satisfactory logical system to which the principles of mechanical selection can be matched, after which a machine can be devised to perform the requisite tasks'. We would strongly contend that this logical system will be a classification, or a method which leans very heavily on classificatory principles.

440. Freeman's interesting article[3] points out that class-numbers have been awkward in mechanised information retrieval because sorters and tabulators require 'fixed fields', that is to say a standard length of notation and this would have to equal the longest class-number; secondly because sorting a classified index on punched cards is very difficult if symbols are represented by more than a

---

[1] See, for instance, R. R. Shaw's article, *Science*, May, 1963, pp. 606–9.
[2] *Classification and Indexing in Science*, 2nd edition, 1959, pp. 118–19.
[3] R. R. Freeman, Computers and classification systems, *Journal of Documentation*, September, 1964, pp. 137–45.

single punch. The 'fixed field' idea need not occur if the right type of computer is available and Freeman suggests that a classification such as the UDC may be useful in that searches can be broadened or narrowed by adding or dropping class-numbers; other writers consider that UDC is not suitable for such work, although its hierarchies may help in the making of classifications suited to computer searching. Freeman also suggests other uses for a computer with regard to classification. If a classification can aid computer searching, so the work of computers can be applied to the development of classifications. They can be employed to measure statistically the associations between groups of words, thus enabling vocabularies to be more closely controlled and, he adds, the revision of the UDC could be speeded up through the use of computer technology. In this last idea, he is echoing a recommendation of the American National Committee for UDC revision, as we have noted elsewhere.

441. It is worth while for us to examine one or two situations where references have been fed into a computer in classified or alphabetical form. At the National Engineering Laboratory at East Kilbride[1] a DEUCE computer, illustrated opposite page 367, has been used to retrieve details of periodical articles in the subject field of instrumentation. A classified method of recording data has been employed. The UDC was rejected, not because it is in any way inapplicable to computer searching, but because it was considered that the adherence to the DC framework of the late nineteenth century makes it rather cumbersome and unsatisfactory for dealing with the subject fields covered at the N.E.L. Indeed it was necessary to develop a separate system with a notation of capital letters, similar to UDC in some respects, but designed specially for the organization of the literature of instrumentation.

442. The United States offers us many examples of information indexing programmes of great importance, although the emphasis on classification, at least in the conventional sense of the term, is comparatively slight. In the National Library of Medicine's Medical Literature Analysis and Retrieval System (MEDLARS), a computer is used to compile bibliographies on demand, to speed up the production of reading lists on topics which are always important to specialists in the field, and to produce the bibliographical service Index Medicus. The latter can be produced more rapidly and in a

[1] This work is reported by W. H. P. Leslie, Automatic retrieval of technical information, *Aslib Proceedings*, June, 1961, pp. 145–53.

fuller form through the employment of the computer. Another experiment of great consequence, which we refer to again in our final chapter, is the American Society of Metals literature retrieval system which has been developed and tested at Western Reserve University. This owes much to the research and efforts of such information specialists as Allen Kent and J. W. Perry; it relies on semantic factoring which, in many respects, is best thought of as a verbal equivalent of faceted classification. Co-ordination of terminology is achieved largely through *role indicators* (used to indicate the part that each term fulfils) and punctuation, or *links* (these have a classificatory function, indicating words which are linked in the subject of an article and their object is to minimise the risk of false sorts). The work at Western Reserve University has now been modified in the light of experience and following tests of the system at the College of Aeronautics, Cranfield; it remains essentially an alphabetical retrieval system designed for use in conjunction with a computer. Indeed Marjorie Hyslop assures us that 'some of the best talent available is going into adaptation of modern computer technology to the new A.S.M. system'.[1]

443. There are other examples of this kind of work; Barnes's report informs us that EURATOM are organizing the contents of *Nuclear Science Abstracts* for computer searching. But our two main objects here must be to decide to what extent the rapid retrieval of references to documents through the use of computers and other forms of computer employment will affect information work in libraries, and to indicate to what extent classification can play a worthwhile part in such highly mechanised systems. It is clear that, in certain circumstances – an extremely large collection of documents, computer facilities available on the premises, a consistently large number of enquiries to be dealt with, and so forth – the use of a computer in information indexing and recovery can be fully justified. It is equally certain that, in other institutions or circumstances, its employment, at present at least, would be uneconomical. The crux of the information retrieval problem itself is still this; should a retrieval system follow a multi-dimensional, that is fully faceted, classified arrangement or should it be based on alphabetical terms with a strong classificatory or linking structure introduced? It is virtually certain that the enumerative schemes will not be suitable

[1] The A.S.M. retrieval system; after Cranfield, *Journal of Documentation*, March, 1965, pp. 27–42.

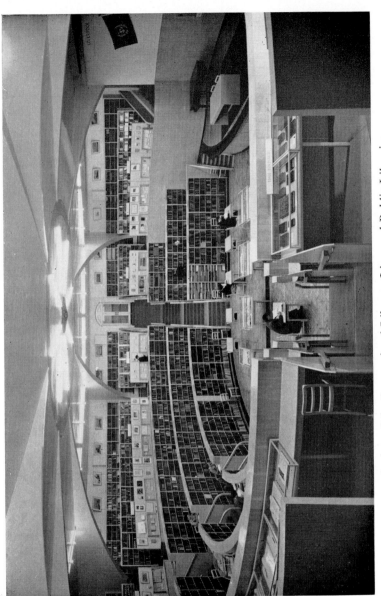

A view of the International Library, Liverpool Public Libraries.

A DEUCE computer which has been used for information retrieval and other tasks at the National Engineering Laboratory, East Kilbride.

for this type of work; to use them in a computer retrieval system is like 'building a locomotive to run with legs', to borrow R. A. Fairthorne's expressive phrase. But then, of course, the older systems were never intended for such a task; there is no doubt that faceted systems are infinitely superior for the work of information retrieval. Thus having decided between the faceted classification and the alphabetical thesaurus as the tool for the organization of the index, the major step is then to select or construct a suitable classification or, if the alternative programme is preferred, to work out principles for the determination of a suitably structured vocabulary which will minimise error and ambiguity and which will correspond to the needs of the system's users. In this respect, the tremendous amount of effort put into research in the sphere of semantic factoring (that is the breaking down of subjects into their simplest possible verbal factors) and roles and links in the American Society of Metals system and the prolonged experiments at Cranfield must surely prove fruitful. The work done in Britain on the classification of language and the association of keywords[1] may well be extremely significant also; we have already noted that a computer may be employed for the task of testing relationships between words as well as for the work of recovering references to documents from a classified or alphabetical store.

444. In conclusion, we would merely re-emphasise our support of some form of classification in all forms of literature searching and reiterate that the increased attention paid to mechanisation in retrieval systems does not remove one whit from the librarian or information officer the onus of thorough subject analysis of documents through faceted classification, co-ordinate indexing, semantic factoring, or other methods. The increasing use of machines presents a danger which is identified for us in these words of Farradane's – 'many have been dazzled by the large memory capacity and fantastic speeds of the computer into thinking that new principles of organization of knowledge have thereby been introduced; they have not. In contrast to older classifications, the machine can keep all concepts separated and uncombined and will make the requisite combinations only at the moment of scanning.'[2] He goes on to say that this can

[1] R. M. Needham and K. S. Jones, Keywords and clumps: recent work on information retrieval at the Cambridge Language Research Unit, *Journal of Documentation*, March, 1964, pp. 5–15.
[2] Fundamental fallacies and new needs in classification, *Sayers Memorial Volume*, 1961.

also be done by faceted classification, but that the latter also permits 'browsing'; such a process is impossible with a computer store. Likewise Barnes tells us[1] 'there is no immediate prospect that the skilled effort needed for indexing and abstracting could be replaced by computer processing' and that 'the most promising applications for computers in the field of information retrieval are in situations where the information threatens to outgrow existing filing methods, and where the overheads of information input, computer programming, and computer operation can be spread over many enquiries'. But if there is a danger that some librarians may think that machine searching will immediately solve most of our difficulties and will be soon applicable to almost all situations, there is certainly no justification for underestimating the powers and performance of a technology which, in its modern form, is scarcely yet twenty years old. The computer provides a method for a more rapid and efficient information service and it challenges the librarian, as it challenges workers in other spheres, to improve his technique so that this method can be exploited to the full in appropriate libraries and research establishments. Far from abolishing the need for classifying and indexing, it gives a new meaning and impetus to research work in this field.

[1] Op cit., p. 21–2.

The Future of Library Classification

445. It will be obvious, both to the professional librarian and to the student of our subject, that there is some overlap and inter-relationship between the final four chapters in this Manual. Our aim in this last chapter is to discuss the need for investigation into the development of classificatory principles and techniques and to make the reader aware of the important research that is at present taking place. This research does not concern special librarians alone by any means, although most of the more dramatic developments in recent years have been most applicable to the special librarian's sphere. The growth of general libraries, and particularly the expansion of their reader's advisory services and their facilities for scholars and research workers, is placing a severe, some would say intolerable, strain upon the older general classifications that are still so popular. This is akin to the difficulties which the special librarian has encountered in using conventional methods to organize such material as periodical articles, patents, and technical reports; the problem has in the past, however, been more acutely felt in special libraries. The need for superior methods for the arrangement and control of literature in all types of library has acted as a great stimulus to research in classification; this has involved both the re-examination of older techniques and attempts to devise new systems which will be suitable for modern libraries and will learn from both the achievement and mistakes of classificationists and indexers of the past.

446. We find that research and investigation in this subject field can take various forms. It may

1. Concentrate on the re-examination of the *principles* of classifi-

cation, the standardisation of terminology, and the appraisal of the functions of notation.

2. Consider chiefly the construction of more special classifications, particularly in areas of knowledge where schemes are badly needed and pay attention also to the problem of improving co-ordinate indexing techniques.

3. Restrict itself, as far as general schemes are concerned, to attempts to improve the existing systems; this might be justified on the grounds that most general libraries are firmly committed to these systems and that complete reclassification, even if theoretically justified, is not economically feasible.

4. Devote most of the labour and energy involved to the production of a new and better general scheme which will gradually replace DC and UDC, at present the widely accepted favourites.

These forms of research are not entirely incompatible, but may well sometimes be in conflict; obviously the third and fourth activities lead ultimately in different directions and can only both be followed wholeheartedly if the time and resources available for research are extremely great.

447. We shall return to this theme later. It is first of all necessary to discuss the work of individuals and organizations who have been prominent in initiating and pursuing classification research. Pride of place here goes deservedly to Dr S. R. Ranganathan. Of all living librarians, he perhaps most merits Putnam's famous description of Melvil Dewey – one who lives librarianship 'throughout the 24 hours, the week, the month and the year'. Ranganathan has, to mention only some of his contributions to classification, carefully distinguished between the 'idea plane' and the 'notational plane' in classification; between the classification of the fairly straightforward subjects found in most books (the world of macrothought, as he terms it) and the needs of documentation (the world of microthought demanding classification in depth); and is working on the development of such ideas as schedules of basic classes and the development of common energy isolates. We owe to him, of course, the clear recognition of the need for completely synthetic classifications, a fact which the older classificationists had only partly revealed, not to mention his development of a rational procedure for dealing with documents which merge ideas from two or more subject disciplines. In his many books on classification, which are

now being revised, and particularly in his far-seeing work, *Philosophy of Library Classification*, he has urged us to ensure that we are not content to rest on the achievements in classification gained by the giants of the past, but to press on with the work of improving systems and principles and to see that organizations such as UNESCO, IFLA, and the International Federation of Documentation are convinced of the need for exploration and improvement in library classification; it is now possible, he assures us, to make better schemes with a longer effective life if appropriate research is done and international co-operation takes place. 'The library profession',[1] he writes, 'should become more aware of the crumbling of the present foundations of classification . . . and put up a case for the redesign of the foundations in the light of the factors which led to its breakdown and the methods of research and growth which prevail now and are likely to prevail in the future'. In conjunction with a growing band of workers in India, he himself is investigating classification in depth and the shaping of optional facets for documentation.[2] Ranganathan has been criticised for the complexity of his ideas and the length of the notations produced by his insistence that close classification be pursued. Yet he wisely points out that the initial effort needed to cope with his distinctive ideas will be well rewarded and that in small libraries the content of most books is simple to classify and will result in simple class numbers even though the system used may have the potential further analysis in depth for more complicated documents.

448. In calling upon us to ensure that the classifications of the future are designed by a team of specialists rather than by an individual or a few solitary workers, Ranganathan is not stating something new; Hulme had recognised the need for this many years ago. Yet it is only comparatively recently that the advice has been fully heeded, although some general schemes have been maintained for years by a vast group of experts. In this country, the most active team by far has been the Classification Research Group, or the C.R.G. as they are now usually termed. The members of the group have been extremely industrious in examining the foundations of the existing schemes, and sometimes in assisting in their revision; in helping to develop the newer principles unearthed by Ranganathan

---

[1] *Philosophy of Library Classification*, 1951, p. 86.
[2] This research is reported chiefly in the Indian journals, especially *Herald of Library Science* and *Library Science with a Slant to Documentation*.

and others; in re-examining the role of notation; and in creating completely faceted schemes for certain areas of knowledge. The work of the group was briefly mentioned in Chapter 11 and some of the special schemes which its members have created have been listed in our chapter on the problems of classifying a special library. The C.R.G. was initiated in 1952 and its members still meet regularly; their work and progress is reported at sporadic intervals in special bulletins in ASLIB's *Journal of Documentation*. The writings of individual members of the group have proved remarkably stimulating and have injected much enthusiasm for the newer ideas on our subject into British librarians. A similar group was formed a few years ago to unite those interested in classification who reside in the north of England, but the Northern Classification Study Group as it is called is now, unfortunately, virtually dormant. It seems likely also that, if its activities are resumed, it will concentrate mainly on the investigation of indexing problems rather than on classification as such.

449. Meanwhile the C.R.G. continues to flourish. It is now, in conjunction with appropriate individuals and organizations in other countries, chiefly interested in the possibility of creating a new general classification based on facet analysis. CC will certainly not, however, be the only general classification to influence the proposed new scheme; for example, the order of major disciplines as conceived by Bliss has won the support and admiration of many librarians. A grant of $14,000 has been supplied by NATO towards the task of creating a new general system and preparation is proceeding steadily, although the task is, of course, one which will take some time. The C.R.G. suggestions for the new scheme can be read in a report of a conference which they held in 1964; in this document, published by the Library Association, Mills, Coates, Miss Kyle and others offer us remarkably thoughtful and interesting papers. One idea which is clearly emerging from the work of the group is the possibility of creating the new general scheme partly through the merging of suitable special classifications. Here the idea of the theory of *integrative levels*, as put forward in this country by the biologist Joseph Needham and as expounded in France by such writers as Glangeaud, assumes some significance. The essence of this idea can be explained in the words of Needham.[1] He considers

---

[1] J. Needham, *Time the refreshing river* (a collection of addresses and essays), 1943, p. 234.

'the existence of levels of organization in the universe, successive forms of order in a scale of complexity' and suggests that 'a sharp change in the organizational level often means that what were wholes on the lower level become parts on the new, e.g. protein crystals in cells, cells in metazoan organisms, and metazoan organisms in social units'. The application of such a theory as this to library classification has been discussed in an excellent paper by Foskett[1] and also in one of the recent C.R.G. bulletins. It is a notion which seems to revive, in a more fully developed form, the ideas of writers such as Richardson, in that it suggests that library classification can benefit from the observance of a form of natural order discernible in the world around us. The idea was held strongly at the end of the nineteenth century and has persisted in the writings of Bliss and Foskett. True, it is an approach that could become too theoretical, as Hulme recognised; yet the tools now available for the analysis of knowledge as found in books should ensure that this does not happen. But, whether the theory of levels of integration proves of value to our studies or not, it is certain that a new general classification should be available comparatively soon. In addition to its possible use in public and academic libraries and in bibliographies, this scheme may well provide fresh encouragement for the making of further special schemes – thus repaying the debt which the new classification will owe to the faceted schemes for special subject fields.

450. If emphasis is now placed on international co-operation in the making of a faceted general scheme, it must not be forgotten that the work of the C.R.G. in the realm of special librarianship has also been very significant. Here, however, its activities have been partly overshadowed by the research taking place at the College of Aeronautics, Cranfield. This is an ASLIB project on the comparative efficiency of classification and indexing systems, supported by a generous grant from the National Science Foundation, Washington. A number of aeronautical documents were classified or indexed, in the first stage of the project, by each of four systems. The systems selected were UDC; a faceted classification for aeronautics prepared by Vickery and Farradane; an alphabetical list of subject headings and the Uniterm system of co-ordinate indexing. In addition to the full-time staff working under the direction of C. W. Cleverdon, some assistance was given by classifiers and indexers in industrial and

---

[1] Classification and Integrative Levels. In *Sayers Memorial Volume*, 1961.

college libraries and other interested organizations. Following the compilation of the four parallel indexes, testing has taken place on the relative merits of the rival systems. Reports on the project tend to distinguish between the recall ratio (the number of documents actually recalled from an index in response to a question on a given theme, in proportion to the number of documents on that theme which are known to be indexed) and relevance ratio (the number of documents which are actually wanted in proportion to the number of documents retrieved in response to a question on a given theme). Of these, although each is significant, the recall ratio is surely the more important unless the relevance ratio is extremely low; it has been found that all four systems have a recall performance of about eighty per cent and all *can* prove efficient for information retrieval purposes. As Barbara Kyle[1] puts it: 'We certainly owe to Cranfield and similar projects our ability to say that there is no one best system of information retrieval applicable to all circumstances'. This does not mean that the work at Cranfield has been inconclusive; indeed the project has thrown a great deal of light on the problems of co-ordinate indexing and the merits and faults of UDC for retrieval purposes. It has also provided an opportunity to put modern theories of faceted classification to a practical test. We can be sure also that the full harvest of experience from this research has not yet been gathered in. Testing and experiments are still taking place and attention is being paid to similar projects in the United States. In fact, the important Western Reserve University system has been tested at Cranfield and modified as a consequence.

451. But our survey so far has been too insular and classification research is now being pursued in many countries. We have already commented on some of the retrieval systems being tested in the U.S.A. in our previous chapter; it is certain that, with the growing use and value of machine literature searching and with the greater funds that are available for such work in the United States, many of the future significant advances in information indexing will take place in that country. As far as general libraries are concerned, classificatory research in the U.S.A. has taken a far less spectacular form. The majority of librarians there seem to hold the view which was put forward in an article ten years ago,[2] that any order of arrangement

---

[1] See her article in *Journal of Documentation*, June, 1964, pp. 55–69.
[2] R. Gjelsness; Research in cataloguing and classification, *Library Trends*, October, 1957, pp. 171–86.

on the shelves must have certain imperfections and that the alphabetical order is to be preferred in catalogues; the consequence being that research in classification for the public and academic library should concentrate on the revision and gradual improvement of the well tried systems. To librarians in the United States this means DC and LC. Yet it is interesting to note that a Classification Research Group was set up in the U.S.A. in 1959; possibly there will be a slow recognition of the value of the techniques of facet and phase analysis and they may begin to gradually influence shelf classification in the general libraries of the United States.

452. In Europe, in addition to the work of the late Donker Duyvis and other stalwarts engaged in the revision of the UDC, it is important to note the very significant contributions made to our subject by Eric De Grolier. The range of his reading and the quality of his thought are evident in his *Théorie et pratique des classifications documentaires* (1956) – the fruit of some twenty years study and labour in our subject field, and *Categories applicable to classification and coding in documentation* (1962). The latter work reports concisely but in most interesting fashion, on the classification research that is being carried out in the different countries of the world. De Grolier has devised a synthetic system of his own – ALSYN (alpha-synthétique), and his plea for the more effective interchange of ideas and for international co-operation in classification is, fortunately, now being heeded. It is clear from his work and from that of compatriots such as G. Cordonnier, that there is a considerable amount of sympathy in France towards the newer techniques and the work of the British C.R.G.

453. From France also comes the ingenious retrieval system SYNTOL, devised by J. C. Gardin. This is typical of the advanced alphabetical co-ordinate indexing systems which lean heavily on the principles of classification. It distinguishes between paradigmatic (vertical) word relationships and syntagmatic (horizontal) relations. It is still in the experimental stage and may be used in a computer retrieval system, although it need not be associated with such a highly mechanised retrieval programme. It is unfortunate that one of the fullest statements of the object and methods of the system, the volume in the Rutgers University series, is somewhat lacking in clarity.

454. The desire for improvement or change in our classifications that is felt in so many countries has resulted in two international

conferences on the subject. The first of these was held at Dorking in 1957 with four British speakers – Mills, Vickery, Coates and Farradane – and four from overseas nations. Definite conclusions and recommendations resulted; these concerned the making of new schemes, the character of notation, the place of the machine in literature searching, and the need for research work in the various countries to be co-ordinated. The addresses and theme papers of this conference remain rewarding reading for the diligent student of our subject. Classification has loomed large in papers and discussions at other conferences also; the Scientific Information Conference at Washington in 1958, for instance, gave due attention to the subject. But the second international conference on classification was not held until 1964. This time the venue was Elsinore and it is significant that, whereas the Dorking Conference had representatives from France, Germany, India, Italy, the Netherlands, the U.S.A. and the United Kingdom, sixteen nations were represented in Denmark; surely a sign of the growing interest in the development of classification! At this conference, it was suggested that efforts should be made to standardise internationally the terminology used in classification, and that a register of research projects should be maintained to facilitate international co-operation in the subject.

455. Although, in many ways, research by teams of workers on classification and indexing is still in its infancy, it must be clear by now to our reader that the making of *special* classifications and alphabetical systems for retrieval purposes has been given, and will continue to receive, a great deal of attention; there can be no doubt of the enormous value of research at an international level in this sphere. In some countries, such as Holland, the UDC remains extremely popular and, as we have seen, that system is compulsory in scientific libraries in the U.S.S.R., for it is considered that the expert attention which its schedules receive and its international character and recognition more than offset its structural flaws. Yet one is inclined to predict that it is the faceted special scheme and the co-ordinate indexing systems which rely heavily on classification principles which will ultimately prevail in most special libraries.

456. But, as we are equally concerned with general systems and as many librarians will continue to use established classifications in this category and to enjoy (or endure) the fruits of their employment, it behoves us to conclude by attempting to briefly estimate the future of the general classifications. The case for a new general scheme is

perhaps a more controversial one to uphold than even the argument for the ultimate triumph of the special faceted classifications, since reclassification of a vast academic or public library, even by the osmosis method, is rarely a practical proposition. True a modern general system could be adopted by new general libraries, but comparatively few of these are created except in countries where libraries and library science have been comparatively late in developing. It is quite clear that in some countries it is preferred that research should concentrate upon the improvement of existing systems. Librarians in the United States, as we have already pointed out, have relatively little interest in any general scheme except DC and LC. Many British librarians think in similar fashion, except that they see UDC rather than LC as still the greatest challenger to the almost ubiquitous Dewey Decimal Classification. Thus we find a recent textbook[1] recommending that advanced colleges should use UDC, others DC in their libraries. The Library Association Research Committee has also received a grant from the U.S.A. to carry out research with regard to DC.[2] It would almost seem to be law in general classification that the most used schemes are the ones which must survive and that the rate at which a scheme can afford to change in order to keep pace with new knowledge is in inverse proportion to the number of its users; DC, therefore, is not completely satisfactory, despite its regular revision, as a system for modern knowledge – to make it such would demand a rate of change and expansion which few users would willingly bear!

457. It is thus more difficult to predict the trends in classification in general libraries in the near future than it is to anticipate the development of classification and indexing techniques in special libraries, which are chiefly concerned with the provision of a rapid information service. Public and college librarians who favour the retention of the long established methods suggest that some limitations are inevitable in all classifications and that one which works reasonably well, and to which many general libraries are firmly committed, must be retained. They virtually reiterate what Dewey argued for years – that it is a waste of time to attempt to supplant DC in most general libraries; it is perhaps significant that Rider accepted this when producing the *International Classification*, which, despite his careful definition of its purpose, nevertheless lies un-

[1] D. L. Smith and E. G. Baxter, *College Library Administration*, 1965.
[2] See *Liaison*, June, 1965, p. 36.

used. There is also the grim warning of BC; little more than a decade ago this was recommended with confidence for new general libraries by the British reviewers, yet certain deficiences have now come to light[1] which could have made its widespread adoption, despite many excellent features, most unwise. It could, one supposes, be argued that the new faceted general classification might meet with similar problems.

458. Yet a large, perhaps more perceptive, minority in Britain and in several other countries stress vehemently the need for a new general system in addition to the creation of more special schemes. They can say, with some justice, that it is unreasonable to expect the DC to last for ever, that its structure becomes more and more unsuited to library requirements with the passage of time, and that the general library cannot afford to lag behind in the bringing up-to-date of classification systems. Certainly the new principles provide a foundation for us to build upon which holds out more hope for a durable classification than did the traditional 'tree of knowledge'. It can be said indeed that an enumerative classification is very like a photograph, or portrait, of a person. As a photograph shows an individual at a particular time and from a particular angle, so the enumerative classification arrests knowledge at a given stage of its development and organizes it rigidly in a selected form. Thus only certain basic concepts are combined; many topics cannot be accurately specified. Likewise, as a photograph is inanimate and unchanging, so the enumerative classification has great difficulty in keeping up with a world in which knowledge is in a constant state of flux. It may be that no classification can be fully self-perpetuating or can be completely abreast with modern thought in every subject field, but the entirely synthetic system is much more flexible in this respect than its older rivals.

459. The new general scheme will also differ from BC in that it will be the product of an international team of experts and revision should be assured. The objection, of course, may be raised that any classification applied to the shelves can offer but a linear arrangement and can never hope to reveal there the multi-dimensional relationships which exist between subjects. This is true but, in European countries, librarians will expect classified catalogues and bibliographies to aid the shelf classification; here the value of modern ideas

---

[1] Renewed efforts are now being made to overcome these and to mprove the revision policy.

in gathering basic concepts into categories and permitting their combination, and in offering a rational procedure for coping with complex works, may prove decisive.

460. It is unwise for any single individual to assume emphatically the role of prophet in this matter. The appeal of a new scheme based on superior principles is undoubted, but many still see the greatest strength of DC and UDC in the universality of these systems and argue that a reasonable classification which is an acknowledged standard is better than an untried new general scheme. The tremendous enthusiasm for the newer techniques and the continued esteem in which the older systems are held by so many librarians suggests that continued research on both improvement and innovation, with regard to the general classifications, may be best. This seems to be most uneconomical, yet it may be the course of action which is dictated by circumstances. While all such speculation on the future of the general schemes tends sometimes to be gyratory and inconclusive, one fact at least can be stated with full confidence. This is that mere demolition and destructive criticism will not do. If there is a genuine need for a new general scheme it must be for one which offers a demonstrably better arrangement, which acknowledges the impact which mechanisation is making upon librarianship, and which is based on satisfactory and lasting principles. Such a scheme must be made and tested in bibliographies and in new general libraries before any change could possibly be contemplated in most of the older ones and the enumerative schemes gradually cast into the fires of Gehenna.

461. What is certain too, and what we hope has become crystal clear to those who have read this section and followed up some of the relevant items in our bibliography, is that information retrieval systems will continue to improve and the status and capabilities of the general library will suffer if it lags, to a very great extent, behind the progress made in the sphere of special librarianship. We can say also with conviction that bibliographical classification, whatever form it may take, has a tremendous future which will more than bear comparison with its most interesting history. It is necessary, therefore, to finish our work as we began it; by stressing that classification must not be dismissed as a mere technique for it is invaluable in organizing our libraries. The good classification locates material on each subject, demonstrates the most important subject relationships and, by revealing the structure of each subject field, marshalls

knowledge in a way which means that a library's resources will be employed to the maximum advantage. Classification assists both reader and librarian in ensuring that books are shelved in a way in which they will lend support to one another; likewise, in bibliographies, abstracts, and catalogues, its helpful arrangement pinpoints literature on any specific theme and shows the existence of material on closely allied themes, facilitating browsing and permitting specific or generic searches to be made. It moulds literature into an organized form for service and thus helps to promote the advancement of knowledge and to obviate the futile repetition of work which another has already done. Its use and value will increase in the libraries of the future with the growth of literature, of information services, and of the demands made on all types of library. Although the emphasis in classification may change as mechanisation increases and as general libraries tend to acquire more and more non-book material, the process remains a systematic 'time saving operation for the discovery of knowledge in literature'; in many ways, the fully effective role of classificatory principles in libraries may have only just begun.

Bibliography

CONTENTS

I. Major works on Library Classification.

II. Suggested readings to follow the various chapters in this Manual.

The Bibliography that follows is by no means exhaustive; it is designed chiefly to support the Manual in its role as a textbook for the Part II Examination in Classification Theory of the British Library Association, for no single volume could hope to provide the student with the breadth of reading which is now so necessary in this subject. The first section of the Bibliography, therefore, lists and briefly describes most of the major textbooks on library classification, while its second part attempts to furnish the advanced student with some possible readings from these and other texts to support his perusal of the individual chapters of this Manual.

It must be stressed once again that reading about classification systems is no substitute for the careful examination of general and some special schemes and that the modern student will find, ever increasingly, much of his material in the current library journals such as the *Library Association Record*, *Aslib Proceedings*, *the Journal of Documentation* and *Library Resources and Technical Services*.

Part I. Major works on Library Classification.

ALLERTON PARK INSTITUTE. *The Role of Classification in the Modern American Library*, (1960.)

> (This is a symposium, edited by Thelma Eaton and Donald E. Strout, based on papers given at a 1959 autumn institute conducted by the University of Illinois Graduate School of Library Science. The student will find the papers useful and thought provoking.)

N*

BLISS, HENRY EVELYN. *The Organization of Knowledge in Libraries*. 2nd edn.
H. W. Wilson Company, 1939.
(A valuable discussion of general principles and the functions of notation plus a
discerning critique of the major bibliographical schemes. There are also some useful
bibliographical notes.)

DAVISON, KEITH. *The Theory of Classification*. Clive Bingley Ltd., 1966.
(Specially designed as a compact text for examination revision. Gives many helpful
readings and comments.)

FOSKETT, DOUGLAS J. *Classification and Indexing in the Social Sciences*.
Butterworth, 1963.
(A most valuable discussion of the problems of organizing social science literature
with comments on the merits and failings in this field of the major general schemes.)

Science, Humanism and Libraries. Crosby Lockwood, 1964.
(A collection of eighteen stimulating papers, several of which relate to classification.)

GROLIER, ERIC DE. *Théorie et pratique des classifications documentaires*.
Union française des organismes de documentation, 1956.
*Study of general categories applicable to classification and coding in
documentation*. Unesco, 1962.
(Two excellent detailed studies from an authoritative writer; the student who
consults the latter work will encounter De Grolier's knowledge of developments in
classification in many countries.)

KELLEY, GRACE O. *The classification of books*. H. W. Wilson Company, 1937.
(Still worthy of examination. As a result of experience, Dr Kelley concludes that
classification does not reveal all the material on subjects and, indeed, may even
obscure the main work on a subject. Her admirable chapter in *The acquisition and
cataloguing of books*, edited by *W. M. Randall*, 1940, tones down the criticism of
the 1937 volume. The quotation which follows our title page comes from the later
work.)

LAMONTAGNE, LEO. E. *American Library Classification*. Shoe String Press,
1961.
(An excellent historical account: a detailed history of the development of the
Congress classification is given.)

METCALFE, JOHN. *The subject classifying and indexing of libraries and
literature*. Angus and Robertson, 1959.
(Covers a wide area of ground and is often highly controversial. Metcalfe's earlier
book on information indexing might also be consulted.)

MILLS, J. *A modern outline of library classification*. Chapman & Hall, 1960.
(An excellent textbook. The student should not allow the crowded varityped pages
to deter him from following the sound description of schemes and modern principles
and the author's original thought with regard to classification theory.)

NEEDHAM, C. D. *Organizing Knowledge in Libraries*. Andre Deutsch, 1964.
(Concerned mainly with cataloguing and is designed to serve as a textbook for the
Part I examination. The chapters on classification stress modern principles very
strongly.)

PALMER, BERNARD I. *Itself an education : six lectures on classification*. The
Library Association, 1962.

PALMER, BERNARD I. and WELLS, ARTHUR J. *Fundamentals of Library Classification*. Allen & Unwin, 1951.
(The above works are important: the latter is an English restatement of the CC principles which focuses them on classification by DC. The later work is a valuable and informative collection of papers.)

PARKHI, R. S. *The Decimal Classification and the Colon Classification in perspective*. Asia Publishing House, 1964.
(A detailed comparison of the two schemes, their history and principles. The British student will find that this work is chiefly of use to him for the information which it gives about Colon.)

PHILLIPS, W. HOWARD. *A Primer of Book Classification*. 5th edn. Association of Assistant Librarians, 1961.
(Declared by some writers to be out of date. Yet it gives a sound survey of the general schemes and a valuable account of the older principles. It is to be considered a useful complement to Mills's work in the latter respect and is modelled on the earlier editions of Sayers' *Introduction*, from which it differs in some particulars.)

RANGANATHAN, S. R. Among several important books, we would merely cite the following:
Elements of Library Classification. 2nd edn. (British), edited by B. I. Palmer. Association of Assistant Librarians, 1959. There is also a 3rd (Indian) edition, 1962.
Philosophy of Library Classification. Munksgaard, 1951.
Prolegomena to Library Classification. 2nd edn., Asia Publishing House, 1957.
(The last of these works gives a detailed account of some of the major ideas behind the Colon Classification and the canons of classification held by its creator. The student may find the explanation of the *Elements* more straightforward or he may prefer to read the most interesting and prophetical *Philosophy*.)

RICHARDSON, E.C. *Classification : theoretical and practical*. 3rd edn., 1930, reprinted by the Shoe String Press, Connecticut, 1964.
(Extremely useful still for the clarity with which the author sets forth his idea that a classification of knowledge is the foundation for the durable book classification, and for the historical detailed provided.)

RUTGERS UNIVERSITY. GRADUATE SCHOOL OF LIBRARY SERVICE. *Systems for the Intellectual Organization of Information*, edited by DR SUSAN ARTANDI. These include:
Volume I: *The U.D.C.*, by J. MILLS, 1964.
Volume II: *SYNTOL*, by J. C. GARDIN, 1965.
Volume III: *Alphabetical subject indication of information*, by J. METCALFE, 1965.
Volume IV: *Colon Classification*, by S. R. RANGANATHAN, 1965.
Volume V: *Faceted Classification*, by B. C. VICKERY, 1966.
(An extremely useful series which should certainly be consulted, if available.)

SAVAGE, E. A. *Manual of book classification and display for public libraries* Allen & Unwin, 1946.
(Dr Savage's work deals mainly with book display. The brief study of classification

is individual and is based, to some extent, on the principles of Hulme and of the LC classification. Although somewhat dated, the book remains readable, vigorous and challenging even to extravagance.)

SAYERS, WILLIAM CHARLES BERWICK. *Introduction to Library Classification.* 9th edn., Grafton, 1954.
(Useful for practical hints and as a possible supplementary text to Phillips's *Primer* for traditional theories.)

The Sayers Memorial Volume. Edited by D. J. FOSKETT and B. I. PALMER. The Library Association, 1961.
(Contains papers from 16 contributors; most papers relate to classification, information retrieval, or indexing.)

SHERA, JESSE H. Collected essays and addresses, edited by D. J. FOSKETT. Crosby Lockwood, 1965.
Volume I. *Libraries and the Organization of Knowledge.*
Volume II. *Documentation and the Organization of Knowledge.*
(The chief papers of an outstanding modern American thinker and writer on classification.)

SRIVASTAVA, A. P. *Theory of knowledge classification in libraries.* Lakshmi Bookstore, 1964.
(The development of classification theory is shown and discussed, with special reference to DC and CC examples.)

VICKERY, BRIAN C. *Classification and Indexing in Science.* 2nd edn., Butterworth, 1959.
Faceted classification : a guide to the making and use of special schemes. Aslib. 1960.
(Two important works by another outstanding British writer, whose important book *On Retrieval System Theory* might also be consulted along with other texts on information retrieval. The 1959 volume deals with the problems of classification in the sciences and the value of modern classification theory in this field. *Faceted Classification* is a much smaller work; the student should find it lucid and extremely helpful.)

The proceedings of the two international conferences on our subject should also be referred to:

Proceedings of the International Study Conference on Classification for Information Retrieval, Dorking, 1957. Aslib, 1957.
Proceedings of the Second International Conference on Classification Research, Elsinore, 1964. Munksgaard, 1965.
(Of special value in the 1964 Conference papers are those by Borko and Gardin on classification and computers, and one by Ranganathan on the history of library classification.)

Part II. Suggested readings to follow the various chapters in this Manual.[1]

[1] Readings from works already cited in Part I of the Bibliography are listed as briefly as possible in Part II. Further bibliographical information is provided for any item not listed in Part I.

SECTION I

CHAPTER 1.
RICHARDSON. *Classificalion.* pp. 1–6.
SAYERS. *Introduction to library classification.* Chapter 1.

CHAPTER 2.
BLISS. *Organization of Knowledge in Libraries.* Chapter 1.
MILLS. *Modern Outline of Library Classification.* Chapter 1.
PALMER AND WELLS. *Fundamentals of Library Classification.* Chapter 1.
RANGANATHAN. *Elements of Library Classification.* Chapters 1–4.

CHAPTER 3.
BLISS. *Organization of Knowledge in Libraries.* pp. 1–20.
E. W. HULME. *Principles of Book Classification.*
(Hulme's articles, reprinted in pamphlet form by the A.A.L. stress the need for book classification to observe constantly the volume and character of published literature. They may be regarded as a valuable lead up to the more complete and satisfactory theories of today.)
RICHARDSON. *Classification.* pp. 9–42.

CHAPTER 4.
MILLS. *A Modern Outline of Library Classification.* Chapters 2–4.
PALMER. *Itself an education.* Lecture 2. Formation of Main Classes.
PALMER and WELLS. *Fundamentals of Library Classification.* Chapters 2–5.
RANGANATHAN. *Elements of Library Classification.* Chapters 7 and 10.

CHAPTER 5.
E. J. COATES. *Notation.* (In *Proceedings of the International Study Conference on Classification for Information Retrieval,* 1957.)
MILLS. *Modern Outline of Library Classification.* Chapter 5.
PALMER. *Itself an education.* Lecture 4. The Development of notation.

CHAPTER 6.
PHILLIPS. *Primer of Book Classification.* pp. 21–57.
(Useful reading at this stage to revise basic ideas encountered in this and earlier chapters of the Manual.)
SAYERS. *Introduction to library classification.* Chapter 4.
(May be read instead of, or in addition to, the above reference.)

CHAPTER 7.
BLISS. *Organization of Knowledge in Libraries.* pp. 21–71.
MILLS. *Modern Outline of Library Classification.* Chapter 6.
PARKHI. *Decimal and Colon Classification in Perspective.* pp. 307–411.
RANGANATHAN. *Elements of Library Classification.* Chapters 5–6.

This is a useful stage in one's studies to read also:

D. W. LANGRIDGE. *Teaching classification and cataloguing for the new syllabus. Library Association Record*, April 1965, pp. 127–30. (An interesting and perhaps somewhat controversial article.)

PALMER. *Itself an education.* Lecture 6. *Classification as a foundation study for librarians.*

SECTION II

CHAPTER 8.

Although no modern student will wish to consult all these works, unless studying in detail the history of our subject, we consider it necessary to mention some of the major sources of information on the early history of book classification:

H. E. BLISS. *The organization of knowledge and the system of the sciences.* H. W. Wilson Company, 1929.

(A detailed and scholarly study of the methods used by intellectual workers in the various fields for the analysis and synthesis of knowledge in all forms. Its ultimate aim is to deduce the most practical, permanent and valid arrangement, in order that this may become the basis of a bibliographical system. Bliss's *Organization of Knowledge in Libraries* and his *Bibliographic Classification* are the outcome of this work.)

J. C. BRUNET. *Manuel du Libraire et de l'Amateur de Livres.* 9 vols in 8. Edn. 1860–80. (Volume 5 contains the classification.)

A. CIM. *Le Livre : historique, fabrication, achat, classement, usage et entretien.* 5 vols. Flammarion, 1905.

(Vol. 4 deals with classification very fully with outlines of many schemes as far as Brunet and his followers.)

E. EDWARDS. *Memoirs of Libraries.* 2 vols. Treubner, 1859.

(Volume 2 contains the most valuable history, in English, of book classification systems up to 1850.)

R. FLINT. *History of Classification of the Sciences.* Blackwood, 1904.

(An excellent critical and descriptive view of knowledge classifications.)

E. C. RICHARDSON. *Classification.*

(Includes an appendix containing an essay towards a bibliographical history of the systems of classification.)

The student with less time available for a study of historical detail may merely consult *Richardson*, *Bliss* and the relevant portion of *Sayers' Introduction to library classification*.

CHAPTER 9.

LEO LAMONTAGNE. *American Library Classification* is the standard work of reference for nineteenth century developments in classification in the United States; one might read too, either his account of the *Historical background of classification in the U.S.A.* which appears in *The Subject Analysis of Library Materials*, edited by *Maurice F. Tauber*, 1953 or *Thelma Eaton*'s paper on this theme in *The Role of Classification in the Modern American Library*.

PHILLIPS. *Primer of Book Classification.* pp. 83–94.
(Gives a useful account of the Expansive Classification.)

F. RIDER. *Story of DC 1896–1951. Library Journal*, 15th March 1951, pp. 473–476.
Useful for the very early history of Dewey's scheme.)

CHAPTER 10.

L. S. JAST. *Classification in public libraries with special reference to the Dewey Decimal system. The Library*, 1895, pp. 169–78.
The Dewey Classification in the Reference Library and in an Open [Access] Lending Library. The Library, 1896, pp. 335–50.
The Dewey Classification and some recent criticism, The Library, 1897, pp. 340–345.
Classification in British Public Libraries. Library Association Record, April 1903, pp. 175–82.
(Jast was one of the pioneers of DC in this country. He deals with notation in the first of these papers, but in later ones he meets the critic on the grounds of theory. The third paper replies to criticisms in *Lyster's Some Observations*. The final paper sums up the advances of a decade. This, especially, is worth reading as an early account of the effects the DC produced in England.)

T. W. LYSTER. *Notes on shelf classification by the Dewey system. The Library*, 1897, pp. 329–39.
Observations on the Dewey notation and Classification. The Library, 1896, pp. 482–90.

CHAPTER 11.

There are many diverse readings that could be mentioned here; we would suggest that the student should, at this stage, make sure he has mastered other reading done on the history of classification in libraries. He might then refer to some of the following.

D. J. FOSKETT. *Library Classification and the Field of Knowledge*, 1958.
(A remarkably stimulating pamphlet which surveys the growth of knowledge over the centuries and suggests that the twentieth century needs a better general classification than DC. The pamphlet is based on an address given to the North Western Group of the Library Association's Reference and Special Libraries Section).

H. HOPWOOD. *Dewey Expanded. Library Association Record*, 1907. pp. 307–322.
(A useful early paper on the initiation of UDC.)

F. RIDER. *The International Classification.* 1961.
(This scheme should be examined briefly, if possible. Alternatively the accounts referred to in the footnote to paragraph 145 might be read.)

W. C. BERWICK SAYERS. *Library Classification in retrospect and prospect. Library World*, April 1959, pp. 206–12.
(Mainly of interest as a concise survey of historical developments in the twentieth century.)

SECTION III

CHAPTER 12.

BLISS. *Organization of Knowledge in Libraries*, Chapter 10.
(A searching example of the adverse criticism which Bliss has valiantly delivered
against the most popular of schemes. Still relevant.)

E. J. COATES. *Dewey Decimal Classification. Edition 16. Library Association
Record*, August 1959, pp. 187–90.
(A thorough critical review which is one of the best concise modern indictments of
DC.)

B. CUSTER. *Dewey lives. Library Resources*, Winter 1967, pp. 51–60.

B. CUSTER. *Dewey 17 : a preview and a report to the profession. Library
Association Record*, March, 1965, pp. 79–83.
(The most important description of the latest edition and the changes introduced;
a similar article by Sarah Vann can be found in *Library Resources and Technical
Services*, Spring 1964. The student of DC should also read one or two reviews of
the 17th edition.)

MILLS. *Modern Outline of Library Classification*. Chapter 7.

PHILLIPS. *Primer of Book Classification*. pp. 60–82.

S. VANN. *Dewey abroad : the field survey of 1964. Library Resources*,
Winter 1967, pp. 61–71.

H. H. YOUNG. *The enduring qualities of Dewey*. In *The Role of Classification
in the Modern American Library*. 1959.
(Discusses whether DC is an 'enduring' scheme or simply the general classification
which most libraries must continue to endure.)

CHAPTER 13.

BLISS. *Organization of Knowledge in Libraries*. Chapter 13.
MILLS. *Modern Outline of Library Classification*. Chapter 10.
PHILLIPS. *Primer of Book Classification*. pp. 110–24.

CHAPTER 14.

There is a wealth of reading on the UDC. In addition to the introduction to the British
abridgement we would recommend that the student consults some of the following:

S. C. BRADFORD. *Documentation*. 2nd edn., edited by *J. H. Shera*, 1953.
(Still in many respects an excellent account of the scheme which Bradford advocated
so well.)

BRITISH STANDARD 1000 C. *Guide to the UDC*, edited by *J. Mills*, 1963.
(An excellent account of the scheme.)

S. F. HARPER. *The Universal Decimal Classification. American Documentation*, October 1954, pp. 195–213.
(A good introductory account.)

B. KYLE. *The UDC : present position and future developments. Unesco
Bulletin for Libraries*. March–April 1961, pp. 53–64.
(Considers the value of UDC in the humanities and makes some suggestions which
would involve drastic changes. The same periodical contains in its next issue a
similar article, but one which criticises the UDC as a classification for science and
technology, by *B. C. Vickery*.)

MILLS. *Modern Outline of Library Classification*. Chapter 8.
(The advanced student may also refer to Mills's volume in the Rutgers University series.)
PHILLIPS. *Primer of book classification*, pp. 125–40.
M. SCHUCHMANN. *The U.D.C. – yesterday, today, tomorrow*. (In Elsinore Conference Proceedings, pp. 113–17.)

Many excellent articles on this classification appear in *Aslib Proceedings, Journal of Documentation* and, especially of course, in the F.I.D. *Review of Documentation*. There is an important series of articles in the last named periodical on the revision policy of the scheme which were written by *Donker Duyvis*. They appeared in the late nineteen fifties.

CHAPTER 15.

BLISS. *Organization of Knowledge in Libraries*. Chapter 12.
F. E. GATTINGER. *Reclassification – are you converted yet? A.P.L.A. Bulletin*, February 1965, pp. 16–22.
(Recommends LC for Canadian academic libraries.)
M. MANN. *Introduction to the cataloguing and classification of books*. 2nd edn. 1943.
(Now dated in many respects. But Chapter 5 gives a readable account of LC.)
MILLS. *Modern Outline of Library Classification*. Chapter 9.
PHILLIPS. *Primer of Book Classification*. pp. 95–109.

News of developments can be found in the revision bulletins and in the *Annual Reports of the Librarian of Congress.*

CHAPTER 16.

MILLS. *Modern Outline of Library Classification*. Chapter 12.
PHILLIPS. *Primer of Book Classification*, pp. 151–66.
The scheme itself and Bliss's introduction to it must be studied carefully; the wise student will examine some of the reviews[1] that appeared in 1953 or, for a brief and highly critical account of BC, he may turn to the appropriate appendix of METCALFE'S *Subject Classifying and Indexing of Libraries and Literature*.

CHAPTER 17.

P. ATHERTON. *Ranganathan's classification ideas: an analytico-synthetic discussion. Library Resources and Technical Services*, Fall 1965, pp. 463–72.
C. D. BATTY. *Introduction to the Colon Classification*. 1966.
(A valuable programmed text on the practical application of the scheme.)
H. C. JAIN. *Colon Classification; a review article. Library Association Record*, August 1964, pp. 345–9.
MILLS. *Modern Outline of Library Classification*. Chapter 11.
(The best brief account of the scheme. Indeed all the chapters on the schemes in this textbook are essential reading for the student of the Part II syllabus of the British Library Association.)

---

[1] Copies of the *Bliss Classification Bulletin* should not be neglected, if these are accessible to the student.

R. MOSS. *Categories and relations. American Documentation*, October 1964, pp. 296–301.
(A good example of a critical study of Ranganathan's theories.)

There are many more writings on CC. Ranganathan's own books should not be neglected and there is, as in the case of BC, a critical account in an appendix to Metcalfe's book (cited above).

SECTION IV

CHAPTER 18.

W. S. MERRILL. *Code for Classifiers*. 2nd edition, 1939.
(Should be used continually as a reference book by the practical classifier.)

MILLS. *Modern Outline of Library Classification*. Chapter 14.

PHILLIPS. *Primer of Book Classification*, pp. 167–175.

There are two concise volumes published by Clive Bingley Limited that will be most useful to the student of practical classification:

C. D. BATTY. *Introduction to the Dewey Decimal Classification*, 1965.

W. DENT. *Practical cataloguing*, 1966.

CHAPTER 19.

Once again, there is a wealth of reading and the wise student should think carefully about the administrative problems dealt with in this chapter. Possible reading includes:

K. DAVISON. *Classification practice in Britain*. 1966.
(A splendid statistical survey of current methods and opinions, with special emphasis on the DC.)

R. B. DOWNS. *The administrator looks at classification*. In *The Role of Classification in the Modern American Library*, 1959.

M. F. TAUBER and OTHERS. *Technical Services in Libraries*, 1953.
(Chapter 13 gives a good account of the administrative obstacles which hinder reclassification).

J. THOMPSON. *Book Classification in New University Libraries. Library Association Record*, September, 1963, pp. 327–30.
(A plea for broad classification: the ensuing correspondence should be read also.)

In addition to readings such as these, the British student of classification theory should certainly examine the British National Bibliography's modifications of DC and the reasons for these. He could read the letter from CUSTER (*Library Association Record*, December 1960) and WELLS'S comments (*Liaison* August 1961).

CHAPTER 20.

NEEDHAM. *Organizing Knowledge in Libraries*. Chapter 11.

PHILLIPS. *Primer of Book Classsification*. pp. 177–85.

SAVAGE. *Manual of Book Classification and Display*, 1946.
(May profitably be consulted on display work.)

R. S. WALKER. *The theory of library display. Library Association Record*, January 1956, pp. 1–6.
(Useful in stressing the need to present bookstocks in a thoughtful and attractive manner in public libraries.)

CHAPTER 21.

J. H. SHERA and M. EGAN. *The Classified Catalogue*, 1956.
There are several references that could be followed up on chain indexing. The following are recommended.
D. DOUGHTY. *Library Association Record*, May 1955, pp. 173–8.
J. MILLS. *Ibid.*, April 1955, pp. 141–8.
> (These could well be prefaced by some elementary reading such as the relevant article from the *Encyclopaedia of Librarianship*, edited by *T. Landau*.)

CHAPTER 22.

KELLEY. *The Classification of Books*. Chapters 1 and 4.
J. LUND and M. TAUBE. *A non-expansive classification system. Library Quarterly*, July 1937, pp. 373–94.
MILLS. *Modern Outline of Library Classification*. Chapter 15.
R. MOSS. *How do we classify? Aslib Proceedings*, February 1962, pp. 33–42.
R. RUTZEN. *A classification for the reader*. In *Role of Classification in the Modern American Library*, 1959.
> (One of the best accounts of the 'reader interest' classification idea.)
J. H. SHERA. *Classification : current functions* ... In *M. Tauber, editor. The Subject Analysis of Library Materials*, 1953.
> (This paper can also be found, along with many of Shera's other writings in the volumes mentioned in the first part of the bibliography.)

CHAPTER 23.

The student is advised to follow up his reading of this chapter with a more extensive study of one or two types of specialized material. The following readings may be of assistance:

J. BURKETT and T. MORGAN, editors. *Special materials in the library*, 1963.

Local Collections
J. L. HOBBS. *Libraries and the material of local history*, 1962. Chapters 17–18.

Maps
D. MASON. *Primer of Non-Book Material in Libraries*, 1958. pp. 7–11.
A. M. FERRAR. *Management of map collections* ... *Library Association Record*, May 1962, pp. 161–5.

Music
B. REDFERN. *Organizing music in libraries*, 1966.

Illustrations
E. V. CORBETT. *The Illustrations Collection*, 1941. Chapters 6 and 7.

Classification of Fiction
L. A. BURGESS. *A fiction policy. Library Assistant*, 1943. pp. 76–81.
R. S. WALKER. *Problem Child. Librarian*, February 1958, pp. 21–8.

SECTION V

CHAPTER 24.

C. A. CROSSLEY. *New schemes of classification. Library Association Record*, February 1963, pp. 51–59.

D. J. FOSKETT. *Classification.* In *Aslib Handbook of Special Librarianship.* 2nd edn. 1962.

Science, Humanism and Libraries. Chapters 12 and 13.

MILLS. *Modern Outline of Library Classification.* Chapter 13.

NEEDHAM. *Organizing Knowledge in Libraries.* Chapter 7.

(Extremely useful in describing how to make a special faceted scheme.)

VICKERY. *Faceted classification.*

(A good alternative to the Needham reference above. This writer's book in the Rutgers University series also merits attention.)

B. WHITE. *The S f B system. Library Association Record*, December 1966, pp. 428–32.

CHAPTER 25.

On indexing in general one could read *D. W. Langridge's* paper *Classification and Book Indexing*, in the *Sayers Memorial Volume.*

The following are some references on post co-ordinate indexing:

J. C. COSTELLO. *Uniterm indexing: principles, problems and solutions. American Documentation*, January 1961, pp. 20–6.

A. JOHNSON. *Unit concept co-ordinate indexing of technical reports. Journal of Documentation*, September 1959, pp. 146–55.

(A lucid explanation of the application of the system; in *Aslib Proceedings*, June 1963, Johnson discusses the circumstances in which it might be profitable to apply the process to a special library's bookstock. This issue of the *Proceedings* has several pertinent articles. K. Baker of B.I.C.C. has published an excellent paper on the costs of co-ordinate indexing. *Northern Aslib Bulletin*, October–December 1966, pp. 3–27.)

R. MOSS. *Vocabularies for Batten Card (Peek-a-Boo) Indexing.* Liverpool School of Librarianship Occasional Paper No. 2.

V. SLAMECKA. *Classificatory, alphabetical and associative schedules as aids to co-ordinate indexing. American Documentation*, July 1963, pp. 223–8.

(There is a paper of rather similar scope by R. M. A. McClelland and W. W. Mapleson in *Aslib Proceedings*, October 1966, pp. 290–9.)

Less favourable accounts of co-ordinate indexing can also be found. See, for example, *I. A. Warheit, College and Research Libraries*, July 1955, pp. 278–84.

CHAPTER 26.

This branch of our subject is developing very rapidly. In the examinations of the British Library Association, classification overlaps here with the paper on the Dissemination of Information.

The student wishing to read a textbook on information indexing is recommended to consult one or more of:

A. KENT. *Textbook on Mechanized Information Retrieval.* Wiley, 1962.

J. R. SHARP. *Some Fundamentals of Information Retrieval.* Deutsch, 1965.

B. C. VICKERY. *On Retrieval System Theory.* 2nd edn., Butterworths, 1965.
(This writer's *Classification and Indexing in Science* is relevant here, especially chapters 1 and 5 and chapters 5 and 6 of Foskett's volume relating to the social sciences are also of great merit on this theme.)

The following are papers, reports or articles of importance:

R. C. M. BARNES. *The Present State of Information Retrieval by Computer.* Atomic Energy Research Establishment Report No. R4514. 1964.
(His short paper in *Atom*, August 1965, pp. 162–63 is also of interest.)

J. E. L. FARRADANE. *Classification and Mechanical Selection.* In *Proceedings of the International Study Conference on Classification* . . . 1957.
Fundamental fallacies and new needs in classification. In *Sayers Memorial Volume.*

R. R. FREEMAN. *Computers and Classification Systems. Journal of Documentation*, September 1964, pp. 137–43.

M. HYSLOP. *The A.S.M. Retrieval System: after Cranfield. Journal of Documentation*, March 1965, pp. 27–42.

J. MILLS. *Information Retrieval: a revolt against conventional systems? Aslib Proceedings*, February 1964, pp. 48–63.

J. NEGUS. *Practical experience with the A.S.M. Metallurgical Literature Classification* (at the British Iron & Steel Research Association). *Aslib Proceedings*, October 1961, pp. 274–89.

R. J. TRITSCHLER. *A computer integrated system for centralized information dissemination. Aslib Proceedings*, December 1962, pp. 473–500.

CHAPTER 27.

The student should consider carefully the ideas suggested in this final chapter and should be on the look-out for current articles concerning them. The C.R.G. Bulletin appears at intervals in the *Journal of Documentation* and often provides information on contemporary theories. The September 1964 issue, for example, dealt with integrative levels. The reports issued on the Cranfield experiment should certainly be studied, if they are available. Articles and papers which might be read include:

S. ARTANDI. *SYNTOL. Library Resources and Technical Services*, Fall, 1965, pp. 443–47.

FOSKETT. *Science, Humanism and Libraries.* Chapters 15 and 16.

B. KYLE. *Information retrieval and subject indexing: Cranfield and after. Journal of Documentation*, June 1964, pp. 55–69.

LIBRARY ASSOCIATION. *Some problems of a general classification scheme.* 1964. (Report of a 1963 conference. The paper by *Mills* on the faults of existing schemes and that by *Coates* on the C.R.G. proposals for a new scheme are especially important.)

A. MALTBY. *Classification at the Crossroads. Library World*, October 1965, pp. 102–5.
(Some thoughts on the future of the general schemes.)

V. M. PINGS. *A Universal Classification – untenable. Library Resources and Technical Services*, Winter 1960, pp. 5–13.

RANGANATHAN. *Philosophy of Library Classification.* Chapter 8.

SHERA. *Libraries and the Organization of Knowledge.*
(The chapter entitled 'What lies ahead in classification?' is particularly relevant.)

D. R. SWANSON. *The evidence underlying the Cranfield results. Library Quarterly*, January 1965, pp. 1–20.
(One of the best of the many articles on the project. See, too, Cleverdon's rejoinder in the April issue; the *reports* of the Cranfield project issued by Aslib should certainly be examined by any student of classification who has access to them.)

Index

GUILDFORD COUNTY TECHNICAL
COLLEGE LIBRARY

Synthesis in classification—*cont.*
—— in BC, 252–4
—— in CC, 267 ff., 275
—— in DC, 159–61
—— in EC, 123
—— in LC, 231–3
—— in SC, 183–5
—— in UDC, 202–8
Syntol, *see* Gardin, J. C.
Systematic mnemonics, 63
Systematic schedules, *see* Auxiliary schedules

Taube, M., 260, 366–7, 420
Tauber, M. F., 284, 318
Terminology of book classification, 24, 39
Thesaurus (for co-ordinate indexing), 431
Thompson, J., 310, 370
Thou, de, library of, 103
Tier guides, 327
Tool phase, 41
Trade, Board of, Library, 404
Tree of Knowledge, 26, 38
Tree of Porphyry, 27
Typography, classification by, 13

Uniformity in classification, case for, 305–6, 460
United Kingdom Atomic Energy Authority, 211
Uniterm system of co-ordinate indexing, 420–2
—— used in Aslib test, 450
Universal Decimal Classification,
—— DC, as basis, 196–9
—— *description and evaluation*, 193–218
—— initiation, 137
—— most synthetic of older schemes, 34, 36
—— suitability for special libraries, 401 ff.

—— use compulsory in Russian scientific libraries, 214, 455
—— used in Aslib test, 450
University College, London, 316
Unscheduled mnemonics, *see* Seminal mnemonics
Unsought links (in chain indexing), 348
Utilitarian classifications, early, 102 ff.

Variable mnemonics, 63
Vertical file, 387–9
Vickery, B. C.,
—— aeronautics scheme, 450
—— on CC, 268
—— on faceted classification, 412–13
—— on laws of library science, 95
—— on mechanical selection, 438–9
—— on notation, 50, 68
—— on special classification, 400
—— on UDC, 217
—— soil science classification scheme, 409
Vocabulary for co-ordinate indexing, 431

Wales, Library School of, *see* College of Librarianship, Aberystwyth
Walker, R. S., 333, 381
Washington, Scientific Information Conference, 1959, 454
Waste paper basket class (Generalia), 72
Wells, A. J., 39, 89, 142, 296
Western Reserve University, U.S.A., 442, 450
West Riding County Library, 335
Wheatley Medal Award, 416
Woolwich, Bishop of, *see* Robinson, J. A. T.

Young, H. H., 169

Zatocoding, *see* Mooers, C.

30052